Mood

OXFORD SURVEYS IN SEMANTICS AND PRAGMATICS

GENERAL EDITORS: Chris Barker, *New York University*, and Chris Kennedy, *University of Chicago*

ADVISORY EDITORS: Kent Bach, *San Francisco State University*; Jack Hoeksema, *University of Groningen*; Laurence R. Horn, *Yale University*; William Ladusaw, *University of California Santa Cruz*; Richard Larson, *Stony Brook University*; Beth Levin, *Stanford University*; Mark Steedman, *University of Edinburgh*; Anna Szabolcsi, *New York University*; Gregory Ward, *Northwestern University*

PUBLISHED

1 *Modality*
Paul Portner

2 *Reference*
Barbara Abbott

3 *Intonation and Meaning*
Daniel Büring

4 *Questions*
Veneeta Dayal

5 *Mood*
Paul Portner

IN PREPARATION

Aspect
Hana Filip

Lexical Pragmatics
Laurence R. Horn

Conversational Implicature
Yan Huang

Mood

PAUL PORTNER

OXFORD

UNIVERSITY PRESS

OXFORD
UNIVERSITY PRESS

Great Clarendon Street, Oxford, OX2 6DP,
United Kingdom

Oxford University Press is a department of the University of Oxford.
It furthers the University's objective of excellence in research, scholarship,
and education by publishing worldwide. Oxford is a registered trade mark of
Oxford University Press in the UK and in certain other countries

First Edition published in 2018

Impression: 1

Published in the United States of America by Oxford University Press
198 Madison Avenue, New York, NY 10016, United States of America

British Library Cataloguing in Publication Data
Data available

Library of Congress Control Number: 2017939633

ISBN 978-0-19-954752-4 (hbk.)
      978-0-19-954753-1 (pbk.)

Printed and bound by
CPI Group (UK) Ltd, Croydon, CR0 4YY

Contents

General preface

Oxford Surveys in Semantics and Pragmatics aims to convey to the reader the life and spirit of the study of meaning in natural language. Its volumes provide distillations of the central empirical questions driving research in contemporary semantics and pragmatics, and distinguish the most important lines of inquiry into these questions. Each volume offers the reader an overview of the topic at hand, a critical survey of the major approaches to it, and an assessment of what consensus (if any) exists. By putting empirical puzzles and theoretical debates into a comprehensible perspective, each author seeks to provide orientation and direction to the topic, thereby providing the context for a deeper understanding of both the complexity of the phenomena and the crucial features of the semantic and pragmatic theories designed to explain them. The books in the series offer researchers in linguistics and related areas—including syntax, cognitive science, computer science, and philosophy—both a valuable resource for instruction and reference and a state-of-the-art perspective on contemporary semantic and pragmatic theory from the experts shaping the field.

Paul Portner's survey on mood provides a welcome new platform for the work on a major but understudied topic in the semantics of natural language. The vast majority of modern semantic studies have focused on the ways in which the morphosyntactic and semantic properties of the constituent elements of declarative sentences—and to a somewhat lesser extent, interrogatives and imperatives—interact with each other and with aspects of the context of utterance to determine truth-conditional content. However, as an increasingly large number of scholars have begun to appreciate, the full set of linguistically marked distinctions in clause type is finer-grained than the traditional three-way distinction between declarative, interrogative, and imperative reflects, richly subtle in its detail, and indicative of a systematic relation between clausal and verbal morphosyntax and constraints on the ways that a sentence can be used to perform a speech act. Comprehensive, careful, instructive, and insightful, Portner thoroughly explores the intricate tension between clausal and verbal morphosyntax and illocutionary content, covering performativity, speech act theory, dynamic update, and evidentiality. This volume bridges traditional studies of clause typing and contemporary semantic and pragmatic theory, and lays the foundation for future advances in our study of the relation between sentential morphosyntax and illocutionary force.

Chris Barker
New York University

Christopher Kennedy
University of Chicago

Acknowledgments

The idea for this book goes back to a proposal I made in 2003 to Oxford University Press for a volume on modality and mood, and from that time I have appreciated the patience and support of both the editors of the Oxford Surveys series, Chris Barker and Chris Kennedy, and the editors at the press, especially John Davey and Julia Steer. It turned out that it was far from feasible to include my thoughts on mood and modality, and the relation between them, in a single volume. I am very grateful that the press allowed me to pursue this project in two parts. I revised the portion of the manuscript on modality into *Modality* (Portner 2009), and then set out to write a second volume on mood. This latter part of the project turned out to be much more difficult, because the range of relevant ideas in the literature is so much more varied and disconnected, but for me the process of engaging with that literature has also led again and again to the feeling that a new insight is waiting to be understood. I hope that readers will experience to some extent the benefits, as I have, of finding new ideas and connections within the literature on mood.

As I wrote the book I continued my various research projects on modality and mood, and my collaborators, discussants, and reviewers during that time have helped me immensely in this project. I can mention especially my collaborators Graham Katz, Elena Herburger, Miok Pak, Aynat Rubinstein, and Raffaella Zanuttini. I received helpful comments on Chapter 3 from Malte Willer and on the entire manuscript from an anonymous reviewer. In presentations of ideas which flow from the perspective on mood adopted in this book, I have received crucial feedback from Maria Aloni, Gennaro Chierchia, Nate Charlow, Liz Coppock, Kai von Fintel, Anastasia Giannakidou, Magda Kaufmann, Angelika Kratzer, Alda Mari, Craige Roberts, and Steve Wechsler. This feedback has in many cases led me to rethink my understanding of the literature and trends present in current research. I thank my students for sharing their insights and for help with research and editing, in particular Lissa Krawczyk, Hillary Harner, and Akitaka Yamada.

My family has remained confident in my ability to complete this project and, amazingly, convinced of its value through the long years that it hung about the house as a competitor for my attention. I love the fact that my kids Noah and Ben believe in the importance of research and writing, and I deeply appreciate the respect my wife Sylvia holds for any project which has value to me. The feeling that what one of us cares about, we all do, has given me the confidence to move forward whenever the project seemed too complex and difficult. I dedicate the book to my family and especially to Sylvia.

List of figures and tables

Figures

Tables

1

Introduction

Mood is a fundamental and traditional concept used in the description of human language and in theoretical inquiries into the nature of language. Because it is fundamental and traditional, one might think that the theory of mood is an important topic within linguistics. Yet mood as such, in its most general sense, is not a topic of research, and there are several reasons for this. One is that the concept of mood is so fundamental that different scholarly traditions have molded their understanding of what mood is to fit their conception of the nature of language. We see it used in different ways in philosophy, formal semantics and pragmatics, and descriptive/typological linguistics. And even setting aside broad differences in approach to the study of language, mood is a difficult topic because all linguists agree that it relates to at least the two different grammatical phenomena: **verbal mood**, the category which includes indicatives and subjunctives, and **sentence mood**, the category which includes declaratives, interrogatives, and imperatives. It has generally not seemed likely that a general theory of mood incorporating both of these categories would be possible, and so, in many instances, linguists take care to explain that they are talking about one kind of mood and not the other. It will emerge as we go forward, however, that similar ideas and puzzles recur as we try to understand the two kinds of mood. They might not be as different as we often assume.

In writing this book, I have two primary goals. The first is to provide scholars interested in the semantics and pragmatics of mood with a deeper source of background than is found in any single previous work. In doing this, I draw on as much of the literature on mood as I am able, but I think and write from within the formal semantics tradition. And second, I seek to formulate and advance new ideas about the semantics and pragmatics of mood. As I survey, organize, and explain the literature, I will sometimes sketch out novel analyses. In some cases, I do this as a model for discussion without entirely endorsing the analysis, while in others, I advocate for a certain hypothesis.

It must not go without saying that there is a great deal of insightful research on mood which will not be mentioned in this book. The fields of linguistics and philosophy are too large and the concepts of mood are too useful—they lead to such a vast literature that even the subset of it that is worth studying today is so extensive that no single book can incorporate a responsible discussion of it all. What is included here is the result of my best judgment about what combination of literature, explanation, and new ideas can best further the goals of the book.

Mood. First edition. Paul Portner.
© Paul Portner 2018. First published 2018 by Oxford University Press.

There is a great deal of additional important scholarship on mood which I would recommend. I hope that this book can help readers make better use of it.

Some terms and conventions.   Before beginning the substantive discussion, I would like to specify some of my terminology and conventions.

1. Notational conventions. In mentioning a word, phrase, or sentence:

   (a) The use of SMALL CAPS indicates a technical term whose precise meaning is being discussed in the immediate context; in many cases, the term is actually defined there.

   (b) The use of **boldface** merely serves to draw the reader's attention to a particular word or words.

   (c) The use of *italics* indicates that the material is being referred to as a linguistic object. Exception: Within numbered examples and figures, such material will not be italicized, unless there is other material within the numbered example which is not being referred to as a linguistic object.

   (d) The use of 'single quotes' indicates that the material stands for the linguistic objects in a number of languages, under the assumption that all of those objects are similar enough across the relevant languages to be spoken of as if they are the same. Example: "In most Romance languages, 'believe' selects the indicative." Single quotes are also used for glosses and paraphrases.

   (e) The use of "double quotes" indicates that the quoted material should be understood as spoken or written by someone. Double quotes are also used in the traditional way as "scare quotes," indicating that the quoted material should not necessarily be taken literally.

   (f) [Brackets] indicate some aspect of the context in which an example is to be understood.

2. I use the term LOGICAL FORM in two ways:

   (a) When capitalized, as "Logical Form," it refers to a level of linguistic representation at which certain semantic properties, such as scope, are explicitly represented. Logical Form can be a level of syntax or an independent level between syntax and semantics.

   (b) When not capitalized, as "logical form," it refers to a representation which displays or elucidates important abstract properties of meaning. The logical form usually has some logic-like properties, such as a simple vocabulary and an unintuitive syntax. Unlike Logical Form, a logical form is not understood to be a level of linguistic representation.

3. When using a pronoun anaphoric to an antecedent which could refer to a male or female individual, I roughly alternate genders. Example: "If a philosopher reads this, she might disagree" (next time "he"). Occasionally, however, it will be better to use "he or she," "s/he," or singular "they."

In difficult cases, I will apply these conventions in the way I feel is most helpful.

1.1 What do we study when we study mood?

1.1.1 Conceptual preliminaries

One of the most fundamental issues to be addressed by semantic theory concerns the kind of meanings that simple declarative sentences have, and we can judge any approach by how well it helps us understand such basic properties as: they can be (and typically are) either true or false; they can be used to share factual information; they are appropriate for representing the contents of thought and some other cognitive states; and they stand in logical relations to one another like entailment and synonymy. Consider the declarative sentence (1a). It has all of these properties:

(1)   a. Ben is holding a bird.
       b. This is true because: Ben is holding John Fei.
       c. Noah told me: "Ben is holding a bird." And now I know what Ben is holding.
       d. Noah thinks that Ben is holding a bird.
       e. *Ben is holding a bird.* Entails: *Ben is in close proximity to a bird.*

Moreover, semanticists think they have a good (though not yet perfect) understanding of how each of these properties should be explained, an understanding which is based on the theoretical construct of a PROPOSITION.

In formal semantics, our theories of sentence meaning most commonly work with the idea that propositions can be defined in terms of POSSIBLE WORLDS. A possible world is a way things could be, complete through space and time, an alternative history of the universe. Our own universe-history can be referred to as the "actual world" or "real world." For the purposes of linguistic semantics, let us assume that we have a set of possible worlds conceivable by humans. By this I mean that any difference in how things could be which a human could recognize, imagine, or describe corresponds to a difference between possible worlds in the set of all worlds W. For example, if I tell you that Ben has a cockatiel, you can imagine that it is grey, or that it is white. Therefore, W should contain at least one possible world in which it is grey and at least one in which it is white. The set of worlds conceivable by humans seems sure to be adequate for doing natural language semantics, if any theory based on possible worlds is.

A proposition in possible worlds semantics is a subset of W. For example, the meaning of (1a) is, or can be characterized in terms of, the set (2):

(2)   {w : Ben is holding a bird in w}
       (= the set of worlds in which Ben is holding a bird.)

This definition of proposition helps to explain the properties summarized in (1). For example, (1b) amounts to the claim that the actual world is one of the worlds in the set. Though the conception of propositions as sets of possible worlds is not without its problems, we can ignore them for now. Our goal is to use it to develop a useful way of thinking about mood.

Another feature of language we need to understand if we are to get a handle on the concept of mood is MODALITY. Modality is "the linguistic phenomenon whereby grammar allows one to say things about, or on the basis of, situations which need not be real" (Portner 2009, p.1). The noun *Ben* in (1a) is not modal; it is used to refer to a particular, actual person. In contrast, the auxiliary *should* in (3) is modal:

(3)   Ben should put down the bird.

This sentence says that situations in which Ben puts down the bird are in some respect better than, or preferable to, situations in which he does not. Since he either will or will not put down the bird, some of these situations will never be real, and so the word *should* counts as modal.

1.1.2 The general concept of mood

With these preliminaries in place, we can attempt a definition of mood:

MOOD is an aspect of linguistic form which indicates how a proposition is used in the expression of modal meaning.

As we start out, it's acceptable to be vague about what we mean by the "use" of a proposition, because linguists have employed the term "mood" in many different ways. Let us consider two examples:

1. In many languages, subordinate clauses (and sometimes root clauses as well) come in different forms, known as VERBAL MOODS, such as indicative mood and subjunctive mood. These clauses can be used to help represent various cognitive states and mental events, such as beliefs, desires, and dreams. When they are used in a subordinate clause to help talk about a desire (as in (4)), they typically take the subjunctive form; in contrast, when they are used to describe a dream ((5)), they typically take indicative form.[1]

   (4)   *Pierre veut   que Marie soit   heureuse.* (French)
         Pierre wants that Marie is.SUBJ happy
         'Pierre wants Marie to be happy.'

   (5)   *J'ai rêvé   qu'il   était   président.*
         I dreamed that he was.INDIC president
         'I dreamed that he was president.'

---

[1] Under certain circumstances, they may take a different form, such as infinitive. For our purposes here, it's helpful to pretend there are only two possibilities.

We call this kind of mood "verbal mood" because it is frequently (though not always) marked in a grammatical sense on the verbal head of the clause; for example, the verb *soit* is a subjunctive form of 'be' in French.

2. In all languages, root sentences have various functions, including easy-to-intuit ones like directing somebody to do something (as in (6a)), requesting information ((6b)), and providing information ((6c)).

(6) a. Pick up a bird!
     b. Is Ben holding a bird?
     c. Ben is holding a bird.

Each of these functions is associated in an intuitively clear way (which is nonetheless hard to define) with particular members of a paradigm of forms known as SENTENCE MOODS. The most prominent sentence moods are the three just illustrated: the imperative, interrogative, and declarative.

Each of these two important concepts of mood realizes the general description of mood indicating how a sentence's proposition is to be used: verbal mood tells us something about how it is to be used, within the compositional computation of meaning, to describe an individual's mental life, while sentence mood indicates how it is to be used, in a multi-party exchange, to achieve specified communicative functions.

Given an understanding of mood like the one just developed, what would a linguistic theory of mood look like? We could spell out a too-simple theory of verbal mood like this: Assume that verbs like *want* and *dream*, verbs which take sentential complements and talk about some aspect of their subject's mental life, are modal words which express a relation between two arguments, an individual and a proposition. Their logical form can be represented as $V(x, p)$, for example wants(Pierre, {w: Marie is happy w}). Mood choice is determined by the following principle:

(7) If the relation expressed by the verb concerns a preference about how the future will be, the clause which denotes the proposition argument of this relation should be in the subjunctive mood. Otherwise, it should be in the indicative mood.

Given this principle, if you want to say something which means wants(Pierre, {w: Marie is happy w}), the verb 'be' will be subjunctive, but if you want to say something which means dreams(I, {w: Pierre was president w}), it will be indicative. Nothing semantic changes between the two cases, other than the main relation, wants or dreams.

And we could spell out a too-simple theory of sentence mood like this: Assume that the function of a root sentence used in dialogue is to adjust the speaker's and hearer's shared assumptions. For example, sometimes the speaker may want to create a shared assumption that one way the future could be is preferable to another, perhaps threatening some sort of punishment upon the addressee if the preferred future does not come about. We can describe this as the speaker directing the addressee to do something. There is a particular grammatical form, the imperative, for a sentence used with this purpose, as in (6a). This reasoning suggests the following principle:

(8)   If a sentence is used to create an assumption that it is preferable that the proposition expressed by the sentence comes to be true (as opposed to false), it should be expressed using imperative mood.

There would be similar principles for interrogative sentences (*Will Ben put down the bird?* creates an assumption that the addressee will help the speaker know something) and indicative sentences (*Ben will put down the bird* creates an assumption that a certain fact holds). Nothing would differ among these cases in terms of the proposition involved, but there would be crucial differences in the goal which the speaker aims to achieve by using a sentence which denotes that proposition.

These pictures of subjunctive and imperative clauses have been presented to help convey an understanding of the idea behind the informal definition of mood. This conception of mood will be very important in the book, as it serves as an unarticulated intuition behind the actual practices linguists have in describing phenomena as "mood," and because it plays a role in many attempts to provide concrete semantic or pragmatic analyses of mood forms. However, the specific statements about the subjunctive and imperative above are not to be taken as serious proposals. Besides oversimplifying the relevant phenomena, they make many assumptions which could turn out to be wrong: for example, they assume that all sentences have propositions as their basic meanings and that the various moods have no effect themselves on the meaning of a given sentence. All such assumptions must be carefully evaluated as part of any serious investigation of mood. Much of the work in this book is to examine some of the phenomena which meet the characterization of mood based on the concept of "modal use" and to consider various theories of them. In the next subsection, I give a preview of where this way of thinking about mood will lead us.

1.2 Main findings about the nature of mood

The literature on mood is extensive, contradictory, and at times confusing. Nevertheless, I hope we won't end up in a muddle. The discussion will lead not only to lots of questions, but to a few linguistically significant conclusions as well. Here at the outset, I would like to highlight the work's most basic, broadly conceptual findings:

1. While verbal mood and sentence mood are distinct both in terms of morphosyntax and in terms of meaning, they are closely related. They are related because of tight parallels between the modal semantics of sentence-embedding constructions, which determine verbal moods, and the

communicative functions served by root sentences in conversation, in terms of which sentence moods are characterized.

2. At a formal level, many theories of verbal mood and sentence mood can be expressed within a unified framework. This framework states that both kinds of mood encode the interaction between a clause's meaning and a contextually given PARTIALLY ORDERED SET OF WORLDS (the POSW). The POSW may be derived from either the grammatical or the discourse context. Though the POSW-framework is clearly not the last word on the relation between verbal mood and sentence mood, it can point the way towards a more general and explanatory theory of the two kinds of mood and the relation between them.

   On the assumption that some types of verbal mood and some types of sentence mood can be analyzed in terms of a single theoretical system (be it the POSW or something else), I label the broader linguistic category which includes them both CORE MOOD.

3. There is a range of forms and constructions across languages whose relation to core mood is not currently well understood. Among these are evidentials, the kinds of forms which Elliott (2000) describes as marking "reality status," and numerous other specific moods and modes used in the description of languages typologically different from those which have been the focus of research on verbal mood. We do not yet have a good enough understanding of all the forms with labels like "realis," "irrealis," "conjunct," "inferential," "hearsay," "conjecture," "potential," "desiderative," "assertive," and "contingent" to say how they are related to core mood.

I think that core mood covers more than what linguists typically think of as mood, rather than less, and I don't know of any linguistic forms which at once should clearly be classified as mood, yet also clearly not as core mood. However, some types of elements, for example evidentials, which I think could reasonably be thought of as core mood, are not typically thought about in that way, and so they may exemplify non-core mood. More significantly, few phenomena which have been described in terms of the concepts of reality status have been analyzed in a precise enough way for it to be clear what their relation to core mood is. Table 1.1 outlines

TABLE 1.1 Semantic classifications for mood and modality

	Modality			
	Core mood		Non-core mood	(The rest of modality)
Verbal mood	Sentence mood	Other core mood		
indicative, subjunctive, certain infinitives	imperative, declarative, interrogative	evidentials? reality status?	evidentials? reality status?	epistemic, priority, deontic, dynamic modals; modal adjectives, adverbs

this way of thinking about the relationships among various kinds of mood and between mood and modality.

1.3 Background on modality

As described above, for the purposes of this book I define modality as the linguistic phenomenon whereby grammar allows one to say things about, or on the basis of, situations which need not be real. Since, on this conception, mood fits within this broader category of modality, it will be essential to have an understanding of the semantics of modality. In this section I will provide an overview of some key ideas in the semantic theory of modality, drawing on the more extensive discussion by Portner (2009).

1.3.1 Classifications of modality

We begin with two ways of classifying modal expressions: by the linguistic level at which they are expressed and by the meanings they convey.

Classifications of modality by level of linguistic organization.   Modality may be classified according to the level of linguistic organization on which it operates. Specifically, it's useful to distinguish SUBSENTENTIAL, SENTENTIAL, and DISCOURSE modality.

1. Subsentential modality operates below the level of proposition expressed by a complete sentence. It includes modal adjectives, modal nouns, propositional attitude verbs (verbs which take an argument which expresses a proposition), verbal mood, and infinitives, among other types.

   (9) (a) A *possible* solution to this problem is to call the recalcitrant reviewer.
        (b) The *probability* of success is low.
        (c) I *think/hope/regret* that she arrived on time.
        (d) I hope *to be* happy.

   Of course, many of these elements also affect the meaning of the complete sentence, but they do so via the meaning of some smaller constituent. For example, the subject phrases in (9a–b) have noun phrase-type meanings which have been built up using the modal concepts expressed by *possible* and *probability*, and the predicate in (9c) denotes a property, like other predicates do, but this property involves consideration of not-necessarily-real situations which are important in the speaker's mental life.

2. Sentential modality operates at the level of the complete proposition. In other words, if a sentence contains a constituent which denotes a proposition, and then a modal element combines with this to create another propositional constituent, we have a case of sentential modality. In grammatical terms, this means that it is typically realized above the level of the main subject–predicate structure in the clause, that is, above the S, IP, *v*P, or other roughly

equivalent syntactic unit. Sentential modality affects the primary meaning of the sentence; thus, in the case of a root declarative clause, it affects the truth conditions of the sentence; in the case of a root interrogative, it affects what information is literally requested, and so forth.

Sentential modality has commanded the vast majority of scholarly attention on modality within linguistics. In English, there has been a great deal of work on the modal auxiliaries like *can* in (10a). We can also classify as expressing sentential modality such elements as modal verbs (by this I mean verbs which are not auxiliaries, but which are distinct from regular lexical verbs as well, as in (10b)), modal adverbs, and some tense and aspect forms.

(10) (a) Noah *can* swim.
     (b) *Devo*   partire domani.   (Italian; Squartini 2004)
         must.PRES-1SG leave   tomorrow
         'I must leave tomorrow.'
     (c) *Probably*, Ben was there.
     (d) She *will* be late.
     (e) The team *is building* a bridge.

In some cases, the decision whether to treat a given modal element as representing subsentential or sentential modality requires a careful syntactic and semantic analysis. For example, my labeling (10b) as sentential is based on the assumption that *dovere* ('must') is syntactically distinct from regular lexical verbs, and the idea that the progressive in (10e) exemplifies sentential modality assumes that it is a sentence-level operator. If either of these points turns out not to be correct, then they are not examples of sentential modality.

3. Discourse modality is the direct contribution of modality to meaning in discourse. I say "direct contribution" because, of course, any type of modality ultimately contributes to the broader discourse; what distinguishes discourse modality is that it does not do so via an effect on the regular semantic meaning expressed by a sentence. Though (10b) may cause the discourse to contain the information that the speaker favors future situations in which she leaves over ones in which she does not, this effect is mediated by its ordinary sentence-level semantics; hence, it is not discourse modality. In contrast, discourse modality is separate from any modal contribution towards regular sentence meaning. Some plausible examples of discourse modality are evidentiality, sentence mood, and the performative meanings of modal auxiliaries and modal verbs.

(11) (a) Para-sha-n-*mi/-si/-chá*.   (Cusco Quechua, Faller 2006b)
         rain-PROG-3-BPG/REP/CONJ
         'It is raining.' (Direct evidence/Reported/Conjectural.)
     (b) Leave right away!
     (c) It *might* rain.

In (11a), we see the three evidential markers in Cusco Quechua, the first indicating that the speaker has direct evidence (what Faller calls 'best possible grounds'), the second that he is conveying a report, and the third that he is making a conjecture. In (11b), we have an imperative. These two exemplify discourse modality on the assumption that the evidentials and imperative form do not cause the sentence to denote a modalized proposition—for example that (11a) does not mean 'I have direct evidence that it is raining' (if it did mean this, it would show sentential modality), but rather conveys this meaning without affecting the primary proposition 'it is raining.' Example (11c) can be considered discourse modality if we accept the claim (Portner 2008) that it not only means that rain is compatible with our information (its sentential modality), but also makes the question of whether it will rain a topic of conversation (additional discourse modality).

The examples of each subtype above are given only in order to help make clear what should fall under each subcategory. It wouldn't be surprising if further research showed some of them to be miscategorized or even not modal at all. For example, while many think that the progressive is modal, this is somewhat controversial (Portner 2011a).

Classifications of modality by meaning. Modality involves saying something about, or on the basis of, situations which need not be real, and it is useful to classify modal elements according to the way in which its meaning is based on those situations. Roughly speaking, (12) says that the relevant situations (those in which the girl gets the prize) are good (perhaps more specifically, they are good in relation to the criteria set up for the contest):

(12)   That girl should get the prize.

In the literature on modality, we find various systems for classifying modal elements, especially sentential modals, along such parameters; in Portner (2009), I outline a top-level classification into epistemic, priority, and dynamic modality, with various subtypes:

1. EPISTEMIC MODALITY has to do with what can be concluded based on someone's knowledge.
   True epistemic modality is not commonly divided into subtypes, but in logic and philosophy, there is consideration of such related concepts as ALETHIC modality (concerning concepts of logical possibility and necessity) and METAPHYSICAL modality (concerning metaphysical possibility and necessity). It is not clear that natural language modal elements ever express these concepts, except in the context of technical logical/philosophical discourse. HISTORICAL modality is a kind of metaphysical modality where the relevant worlds are those with a future that is compatible with everything that has already occurred, and should perhaps be classified as a kind of dynamic modality.
2. PRIORITY MODALITY has to do with reasons for assigning priority, or preference, to one type of situation over another.

There are several subtypes, such as: DEONTIC modality concerns priority based on rules or right and wrong, BULETIC modality concerns priority based on desire, and TELEOLOGICAL modality concerns priority based on goals. We do not assume that these subcategories are mutually exclusive.

3. DYNAMIC MODALITY has to do with the possible courses of events in the world, based on the factual circumstances.

The most prominent subtype is VOLITIONAL MODALITY. Volitional modals concern the actions available to a volitional individual, with sub-subtypes including ABILITY modality (focus on the individual's abilities), OPPORTUN-ITY modality (focus on the circumstances surrounding the individual), and DISPOSITIONAL modality (focus on the individual's dispositions). There are also forms of dynamic modality which are not tied to a volitional individual, and I will call these INTRINSIC MODALITY. A somewhat special variety of dynamic modal are the QUANTIFICATIONAL MODALS, which seem to involve quantification over individuals.

Examples of all of these subtypes from Portner (2009, ch.4) are given in (13)–(15):

(13) **Epistemic**
 (a) A typhoon may hit the island.
 (b) Mary must have a good reason for being late.

(14) **Priority**
 (a) Deontic: The rich must give money to the poor.
 (b) Buletic: You should try this chocolate.
 (c) Teleological: You could add some more salt to the soup.

(15) **Dynamic**
 (a) Volitional:
   (i) John can swim. (ability)
   (ii) You can see the ocean from here. (opportunity)
   (iii) Mary will laugh if you tell her that. (dispositional)
 (b) Intrinsic:
   (i) The cup is breakable.
   (ii) Every empire eventually falls. (historical)
 (c) Quantificational:
   (i) A spider can be dangerous. (existential)
   (ii) A spider will be dangerous. (universal)

Following Kratzer (1981, 1991), priority and dynamic modality are often grouped together as CIRCUMSTANTIAL MODALITY (i.e. modality which makes reference to factual circumstances, rather than only an individual's knowledge or beliefs), and following this terminology, dynamic modality can be called "pure" cir-cumstantial modality (circumstantial modality where priorities do not play a role).

One feature of traditional classifications which might be less than ideal is the great difference it implies between two uses of words like *likely*, *certain*, and *chance*.

According to the standard classification above, *likely* is ambiguous between an epistemic meaning in (16a) and a dynamic meaning in (16b).[2]

(16)　a. Given the evidence, Bob is likely to be hiding in the basement.
　　　b. The way that storm is developing, it is likely to spawn a tornado.

It is useful to have a cover term for types of epistemic and dynamic modality which express either subjective or objective chance; we can use the term PREDICTIVE MODALITY for this class.

I will refer to the differences in meaning along the dimensions outlined in (13)–(16) as differences of JUDGMENT TYPE. (In the literature and especially in the spoken jargon of semantics, they are often described as "flavors" of modality.) See Portner (2009) for discussion of other classification schemes. Note that many of the above examples involve English modal auxiliaries. Other varieties of modality are found in other languages, and in other constructions within English, but these have not made their ways into the generally shared terminology of semanticists.

Yet another parameter along which modal meanings vary is that of STRENGTH. Scholars who study modality make at least a two-way distinction between strong and weak modals, although not every language may actually have modals of both strengths (Deal 2011). Both *should* and *may* can be deontic, but (17a) is stronger than (i.e. it entails) (17b):

(17)　(a) He should vote for her. (strong)
　　　(b) He may vote for her. (weak)

Similar oppositions exist within each of the other subtypes of modality, as can be seen in (13)–(15). In those examples, *must*, *should*, and *will* would be classified as strong modals, while the others would be classified as weak. Strong modals are sometimes called NECESSITY modals, and weak ones POSSIBILITY modals, on the grounds that *it is necessary that* is strong and *it is possible that* is weak.

When we look beyond modal auxiliaries, it becomes clear that strength is not a two-way distinction. In the following, (18a) is stronger than (18b), and so forth down the line:

(18)　(a) It will certainly rain.
　　　(b) It will almost certainly rain.
　　　(c) It will probably rain.
　　　(d) There is a reasonable chance that it will rain.
　　　(e) It is just possible that it will rain.

It seems that modal strength is gradable, and it is natural to think of this gradability as being similar to the gradability of concrete properties, such as height and weight. (Gradable modality is currently a topic of much study in semantics; see for example

---

[2] Rubinstein et al. (2013) find that speakers have significant difficulties making the distinction between epistemic and dynamic modality in certain texts.

Portner 2009; Yalcin 2010; Katz et al. 2012; Klecha 2014; Lassiter 2016.) As we see in these few examples, variation in strength can arise from a combination of lexical choice (*certainly* is stronger than *probably*) and compositional semantics (*almost certainly* is weaker than *certainly*). Among strong modals, elements including *should* and *ought* are sometimes called "weak necessity modals," because they feel weaker than other ("strong") necessity modals like *must*. (The terminology is somewhat confusing here, because a weak necessity modal is still a strong, or necessity, modal by our terminology. A weak necessity modal is the weaker subtype of strong modal.) It's not yet clear whether weak necessity modals are logically weaker than their strong counterparts, or whether they differ in meaning in some other way (e.g. von Fintel and Iatridou 2008; von Fintel and Gillies 2010; Rubinstein 2012).

1.3.2 Modality in possible worlds semantics

In order to fully engage with the ideas and debates in the analysis of mood which will occupy the bulk of this book, it is important for readers to have a good understanding of semantic theories of modality. The goal of Portner (2009) was to introduce the analyses of modality within four semantic frameworks: modal logic, Kratzer's ordering semantics, dynamic semantics, and cognitive semantics. I cannot recapitulate that discussion here, but instead suggest that readers without sufficient background begin with that book or other resources on the semantics of modality. In this section, I will review some of the key ideas of the important tradition of modal semantics based on possible worlds. This tradition began within modal logic and has evolved into the standard account within formal (linguistic) semantics. It is of the most relevance here because the bulk of theoretically-informed work on mood takes place within this framework. My goal with this review of possible worlds analysis of modality is to emphasize aspects of the approach which will prove especially important in the rest of the book, to establish my own terminological and notational preferences, and to jog the memories of readers who may know about the semantics of modality, but not have thought about it in a while.

The standard theory of modality within possible worlds semantics focuses on sentential modal constructions,[3] and aims to explain their judgment type and strength.

Judgment type.   Within possible worlds semantics, judgment type is determined by the particular set of possible worlds on which the modal's meaning is based. For example, with the epistemic example (13a), the judgment being made is that a

---

[3] Subsentential and discourse modality are considered important topics to which the theory should be extended (and much of this book concerns such attempts), but not exemplars of the standard theory as it stands. An exception to this statement is subsentential modality that gets treated as if it were sentential modality, for example the use of modal adjectives with sentential complements: *It is necessary/likely/possible that it is raining.* These treatments generally ignore features of the subsentential modal constructions which are not shared by sentential modals.

typhoon hitting the island is compatible with the speaker's knowledge. Suppose we identify the set K of worlds compatible with what the speaker knows; in that case, we can express the judgment of (13a) by saying that some of the worlds in K contain situations in which a typhoon hits the island. In more formal terms, modal logic bases the semantics of a particular modal element on an ACCESSIBILITY RELATION between worlds R. In (13a), we might use R_{ep}:

(19)   For any worlds w_*, and w: $R_{ep}(w_*, w)$ iff everything the speaker knows in w_* also holds in w.

Taking w_* to be the actual world, the set of accessible worlds K is $\{w : R_{ep}(w_*, w)\}$. We can define the truth conditions of (13a) as follows:

(20)   *A typhoon may hit the island* is true in a world w_* iff there is some world w such that both $R_{ep}(w_*, w)$ and a typhoon hits the island in w.

Though the definitions in (19)–(20) show technically how an accessibility relation works (and so might be useful for some purposes), it is far too simple. For instance, it assumes that the only person whose knowledge we care about is the speaker's and the only knowledge of his that we care about is that which he has at the present moment. If there are examples where the knowledge of an individual other than the speaker, or at a time other than the present, is relevant, we'd need a different accessibility relation.

   Let us examine some data to see who can be the "knower" and what can be the "knowing time" in cases of sentential epistemic modality.

(21)   [Two children are discussing whether the creature they caught is a newt or a salamander.]
   (a) This might be a salamander.
   (b) It might have been a salamander.
   (c) Ryan said that it might be a salamander.

In (21a), the knower is either the child speaking or the two children jointly, and the knowing time is the speech time. In (21b), the knower is again the speaker or two children jointly, while the knowing time could be either the speech time or some time in the past, for example, when the children still had the creature in their hands. (To see the latter possibility, consider the continuation . . . *but it turns out it wasn't.*) In (21c), Ryan is the relevant knower, and the knowing time is the (past) time at which he spoke. Clearly, the details of the accessibility relation can vary from case to case, and yet this variation is very much limited by grammatical factors. It would be very difficult for one of the children to use (21a) to make a modal statement based on what Ryan knew.

   It is an important goal for modal semantics to come up with an adequate theory of the kind of variation illustrated in (21). One way to do this is to incorporate a context situation s into the definition of the accessibility relation. The knower and knowing time are extracted from the context situation, while the context situation itself (as the name suggests) is determined by the linguistic or extralinguistic context, in ways to be determined:

(22) For any context situation s and worlds w_*, w: $R_{ep}(s)(w_*, w)$ iff everything that the thinking participant(s) of s know in w_* at the time of s also holds in w.

There is some redundancy in (22) because the set of accessible worlds depends on both a context situation s and a world w_*. But if we assume that each situation is only part of a single world, and that it only determines accessibility from the world of which it is a part, we can base the accessibility relation on the context situation alone, as follows:[4]

(23) For any context situation s and world w: $R_{ep}(s, w)$ iff everything which the thinking participant (or participants) of s know in s also holds in w.

In root sentences, it is always possible (and usually preferred, if not outright required) for s to include the speaker as among the thinking participants, and for the time of s to include the time at which the sentence itself was used. Thus, the typical interpretation of a root sentence with *might* concerns the speaker's knowledge at the time of utterance. This is what we see in (21a). However, the time can diverge from the speech time, particularly in the presence of perfect aspect (*have been* in (21b)), and it's even possible for the thinking participants not to include the speaker, for example in a narrative. In embedded clauses, the situation s is typically determined by grammatical factors; in (21c), we see the matrix verb *said* controlling the interpretation of the modal in the embedded clause by making sure that Ryan is the thinking participant of s.

Other judgment types can be associated with accessibility definitions similar to (23), such as the following for a deontic modal used to make a statement about what the law requires (for example, *That guy should put a coin in the parking meter*):

(24) For any context situation s and world w: $R_{legal}(s, w)$ iff all of the laws in force in s are fully complied with in w.

We describe a world accessible by the relation associated with an epistemic modal as an EPISTEMICALLY ACCESSIBLE WORLD. Similarly, we may talk about DEONTIC-ALLY ACCESSIBLE WORLDS, BULETICALLY ACCESSIBLE WORLDS, and so forth. We can also use less esoteric language like "knowledge worlds" (for epistemically accessible ones) and "desire worlds" (for buletically accessible ones).

Strength.   Differences in strength are analyzed within modal logic and semantic systems closely based on modal logic as a difference between universal and existential quantification. The strength of a given modal is also known as its

---

[4] Hacquard (2010) argues that the meanings expressed by modal auxiliaries are relative to events in a way analogous to (23). She also assumes that the judgment type can be determined from s, so that a single general-purpose R can work for all flavors of modality.

MODAL FORCE. Within the meaning of the weak modal *might* in (13a), we find the phrase "there is some world," an existential quantifier over accessible worlds. A strong modal like *must*, in contrast, is used to make a statement to the effect that all relevant worlds have a certain property. In other words, it is a universal quantifier over accessible worlds. The universal meaning of epistemic *must* in (13b) can be stated as follows:

(25)   *Mary must have a good reason for being late*, used in a context situation s in w_*, is true in w_* iff, for every w such that $R_{ep}(s, w)$, Mary has a good reason for being late in w.

This is like (20) except that it involves universal quantification and it has been improved through the inclusion of the context situation motivated above.

The quantificational analysis of modal strength in standard possible worlds semantics only can distinguish two strengths, strong (universal quantification) and weak (existential quantification), and it is clear that this is not enough to explain the full range of variation in strength. This point is most clear with subsentential modality, as illustrated by (18) above, but it may also be seen in the relation between strong and weak necessity modals. Many authors (including von Fintel and Iatridou 2008; Finlay 2010; Kolodny and MacFarlane 2010; Rubinstein 2012; Lassiter 2016) discuss the fact that the strong necessity *must* and *have to* appear to be stronger than weak necessity *should* and *ought to* (example from von Fintel and Iatridou):

(26)   Everybody ought to wash their hands; employees must.

The simplest approach to explaining intuitive differences in strength beyond the basic strong–weak contrast focuses on the choice of accessibility relation. The idea here follows from a logical observation. Suppose we have two accessibility relations R and R' such that the set of worlds accessible by the former is always a subset of the set of worlds accessible by the latter:

(27)   For any context situation s: $\{w : R(s, w)\} \subseteq \{w : R'(s, w)\}$.

Then, if we have weak (existential) modal sentences differing in that the first uses R and the second R', the first will entail the second. The reverse holds for strong (universal) modal sentences. To see why, consider Figure 1.1, based on Portner (2009). At a given situation s, R makes accessible the set of worlds indicated by the arrow labeled R, and R' makes accessible a superset of that set. A weak modal is true, using a given accessibility relation, if some accessible world is one in which the portion under the scope of the modal (call it S) is true. The portion of the diagram on the left shows the situation relevant to a weak modal: if S is true at some world in the smaller set accessible by R, it will obviously be true at some world accessible by R' (at least, the very same world). The right-hand side of the diagram shows that the opposite holds with a strong modal: if S is true at all worlds accessible by R', it will obviously also be true at all worlds accessible by R. To summarize, we have the following:

(28)   For any sentence S and any accessibility relations R and R' related as in (27):
  (a) $\Diamond_R(S)$ entails $\Diamond_{R'}(S)$
  (b) $\Box_{R'}(S)$ entails $\Box_R(S)$

(The symbol $\Box$ is drawn from modal logic to indicate any modal whose meaning is expressed using universal quantification over worlds, while $\Diamond$ is the corresponding symbol for a modal whose meaning is expressed using existential quantification.) We might use the observations in (28) to analyze (26) by saying that the accessibility relation associated with *ought* makes accessible a subset of the worlds made accessible by that associated with *must*. In other words, *ought* is like $\Box_R$ in (28), while *must* is like $\Box_{R'}$.

The main issue with trying to explain differences in modal strength in terms of subset relations among accessibility relations is that it becomes unclear precisely what content is associated with each relation. In the case of (26), we are to assume that *ought*'s R determines a subset of *must*'s R', but precisely which worlds do $R(s)$ and $R'(s)$ make accessible? Intuitively, we want to say that $R(s)$ makes accessible all worlds in which both the very important and the less important rules applicable in s are followed, while $R'(s)$ makes accessible all worlds in which the very important rules in s are followed, but possibly not the less important rules. It would be helpful if we could explicitly define the accessible worlds for *ought* and *must* in terms of the rules of varying degrees of importance. Kratzer's premise-based ordering semantics for modality discussed next allows us to think of differences in modal strength in precisely this way.

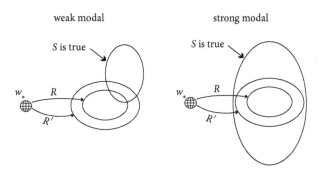

FIGURE 1.1   Strength via accessibility relation

Kratzer's ordering semantics.   In Portner (2009), I presented two versions of modal logic based on the ideas about modal force and judgment type outlined above. These theories, a basic modal logic similar to what is taught in introductory modal logic texts and a "modal logic for linguists" which modifies it to deal with some of the most obvious differences between natural languages and logical ones, are useful because they are widely understood and serve as a precise baseline against which other theories can be measured. While forms of modal logic like those are useful, they are not taken as realistic theories of modal semantics in natural language. They simply do not allow one to express in a theoretically perspicuous way many important ideas about modal semantics and pragmatics.

For this reason, linguists have extended and modified the framework of modal logic to produce more linguistically useful theories of modality.

The standard theory of modality within formal semantics was developed by Kratzer (1977, 1981, 1991, 2012). This influential approach extends the basic possible worlds analysis of modality in several ways. Perhaps the most important development is that the modals do not simply classify a possible world as either wholly accessible or inaccessible, but rather rank or order them according to some relevant criteria. Exactly which worlds are accessible in a given case can be determined in a flexible way based on this ordering. We can label Kratzer's theory as a prime example of the ORDERING SEMANTICS approach to modality.

Portner (2009) provides a detailed introduction to Kratzer's theory, but it will be useful to have a brief review here. One key concept in her framework is that of a CONVERSATIONAL BACKGROUND. A conversational background is a function from situations to sets of propositions, and can be given by context, linguistic material, or a combination of the two.[5] A conversational background can serve either of two basic functions. It can specify a set of relevant worlds or it can define an ordering of worlds. In its former function, a conversational background is known as a MODAL BASE, while in the latter function, it is known as an ORDERING SOURCE.

(29) **Conversational backgrounds**
    (a) A conversational background is a function from situations to sets of propositions. (Its domain is S and its range $\mathcal{P}(W)$.)
    (b) Functions of conversational backgrounds
        (i) Modal base. For any situation s, a conversational background $\mathbf{m}$ (functioning as a modal base) defines a set of relevant worlds $\bigcap \mathbf{m}(s)$.
        (ii) Ordering source. For any situation s, a conversational background $\mathbf{o}$ (functioning as an ordering source) defines an ordering $\leq_s$, as follows:
        For any worlds w and v, $w \leq_s v$ iff, for all $p \in \mathbf{o}(s)$, if $v \in p$, then $w \in p$.

The modal base defines as relevant (at a given situation s) those worlds in which all propositions in the modal base are true. The ordering source ranks worlds so that one world is ordered $\leq$ another (with respect to a given situation s) if and only if all of the propositions in the ordering source which are true in the latter are also true in the former. So for example:

(30) (a) Modal base: {'It is hot', 'It is sunny'}.
    (b) Ordering source: {'We have cold drinks', 'We have a parasol'}.

The relevant worlds defined by the modal base are ones in which it's both hot and sunny. The ordering defined by the ordering source ranks those worlds in which

---

[5] In Kratzer's work, a conversational background is a function from worlds to sets of propositions. I will treat the domain as situations rather than worlds, in order to incorporate the idea of a context situation.

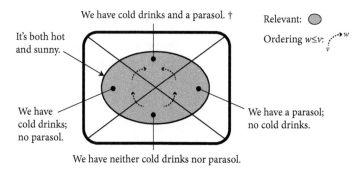

We have cold drinks and a parasol. †

It's both hot and sunny.

We have cold drinks; no parasol.

We have a parasol; no cold drinks.

We have neither cold drinks nor parasol.

Relevant:

Ordering $w \leq v$:

FIGURE 1.2   Modal base and ordering source

we have both cold drinks and a parasol the highest, worlds in which we have either cold drinks or a parasol less high, and worlds in which we have neither cold drinks nor a parasol the lowest. (Worlds in which we have cold drinks but no parasol, and those in which we have a parasol but no cold drinks, are not ordered with respect to each other.) These relations are illustrated in Figure 1.2.

Within ordering semantics, the meanings of modal operators are defined in terms of structures like the one illustrated in Figure 1.2. In simple cases (like the one in the figure), the modal base and ordering source combine to define a set of accessible worlds which can be thought of in pretty much the same way as the accessibility relation in modal logic. The accessible worlds are the best-ranked relevant worlds; this set is indicated by † in Figure 1.2 (i.e. the grey-shaded worlds in the upper sector). The meanings of strong and weak modal operators can then be defined in terms of this set in the usual way. However, the ordering structures can be more complicated; for example, there may be multiple, incompatible sets of "best-ranked" worlds (worlds compared to which there are no higher-ranked worlds), or infinite series of ever-better worlds, with no stopping point at a highest-ranked world. In those cases, more sophisticated definitions will be called for; see Kratzer's papers or Portner (2009) for details.

Kratzer's framework has been used to provide a better analysis of modal strength than the one which comes from modal logic. Recall the problem of *must* and *ought* illustrated in (26). In order to explain the fact that *must* is stronger, we want to say that the set of accessible worlds for *must* is always a superset of the set of accessible worlds for *ought*. Within Kratzer's system, the set of accessible worlds for a modal is determined by the conversational backgrounds which function as modal base and ordering source. Suppose that it is part of the lexical meaning of deontic *must* that it uses a particular conversational background which includes only the most important priorities and rules in the context; in contrast, deontic *should* uses both this conversational background and another one which includes some less-important priorities and rules. From this intuitively reasonable difference between *must* and *should*, we can derive that the sentence with *must* is stronger than the corresponding sentence with *should*.

Let me show this by way of example. Consider the following conversational backgrounds:

(31) a. For any situation s, $cb_{crucial}(s) =$ the set of the most important priorities and rules in s (for example: you wash hands, you cook dinner).
    b. For any situation s, $cb_{good}(s) =$ the set of relevant but lesser priorities in s (for example: you clean up the house before dinner).

Now consider (32):

(32) a. You must cook dinner.
    b. You must clean up the house beforehand.
    c. You should clean up the house beforehand.

The ordering source for (32a–b) is $cb_{crucial}$, while that for (32c) is a combination of cb_{good} and $cb_{crucial}$.[6] Given this, (32a) and (32c) will be true, but (32b) will be false because there are best-ranked worlds accessible according to $cb_{crucial}$ in which you do not clean up the house. This example illustrates how the notion of conversational background allows us to state in an explicit and intuitive way how various contextual factors combine to determine which worlds are accessible in modal semantics.

Ordering semantics is useful for dealing with a number of other problems in the semantics of modality, including further variation in modal strength (as in (18)), comparative modality, and the interaction between modals and conditionals, but it would take us too far from our main concerns to pursue them here. Our discussion so far has been enough to highlight two points at which the ordering semantics approach is helpful in the theory of mood. First, Figure 1.2 is an example of the kind of partially ordered set of worlds (or POSW) which will show up in analyses of both verbal mood and sentence mood, and which may serve as the basis for developing a general theory of core mood. And second, the discussion of *must* and *ought* gives a sense of how we can formalize intuitively meaningful factors (like "the most important priorities and rules") to give an account of the lexical semantics of modal expressions. In order to understand verbal mood, we will develop techniques for explaining a variety of features of lexical meaning within a formal theory of modal semantics.

Before moving on, it is important to note that ordering semantics as sketched above is not the last word on the semantics of modality. At the current time, we see both a great deal of work aiming to modify and extend the basic framework and some important arguments that the entire framework should be replaced. When it comes to the semantics of mood, however, ordering semantics remains the touchstone (though not necessarily the precise form of ordering semantics proposed by Kratzer). Given the tight link between verbal mood and modality in human language, it is certain that the correct theory of modality will play an important role in the correct theory of mood, and so it should be seen as a test of

---

[6] There are several different possibilities for how to combine them. We might combine the ordering sources as $\lambda s[cb_{crucial}(s) \cup cb_{good}(s)]$ or merge them in another way. Or we might assign *ought* both $cb_{crucial}$ and cb_{good} ordering sources, adjusting the definition of $\leq_s$ to allow for multiple ordering sources. See von Fintel and Iatridou (2008), Rubinstein (2012), and Katz et al. (2012) for discussion.

old and new theories of modal semantics whether they can produce useful insights when used for thinking about mood.

1.4 The flow of information in discourse

Linguistic research on sentence mood builds on a very diverse range of ideas about discourse meaning from pragmatics, philosophy, and logic, and there is no foundational framework with the same near-standard status that the possible worlds semantics for modality has in research on verbal mood. In order to investigate sentence mood, we need some ideas about the nature of "information flow" in discourse. That is, we need some understanding of how information is introduced, solicited, and deployed for planning, reasoning, and social interaction in conversations or other genres like narratives and records. (Exactly what falls under this term "flow" must be left vague at this point. Theories differ, and it is up to a specific theory of discourse meaning to state what it encompasses and what it does not, and to justify its choices.) In this section, I will give a brief overview of two approaches to information flow which are important in contemporary research on sentence mood: the dynamic approach and classical speech act theory.

1.4.1 The dynamic approach

The central virtue of the dynamic theories is that, through all their variations, they give an explanation of the nature of information in discourse which is both precise and amenable to a simple account of how that information changes. I will introduce the ideas of dynamic semantics from a slightly unorthodox direction, beginning with the work of Robert Stalnaker (1970, 1974, 1978, 1984), and then discuss how Stalnaker's ideas develop into dynamic semantics in the form of the File Change Semantics of Irene Heim (1982, 1983, 1988, 1992). I will then give overviews of two other important, and somewhat different, theories of dynamic semantics: Kamp's Discourse Representation Theory (Kamp 1981; Kamp and Reyle 1993) and the "Amsterdam school" of Dynamic Logic (Groenendijk and Stokhof 1990, 1991; Groenendijk et al. 1996). In this section, we will not go into more recent work which explicitly applies the dynamic approach to understanding verbal mood or sentence mood; we will delve into such material in Chapters 2 and 3.

Stalnaker on pragmatic presupposition and assertion. Stalnaker (1978) proposes that "the central concept needed to characterize speech contexts" is SPEAKER PRESUPPOSITION:

A proposition is presupposed if the speaker is disposed to act as if he assumes or believes that the proposition is true, and as if he assumes or believes that his audience assumes or believes that it is true as well.   (Stalnaker 1978, p.321)

Building on this concept of presupposition and the associated model of the discourse context, we will be able to characterize the dynamic perspective on information flow in discourse.

Stalnaker takes propositions to be sets of possible worlds (as we have done above), and so it is possible to conjoin all of the speaker's presuppositions into a single proposition which represents all the ways the world could be which match all of those presuppositions. This proposition is the CONTEXT SET of the speaker. More generally, any participant in a linguistic exchange has a context set (relative to that exchange):

(33)   The **context set** of A in speaking to B =
       $\bigcap\{p : A$ presupposes p in speaking to audience $B\}$

In a given conversation, each participant has her own context set.[7] These context sets might be different, since one or more participants could be mistaken about what her audience assumes or believes. If the participants in the conversation have the same presuppositions in speaking to one another, we have a NON-DEFECTIVE CONTEXT, and theories of dynamic semantics typically make the idealizing assumption that our understanding of language and communication can make progress by considering only non-defective contexts. While one might fear that this idealization takes us too far from the nature of real conversation, in that most contexts are probably defective, it is perhaps reasonable to assume that most contexts are "close enough to non-defective" (as Stalnaker says) that their deficiencies do not matter.

In a non-defective context, we can speak of the COMMON GROUND OF THE CONTEXT and the CONTEXT SET OF THE CONTEXT:

(34)   a. The **common ground** of a non-defective context c:
          cg_c = the set of presuppositions of all of the participants in c in speaking to one another.
       b. The **context set** of a non-defective context c: $cs_c = \bigcap cg_c$

The context set of a non-defective context is identical to the context set of any participant in the conversation (in speaking to any other participant).

In thinking about Stalnaker's notion of context, it is worth noticing that the discussion has moved quickly from a definition of presupposition based on a speaker's disposition to act as if he assumes or believes some things (in speaking to an audience) to an analysis of context which relies on the concept of "the conversation." Specifically, the definitions of defective and non-defective contexts only make sense relative to a delineation of a set of participants all of whom count as speakers towards and audiences of one another. Thus, Stalnaker's approach seems to make the assumption that the nexus of speakers and auditors which constitutes a conversation is clear and unproblematic. Although Stalnaker's approach to defining the common ground of a context is sufficient for the purposes for which he and other dynamic semanticists use it, a more precise definition of context will require

---

[7] He or she might even have different context sets for each other addressee in the conversation, for example if he or she is talking to two people, trying to deceive one with the support of another.

a better-developed notion of conversation and with it a clearer understanding of what it means to be a speaker's "audience" (cf. Bell 1984).

Given the ability to model the conversational context with the common ground and context set, Stalnaker discusses the concepts of assertion and linguistic pre-supposition. He writes that

... the essential effect of an assertion is to change presuppositions of the participants in the conversation by adding the content of what is asserted to what is presupposed. This effect is avoided only if the assertion is rejected.   (Stalnaker 1974, p.323)

These ideas about assertion can be expressed in terms of a rule affecting the common ground or context set:

(35)   a. The essential effect of an assertion of S with respect to a non-defective context c with common ground cg_c is to change cg_c to $cg_c \cup \{[\![\, S \,]\!]^c\}$.
   - As a formula: $cg_c + S = cg_c \cup \{[\![\, S \,]\!]^c\}$
   This effect comes about unless the assertion is rejected.

   b. The essential effect of an assertion of S with respect to a non-defective context c with context set cs_c is to change cs_c to $cs_c \cap [\![\, S \,]\!]^c$.
   - As a formula: $cs_c + S = cs_c \cap [\![\, S \,]\!]^c$
   This effect comes about unless the assertion is rejected.

The formulaic versions above rely on interpreting the '+' symbol appropriately, as shorthand for the extended description given by Stalnaker.

Heim's File Change Semantics.   Irene Heim (1982, 1983, 1988) takes us from Stalnaker's concepts of assertion and presupposition to the core ideas of dynamic semantics. In Heim's work, we can see a number of important developments which lead from the philosophical and somewhat abstract perspective of Stalnaker to a framework more suited to research into linguistically interesting questions about assertion and presupposition. The most obvious differences result from Heim's concern for a much wider range of presupposition phenomena. First of all, whereas Stalnaker expressed skepticism that it is ever crucial to talk about the presuppositions of linguistic forms (as opposed to the pragmatic presuppositions of the speakers who use those forms), Heim develops a notion of the FELICITY CONDITIONS of a presupposition trigger within dynamic semantics. For example, Heim (1992) defines the felicity condition of *too* in such a way that the second sentence in (36a) (uttered in that context and with the coindexing indicated) is subject to the condition (36b):

(36)   a. Mary$_1$ is happy. Susan$_F$ is happy too$_1$.
   b. Felicity condition of *too*, given context c indicated by (36a): $cs_c + Susan_F$ *is happy too*$_1$ is defined iff Mary is happy in every world in cs_c.

Intuitively, the second sentence of (36a) presupposes that the referent associated with index 1, Mary, is both distinct from Susan and happy. Heim does not formulate this presupposition directly in terms of the speaker's disposition to act as if he assumes or believes something, but rather expresses it as a condition on when $cs_c + S$ is defined. This way of formalizing the felicity condition triggered by *too* ultimately leads back to Stalnaker's pragmatic speaker's presupposition, since on the assumption that cs_c is non-defective, if the condition in (36b) fails, this is because the speaker and addressee do not presuppose (in the sense of pragmatic presupposition) that Mary is happy. However, crucially it is not identical to Stalnaker's notion of presupposition, because it is seen as a linguistic property of the sentence which constrains speakers' utterances based on their (speaker) presuppositions.

In the context of (36a), the felicity condition of *too* will be satisfied, if the assertion of the first sentence is not challenged, because the first sentence entails that Mary is happy and the assertion adds this information to the context set. Heim uses similar ideas about presupposition to attack the famous Projection Problem for presupposition (see for example Karttunen 1973; Karttunen and Peters 1975; Gazdar 1979; Soames 1982; Heim 1988, 1992).

Other crucial differences between Heim's work and Stalnaker's flow from Heim's concern for presupposition phenomena related to anaphora and definiteness. Example (37b) is felicitous if preceded by (37a), intuitively because *a soldier* in (37a) provides a referent for *he* in (37b):

(37)   a. I saw a soldier in the park.
        b. He waved to me.

To be more precise, within Heim's theory the felicity of a pronoun depends on both the preceding context and indexing of noun phrases in Logical Form. On the reading indicated by the indexing (38a), the second sentence is felicitous. On the reading indicated by the indexing in (38b), in contrast, it is not felicitous unless the referent for *he* is determined by previous material or extralinguistic context.

(38)   a. I saw [a soldier]$_1$ in the park. He$_1$ waved to me.
        b. I saw [a soldier]$_1$ in the park. He$_2$ waved to me.

Definite and indefinite noun phrases show complementary patterns:[8] A definite is felicitous if it is coindexed with an antecedent and it is entailed that the referent has the property denoted by the definite's common noun phrase. (It can also be felicitous due to extralinguistic context.) An indefinite is felicitous unless it is coindexed with an antecedent.

(39)   a. I saw [a soldier]$_1$ in the park. The soldier$_1$ waved to me.
        b. I saw [a soldier]$_1$ in the park. *A soldier$_1$ waved to me.

---

[8] The description here leaves out many complexities which are well-studied in the literature on anaphora and definiteness, but this oversimplified version is sufficient to allow us to understand Heim's contributions to dynamic semantics.

In (37)–(39) we see, in each case, that the initial sentence *I saw a soldier in the park* introduces a soldier into the context, and that soldier can serve as a referent for a pronoun or definite; it cannot, however, serve as the referent for a subsequent indefinite, and indeed each indefinite must introduce its own, new individual into the context. The main effort of Heim's work on definiteness is to take this intuitive description and develop it into an explanatory formal theory.

Under the inspiration of Stalnaker's ideas about presupposition and assertion, one can see (37)–(39) as showing that the common ground and context set contain information not just about what is presupposed to be the case, but also about which individuals the participants presuppose they are able to talk about. For example, assertion of the first sentence in (38a) results in a context set which represents a speaker presupposition that the speaker saw a soldier in the park and a speaker presupposition that subsequent assertions can affect the speaker presuppositions about this same presupposed soldier. Thus, after the second sentence in (38a) is asserted, the context set encodes a speaker presupposition that the speaker saw a soldier in the park who waved at her. The beauty of analyzing anaphora in terms of the context set is that this overall presupposition of (38a) can be recorded without there needing to be any actual soldier in the park—in the end, the context set encodes a speaker presupposition to the effect that the speaker is disposed to act as if she assumes or believes that she saw a soldier in the park who waved at her. The soldier being talked about is a mere DISCOURSE REFERENT, in Karttunen's (1976) terminology. We can understand discourse referents to be the referential component of speaker presupposition.

The technical side of Heim's work focuses on giving a precise, compositional version of the above ideas. She replaces Stalnaker's notion of the context set of the context cs_c, a set of possible worlds, with the SATISFACTION SET of the context sat_c, a set of pairs $\langle w, g \rangle$ consisting of a world w and assignment of values to indices g. Note that g is a partial function from indices to values (not every index need be in its domain), but all of the assignments in a satisfaction set must have the same domain.[9] The satisfaction set allows her to represent contextual information both about what is the case (via w) and about discourse referents (via g). Specifically, if index i is assigned a value by the assignments in the satisfaction set, i corresponds to a discourse referent in the context. For example, sat_c in (40) represents a context in which Max is a soldier, Al is a baker, we're not sure whether Max walked, the first discourse referent is one of the two men Max or Al, and there are no other discourse referents.

(40) $sat_c = \{\langle w_1, g_1 \rangle, \langle w_1, g_2 \rangle \langle w_2, g_1 \rangle, \langle w_2, g_2 \rangle\}$, where
   i. $\langle w_1, g_1 \rangle$:
         w_1: Max is a soldier, Al is a baker, Max walked.
         $g_1(1) = $ Max. For all $i \neq 1, g_1(i)$ is not defined.
   ii. $\langle w_1, g_2 \rangle$:
         w_1: (as above)
         $g_2(1) = $ Al. For all $i \neq 1, g_2(i)$ is not defined.

---

[9] Instead of talking about the context, Heim talks about the satisfaction set of the "file," a metaphorical picture of context as a file cabinet filled with shared information.

iii. $\langle w_2, g_1 \rangle$:

w_2: Max is a soldier, Al is a baker, Max didn't walk.

g_1: (as above)

iv. $\langle w_2, g_2 \rangle$:

w_2: (as above)

g_2: (as above)

Heim has to adjust Stalnaker's analyses of pragmatic presupposition and assertion to make sure that pronouns and definite and indefinite noun phrases affect discourse referents in the way observed in (37)–(39). Let's work with a simpler example than those, (41a):

(41)   a. [A soldier]$_1$ walked. He$_1$ waved.
       b.   i. soldier(x_1) $\wedge$ walked(x_1)
           ii. waved(x_1)

Building on ideas of Lewis (1975), Heim proposes that pronouns and definite and indefinite noun phrases are realized as variables at logical form, and that, while these variables become bound in some cases, in simple ones like this they do not. The logical form of the sequence (41a) is a pair of open sentences (41bi–ii). Although an open sentence does not have proper truth conditions, we can talk about the conditions under which an assignment of individuals to the free variables leads to its being true in a world. For example, a pair consisting of a possible world w and assignment of individuals to indices g satisfies (41bi) if and only if the individual $g(1)$ assigned to index 1 is a soldier who walked in w. The SATISFACTION SET of a sentence S, $Sat(S)$, is the set of world-assignment pairs which satisfy S.

Satisfaction sets allow a treatment of assertion parallel to Stalnaker's:

(42)   The essential effect of an assertion of S with respect to a non-defective context c with satisfaction set sat_c is to change sat_c to $sat_c \cap Sat(S)$.
       • As a formula: $sat_c + S = sat_c \cap Sat(S)$
       This effect comes about unless the assertion is rejected.

The assertion of (41bi) in a context c results in a satisfaction set in which every $\langle w, g \rangle$ pair has $g(1)$ a soldier who walked in w. For example, if it is asserted in the context with sat_c as in (40), the result is $\{\langle w_1, g_1 \rangle\}$.

The satisfaction set also allows an attractive theory of the presuppositions of definites and indefinites. In the first sentence of (41a), the index 1 is associated with an indefinite. This means that index 1 is "new"; in other words, it is presupposed not to be in the domain of the satisfaction set. When we get to the second sentence, however, 1 is associated with a definite; at this point, 1 is presupposed to be in the domain of the satisfaction set:

(43)   Presuppositions of indefinites and definites:
       a. If variable x_i is associated with an indefinite NP_i in S, then $sat_c + S$ is only defined if i is not in the domain of sat_c.

b. If variable x_i is associated with a definite NP_i in S, then $sat_c + S$ is only defined if i is in the domain of sat_c.

What's important here for us is that (43) encodes lexically triggered presuppositions which pertain to discourse referents, not propositional information.

Although it was not explicit in her earliest work, Heim comes to see the formula in (42) not just as a description of what happens when someone asserts a sentence, but rather as giving the very meaning of the sentence.[10]

the meaning of a sentence is its context change potential (CCP).... A CCP is a function from contexts to contexts.   (Heim 1992, p.185)

In this quote, Heim goes beyond Stalnaker's perspective on assertion, according to which a sentence has semantic content (a proposition) which gets used to change the context when it is asserted. Instead she adopts a more radical view according to which the context change potential is itself the semantic content.[11] This view is the central hypothesis of dynamic semantics, and so we can see Heim's work as realizing a dynamic semantics analysis of speaker presupposition, assertion, and felicity conditions.

Versions of the dynamic approach.   For the purposes of discussing theories of mood in Chapters 2 and 3, it will be useful to have terms for a range of broadly "dynamic" perspectives on meaning. We will use the term DYNAMIC PRAGMATICS for the Stalnakerian view that sentences have a static (i.e. non-dynamic) semantic content such as a proposition, which is then used to define a context change potential (for example, assertion).[12] We will use DYNAMIC SEMANTICS for the view which says that the content of a sentence is precisely its context change potential. The difference between dynamic pragmatics and dynamic semantics concerns the relative priority between static content and context change potential. For dynamic pragmatics, static content is basic and is dynamicized through operations native to pragmatics; for dynamic semantics, context change is basic, and if static content is needed for some analytical purpose, it has to be recovered from the context change potential. We should note that hybrid views are possible: perhaps some sentences have a static content while others do not, or perhaps sentences have two aspects of meaning, one of which conforms to the dynamic pragmatics view and the other of which requires dynamic semantics.[13] As I will use it, the broad term DYNAMIC

---

[10] To give the complete meaning of the sentence in this framework would be to define $c+S$ generally, not just the effect of S on the satisfaction set of c, $sat_c + S$.

[11] One might wonder whether the difference is more than terminological, since the $Sat(S)$ plays a role in (42) parallel to the content of S in Stalnaker's (35b), but be that as it may, Heim is clearly endorsing a move to understanding sentence meaning in essentially context-change terms.

[12] Lauer (2013) uses "dynamic pragmatics" for a rather different approach to discourse meaning. Schlenker (2010) employs the phrase to describe Stalnaker's theory of presupposition and assertion, and Stalnaker (to appear) uses the term in the way I do here. Stalnaker (2014) further explores and advocates for the dynamic pragmatics approach.

[13] The discussion of the performativity of modals by Portner (2009) suggests this last possibility.

TABLE 1.2   Versions of the dynamic approach

The dynamic approach		
Dynamic pragmatics	Dynamic semantics	Combined approaches
Static semantic content, and CCP via pragmatics	Semantic content = CCP	Semantic content is varied

APPROACH encompasses dynamic pragmatics, dynamic semantics, and all of these other possibilities. These versions of the dynamic approach are summarized in Table 1.2.

Discourse Representation Theory.   Beginning at the same time as Heim's work on File Change Semantics but continuing for a longer time, Hans Kamp and colleagues developed an important representative of the dynamic approach, Discourse Representation Theory (DRT; Kamp 1981; Kamp and Reyle 1993, among others). DRT differs in an important way from File Change Semantics and the Stalnakerian ideas on which the latter is based: According to DRT, the dynamic aspects of meaning are computed with the essential mediation of a new level of representation known as the DISCOURSE REPRESENTATION STRUCTURE. A discourse representation structure, or DRS, is a level of Logical Form which can incorporate the contributions of a sequence of sentences in discourse. For example, the operation of DRS-construction applied to the sequence (41a) from above results in, first, (44b), and then (44c):

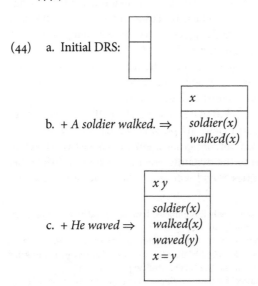

(44)   a. Initial DRS:

b. + *A soldier walked.* ⇒

c. + *He waved* ⇒

The box structures in (44) are the conventional way of representing DRSs; officially, they are just set-theoretic pairs consisting of a set of variables (discourse referents, on top) and formulas in a logical language (conditions, at bottom). A DRS is interpreted through techniques familiar from logic, and the simple examples in (44) can be interpreted extensionally in a first-order model. Specifically, the DRS in (44b) is true in a model M iff there is a soldier who walked in M, and the one in (44c) is true in M if there is a soldier who walked and waved in M.

From the above sketch, it should be apparent that the semantic mechanisms of DRT are not dynamic since each DRS is interpreted with a standard static semantics. What is special about DRT is that the dynamism in the theory is realized through the DRS-construction process. For example, the dynamic meaning of *He waved* in (44c) is captured by the introduction into the DRS of discourse referent y and conditions $waved(y)$ and $x = y$. In this way it differs crucially from Heim's framework in which the context change potential of a sentence is a function from contexts (represented in a simplified way as satisfaction sets) to contexts.

I am not aware of any research on the semantics and pragmatics of mood in which the representationalism of DRT would differentiate it in a crucial way from other dynamic approaches. In the very basic example used here, note the similarity between the logical forms used by File Change Semantics, (41), and the DRSs constructed by DRT, (44). The differences are merely (i) that the DRSs contain a layer enumerating the discourse referents (x, y) and (ii) that they introduce a separate discourse referent y for the pronoun which is equated with the previously introduced one, x. The first difference is due to the fact that, in order to assign traditional static semantic values to DRSs, all discourse referents must be implicitly bound at some point, and the discourse referent layer identifies the scope at which this occurs. (If box (44b) is nested inside a larger box, the value of x cannot be accessed from the containing box.) The second difference corresponds to the fact that Heim assumes that anaphoric relations are already resolved in syntax (and represented by coindexing, as in (41a)), while Kamp assumes that they are resolved in a "pragmatic" phase of DRS-construction which follows the introduction of syntactically overt material.

Dynamic logic. Beginning with an important series of papers by Groenendijk and Stokhof, dynamic logic developed the dynamic approach to meaning through a series of formal innovations (e.g. Groenendijk and Stokhof 1990, 1991; Groenendijk et al. 1996). The earliest work in dynamic logic explored the best ways to formally analyze anaphora in a dynamic framework; the approach opposes the representational analysis of DRT and in this way is similar to File Change Semantics. However, in contrast to the way in which Heim's commitment to dynamic semantics became clear only gradually, the founders of dynamic logic were interested in dynamic semantics from the start. Based on these initial results focused on anaphora, dynamic logic went on to explore many other important topics, including modality and sentence mood. In this section, we will briefly review some important ideas about anaphora and epistemic modality developed within dynamic logic. For a more detailed introduction, see Portner (2009). We will return to dynamic logic in Chapter 3 as we study its contribution to theories of sentence mood.

Dynamic logic is, as the name indicates, a logic, meaning that it is a syntax and semantics for a syntactically simple artificial language. It is important to note that the fundamental ideas of dynamic logic have been employed in several different ways; they have been used to give a semantics to the standard syntax for predicate logic according to which quantifiers have non-standard scope (Groenendijk and Stokhof 1991), to interpret a logical language which translates sentences of English in a Montague Grammar-like fragment (Groenendijk and Stokhof 1990), and to give an explicitly dynamic semantics to modal predicate logic (e.g. Groenendijk et al. 1996). Because of the attention it pays to modal semantics, we will focus on the last of these here.

We can begin thinking about dynamic logic by relating some of its ideas to what we've already discussed about Heim's work. In File Change Semantics, the context change potential of a sentence is defined in terms of the satisfaction set of the context, sat_c, and the satisfaction set of the sentence, $Sat(S)$. In dynamic logic, in place of the satisfaction set of the context, we talk about an INFORMATION STATE. An information state is essentially a model of the context which focuses on the same type of information present in a satisfaction set. Similarly, in place of the context change potential, we say that the semantic value of a sentence is its UPDATE POTENTIAL. The update potential of ϕ is notated as $[\phi]$. Update potentials are formally functions from information states to information states, and we write $s[\phi]$ to indicate the result of using ϕ to update s. Note that the meaning of a sentence is precisely its update potential, and so when dynamic logic is applied to analyze the meaning of natural language expressions, the result is clearly an example of dynamic semantics as we have defined it above.

We begin with the concept of an information state. In basic dynamic logic, information states are sets of POSSIBILITIES, where a possibility is a triple $\langle w, r, g \rangle$ whose three parts function as follows:[14]

(45) A possibility is a triple $\langle w, r, g \rangle$, where:
      1. POSSIBLE WORLD: w is a possible world.
      2. REFERENT SYSTEM: r is a partial function from variables to **pegs**.
      3. ASSIGNMENT TO PEGS: g is a function from the pegs in the range of r to individuals (in the domain D of the model).

Together, r and g serve to assign values to variables, and so serve the function of the assignment function components of the elements of the File Change Semantics satisfaction set, but instead of assigning values to the variables directly, a possibility first associates variables with a computation-internal representation of the discourse referent, a PEG, and then assigns an individual as the referent of the peg. The role of pegs is not too important for our purposes in this book, and we can think of them as just keeping track of which variables correspond to discourse referents that are currently accessible.

Given the definition of a possibility, an information state will look like this:

---

[14] I have reordered the components to make the presentation connect in a more simple way to that which has come earlier in this section.

(46) $s = \{\langle w_1, r, g_1 \rangle, \langle w_2, r, g_1 \rangle \, \langle w_1, r, g_2 \rangle, \langle w_2, r, g_2 \rangle\}$, where

    i. $\langle w_1, r, g_1 \rangle$:

        w_1: Max is a soldier, Al is a baker, Max walked.

        $r(x_1) = d_1$. For all $i \neq 1, r(i)$ is not defined.

        $g_1(d_1) =$ Max. For all $i \neq 1, g_1(d_i)$ is not defined.

    ii. $\langle w_2, r, g_1 \rangle$:

        w_2: Max is a soldier, Al is a baker, Max didn't walk.

        r: (as above)

        g_1: (as above)

    iii. $\langle w_1, r, g_2 \rangle$:

        w_1: (as above)

        r: (as above)

        $g_2(d_1) =$ Al. For all $i \neq 1, g_2(d_i)$ is not defined.

    iv. $\langle w_2, r, g_2 \rangle$:

        w_2: (as above)

        r: (as above)

        g_2: (as above)

This information state is the dynamic logic counterpart of the satisfaction set in (40). It represents a context in which one discourse referent (i.e. one peg), d_1, is active and associated with the variable x_1. This discourse referent could refer to Max (a soldier) or Al (a baker), and it's not known whether Max walked or not.

Whereas File Change Semantics treats indefinite noun phrases as open sentences, one of the most apparent innovations of dynamic logic is that it produces a dynamic meaning for the existential quantifier $\exists$. The job of $\exists$ is to introduce a new discourse referent (or peg) associated with its variable, and then generate the information state which corresponds to all of the ways that an individual can be associated with that peg while meeting the conditions set out in the formula in its scope. Formally, the rule looks like this:

(47) $s[\exists x\phi] = \bigcup_{d \in D}(s[x/d][\phi])$

The sentence *A soldier walked* would be represented as (48):

(48) $\exists x_1[soldier(x_1) \wedge walked(x_1)]$

And the result of updating an information state s with (48) is an information state (call it s') in which every possibility $\langle w, r, g \rangle$ has $r(x_1) = d_1$ and $g(d_1)$ is a soldier who walked in w. The dynamic feature of $\exists$'s meaning here is that it leaves a trace in the output state s'; specifically, r records that there is a discourse referent d_1 active and linked to the variable x_1. So, if the formula *waved*(x_1) with a free occurrence of x_1 is used after (48), r will associate its x_1 with d_1. So, when we compute $s'[waved(x_1)]$, the information state will gain the information that this same discourse referent waved (by losing those possibilities where $g(d_1)$ did not wave in w).

In addition to this analysis of indefinites and discourse anaphora, similar to the earlier frameworks of File Change Semantics and DRT, dynamic logic develops some innovative ideas about epistemic modality. As with the analysis of ∃, the semantic rules for the modal operators □ and ◊ have something in common with the standard treatments in modal logic, but they relate to the discourse context in a different, inherently dynamic way.

Epistemic modality is the judgment type which concerns someone's knowledge, and within standard modal semantics, this judgment type is analyzed using an epistemic accessibility relation. The key to understanding the dynamic logic analysis of □ and ◊ is to note that the information state s plays a role very similar to the set of accessible worlds in the standard analysis, but that, because s only provides a set of worlds, and not an accessibility relation, it is impossible to give a modal formula like $◊\phi$ a standard propositional meaning; that is, it is impossible to say that it denotes the set of worlds from which some ϕ world is accessible. Instead, its meaning must be defined in terms of the set of the "knowledge worlds," that is the worlds in s, directly.

Intuitively, one can think of $◊\phi$ as performing a check on whether any ϕ worlds are accessible—in other worlds, as checking whether there are ϕ worlds in s. If there are, s is left unchanged and the conversation can proceed as if $◊\phi$ had never been uttered; but if there are not, the conversation has reached a dead end. Formally speaking:

(49)   a. $s[◊\phi] = s$, if $s[\phi] \neq \emptyset$;
         b. $s[◊\phi] = \emptyset$, otherwise.

The "absurd" state $\emptyset$ can also be reached by accepting a contradiction (that is, by updating s with a sentence which is inconsistent with the information in s), and so the outcome in (49b) is a clear signal that something has gone wrong with the discourse. As an example, suppose we have the information state (46). In that case, updating for (50a) leaves the information state unaffected, while updating for (50b) leads to the absurd state:

(50)   a. Max might not have walked.
         b. Max might not be a soldier.

Dynamic semantics and assertion.   In Stalnaker's model of presupposition and assertion, sentences have a classical, propositional denotation and their effect on the context set, if they are felicitous, is defined by an intersective assertion operation (35b). Heim maintains the idea of a general intersective update, although her writings show some ambivalence in whether it is a separate operation which applies to the non-dynamic sentence meanings (satisfaction sets) or a property of dynamic sentence meanings (context change potentials). But either way, within Heim's theory, the final CCP can always be broken down into an intersective operation applied to a satisfaction set. Dynamic logic is different in that there are several operators, including ∃ and ◊, which cannot be defined in terms of the intersection of s with any proposition-like set defined within the theory. In the case of ◊, what is crucial is that $\Diamond\phi$ cannot be assigned a meaning independent of the information state s which it is used to update. That is, there is no single $[\![\, \Diamond\phi\,]\!]$ such that $s[\Diamond\phi] = s \cap [\![\, \Diamond\phi\,]\!]$. In this respect, these operators are "essentially dynamic" (see Portner 2009 for discussion).

We should not overstate how essential the dynamism of the inherently dynamic operators is, however. It is possible to reproduce the effects of $\Diamond\phi$ on an information state s in terms of an intersective assertion operator if the static meaning of $\Diamond\phi$ is allowed to depend on s. More specifically, $\Diamond$ can be given a standard modal logic semantics if it may use an accessibility relation which always makes accessible all of the possibilities in s. In that case, $\Diamond\phi$ will always denote a superset of s or the empty set, and by intersecting with s we will always get s or $\emptyset$, as on the dynamic logic analysis.

To see how this semi-dynamic meaning for $\Diamond$ would work, suppose that among the accessibility relations available to modal semantics, we have R_s:

(51)   For any information state s, $R_s = \{\langle i, i' \rangle : i \in s$ and $i' \in s\}$

Notice that what this accessibility relation relates are dynamic logic possibilities, not possible worlds.

(52)   For any information state s:
    a. $[\![\, \Diamond\phi\,]\!]^s = \{i : $ for some $i', \langle i, i' \rangle \in R_s$ and $\{i'\}[\phi] = \{i'\}\}$.
    b. $s[\Diamond\phi] = s \cap [\![\, \Diamond\phi\,]\!]^s$

Seen this way, the dynamic $\Diamond$ is an epistemic possibility modal whose judgment type is based on the "knowledge" in the common ground.

The expanding range of the dynamic approach.   Early work within the dynamic approach contributed important ideas concerning assertion, presupposition, discourse referents, and modality. Since that time, the approach has been improved in various ways, both by incorporating findings from other areas of semantics and by expanding the range of the dynamic approach itself. For the purpose of understanding mood, two developments have been most crucial: first, an attempt to integrate the mechanisms of dynamic semantics into subsentential, compositional semantics; and second, a variety of proposals which extend our notion of context change beyond assertion. Both of these developments will be important in later chapters, but it may be useful to have a very brief preview here:

1. Several scholars have used the assertive update operation '+' as part of the compositional mechanism by which certain subsentential modal expressions combine with their arguments. In Chapter 2, we will see how this strategy develops from several directions, including Heim's (1992) analysis of presupposition projection with attitude verbs and Farkas's (2003) attempt to account for verbal mood selection in a File Change Semantics framework. (Other work on verbal mood hints at the connection to the dynamic approach, but

does not make it explicit; see, for example, Portner 1997; Giannakidou 1999; and Quer 2001.)

2. In Chapter 3, we will see that the dynamic approach has been used to account for other ways of updating the context beyond assertions. Building on a long tradition of research on the semantics and pragmatics of interrogatives, scholars have developed various strategies for incorporating questions into the dynamic approach to meaning. Some of the most representative work along these lines is Hamblin (1971), Gazdar (1981), Ginzburg (1995a,b), Roberts (1996/2012, 2004), and Ciardelli et al. (2013). More recently, imperatives have also been discussed within the dynamic approach, for example by Portner (2004, 2007, 2016), Roberts (2004), Mastop (2005), Charlow (2011, 2013), and Starr (2010, 2013). Portner (2004, 2007) and Starr (2010, 2013) try to explain the universal properties of clause type systems from the perspective of the dynamic approach.

A related theme has been the idea that our model of discourse meaning should make a place for propositions which do not yet have the presupposed status represented by inclusion in the common ground. Hamblin (1971) and Gunlogson (2001) develop models of the context containing representations of the individual commitments of each participant in the conversation. Using such a framework, we can model the state of a conversation which is biased in favor of a proposition and the status of a proposition which has been proposed for acceptance into the common ground but not yet accepted. We see similar ideas in Portner's (2008) work on epistemic modals, Farkas and Bruce's (2010) on polar particles, and Murray's (2014) on evidentials.

There is, of course, much additional important work on both of these topics. Here I only mean to point out the fact that much of it grows out of the dynamic perspective in a more or less direct way. We will study these and other theories of verbal mood and sentence mood in Chapters 2 and 3.

1.4.2 Speech act theory

Most readers of this book are no doubt familiar with the basic tenets of our second framework for understanding the flow of information in discourse, classical SPEECH ACT THEORY. Austin (1962) described the differences between CONSTATIVE utterances, those for which the main point is whether they are true or false, and PERFORMATIVE utterances, those which perform some action in the world. While some of the actions performed by utterances bring about dramatic changes in the social world ("I pronounce you married") or in linguistic convention ("We're naming her Bea"), others pertain only to someone's temporary psychological state ("Let me warn you not to trust her"). The relevance of speech act theory to sentence mood is obvious even at this initial level of understanding; clearly imperatives and interrogatives normally do things the main point of which is not whether they are true or false. And while there are seemingly clear cases of declaratives used constatively to make a factual statement, like (53), it is very difficult to explicate an understanding of sentence types and speech act theory according to which imperatives and interrogatives are performative, while declaratives are constative.

(53)   The bird is out of the cage.

Austin (1962) writes:

> Would it be correct to say that when we state something . . . we are doing something as well as and distinct from just saying something?
>   . . . Surely to state is every bit as much to perform an illocutionary act as, say, to warn or to pronounce.   (Austin 1962, p.573)

Even in its most canonical constative use, (53) does something, and in the passage Austin calls what it does *stating*.

Austin recognized that his ideas were most likely to prove fruitful if used to understand better all of the speech acts which various sentences may perform, including those performed by constatives. To this end, he distinguishes three levels of speech acts:

1. The LOCUTIONARY ACT lumps together all of the acts intrinsic to the language system, including phonetics, phonology, morphology, syntax, and truth-conditional semantics, which the speaker performs when he utters a sentence.
2. The ILLOCUTIONARY ACT is the central act of intentional communication which the speaker performs in making the utterance.
3. The PERLOCUTIONARY ACT, or acts, are those which the speaker performs through, or as an effect of, the locutionary and illocutionary acts.

In the case of (53), the locutionary act includes subacts like moving the tongue to an interdental position, using the English word 'the', referring to a particular bird, and (I will assume) expressing the proposition which (53) literally denotes in the context in which the utterance is made. The illocutionary act might be to state this proposition, or it might be something else (or in addition),[15] such as to warn the addressee that it's not okay to open the window. The perlocutionary act might be to convince the addressee not to open the window.

Illocutionary force and the logical form of illocutionary acts.   Illocutionary acts, as described by speech act theorists beginning with Austin, serve the many diverse functions of language, including communication, planning, and managing social relationships. The acts which serve these functions are correspondingly diverse. We have acts such as asking one's interlocutor a question, giving a subordinate an order, providing a stranger with needed information, making a motion in a formal meeting, promising to help a friend with his problems, and threatening an enemy.

---

[15] Though it is not part of the original framework of speech act theory, the theory probably should allow a single utterance to perform multiple illocutionary acts, as noted by Levinson (1981) among others.

The type of act of which a particular illocutionary act is an example is known as its ILLOCUTIONARY FORCE. Thus, we can speak of an utterance as having the force of asking, the force of ordering, etc. Every illocutionary act has a force, and many scholars who take a functional approach to language have seen the concept of illocutionary force as providing a framework for explaining some important properties of language and dialogue.

Searle (1965, 1969) offers a reassessment of Austin's locutionary act which makes explicit where the crucial components of semantic interpretation fit into speech act theory. In the place of the locutionary act, he gives us both utterance acts (uttering words, phrases, and sentences) and propositional acts. PROPOSITIONAL ACTS are the speech acts of semantics; among them are the acts of referring, predicating, and expressing a proposition. In uttering a sentence like (53), one normally performs propositional acts like referring to a particular bird, predicating of it the property of being outside of the cage, and expressing the proposition that the bird (the particular one referred to) is not in the cage.

While the propositional acts are not part of the illocutionary act, they play a special role in the illocutionary act. Searle proposes that illocutionary acts in general have the logical form $F(c)$, where F is its illocutionary force and c is its CONTENT. The propositional acts determine the content of the illocutionary act. In most cases discussed by philosophers, the content is the proposition expressed as a propositional act, or in some cases it can be the object referred to (for example, *Down with Caesar!*; Searle 1969). For example, when (53) is used to make an assertion, the content is the proposition that the bird is outside of the cage and the illocutionary force is assertion.[16] In the case of wh-questions, Searle (1989) proposes that the content is a propositional function.

As for the force of an illocutionary act, in many cases it is obviously determined by some grammatical or lexical feature. Such linguistic material is known as the FORCE INDICATOR. For example, the declarative sentence form (in English, indicative verbal mood plus non-interrogative syntax) is an indicator of assertive force, while interrogative syntax would serve as an indicator of the force of asking. According to the LITERAL MEANING HYPOTHESIS (Gazdar 1981), every sentence has a force indicator, and any utterance of it which is an attempt to perform an illocutionary act includes an attempt to perform the illocutionary act $F(c)$ where F is the force indicated by the force indicator and c is the proposition expressed by the propositional act. As we will see, this literal meaning hypothesis (alternatively called the LITERAL FORCE HYPOTHESIS, when focusing on the status of F) is critiqued in later literature.

Searle (1965, 1969) also clarifies the status of the rules which govern the performance of illocutionary acts. By and large, speech acts are defined by linguistic and social conventions, and those conventions place conditions on when an individual can perform the act. Illocutionary acts, in particular, are associated with felicity conditions pertaining to the propositional content, the speaker's psychological state, and the actual state of affairs. (We will not go into the details of the kinds of

---

[16] As Searle notes, the idea that the use of a sentence has a logical form divided into a force-like part and a content-like part has deep roots, at least to Frege's judgment stroke. See Pagin (2014) for a recent overview. I find Dudman (1970, 1972) to provide very helpful insights.

conditions and rules which apply in this version of the theory, because they will be incorporated into more recent versions of the Searlean approach discussed below.)

The ideas just outlined comprise what we may call the classical version of speech act theory. In this framework, each of the utterances listed in (54) has the logical form indicated (see Searle 1969, ch. 2):

(54)   Where $p = $ the proposition that the bird is out of the cage:
  a. The bird is out of the cage. (asserted)
     $\vdash(p)$
  b. I warn you that the bird is out of the cage. (warned)
     $W(p)$
  c. The bird is out of the cage. (warned)
     $W(p)$
  d. Is the bird out of the cage? (asked)
     $?(p)$
  e. What is out of the cage? (asked)
     $?(\lambda x[x \text{ is out of the cage}])$
  f. Let the bird be out of the cage! (ordered)
     $!(p)$

In the case of (54a), the indicative verbal mood and lack of interrogative structure indicates the sentence's assertive force, $\vdash$. In (54b), the performative verb and its two nominal arguments *I warn you* is the force indicator, while the complement clause *that the bird is out of the cage* gives the content. (Borrowing terminology from the old performative–constative distinction, examples with a performative verb as the force indicator are often called EXPLICIT PERFORMATIVES, or sometimes just "performatives.") In the case of (54c), the force of warning is not indicated in any obvious way (and it is not clear what the indicative verbal mood is doing), but rather inferred from context, while the propositional content continues to be identified with that denoted by the subject–predicate structure. Because its force is not the same as the one for which it contains an indicator, (54c) is known as an INDIRECT SPEECH ACT. (If the literal force hypothesis is correct, it fundamentally has the force $\vdash$, and the logical form with W has some type of secondary status.)

Normally, in this classical version of speech act theory, content is understood to be the meaning computed by standard compositional semantics. Force is officially understood to be indicated in diverse and sometimes complex ways, but in point of practice, the theory largely focuses on cases where force is indicated either by sentence mood or by a performative verb and its associated arguments.

Much research in linguistics has built upon the classical version of speech act theory. For example, we often find claims in syntactic theorizing that a particular piece of structure (e.g. the head of a functional projection, a specified element in C, or a cluster of properties) is the "force indicator."[17] Because this work in linguistics is devoted to analyzing linguistically interesting properties of sentences, it normally

---

[17] See Chapter 3 for discussion. Representative references include Rivero (1994); Rivero and Terzi (1995); Rizzi (1997); Han (1998); for different views, see Michaelis and Lambrecht (1996); Ginzburg and Sag (2001); Zanuttini and Portner (2003).

focuses either on clause types like interrogatives or imperatives, or on syntactically uniform subclasses of these clause types. This literature thereby skirts some of the most difficult challenges for speech act theory concerning explicit performatives and indirect speech acts.

Language games.   Austin was not the only philosopher who saw how important it is to recognize the diversity of functions of language. Wittgenstein (1953) famously presented the metaphor of language use as a variety of games and pursued the idea that the meaning of a sentence is constituted by the ways in which it can be used in the language game (or games). This perspective has a clear resemblance to the speech act model.[18] Stenius (1967) clarifies and develops Wittgenstein's ideas in a way which has been influential in more recent work in semantics and pragmatics. Working within a Wittgensteinian conception of language use, he divides the sentence's logical form into two parts, the MODAL ELEMENT and the SENTENCE RADICAL. The modal element is not a modal in the sense we have used the term in this chapter, but rather a sentence mood, and it indicates the use to which the descriptive content (expressed by the sentence radical) is put in the language game. (Stenius used the term 'mood' to refer to the type of use a sentence has, but this is confusing in the present context, since we are using 'mood' to represent categories of grammatical form. The term 'force' is more appropriate.) An interrogative sentence thus has the logical form $Q(S)$, with Q the force-indicator (his "modal") and S the sentence radical; it has meaning $?(p)$, with $?$ the force ("mood") and p the content. This way of talking about the logical form of sentences obviously has much in common with speech act theory.

   The language game picture lends itself to a certain way of thinking about the role sentences play in interaction. Declaratives, interrogatives, and imperatives play different roles in a game. For example, a game which includes uttering declaratives, imperatives, and yes/no interrogatives as moves might have the following rules (Stenius 1967, pp. 268, 273):

(55)   a. Produce a sentence in the indicative mood only if its sentence radical is true.

   b. React to a sentence in the imperative mood by making the sentence-radical true.

   c. React to a sentence in the interrogative mood by saying 'yes' or 'no,' according to whether its sentence radical is true or false.

Stenius's presentation of the language game metaphor has influenced much work on discourse meaning. Although the rules in (55) are not dynamic (they do not update the context), they lend themselves to further development in that direction, as we see in work by Lewis (1979b) and Krifka (2001), for example. We will return to Stenius's ideas within the context of a broader discussion of sentence mood in 3.1.3.

---

[18] Searle's remarks on the influence of Wittgenstein on Austin are interesting (Searle 2010).

Challenges for classical speech act theory.   Indirect speech acts and explicit performatives are both cases where there appears to be a mismatch between the illocutionary force of a sentence and the force which is marked by overt grammatical means. It is clear that there is no explicit marker of the force of warning in (54c); the explicit marker (here, indicative mood and non-interrogative grammar) normally marks assertion, and speech act theorists have generally assumed that it does mark assertion here as well. That is, they normally assume that the literal force hypothesis is correct for these cases, and therefore that the force of warning comes about through additional pragmatic processes like Gricean implicature (Gordon and Lakoff 1971, 1975; Searle 1975a; Bach and Harnish 1979; Asher and Lascarides 2001). This perspective is critiqued by Gazdar in an influential article (Gazdar 1981); he argues that not every utterance can be assigned a speech act with the force indicated by its force-indicator, and that not every utterance can be assigned a speech act with the content assigned to it by the semantics.[19] For example, considering (56) he argues that there are contexts in which its force cannot be that of questioning and its content cannot be ⟦ can you pass the salt ⟧^{c}.

(56)   Can you pass the salt?

Rather, its force in such contexts is requesting (and only requesting) and its content is ⟦ you will pass the salt ⟧^{c}. Gazdar, in other words, seeks to overturn the literal meaning hypothesis.

Explicit performatives also show a mismatch between the force indicated by their grammatical form (assertion) and the force they are assumed to actually have (in the case of (54b), warning). On this way of looking at things, it is natural to think of explicit performatives as indirect in a sense, deriving their observed force from a (direct) force of assertion by means of additional reasoning (Lewis 1972; Bach and Harnish 1979; Ginet 1979).

We can identify three main responses to these issues.

1. We find scholars who conclude that classical speech act theory is not particularly useful for purposes of understanding language and communication. The problem of indirect speech acts is seen by them as an example of the broader fact that the function or functions of an utterance are dependent in complex ways on the context in which it is used and on the interaction in which it plays a role; Levinson (1981) gives an early statement of this perspective and it has generally led to a decline in interest in speech act theory within sociolinguistics.

2. We have scholars who aim to develop a more sophisticated theory of illocutionary forces, with the goal of allowing a more transparent relation between grammatical form and illocutionary force. Among other goals, Searle and Vanderveken aim to explain the declarative form of explicit performatives through this approach (Searle 1975b, 1989; Searle and Vanderveken 1985;

---

[19] See also Sadock (1974); Searle (1975a); Morgan (1977); Bach and Harnish (1979), among many others.

Vanderveken 1990, 1991), and Beyssade and Marandin (2006) attack the problem of indirect speech acts. We will sketch the basics of Searle and Vanderveken's theory in the remainder of this section and will return to the more general issues in Chapter 3.

3. We can identify a trend of moving away from some of the ideas of classical speech act theory and towards the dynamic approach. The dynamic notion of update potential can be combined with speech act theory in various ways. Most conservatively, it might be incorporated into classical speech act theory to provide a formal model of the essential communicative effect of an illocutionary act; more radically, update potential might replace the entire notion of illocutionary force. While this trend does not resolve the difference of opinion between scholars who assign (56) a literal meaning in which it has the force of asking and those who do not, it shifts the issue by letting it play out within an idealized formal model of discourse. It may well be that there is a level of analysis at which it is correct to say that uttering (56) asks a question, even though language users normally know right away that the speaker is making a request. We will outline the central ideas of this work in Section 1.4.3 and will return to it in Chapter 3.

The compositional structure of illocutionary force. Beginning in the mid-1970s, Searle and Vanderveken undertook to improve upon the classical notion of illocutionary force (Searle 1975b, 1989; Searle and Vanderveken 1985; Vanderveken 1990, 1991). Their goal was to develop a more systematic taxonomy of illocutionary acts and a system which explains both the range of possible illocutionary acts and the logical properties of and relations among those acts. This effort is important for our purposes here because it led to, in the first place, a new approach to explicit performatives, and then eventually to a theory of illocutionary forces according to which the final force of a sentence is to some extent compositionally derived from the sentence's grammatical properties. This compositional approach to illocutionary force provides the most well-developed basis within speech act theory for the analysis of sentence mood. In this section, we will focus on the analysis of illocutionary force presented by Searle and Vanderveken (1985) and the way Searle applied it to the problem of explicit performatives (Searle 1989). In Chapter 3, we will attend to the treatment of sentence mood developed by Vanderveken (1990, 1991, 2002).

According to the system of Searle and Vanderveken, an illocutionary force is determined by six properties:[20]

1. The ILLOCUTIONARY POINT of a speech act is the core conventional pragmatic purpose of the act. When the speech act has a propositional content p, its point can be described in terms of that content.
   (a) The five illocutionary points are:
      i. An act with the **assertive point** says that the world is a certain way; specifically, it represents an actual state of affairs as being p.

---

[20] My wording here draws extensively on Searle and Vanderveken's (1985) and Vanderveken's (1990, ch.4).

Examples of illocutionary forces with the assertive point: asserting, reporting, claiming.

ii. An act with the **directive point** attempts to get the hearer to do something; specifically, it attempts to get the addressee to make it the case that p.

Examples of illocutionary forces with the directive point: ordering, asking, suggesting, advising.

iii. An act with the **commissive point** attempts to commit the speaker to doing something; specifically, it attempts to commit the speaker to making it the case that p.

Examples of illocutionary forces with the commissive point: promising, vowing.

iv. An act with the **declarative point** performs a world-changing action; specifically, the speech act in and of itself makes it the case that p.

Explicit performatives have the declarative point (resigning, nominating).

v. An act with the **expressive point** expresses the speaker's attitude; specifically it expresses a feeling or attitude towards p.

Examples of illocutionary forces with the expressive point: thanking, apologizing.

(b) Each illocutionary point has a DIRECTION OF FIT:

i. The assertive point has the **words-to-world** direction of fit; the speaker has responsibility for choosing p which matches an actual state of affairs.

ii. The directive and commissive points have the **world-to-words** direction of fit; someone has responsibility for making actual state of affairs match p.

(With the directive point, the addressee has responsibility, while with the commissive point, the speaker has responsibility.)

iii. The declarative point has the **double** direction of fit (both words-to-world and world-to-words); the speech act itself guarantees that p matches an actual state of affairs.

iv. The expressive point has the **null** direction of fit; whether p matches an actual state of affairs is not at issue.

2. The MODE OF ACHIEVEMENT of an illocutionary act is the way in which the illocutionary point of that act is achieved. For example, an act of taking an oath achieves the speaker's commitment to do something by calling upon a higher authority to penalize the speaker if the commitment is not fulfilled.

3. The DEGREE OF STRENGTH of an illocutionary act is the theory's way of saying that some speech acts are stronger than others. For example, an oath commits the speaker in a more serious way than a promise does.

4. The PROPOSITIONAL CONTENT CONDITIONS place restrictions on the propositional content p to which the force may be applied. For example, an oath must concern the future.

5. The PREPARATORY CONDITIONS are the presuppositions of the speech act. For example, an oath presupposes that the speaker can make it the case that p and

that the higher authority which is called upon would endorse the speaker's making it the case that *p*.

6. The SINCERITY CONDITIONS identify the psychological states which the speaker expresses in performing the speech act. For example, in taking an oath, the speaker expresses the intention to make it the case that *p*.

The most primitive illocutionary forces may be defined on the basis of the five illocutionary points. For example, the basic force of asserting has the assertive point and only those other properties which follow from having the assertive point, namely it has words-to-world direction of fit, its strength is medium (the default strength), it presupposes that the speaker has reason to believe *p* (a preparatory condition), and it expresses that the speaker believes *p* (a sincerity condition). It has no special mode of achievement and no propositional content conditions.

Other illocutionary forces can be grouped with the basic one with which they share the illocutionary point, and differ from it in changing the degree of strength, adding a mode of achievement, or adding propositional content, preparatory, or sincerity conditions. For example, the act of reminding is based on assertion and differs from assertion only in having the preparatory condition that the speaker believes or presupposes that the addressee previously believed *p* (Vanderveken 1990, p. 174). Searle also admits complex illocutionary acts, built out of simple ones with logical connectives like (illocutionary) conjunction.

Given this framework, we will look next at how Searle addresses the problem of explicit performatives. In our earlier discussion, we noted the problem posed by examples like (54b), repeated here as (57).

(57)   I warn you that the bird is out of the cage.

It is not clear what the force indicator of this sentence is. On the one hand, we can think of it as *I warn you that*, and from that perspective the sentence has the standard logical form $F(p)$. However, the sequence *I warn you that* does not always function as a force marker, and the sentence also contains the normal assertive force indicator (indicative mood). For this reason, many scholars have argued that its basic force is some form of assertion and that its force of warning is indirect (Searle 1989 cites Lewis 1972; Bach 1975; Bach and Harnish 1979; and Ginet 1979). The idea of this indirect approach is that the speaker asserts that, by uttering the very sentence (57) itself, she warns the addressee that the bird is out of the cage; in virtue of this she represents the world as being one in which she warns the addressee (by uttering that sentence), in which she is committed to believing that she has made such a warning, and in which she has good grounds for this belief. All together, according to the proposal, because of all of the entailments, presuppositions and inferences based on the speaker's assertion, the assertive act guarantees that the utterance also performs an act of warning.

Searle, however, is skeptical of this proposal. While an assertion of (57) would (in the right context) commit the speaker to giving a warning, this is not enough to guarantee that she actually does give a warning. In order for a speech act of warning to occur, the speaker must actually intend to give a warning, and even if she is committed to having this intention, she might not (for example, if she intends to mislead the addressee by pretending to care). As a result, according to Searle the assertive utterance of performative-type sentences can at best receive the illocutionary force of the performative verb via inference, that is as an indirect speech act. Yet he thinks the use of (57) to give a warning is not indirect; thus, he thinks that a different account is called for.[21]

Searle's (1989) solution is to analyze explicit performatives not in terms of the force of assertion (or any other force with assertive point) or in terms of the force explicitly named (in the case of (57), not warning), but rather as having a special force designed precisely to account for explicit performatives. This force is DECLARATION. The special property of acts of declaration is that they count as fulfilling the key conditions on the kind of act named by the performative verb in the sentence itself. For example, when she uses (57) in an act of declaration, the speaker meets the key condition on performing an act of warning the addressee that the bird is out of the cage—crucially, she manifests the intention to warn the addressee that the bird is out of the cage. Assuming that all of the other conditions on giving this warning are met (such as that the bird is indeed out of the cage, that the speaker knows this, and that the speaker and addressee agree that it is something to be careful of), the warning will in fact be given. One can think of the force of declaration as a special meta-force which identifies a possible speech act A (which would make true the sentence uttered) and then fulfills as many of the conditions which must be met for A to be performed as can be fulfilled by a speech act. As a result, the act of declaration amounts to a performance of A, provided the remaining conditions on A are met.

Even given this interesting analysis, it is still not clear what the force marker in an explicit performative like (57) is. In form, it still looks like its force should be assertion (or another force with assertive point), so how is the force of declaration assigned in this case? Vanderveken (1991, pp. 140–1) offers some guidance on this issue. After proposing "the law of an assertive commitment in the achievement of the declarative point," which states that "every declaration contains an assertion of its propositional content," he states that the indicative marks the assertive point unless some additional element like *hereby* further specifies the illocutionary act in such a way that the whole construction is a marker of declarative point. The intuition seems to be that the assertive point is somehow entailed by the declarative point and that this relation is realized in the close relation between the ways in which the two points are marked, but the exact mapping between grammatical forms and types of speech acts remains somewhat vague.

1.4.3 Update potential and illocutionary force

Speech act theory was the main approach to information flow in discourse from the mid-1960s through at least the late 1970s, and as a result of its dominance during this formative phase of pragmatics, it dramatically affected the ways in

---

[21] See Condoravdi and Lauer (2011) for a recent analysis of performatives in terms of assertion which aims to address Searle's critique.

which all linguists interested in discourse meaning think and talk about the topic. As the dynamic approach began to emerge with the work of philosophers like Hamblin (1971) and Stalnaker (1978), researchers in pragmatics faced the task of understanding the relation between the two approaches. In this section, we will consider a number of perspectives on their relation; as we will see, some proposals can be seen as incorporating the tools of the dynamic approach into classical speech act theory, while with others, the relation is much vaguer. As we discuss the range of proposals, I will make an attempt to classify them in a way which will prove helpful when we return to a detailed investigation of sentence mood in Chapter 3.[22]

The dynamic force hypothesis.   In an important but often-overlooked early discussion, Gazdar presents a theory which combines speech act theory with the central idea of the dynamic approach. Specifically, he proposes that illocutionary acts should be analyzed as update potentials as understood within dynamic pragmatics. Given the traditional division of the logical form of illocutionary acts into an illocutionary force and a propositional content, this perspective leads to a position I refer to as the DYNAMIC FORCE HYPOTHESIS:

(58)   The dynamic force hypothesis: Illocutionary force is to be analyzed in terms of update potential as understood within the dynamic approach.

The dynamic force hypothesis aims to improve upon classical speech act theory by providing a better explanation of the nature of illocutionary acts.
    The key ideas of Gazdar's model can be summarized as follows:

1. **The content of a speech act.** The semantic value of any sentence can be the propositional content of a speech act. These contents have various semantic types, for example:
   (a) The meaning of a declarative sentence is a proposition.
   (b) The meaning of an interrogative sentence is a set of propositions.
2. **Illocutionary force.** An illocutionary force is a function from contents to update potentials.
3. **Update potential.** An update potential is a function from contexts to contexts.
4. **Contexts.** Though Gazdar doesn't commit to understanding contexts this way, he suggests Hamblin's (1971) commitment slates as a good basis for providing a definition of contexts. (See Section 3.3.1 for a detailed discussion of Hamblin's ideas.)
5. **Speech act assignment.** A speech act assignment is a pair $\langle f, c \rangle$ consisting of a force f and a content c.
6. **Speech acts.** A speech act is $f(c)$, for any speech act assignment $\langle f, c \rangle$.

---

[22] Quite a few important works in dynamic semantics make little or no reference to speech acts (e.g. Aloni and van Rooy 2002; Ciardelli et al. 2013); while Groenendijk et al. (1996) mention speech act theory as an important predecessor, they leave open whether they think it is being improved upon or superseded by their work.

To give an example, (54a: *The bird is out of the cage*) might (on its literal, assertive interpretation) receive a speech act assignment $\langle \vdash, p \rangle$, where $\vdash$ could be defined as follows:[23]

(59)   For any proposition p, $\vdash(p) =$ the function g which assigns to any context c (satisfying the felicity conditions for the assertion of p by the speaker) the context c' just like c except that the speaker is committed to p in c'.

Gazdar uses this framework to express several important criticisms of classical speech act theory. Specifically, he critiques the literal meaning hypothesis in two ways. Recall that the literal meaning hypothesis says that every utterance performs the speech act defined by the sentence's force indicator and semantic content. In Gazdar's terms, this is to say that every utterance e of sentence d receives the speech act assignment $\langle f, c \rangle$, where f is indicated by the force indicator of d and c is the denotation of d in the context. He argues that it is not always possible to make a speech act assignment with content $[\![\, d \,]\!]$, and that it is also not always possible to make an assignment with force f. As noted above, he uses (56), among other examples, to press these points, claiming that there is not good evidence that it can (in the stereotypical type of context) have assignment $\langle ?, Q \rangle$, where ? is the force of asking and Q is the set of propositions {'the addressee can pass the salt,' 'the addressee cannot pass the salt'}.

Recent perspectives.   It remains unclear in Gazdar's discussion whether he sees Points 1–6 above as representing the beginnings of a new approach to speech acts, or as a method of bringing out some serious problems in speech act theory. But whatever Gazdar's intention may have been, the ideas themselves have turned out to be prescient. Indeed, at around the same time, Levinson (1983) identified the dynamic force hypothesis as a promising direction for developing a new and improved theory of speech acts. In his introductory textbook (Levinson 1983, sect. 5.6), Levinson presents the outlines of the dynamic force hypothesis in terms very similar to Gazdar's (citing, in addition to Gazdar, Hamblin 1971; Ballmer 1978; and Stalnaker 1978). Labeling it the "context-change theory of speech acts," Levinson assumes with Gazdar that a theory of speech acts must account for the full range of illocutionary forces identified by classical speech act theory, but he also makes clear that the explanatory value of such a theory depends on its utilizing a limited range of basic types of update. In this way, Levinson identifies a crucial tension which exists within Gazdar's presentation: On the one hand, classical speech act theory treats all illocutionary forces, both basic ones like assertion and more obscure ones like vowing and exhortation, as full-fledged forces; on the other, sentence mood systems in natural language are not so complex, and it is natural to try to explain them in terms of a restrictive theory of context change based on a simple model of context.

---

[23] It's not clear how "the speaker" is represented in Gazdar's speech act model.

More recently, the literature has given more priority to the second horn of this dilemma. In other words, the rich and complex structure of illocutionary acts has played a diminishing role in work on mood and force, while models which focus on a smaller number of basic forces have gained influence. We see this tendency in the work of such modern speech act scholars as Krifka (2001, 2014), Charlow (2011), and Kaufmann (2012). As a result of this trend, the difference between speech act theory (with the dynamic force hypothesis) and the dynamic approach has grown smaller.

It also worth noting that many scholars do not invest much effort in explaining the relation between their ideas and speech act theory. For example, Roberts (1996/2012) states:

Note that moves, on the interpretation I will give them, are not speech acts, but rather the semantic objects that are expressed in speech acts: A speech act is the act of proffering a move.   (Roberts 2012, p. 12)

It is not clear in Roberts' discussion whether the speech acts she is referring to are the illocutionary acts of classical speech act theory, or just a similar construct. We see similar tangential references to speech act theory in a great deal of recent work which makes use of ideas from the dynamic approach (for example, Lewis 1979b; Ginzburg 1995a,b, 1996; Asher and Lascarides 1998, 2001; Portner 2004; Rett 2014; and Murray 2014).

This discussion of the relation between speech act theory and the dynamic approach has touched briefly on a number of quite different theories, and it is important not to get lost in the details. The crucial point is that we can see ideas from dynamic semantics and pragmatics playing important roles in a variety of contemporary theories, some of which are naturally understood as versions of speech act theory, and others of which are not. The term "dynamic force hypothesis" is most useful when applied to theories which aim to contribute to an improved version of classical "Searlean" speech act theory, and I will use it this way. I consider the works of scholars like Krifka, Kaufmann, and Charlow to fall within this category.[24] Other scholars like Portner (2004) and Starr (2013) have clearly set their ideas apart from speech act theory, and these I will treat as falling under the dynamic approach. Still others, like Lewis (1979b) and Roberts (2012), indicate that their ideas can be integrated with speech act theory into a broader conception of information flow in discourse, but do not develop a detailed proposal for the role which will be played by the core ideas of classical speech act theory. These authors' works too will be discussed as falling within the dynamic approach. Of course, in dividing theories into two groups, we simplify them and risk making certain theories seem more similar or dissimilar than they really are. Readers should keep

---

[24] It is worthwhile to point out Condoravdi and Lauer's (2011, 2012) work on performatives and the illocutionary force of imperatives. While their main proposals are explicitly presented as falling within speech act theory, they offer an alternative formulation of their ideas about imperatives which is compatible with the dynamic approach (Condoravdi and Lauer 2012, sect. 6), and the later ideas of Lauer (2013) are not as tightly tied to classical speech act theory.

in mind that, while the classification used here is appropriate for the purposes of this book—specifically, for the goal of determining what type of theoretical framework is best suited to analyzing sentence mood—the same classification may be unhelpful in other contexts.

1.5 Looking ahead

In Sections 1.3–1.4, I have presented some of the most essential background for recent work on verbal mood and sentence mood. Specifically: (i) the possible worlds semantics for modality which developed out of modal logic provides the framework in which the most important analyses of subsentential modality have been developed, and these analyses in turn provide the basis for theories of verbal mood; and (ii) the major theories of information flow in discourse, namely the dynamic approach and speech act theory, serve as the basis for attempts to understand sentence mood. Up until now, there has been a division in semantic research on mood into these two fields, one focusing on verbal mood and the other on sentence mood, with little interaction between them. This is so despite the fact that verbal mood clearly plays a role in the determination of sentential force. The reason for the division seems to be that the phenomena associated with verbal mood and sentence mood overlap in an odd way. The central questions in the analysis of sentence mood (how to analyze the declarative, interrogative, and imperative clause types and associate them with conversational functions) are partially independent of verbal mood, in that both declaratives and interrogatives typically have indicative verbal mood in root clauses and can be indicative, subjunctive, or infinitival in embedded clauses. In contrast, imperatives can have a distinct verbal mood, but the connection between imperative mood and other verbal moods and mood-like forms (indicative, subjunctive, and infinitive) is not well understood.

In the next two chapters, we will examine verbal mood (Chapter 2) and sentence mood (Chapter 3). Only after we have gained a detailed understanding of these two topics will we be able to return to thinking about the nature of mood in general. In Chapter 4, we will investigate whether verbal mood and sentence mood are fundamentally similar enough to be analyzed in a unified theory of core mood, and we will consider their relation to other phenomena like reality status and evidentiality which are usually seen as residing at the margins of the category of mood.

2

Verbal mood

Mood is, as we said in Chapter 1, "an aspect of linguistic form which indicates how a proposition is used in the expression of a modal meaning." In light of this definition, verbal mood can be understood as the subcategory of mood with the primary function of indicating how the proposition is used in the computation of subsentential modal meaning. Such a conception of verbal mood is close to being just a formal statement of the traditional practice of studying mood in particular languages. Both in traditional grammars of languages with a distinction between indicative and subjunctive clauses and in syntactic and semantic studies of those languages within formal linguistics, one finds lists of elements and constructions which require or allow subjunctive or indicative clauses. The subjunctive list will include lexical items like 'want' and 'happy (that)' and the indicative list will include ones like 'know' and 'say'. And, it is important to notice, not only do the elements in the lists for the most part express modal meaning, but they are described, classified, and explained in terms which suggest that their modal meaning is what is crucial for understanding verbal mood. For example, we are told that predicates which express the concepts of desire, will, necessity, and emotion select subjunctive complements (in those languages which have the subjunctive). These types of modality are all examples of the same judgment type, priority modality.

In order to understand verbal mood, we will need prior understanding of subsentential modality. Section 2.1 will lay out this background. Then, in the remainder of the chapter (Sections 2.2–2.3), we will examine the distribution of verbal mood forms and the semantic theories which have attempted to explain their distribution. As we will see, researchers in this area have made slow but steady progress in improving the semantic theory of verbal mood, and we have now reached the point where it seems possible to enumerate many of the key ideas which must be part of an explanatory theory of this domain. We will see that the following are important:

1. Ideas from ordering semantics seem to be important in explaining the **distribution** of verbal mood forms.
2. Differences in the **meanings** of clauses marked by different verbal moods seem to be based on a variety of semantic properties connected to indexicality, including in particular varieties of *de se* interpretation.
3. Scholars have developed a number of detailed, insightful theories of indicative and subjunctive complement clauses, but we do not have such thorough analyses of verbal mood in other grammatical positions or the meanings and

Mood. First edition. Paul Portner.

functions of other forms which may fall into the category of verbal mood, such as infinitives and dependent modals.

Apart from these points about the semantics of verbal mood in and of itself, studying verbal mood yields insights into the nature of modality generally. Verbal mood gives us evidence about how to classify modal expressions in a linguistically relevant way, and highlights grammatically important properties of modals. As a result, the analysis of verbal mood has implications for our understanding of both subsentential and discourse modality.

2.1 Subsentential modality

As mentioned in Section 1.3.2, the standard theory of modality in possible worlds semantics was developed for sentential modal constructions. As a result, we rarely find discussions of the difference between the examples in (1). The fact that *must* is a modal auxiliary (a sentential modal) while *necessary* is an adjective (a subsentential modal) is glossed over by the fact that both can be symbolized in modal logic as $\Box\alpha$ (where $\alpha =$ 'we pay this bill today').

(1)   (a) We must pay this bill today.
      (b) It is necessary that we pay this bill today.

However, modal adjectives show differences from sentential modals in having typical properties of adjectives. First, since adjectives are an open lexical class, there are many more of them and as a result, they distinguish the parameters of judgment type and strength in a more fine-grained way. Second, they are gradable expressions and the fact that they can be combined with degree modifiers leads to even more variation in strength.[1] These points are illustrated in (2):

(2)   (a) It is possible/likely/probable/necessary/desirable/believable that Ben will win.
      (b) It is somewhat/quite/100% likely that Sam will lose.

At a general level, the facts are similar with modal nouns:

(3)   (a) There is a possibility/chance/likelihood that Ben will win.
           He has a strong desire/belief that Ben will win.
      (b) There is a tiny/slight/significant/excellent possibility that Noah will win.

---

[1] The role of the modifiers of modal auxiliaries in (i)–(ii) is not completely clear:

(i) Ben positively must be winning.
(ii) Ben to some extent must be winning.

Positively in (i) is an extreme modifier (Rett 2008b; Morzycki 2012; Portner and Rubinstein 2016) while *to some extent* in (ii) lessens the strength of *must* in some sense.

As mentioned in Section 1.3.2, Kratzer applied her version of ordering semantics to some of the variation in strength among modal adjectives and nouns. We saw how she defined the concept of 'slight possibility,' which can be used to give an account of the English *there is a slight possibility that*. She likewise provides definitions, using ordering semantics, of necessity, weak necessity, possibility, good possibility, and better possibility and associates these with adjectival and nominal constructions in English and German; see Kratzer (1981, 1991) and Portner (2009) for her treatments of these concepts. However, the fact that the concepts are not given a compositional treatment—slight possibility is not derived from possibility through the effects of the modifier *slight*—means that Kratzer's version of ordering semantics cannot be the full correct analysis as it stands.

Lexical verbs with modal meaning have received much more extensive study within semantics than modal adjectives and nouns. While modal verbs which correspond to auxiliaries in English, such as Spanish *poder* ('can'), are typically treated as sentential modals, the set of verbs which describe aspects of the mental lives of individuals has been the focus of much research within semantics and philosophy. Example (4) lists some of these words, known as PROPOSITIONAL ATTITUDE VERBS because they can be thought of as denoting an attitude (mental relationship) which a thinking individual, the attitude holder corresponding to the subject argument *Ben*, holds towards a proposition, corresponding to the sentential complement *that John can fly*:

(4)   Ben believes/hopes/knows/doubts/fears/realizes/says that John can fly.

Note that modal adjectives also sometimes express propositional attitudes. For example, in *Ben is certain that birds can fly*, the adjective *certain* describes a relation between Ben and the proposition that birds can fly very similar to the ones indicated by some of the verbs in (4). Therefore, whatever we have to say about the semantics of the verbs in (4) should be extendable to a significant extent to adjectives like *certain*. But other modal adjectives don't have analogues in the realm of modal verbs—there is no verb which expresses the same basic meaning as *probable* (it's related to *prove*, but *probable* does not mean 'provable'). The realm of subsentential modality is a collection of overlapping types, some based in semantics and some based in syntax, and we can expect that the properties we observe are due to a mixture of interacting semantic and morphosyntactic factors.

Propositional attitude predicates as strong modals.   Since the work of Hintikka (1961), propositional attitude verbs have been treated as modal operators within the framework of possible worlds semantics. Let us see how this works taking the verb *believe* as a case study. In order to treat *believe* as a modal element within modal logic (Section 1.3.2), we need to know two things: its accessibility relation and its modal force. The accessibility relation of a propositional attitude verb is determined by a combination of the lexical meaning of the verb itself and the grammatical context in which it occurs. Specifically, the set of worlds relevant to the meaning of *believe* can be identified from the beliefs of the referent of its subject (the attitude holder) at the time specified by the sentence's tense. For example, in (5), the accessible worlds are those which match Ben's beliefs at the speech time in the actual world:

(5) Ben believes that John flew away.

In terms of the tools of modal semantics outlined in Section 1.3.2, the meaning of *believe* can be stated in terms of a doxastic accessibility relation.[2]

(6) For any situation s: $R_{dox}(s) = \{w :$ everything that the thinking participant of s believes in s at the time of s holds in $w\}$.

Let us assume that the verb sits in a syntactic structure something like the one in (7a). If so, the semantics needed for *believe* will be that in (7b):

(7) (a)

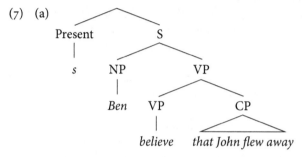

(b) *Believe* denotes the function which takes a proposition p, individual a, and situation s as arguments, and yields true iff a is the thinking participant in s and every world $w \in R_{dox}(s)$ is one in which p is true.

(c) $[\![$ *believe* $]\!] = [\lambda p \lambda a \lambda s$. a is the thinking participant of s and for every world $w \in R_{dox}(s), w \in p]$

The meaning in (7b) can be given as (7c) using the standard λ-notation of formal semantics.

Notice that (7b–c) treats *believe* as a strong modal; it involves universal quantification over accessible worlds. Treating it as a weak (existential) modal would give obviously wrong results. Suppose that Ben has no opinion about whether John flew away; in that case, there will be some worlds compatible with what he believes in which John flew away. On the assumption that *believe* has existential force, (5) would incorrectly be predicted to be true. In contrast, defining the meaning of *believe* as a strong modal gives the right result in this case.

---

[2] It is sometimes clearer to state the accessibility relation as an actual relation, and not a function from situations to a set of accessible worlds. This would look very similar to (6):

(i) For any situation s and world w: $R_{dox}(s, w)$ iff everything that the thinking participant of s believes in s at the time of s holds in w.

In a format closer to modal logic, the accessibility relation would be a relation between worlds:

(ii) For any individual a, situation s, and worlds w and w_*:
$R_{dox(\langle a,s \rangle)}(w_*, w)$ iff everything that a believes in the situation s in world w_* is the case in w.

Applications of strong modal semantics for propositional attitudes. Some other propositional attitude verbs can be treated as strong modals simply by changing the accessibility relation, but as we turn to the full diversity of these predicates, various complexities arise. In some cases, the analysis may be correct as far as it goes, but be incomplete. Consider the situation with *know*. Suppose it is treated in parallel with *believe* above:

(8) ⟦ *know* ⟧ = [$\lambda p \lambda a \lambda s$. *a* is the thinking participant of *s* and for every world $w \in R_{ep}(s), w \in p$]

This meaning fails to give an account for the verb's factivity. We could try to incorporate factivity either by saying more about the accessibility relation in (8), requiring it to be reflexive,[3] or by adding the presupposition that *p* is true as a separate component of the lexical meaning.

Another type of issue can be illustrated with the propositional attitude verb *learn*. If we define the accessibility relation for *learn* as in (9) below, we fail to model the fact that simple sentences with *learn* are eventive rather than stative.

(9) For every situation *s*: $R_{learn}(s)$ is the set of worlds *w* such that everything that the thinking participant of *s* learns in *s* is also the case in *w*.

The reason that *learn* describes an event, of course, is that to learn something is to undergo a change from not knowing it to knowing it. This description indicates that *learn* does not express a simple propositional attitude, but rather has a meaning which can be defined in terms of a more basic propositional attitude, knowledge, as something like the following:

(10) ⟦ *learn* ⟧ = [$\lambda p \lambda a \lambda s$. *a* is the thinking participant of *s* and *s* has an initial part s_1 and a final part s_2 such that:
   i. it's not the case that for every world $w \in R_{ep}(s_1), w \in p$; and
   ii. for every world $w \in R_{ep}(s_2), w \in p$]

These discussions of *know* and *learn* indicate that the possible worlds semantics for modality often provides only one component of the full semantic analysis of a given predicate. Unlike sentential modals, which are often (perhaps wrongly) assumed to be nearly pure exemplars of modal meaning, propositional attitude verbs and other subsentential modals have lexical meanings of which the pure modal component captured by the possible worlds analysis of Section 1.3.2 is only part of the overall meaning.

Desire verbs like *want* and *hope* form one especially complex and important subclass of subsentential modals. Suppose that we analyze *want* as a strong modal in the same way as *believe* above using a buletic accessibility relation:

---

[3] See Portner (2009, ch.2) for explanation concerning the use of properties of accessibility relations in modal logic.

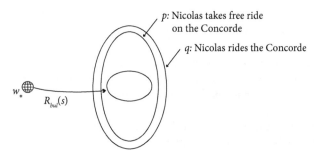

p: Nicolas takes free ride on the Concorde

q: Nicolas rides the Concorde

w_*

$R_{bul}(s)$

FIGURE 2.1   Entailment pattern under strong modal analysis

(11)   For any situation s: $R_{bul}(s)$ is the set of worlds w such that everything the thinking participant of s wants in s is the case in w.

This analysis has problems. Consider the following sentences based on an example of Asher (1987):

(12)   (a) Nicolas wants to ride the Concorde.
        (b) Nicolas wants to take a free ride on the Concorde.

Riding the Concorde (a supersonic airplane now no longer in service) is very expensive, and Nicolas does not think it is worth the money. Therefore (12a) is false. However, it would be fun, so (12b) is true. On the assumption that the subject and situation arguments of *want* are the same in the two examples, this combination of attitudes is not possible according to the analysis which treats *want* as a modal with universal force. Figure 2.1 illustrates how the semantics works: evaluated in a situation s in the real world w_*, the set of worlds accessible by R_{bul} is a subset of the worlds p in which Nicolas takes a free ride on the Concorde. This is what we need to make (12b) true in w_*. Since p is a subset of q, the set of accessible worlds is also a subset of q, and hence (12a) must be true as well. (In general, for any modal '$\Box$' with universal force, if p entails q, $\Box p$ will entail $\Box q$.) Yet obviously, (12b) does not in fact entail (12a), and so a different analysis is needed.[4]

Stalnaker (1984) and Heim (1992) develop ideas about the semantics of desire predicates which use the ingredients of modal semantics in an even more indirect way than we saw with *learn*. The intuition behind this analysis is that desire predicates indicate a preference for one hypothetical scenario over another; for example, to evaluate (12a), Nicolas must consider both what it would be like if he rode the Concorde, and what it would be like if he did not. Then, the sentence is

---

[4] There are similar logical problems with the modal analysis of *believe* in (7) as well, including the famous "problem of logical omniscience." The question remains open whether they show that the entire approach should be modified in a radical way or even abandoned, or whether the unintuitive predictions of the theory outlined in the text can be defended. An introduction to the foundational issues can be found in many handbook and encyclopedia articles on propositional attitudes and possible worlds semantics, for example Swanson (2011b).

true if he prefers the first kind of scenario over the second. This idea is made formal by Heim (1992, (31)) as follows (with adjustments to fit with our notation):

(13) $[\![\,want\,]\!]$ = $[\lambda p \lambda a \lambda s$. a is the thinking participant of s and for every $w \in R_{dox}(s)$, every world in p maximally similar to w is more desirable to a in s than every world maximally similar to w in $\neg p]$

It will be easier to see how Heim's analysis works by introducing several definitions; the following are based on her presentation:[5]

(14) (a) For any worlds w_1 and $w_2, w_1 <_s w_2$ iff w_1 is more desirable to the thinking participant of s in s than w_2.

   (b) For any sets of worlds p_1 and p_2, $p_1 <_s p_2$ iff for every $w_1 \in p_1$ and $w_2 \in p_2$, $w_1 <_s w_2$.

   (c) For any world w and proposition p, $Sim_w(p) = \{w' : w' \in p$ and w' resembles w no less than any other world in $p\}$.

   (d) $[\![\,want\,]\!]$ = $[\lambda p \lambda a \lambda s$. a is the thinking participant in s and for every $w \in R_{dox}(s)$: $Sim_w(p) <_s Sim_w(\neg p)]$

The set of worlds $Sim_w(p)$ represents the scenario that Nicolas rides the Concorde from the point of view of world w; it is the set of worlds most similar to w in which he does so. (Heim's use of similarity to represent what happens if p is true is based on Stalnaker's 1975 analysis of conditionals.) Likewise, $Sim_w(\neg p)$ represents the scenario that he does not ride the Concorde. The ordering $<_s$ indicates Nicolas's preferences. It is defined first as a relation between worlds in (14b), but then applied to propositions in (14c). The definition in (14d) uses an ordinary (doxastic) accessibility relation R_{dox}, putting it together with the preceding definitions to say that, relative to every doxastically accessible world, the scenario that Nicolas rides the Concorde based on that world is preferable (according to Nicolas) to the scenario that he doesn't ride the Concorde.

   These definitions are complicated and important in the discussion later in this chapter, so let's consider in detail how they might work to determine the truth value of (12a) in a particular world w_*. We need to consider worlds doxastically accessible from a speech-time situation s in w_* which has Nicolas as its thinking participant. Pick one of them, w, and suppose that this is a world in which Nicolas does not get to ride the Concorde. Then, since any world is more similar to itself than any other world could be, $Sim_w(\neg p)$ is just $\{w\}$; in other words, from the point of view of w, the scenario in which he does not ride the Concorde is just $\{w\}$. But we also must consider $Sim_w(p)$, the scenario in which he rides the Concorde. $Sim_w(p)$ does not contain w, but rather the world or worlds most similar to it in which he rides the Concorde. Then, the core condition of (14d) will be satisfied if all of the worlds in $Sim_w(p)$ are preferable to this doxastically accessible world w. In other words, it is

---

[5] Heim uses a more traditional system in which the base for the doxastic accessibility relation is a world, rather than a situation. This means that her version of (14d) has the equivalent of $R_{dox}(\langle a, w_* \rangle)$ in the place of our $R_{dox}(s)$.

satisfied if the scenario based on w in which he rides the Concorde is preferable to the world w itself in which he does not. If this condition is satisfied for every doxastically accessible world, (12a) is true.

The meaning in (14) is not the final word on a comparative semantics for desire predicates. Heim discusses several further issues. One is the question of whether the compared sets of worlds, $Sim_w(p)$ and $Sim_w(\neg p)$, should be restricted to belief worlds. Such details will become relevant when we discuss Villalta's (2008) work in Section 2.2.2 below (see also von Fintel and Iatridou 2008; Rubinstein 2012).

Because the contrast between belief predicates and desire predicates is central to patterns of mood selection in many languages, the Stalnaker/Heim analysis of *want* will prove important in what follows. However, the analysis was not developed with the goal of explaining verbal mood. Rather, Stalnaker was interested in the foundations of possible worlds semantics and links to such topics as conditionals, while Heim focused on the behavior of anaphora and presupposition in the complements of attitude predicates. Eventually, the specific form of Heim's analysis will become relevant, but what's important to observe for now is how the analysis uses the ingredients of the theory of modality in a rather complex way to express the meaning of a subsentential modal element. Moreover, even though the Stalnaker/Heim theory did not originate as a theory of mood, it brings out several ingredients of modal semantics which will prove important in the development of such theories. Let us list them briefly:

1. Most obviously, the analysis makes use of a doxastic accessibility relation, R_{dox}. Unlike the accessibility relation of a sentential modal, this one is lexically determined, and its thinking agent and temporal component are grammatically determined.

2. The use of an ordering relation is reminiscent of the function of the ordering source in ordering semantics. While $<_s$ is not defined from an ordering source in the style of Kratzer's theory, this may not be an important difference. On the one hand, ordering semantics can be done without the ordering source (e.g. Brown 1988; Hansson 1990, 2001; Veltman 1996; Halpern 2003; Portner 2009); on the other, one could rewrite the definitions in (14) so as to use an ordering source. There is an important difference between $<_s$ and a Kratzerian ordering source, though: the former is lexically determined, while the latter is given by context.

3. The analysis connects the semantics of *want* to the theory of conditionals. The function $Sim_w(p)$ is included to pick out what things are like if p is or were to be true.

The functioning of accessibility relations, the use of ordering, and connections to conditionals are all important themes in the literature on mood, and we will return to them in subsequent sections.

De se and *de re* interpretations.   According to the ideas about subsentential modality we have discussed so far, modal expressions take as a semantic argument a clause with propositional meaning. The meanings of *believe, know, learn,* and *want* all begin with "λp," and p is understood to be the standard content of a sentence in the possible worlds semantics framework, namely a proposition represented as a set of possible worlds. And in each case, the semantics of the modal expression is stated in terms of a set of accessible worlds being a subset of p; for example, in the simple case of *believe*, all doxastically accessible worlds are described as in p. Yet there is strong evidence that this view of subsentential modality is not always sufficient. Two types of problematical cases are known as *de se* and *de re* interpretation.

Chierchia illustrates *de se* and *de re* interpretations with the following minimal pair in Italian (Chierchia 1989, context quoted from p. 3, examples from p. 24).

(15) Imagine Pavarotti looking at a mirror without realizing it and seeing a man whose pants are on fire. The man Pavarotti is seeing in the mirror is in fact Pavarotti himself, but he does not realize that.

    a. *Pavarotti crede   che i   **suoi pantaloni** siano   in fiamme.*
       Pavarotti believes that the his   pants   be.SUBJ.3PL on fire
       Ma non si è accorto che i   pantaloni sono i   proprio.
       but not REFL is realized that the pants   are the his
       'Pavarotti believes that his pants are on fire. But he hasn't realized that the pants are his own.'

    b. *#Pavarotti crede   che i   **propri pantaloni** siano   in*
       Pavarotti believes that the his   pants   be.SUBJ.3PL on
       fiamme. Ma non si è accorto che i   pantaloni sono i
       fire   but not REFL is realized that the pants   are the
       proprio.
       his
       'Pavarotti believes that his pants are on fire. But he hasn't realized that the pants are his own.'

The examples differ in how the anaphor 'his' is expressed, and they have different truth conditions. The version with *suoi* (15a) can describe a situation in which Pavarotti is not aware that the person whose pants he sees on fire is himself, while the one with *propri* (15b) cannot describe such a situation. Under the assumption that the meaning of a full clause is always a set of worlds, one would think that the complement clauses in (15a) and (15b) denote the very same one, namely the set of worlds in which Pavarotti's pants are on fire. What is the difference between *suoi* and *propri* here which leads to this difference in meaning?

The belief sentence of (15a) has a DE RE INTERPRETATION. It reports that Pavarotti has a belief about a particular pair of pants, identified by us as his pants but identified by him as the pants of the guy he is looking at. The belief sentence of (15b) has a DE SE INTERPRETATION. It reports that Pavarotti has a belief about a pair of pants he identifies as his own. It is even more accurate to describe the *de se* interpretation as one which reports a belief of Pavarotti about himself. He believes himself to be a person whose pants are on fire.[6]

---

[6] There are many important works which investigate the aspects of meaning related to *de se* in more detail. Pearson (2013) and Lasersohn (2017) are especially useful and provide excellent entries into the related literature.

The semantic analysis of *de re* and *de se* interpretations is a complex topic. To begin with, the terminology leads us to think that we should classify sentences as *de re*, *de se*, or neither (we'd call this case *de dicto*), and then assign appropriate logical forms on this basis. On this way of thinking, there would be a *de re* logical form, a *de se* logical form, and a *de dicto* logical form. However, *de re* is really a property of particular expressions within the modal sentence, and not an overall property of the sentence. Sentence (16) can be understood *de se* with respect to Pavarotti's pants, but *de re* with respect to his hat:

(16) *Pavarotti crede   che   i   propri pantaloni siano   dello stesso*
        Pavarotti believes that the his   pants   be.SUBJ.3PL of the same
        colore del   suo cappello.
        color of the his hat
        'Pavarotti believes that his pants are the same color as his hat.'

This sentence reports a situation in which Pavarotti is aware that the pants he's thinking about are his own, but might incorrectly think that the hat is someone else's.

In addition, as Lewis (1979a) points out, all belief can be thought of as, in a basic respect, *de se*. To take the example which we previously described as *de re*, (15a), this sentence can be understood as describing a situation in which Pavarotti believes himself to be someone who is looking at a guy (who happens to be Pavarotti himself) whose pants are on fire. This again shows that we should think of *de re* and *de se* as features of the meanings of propositional attitude expressions, not as readings of potentially ambiguous sentences or expressions.

The semantics of *de re* and *de se* have played a relatively minor role in theories of verbal mood, but we will see evidence that *de se* is actually quite important. As we go forward it will be necessary to have a basic knowledge about each. The key feature of *de re* interpretation is that a phrase identifies a referent and then contributes that referent (but not the way in which it was identified) to the propositional content of the sentence in which it occurs. The mechanism by which it does this is often understood in terms of scope. For example, we can understand (15a) as resolving the reference of *i suoi pantaloni* outside the scope of 'believe.' It means, roughly, 'concerning Pavarotti's pants, Pavarotti believes that they are on fire.' Theories can differ in what they understand to be involved in "resolving the reference" of a definite description like 'his pants.' If 'his pants' is a quantifier, it can simply take wide scope in the ordinary way. If it is an anaphor, the idea would be that it finds its referent in a higher level of discourse representation. Either way, the point is that the pants which Pavarotti believes to be on fire are described as 'his pants' not from Pavarotti's point of view, but rather from the speaker's.

Given the above, the *de re* meaning of (17a) could be represented as (17b), in contrast to the *de dicto* representation (17c):

(17) a. Pavarotti believes that one violinist is beautiful.
       b. $\exists x[\text{violinist}(x) \wedge \text{Bel}(P, x \text{ is beautiful})]$
       c. $\text{Bel}(P, \exists x[\text{violinist}(x) \wedge x \text{ is beautiful}])$

The *de re* reading can be brought out by considering a context in which Pavarotti feels that the orchestra he is working with has a uniformly unattractive violin section, but is entranced by the sight of one woman waiting on the side. He is not aware that she is a violinist.

There are problems with this simple scope-based view of *de re*. The most famous one is due to Quine (1956):

There is a certain man in a brown hat whom Ralph has glimpsed several times under questionable circumstances on which we need not enter here; suffice it to say that Ralph suspects he is a spy. Also there is a gray-haired man, vaguely known to Ralph as rather a pillar of the community, whom Ralph is not aware of having seen except once at the beach. Now Ralph does not know it, but the men are one and the same. Can we say of this man (Bernard J. Ortcutt, to give him a name) that Ralph believes him to be a spy?

(Quine 1956, p.179)

Both of the following sentences appear to be true:

(18)   a. Ralph believes that Ortcutt is a spy.
   b. Ralph believes that Ortcutt is not a spy.

Scope will probably not help with the analysis here. On the assumption that names are scopeless, the only representation of (18a) would be (19a). And even on the questionable assumption that *Ortcutt* can be assigned scope, both the wide scope (19b) and narrow scope logical forms would be equivalent to (19a).

(19)   a. Bel(R, O is a spy)
   b. $\exists x[x = O \wedge$ Bel(R, x is a spy)$]$

Therefore, it is very difficult to see how to account for the compatibility of (18a–b) using a system in which the only tool for assigning meanings distinct from (19a) is scope.

We need to capture the intuition that the beliefs reported in (18a–b) are different because they involve Ortcutt seen in two different ways, as the man on the beach and as the pillar of the community. That is, (18a) is true because of Ralph's belief that the man on the beach is a spy, and (18b) is true because Ralph believes that the pillar of the community is not a spy. Both of these can be expressed with the name *Ortcutt* simply because of the fact that Ortcutt can be identified both as the man Ralph saw on the beach and the man Ralph knows as a pillar of the community. In order to capture the relevance of these two descriptions of Ortcutt to (18a–b), we introduce a RELATION OF ACQUAINTANCE into the logical form. An acquaintance relation $C(x, y)$ holds between x and y iff the first argument x is related to the second y in a specific way which allows x to have a propositional attitude involving y. In Quine's examples, there are two different acquaintance relations in play, roughly 'saw at the beach' and 'pillar of the community'.

(20)   a. $\exists C[C(R, O) \wedge$ Bel(R, the x such that $C(R, x)$ is a spy)$]$
   b. $\exists C[C(R, O) \wedge \neg$Bel($R$, the x such that $C(R, x)$ is a spy)$]$

Example (18a) is true under logical form (20a), because C can take the value 'saw at the beach'; it is true because Ralph saw Ortcutt at the beach, and believes that the man he saw at the beach is a spy. Likewise (18b) is true under logical form (20b) because C can take the value 'knows as a pillar of the community'.[7]

Next we turn to the *de se* feature of meaning. Chierchia's examples (15a–b) show that propositions are not fine-grained enough to differentiate all of the beliefs which can be reported using the verb 'believe.' Within linguistics, the most influential solution to this problem, due to Lewis (1979a) building on Perry (1977), replaces propositions as the objects of attitudes with properties. That is, the proposition that Pavarotti's pants are on fire does not serve as the argument of 'believe,' as we have assumed up until now, but rather one of the following properties does:

(21) a. The property which an individual has in a world iff Pavarotti's pants are on fire in that world =
       $\lambda x \lambda w$. Pavarotti's pants are on fire in w
      b. The property which an individual has in a world iff that individual's pants are on fire in that world =
       $\lambda x \lambda w$. x's pants are on fire in w

We are going to use the λ-bound variable x in the second property to account for the fact that (15b) means that Pavarotti believes that his *own* pants are on fire. But in order to give a truly respectable semantics, we need to come up with a meaning for 'believe' different from the ones given above. Instead of being treated as a strong modal quantifying over the subject's doxastically accessible worlds, it has to accept a property type argument and differentiate (15a–b) in the right way.

The difference between the beliefs reported by the two belief sentences in (15a) and (15b) concerns Pavarotti's knowledge, or lack thereof, of his role in the scene he sees. In the scenario, he believes that a large, handsome man's pants are on fire, but does not identify himself as that man. The scenario thus indicates that belief is not just a matter of what the world is like, but also who one is within the world.[8] We can represent this with a change to our understanding of the doxastic accessibility relation. Instead of being fundamentally a relation between situations and worlds, it should be a relation between a situation and an individual and a world.[9]

---

[7] The semantics of *de re* is a complex topic and the analysis used here is at least oversimplified, if not altogether incorrect. It will suffice, though, as background for investigating verbal mood. See, among many others, the following for more sophisticated discussion: Lewis (1979a), Cresswell and von Stechow (1982), Percus and Sauerland (2003), Maier (2010), Keshet (2011), Charlow and Sharvit (2014), McKay and Nelson (2014).

[8] Cherchia's example does not quite prove this conclusion, since Pavarotti believes that there is a window several feet in front of the man whose pants are on fire, but in reality what he thinks is a window is a mirror.

[9] The formulation of *de se* semantics here is superficially different from Lewis's because I wish to remain consistent with the way modal semantics is presented elsewhere in this work. Note that Lewis proposes that individuals only exist in a single world, and so for him the world component is not needed.

(22)   For any situation s, individual b, and world w: $\langle b, w \rangle \in R_{dox}(s)$ iff everything
       that the thinking participant a in s believes in s is compatible with a being b
       in w.

This new accessibility relation can be used to define a meaning for 'believe' which
takes properties as arguments:

(23)   *Believe* denotes the function which takes a property P, individual a, and
       situation s as arguments, and returns true iff a is the thinking participant
       in s and for every $\langle b, w \rangle \in R_{dox}(s)$, $P(\langle b, w \rangle) = 1$

To use Lewis's way of describing *de se* belief, according to this semantics 'A believes
P' means that A ascribes to himself the property P. This analysis works for (15b): it
says that everything Pavarotti believes in the situation requires that he be a person
who has burning pants. This is not the case in the scenario, and this is why the
sentence is false.

The analysis of (15a) does not work out quite so readily. If we allow 'believe' to
take property (21a) as argument, the sentence would be true if everything Pavarotti
believes in the situation requires that his, Pavarotti's, pants be on fire. This gets right
the fact that he is not aware that the person whose pants are on fire is himself,
but remember that we actually think that *i suoi pantaloni* has the *de re* feature
of meaning. The property in (21a) does not capture the fact that he identifies his
pants indirectly, by seeing himself in a mirror. The right property should involve
an acquaintance relation between Pavarotti and his pants:

(24)   The property which an individual has in a world iff there is one man who
       that individual sees in that world through what appears to be a window, and
       that man's pants are on fire in that world =
       $\lambda x \lambda w$. the pants of the man who x sees in w are on fire in w

The *de re* sentence (15a) as a whole is true because Pavarotti sees himself (through
what appears to be a window frame), and ascribes to himself the property of seeing
(through what appears to be a window frame) the man whose pants are on fire.

Before concluding this subsection, I would like to point out one important fact
which will become relevant later. Chierchia (1989) shows that some elements are
grammatically required to be *de se*. Specifically, the subject of a control infinitive
is always understood *de se* (i.e. as the unsaturated individual argument of the
property complement of a *de se* attitude verb). Consider (25a):[10]

(25)   a. Pavarotti wants to drink espresso.
       b. The property which an individual has in a world iff that individual drinks
          espresso in that world = $\lambda x \lambda w$. x drinks espresso in w

---

[10] Morgan (1970) identified the difference in interpretation between the null subject of a control
infinitive and the corresponding pronominal subject of a finite clause.

Roughly speaking, (25) says that every b who has (in w) what Pavarotti wants in s drinks espresso (in w). The unexpressed subject of *to drink espresso* corresponds to the argument x in (25b), bound by the λx. (A more thorough analysis would combine a *de se* doxastic modal base with a comparative semantics using a *de se* buletic ordering relation, along the lines of (14) but modified to work with properties rather than propositions.) Crucially, it cannot mean that Pavarotti's desires would be satisfied by letting the large man he is looking at drink espresso; to express that meaning, we would need a sentence which supports a *de re* reading of the subject, such as *Pavarotti wants for that man to drink espresso (and amusingly he doesn't know that that man is Pavarotti himself)*. Given that an infinitival subject argument (i.e. PRO) can be obligatorily *de se*, we might consider the possibility that other arguments can be obligatorily *de se* as well. This idea has been taken up in some of the literature on verbal mood (see Sections 2.2.2.4 and 2.3.1.1).

This discussion has been rather subtle at times, and it will be helpful to highlight two important points before moving on to other topics. First, there is good reason to believe that attitude verbs take a property-type, rather than a proposition-type argument. They should be called "property-oriented attitudes" rather than "propositional attitudes." The simple way to put this is to say that attitudes are fundamentally *de se*, with other readings being special cases. Second, when a constituent is understood *de re*, it is analyzed using an acquaintance relation, and moreover the acquaintance relation itself is based on *de se* semantics because it is between the "self" of the attitude and a particular "*res*." But despite the fact that a *de se* semantics is almost certainly appropriate for all attitude verbs, the literature on verbal mood only rarely uses property-oriented meanings; as a result, we will for the most part work with logical forms and meanings which reflect the traditional propositional attiude analysis. We will consider *de se* and *de re* interpretation only when the particular ideas being discussed require it.

Recent issues in the theory of subsentential modality. As mentioned in Section 1.5, there is a developing set of ideas about modality which differs substantially from the more standard approach discussed so far in this chapter. These ideas involve several major claims, in particular: (i) that sentences involving sentential and subsentential modality have a semantics which should be represented in terms of mathematical probabilities;[11] (ii) that root sentences do not have truth conditions, but rather some type of meaning we might call non-factual or "expressive"; and (iii) that the semantic function of clauses embedded under propositional attitude verbs is to impose constraints on mental states which are themselves appropriately modeled in terms of probabilities. I will label this general set of ideas the PROBABILITY-BASED APPROACH.[12]

---

[11] In place of probabilities, we might rather talk of credences. Utilities and expected values might be involved as well for priority-type modal meanings.

[12] Not all authors who will be cited as contributing to the probability-based approach accept all of the major claims I associate with it. For example, Lassiter (2011) assigns truth conditions to modal statements of the form *It is probable that S*, and so does not follow point (ii). For different views on (ii), see Yalcin (2010, 2011, 2012), Swanson (2007, 2015), and Rothschild (2012).

In order to avoid confusion, I would like to be explicit about why I often use phrases like "mathematical probabilities" in discussing the probability-based theory. When we talk about the semantics of a predicate like *probable*, it is no doubt appropriate to say that its semantics concerns probabilities just as it is appropriate to say that the predicate *intelligent* concerns how much intelligence people have. But a crucial part of understanding the semantics of these items is to figure out exactly what types of things probabilities and intelligence are. In both of these cases, there are famous existing concepts which might seem to readily answer the question: Mathematicians have developed a precise formal model of probability no doubt known to all readers of this book in at least a basic form: the theory of probability we invoke when we say things like the probability of a fair coin coming up heads is .5 or 50 per cent. Similarly, psychologists have developed a notion of degrees of intelligence known as IQ. Of course, we would not want to assume that the semantics of *intelligent* involves IQ. Indeed, many believe that the IQ measure is fundamentally misguided, and I doubt anyone would want to claim that *X is intelligent* just means something like '*X*'s IQ is above threshold *i*.' Likewise, we should not simply assume that the probabilities relevant to *probable*'s meaning have anything to do with the mathematical theory according to which they can appropriately be represented as numbers like .5.[13] We need to keep the semantically relevant notion separate from the mathematical one so that we can clearly test the hypothesis that the two should be identified. It is for this reason that, when I wish to consider the idea that the probabilities relevant to the semantics of *probable* do have to do with the mathematical theory, it will sometimes be clearer if I talk about "mathematical probabilities."[14]

The probability-based approach draws its motivation from several major points. The first two are directly relevant to the issue of whether mathematical probabilities should be used to express the semantics of words which express subsentential modality:

1. Subsentential modals are often gradable (see Villalta 2008; Portner 2009; Yalcin 2010; Klecha 2014; Lassiter 2016; Portner and Rubinstein 2016, among others).

(26)   It is more likely that this meat is chicken than squirrel.

(27)   It is highly probable that there will be rain tomorrow.

[13] I don't wish to suggest that mathematical probabilities have anything like the questionable status of IQs. The point of the analogy is simply to make apparent that it's a substantive hypothesis that they play a role in explaining the semantics of such a word as *probable*.

[14] At a deeper level, the issue does not have to do with probabilities represented mathematically, in the sense of using numbers in the familiar way, as opposed to "non-mathematically." Kratzer's ordering semantics is presented in a set-theoretical system which is "mathematical" in its own way. The real issue concerns whether something close to probability theory as standardly presented is needed, or whether a Kratzerian premise semantics giving ordering relations among worlds is more appropriate. Of course, the ideal theory might be based on a formal model somewhere in between, or something altogether different. See Holliday and Icard (2013) for useful discussion.

(28)   Your actions are barely permissible.

The comparative construction and modifiers in these examples show that the modal items *likely*, *probable*, and *permissible* are gradable in much the same way that non-modal adjectives like *tall* and *happy* are. As mentioned above, while Kratzer's semantics for modality gives meanings to some sentences involving gradable modality, it does not do so in a compositional way. It seems natural to analyze gradable modality in terms of the probability-based theory by construing scales associated with modal expressions in terms of probabilities and utilities. Thus, for example, (26) might be analyzed as conveying that the mathematical probability associated with the meat being chicken is higher than that associated with the meat being squirrel. But we should not simply assume that gradability provides evidence for a system based on mathematical probabilities; it may well also be possible to construct an appropriate semantics for gradable modality by extending the ordering semantics system (see Katz et al. 2012; Kratzer 2012; Portner and Rubinstein 2016).

2. Several scholars have argued that Kratzer's analysis cannot correctly model the logic of subsentential modals which intuitively have to do with probability, in particular *likely*, *probable*, and *certain*. The most important of these challenges come from the work of Yalcin (2010), Lassiter (2011), and Moss (2015), and while they raise a number of puzzles, we will focus on only one puzzle for purposes of illustration here. The standard version of Kratzer's analysis (Kratzer 1981, 1991) predicts that if a proposition is as likely as its negation, it is at least as likely as any other proposition whatsoever (Yalcin 2010, p. 922):

(29) ϕ is as likely as $\neg\phi$.

   ───────────────────────

   ϕ is at least as likely as ψ.

It's easy to see why (29) holds if we make the limit assumption.[15] In that case, Kratzer's (1981) semantics says that, when comparing ϕ and ψ in likelihood, we compare the highest ranked worlds making them true. Hence, the premise of (29) says that the highest ranked ϕ worlds have the same ranking as the highest ranking $\neg\phi$ worlds. The conclusion says that the highest ranking ϕ worlds are at least as highly ranked as the highest ranking ψ worlds—and this must be the case, because the highest ranking ψ worlds must be either ϕ worlds or $\neg\phi$ worlds. If a given highest ranked ψ world is a ϕ world, it can't be higher ranked than the highest ranked ϕ worlds, and if it is a $\neg\phi$ world, it can't be higher ranked than the highest ranked $\neg\phi$ worlds. The probability-based theory would analyze the argument as follows: the premise states that the probability associated with both ϕ and $\neg\phi$ is .5, and this clearly does not rule out that there are other propositions with probability above .5.

---

[15] Yalcin's and Lassiter's papers demonstrate the problem without the limit assumption.

There is debate about whether this problem afflicts the whole ordering semantics framework or just the particular version of it cited by Yalcin. Kratzer (2012) proposes a different definition of the world-ordering which avoids the inference in (29), though Lassiter (2011) argues that the new definition fails to fully solve the problem. Klecha (2012) and Katz et al. (2012) provide alternative analyses for some of the data which had been claimed to support the probability-based approach. There is no consensus on whether mathematical probabilities, ordering semantics, or some other tools provide the best basis for the semantics of probability operators; nor is it clear how representative such operators are of the full range of gradable modal expressions. What is important here is simply that points like 1–2 above have motivated the development of a theory of subsentential modality which uses mathematical probabilities.

Within the literature which develops the probability-based approach, scholars have noted other important issues in modal semantics. One of them is especially relevant to this chapter:

3. The semantics for embedded probability expressions does not seem intuitively correct. According to the standard semantics for *believe* (as a strong modal) and *probably* (as expressing Kratzerian human necessity), example (30) would be true if and only if Mary believes that the highest ranked worlds (according to the ordering source for *probably*) are ones in which the thing being talked about is a chicken.

(30)   Mary believes that this is probably a chicken.

Assuming that the ordering source would represent Mary's beliefs, such an analysis amounts to saying that she believes that she holds it likely that it is a chicken. However, the sentence does not seem to report Mary's belief about what she holds likely, but rather a judgment that it's probable, according to her beliefs, that it's a chicken (Yalcin 2007, 2011; Swanson 2011a; Rothschild 2012). One intuition about this case is that the verb and the adverb combine into a single modal operator, "x holds . . . likely in terms of x's beliefs."

Several scholars have argued that embedded probability expressions like *probably* in (30) point to the need to abandon the assumption that sentences like (31) express propositions (e.g. Yalcin 2011; Swanson 2011a, 2015).

(31)   This is probably a chicken.

According to ordering semantics, (31) expresses a proposition which is true if and only if the highest ranked (according to the ordering source) worlds in which the thing is a chicken are more highly ranked than the highest ranked worlds in which it is anything else. A sentence with these truth conditions should be consistent with (32):

(32)   This is not a chicken.

Given that they should be consistent, it is surprising that (33a–b) are incoherent:

(33) (a) ?This is probably a chicken and (but) it's not a chicken.
     (b) ?Suppose that this is probably a chicken and that it's not a chicken.

The embedded version (33b) poses an especially serious problem. As long as the proposition expressed by the complement is consistent, John should be able to suppose that it is true. According to the standard version of ordering semantics, doing so would amount to making the supposition that his own evidence suggests that it is a chicken even though it is not; this is the kind of thing a humble person is willing to suppose. Given that (33b) cannot be directed even towards a humble person, it appears that the complement of (33b) does not have the meaning implied by the standard ordering semantics analysis. From this point, it is a short step for authors like Swanson (2011a, 2015) and Yalcin (2011, 2012) to the conclusion that sentences like (30)–(33) do not denote propositions which describe the world, but rather are "non-factual," "non-descriptive," and "expressive." See the papers cited for details.[16]

Though the usefulness of mathematical probabilities is often broached within the same literature which argues against the assumption that sentences *believe* and *probable* denote assertable, truth-conditional propositions, the claims are largely separable. In what follows, we will focus on the hypothesis that the semantics of certain subsentential modal expressions involves mathematical probabilities. We will return to other issues raised in connection with the probability-based approach later on; specifically, in Section 2.2.2 we will encounter Yalcin's analysis of sentences like (33) as it relates to a particular theory of verbal mood, and in Section 3.3.1 we will briefly discuss Swanson's proposal about the discourse function of sentences like (31).

With these preliminaries out of the way, we can now turn to the question of how one might incorporate probabilities into the semantics. The simplest way is to allow the relevant predicates, which take propositions as their semantic arguments, to describe those propositions in terms of a probability measure derived from the lexical semantics of the predicate, arguments of the predicate, and contextual information. For example, along the lines of proposals made by Lassiter (2011) and Yalcin (2010), *probable* might mean the following:

(34) $[\![\, probable\,]\!] = \lambda p \lambda w[P_w(p) > .5]$

(35) $[\![\, It\ is\ probable\ that\ it\ is\ raining\,]\!] = \{w : P_w([\![\, it\ is\ raining\,]\!]) > .5\}$

---

[16] These authors do not reach exactly the same conclusions about the semantics of attitude verbs and probability expressions. I should note that much of Yalcin's work is presented in an exploratory frame, so it may be going too far to state that he endorses any particular system.

Following Lassiter, we can assign similar meanings to a priority expression like *good* by using a measurement of expected value. A proposition is good if its expected value is above some threshold t:

(36) $[\![\, good\,]\!] = \lambda p \lambda w [V_w(p) > t]$

(37) $[\![\, It\ is\ good\ that\ it\ is\ raining\,]\!] = \{w : V_w([\![\, it\ is\ raining\,]\!]) > t\}$

Under the approach in (34)–(37), probability and value information is only relevant to semantics at the points where a probability operator is being interpreted. It does not challenge the standard assumption that the meanings of sentences should be thought of in terms of truth conditions specified as a set of possible worlds.

A more radical version of the probability approach proposes that sentence meanings themselves involve probabilities. There are several ways to carry this idea out, and for explanatory purposes I sketch an approach based on Yalcin (2012, sect. 5) and Swanson (2015). Within standard possible worlds semantics, sentence-level and modal meanings are all stated in terms of propositions, thought of as sets of possible worlds. In this version of the probability-based semantics, in place of possible worlds, we have probability spaces, and in place of propositions we have CREDAL INFORMATION STATES. A credal information state is a set of probability spaces:[17]

(38) a. A **credal information state** I is a set of probability spaces.
      b. A probability space is a pair $\langle c, P \rangle$, where:
          i. c is a set of worlds, and
          ii. P is a probability measure over a set of subsets of c.

So how can a credal information state represent the meaning of a sentence? Consider the simple example (39):

(39) Willie is happy.

If someone says this to you and you say "thanks for telling me," what have you learned? It seems that, in terms of probability spaces, you've learned that worlds in which Willie is not happy can be put out of mind, and you don't need to assign any probability weight to them. We express this in terms of credal information states by assigning (40) as the meaning of (39):

(40) $[\![\, Willie\ is\ happy\,]\!] = \{\langle c, P \rangle : c \subseteq \{w : \text{Willie is happy in } w\}\}$

---

[17] Note that P need not assign a probability to every subset of c; whether it does or not depends on the exact role we want P to play in relating information states to real cognitive states.

[[*Willie is happy*]] is a set of probability spaces whose domains are limited to worlds in which Willie is happy. Someone who accepts the information in this credal information state does not assign any probability to worlds in which Willie is not happy.[18]

In this approach, an epistemic sentential modal places constraints on the probability measure P. A simple idea about *might* would be that it leads the sentence to denote a set of probability spaces according to which the prejacent has a probability above zero:

(41) a. Willie might be happy.

b. [[*Willie might be happy*]] =
$\{\langle c, P \rangle : P(c \cap \{w : \text{Willie is happy in } w\}) > 0\}$

Although (41b) is not as sophisticated as Swanson's (2015) proposal, it shares the key feature that the meaning of both modal and non-modal sentences are sets of probability spaces.

Now we turn to the semantics of the subsentential modal expression *believe* in the credal information state theory. Within the standard possible worlds approach to attitude verbs, the meaning of *believe* is given in terms of the set of doxastically accessible worlds. Since we have provisionally replaced the notion of proposition (a set of worlds) with a credal information state (a set of probability spaces), it seems that the set of doxastically accessible worlds should translate into a set of probability spaces as well. Here's how that goes:

(42) [[*believe*]] $= \lambda p \lambda x [\{\langle c, P \rangle : c \subseteq$
$\{w : \text{for every probability space } i \text{ which is compatible with } x\text{'s beliefs in } w,$
$i \in p\}\}]$

(43) [[*John believes that Willie might be happy*]] $= \{\langle c, P \rangle : c \subseteq$
$\{w : \text{for every probability space } i \text{ which is compatible with John's beliefs in}$
$w, i \in$ [[Willie might be happy]] $\}\}$

Statement (43) is the set of probability spaces which do not include any worlds in which it is compatible with John's beliefs to assign zero probability to all of the worlds in which Willie is happy.

We have seen two versions of the probability-based approach: a conservative one which uses probabilities as part of the lexical meanings of subsentential modal expressions, and a radical version which replaces possible worlds propositions with credal information states as the central model of semantic content. The question for us here is whether either of these have any significance for our understanding of mood. Unfortunately, the answer is not clear. None of the scholars who have worked on this approach have applied themselves to analyzing verbal mood, and

---

[18] One might think that simply assigning all worlds in which Willie is not happy no probability would be sufficient to record the information that Willie is happy, but Yalcin goes farther than this and excludes them from c entirely.

so it will be up to us to consider whether the probability-based approach suggests any new ways of thinking about the topic. It may be useful to make three points:

1. We see a significant difference between the entries for *probable* and *good* given in (34) and (36). The former involves probabilities, while the latter uses expected values. Expected value is defined as a combination of probability and utility—roughly, how good an outcome is, weighted for how likely it is. Thus, we can say that *probable* uses probability alone, while *good* uses probability and utility. If one wants to explain verbal mood within some version of the probability-based approach, this difference might well be important.

2. We see another significant difference between the entries for *probable* and *good*, on the one hand, and that for *believe* in (42), on the other. Setting aside the fact that the latter is more complex because it was used to explain the radical version of the approach, note that the meanings of *probable* and *good* both involve comparison: they use > to relate the content of their complements to some standard (.5 or *t*). In contrast, (42) uses universal quantification. This difference corresponds to the contrast within Kratzer's theory of modality between predicates which employ an ordering source, and those which do not. As we will see in Section 2.2, one of the most important approaches to verbal mood is based on the difference between comparative and non-comparative predicates—the idea is that comparison of propositions or the use of an ordering source triggers the subjunctive form. While there is as of yet no reason to think that basing our theory of mood on the probability approach, rather than some version of ordering semantics, would result in a better theory of verbal mood, at least we can foresee the possibility of translating the theory based on comparative vs. non-comparative predicates into a system that uses probabilities and utilities.

3. Much of the work in developing a theory of verbal mood comes in trying to analyze particular aspects of the lexical semantics of predicates that embed indicative or subjunctive clauses. The probability-based approach represents the meanings of such predicates using different tools, and so, if one were to develop a probability-based theory of verbal mood, the way to argue in favor of it would be to claim that the lexical semantic properties relevant to verbal mood are better captured using those tools. But there is also the chance that this type of consideration could support the opposite conclusion. The probability-based approach is quite general and powerful, and this might make it too easy to represent all subsentential modality in a simple and uniform way. With such a theory, it might be difficult to explain why the semantic differences which are reflected in verbal mood are important in human language.

In sum, nothing we know about verbal mood rules out the probability-based approach as a theory of subsentential modality, but nothing we know supports the approach either, and moreover we can foresee where some of the pitfalls for it would lie. Linguists should seek to evaluate this approach in terms of whether it can contribute to an explanatory theory of verbal mood.

2.2 Indicative and subjunctive

With this background in place on the semantics of subsentential modal expressions, we can now begin the study of verbal mood. The most basic and well-known categories of verbal mood are the indicative and subjunctive, and the most important theories of verbal mood within linguistics aim to explain the distribution of indicative and subjunctive clauses. In this section, we will study the indicative/subjunctive contrast with the ultimate goal of developing an integrated theory of subsentential modality and the semantics of the different verbal moods. To begin with, in Section 2.2.1, I will give some high-level orientation on the main ideas in the semantics literature concerning the distribution of indicatives and subjunctives. Then we will focus in Section 2.2.2 on the main grammatical contexts in which the subjunctive/indicative contrast has been studied: complement clauses. That subsection both outlines the empirical patterns which inform semantic theories of verbal mood and reviews a number of the most important such theories. As a conclusion to the discussion of indicatives and subjunctives, Section 2.2.3 reviews recent research on non-argument clauses, including adverbial clauses, relative clauses, *if* clauses, and root clauses. My aim in this section and more broadly in Chapter 2 is to contribute to a better understanding of verbal mood by identifying the most useful and promising ideas in the existing literature and by suggesting how to refine those ideas and integrate them with one another. I think that the results of this chapter point very clearly in the direction of a better theory of verbal mood, though I will not be proposing a new theory of indicatives and subjunctives here.

A major difficulty in following the line of research just outlined concerns crosslinguistic variation. Almost all semantically-oriented work on verbal mood focuses on a small number of European languages, and while the mood systems of those languages have much in common, there are also significant differences.[19] Anyone who wants to understand the literature in this area has to give a lot of weight to the major, crosslinguistically valid patterns, but also must keep track of the areas of difference between languages. And it is not at all easy to know which differences among languages are as important as the general patterns, and which are idiosyncrasies which should be understood in terms other than semantic theory.[20] In terms of presentation, this chapter faces a problem of wanting to identify important cases of variation while not getting bogged down in a detailed description of every language which has been carefully studied by linguists within a more or less well-developed semantic perspective. So, as I aim to maintain the correct balance, readers should keep in mind that many details are not discussed,

---

[19] If we look beyond these European languages whose verbal mood systems have been the subject of formal theories, the variation is much greater, and it is by no means clear that we are dealing with a unified category. See Wiltschko (2016) for an approach which aims to extend the theory of subjunctive to languages which are quite different from the standard European ones. In Section 4.2, we will discuss the notions of reality status and mode and consider their relation to mood.

[20] For example, they may have historical, morphological, or psycholinguistically-based explanations which are important to our understanding of language.

and that undiscussed details could turn out to be important. It is up to future research to figure out whether this is so.

2.2.1 Ideas about the indicative/subjunctive contrast

Semantically oriented research on verbal mood has developed two main intuitions about the basis of mood selection:

1. **Comparison:** The subjunctive mood is associated with grammatical contexts which express a comparison between alternatives in which the clause is true and some other relevant alternatives. The comparison-based approach has been connected explicitly to ordering semantics from the time of Giorgi and Pianesi's (1997) important book on tense, aspect, and mood.
2. **Truth:** The indicative is associated with contexts which imply that the clause is true throughout some designated set of possible worlds. This approach finds its roots in the work of Farkas (1985, 1992b), and we see an early, direct implementation of the idea in Portner's (1997) analysis of Italian.

Both intuitions have their basis in traditional ideas about the contribution of mood: Comparison connects directly to the idea that mood choice in complement clauses is determined by a distinction between evaluative/emotive predicates (the subjunctive) and intellectual/cognitive ones (indicative). Truth relates to the idea that indicative clauses are *realis* and subjunctives *irrealis*.[21]

It is important to keep in mind at this point that we are entertaining two intuitions about the indicative/subjunctive contrast, but not necessarily two competing theories. Indeed, in Giannakidou's important work on mood in Greek, we see references to both ideas as she develops her analysis (Giannakidou 1994, 1995, 1997). There are two points I'd like to make about the relation between "comparison" and "truth." First, they could be two ways of making the same semantic distinction. To see the plausibility of this, note that under standard versions of ordering semantics, a predicate with a comparative meaning like 'want' fails to entail that its argument proposition is true throughout the set of worlds compatible with the modal base; instead, it only entails that the complement is true throughout the best-ranked subset of the worlds compatible with the modal base. If we assume that the worlds compatible with the modal base constitute the "relevant" worlds for the truth-based approach, a comparative predicate is predicted to take subjunctive according to both the idea that comparison triggers subjunctive and the idea that truth triggers indicative. In contrast, a non-comparative predicate like 'believe' does entail that its complement is true throughout the set of worlds compatible

---

[21] A list of basic references on the semantics and pragmatics of verbal mood from outside of the formal semantics tradition would include the work of Bolinger (1974, 1976), Terrell and Hooper (1974), Givón (1994), Lunn (1995), Bybee (1998), Bhat (1999), Palmer (2001), Haverkate (2002), Jary (2011), de Haan (2012), and Gregory and Lunn (2012).

with the modal base, and so should take indicative according to both criteria.[22] It is this perspective—where both of the ideas mentioned above are seen as correct when expressed within a version of ordering semantics—which we can consider to be the current state of the art in mood semantics.

The second point about the relation between the two ideas under discussion is that, rather than being unified into a single idea as part of a deeper analysis, the two ideas may have independent roles to play in the overall theory of mood selection. We will see Farkas (2003) pursue this strategy as she attempts to analyze variation in mood selection crosslinguistically in terms of partially competing requirements. The idea is that each of the leading ideas above corresponds to a real requirement on verbal mood, with one favoring indicative, the other subjunctive. When they impose contradictory requirements, a language-specific principle determines which holds sway. Of course, such a strategy cannot work if the ideas are really two sides of the same coin.

In the review of particular theories of verbal mood in the following subsection, I have done my best to appropriately classify particular scholars' work in terms of the two main intuitions outlined above, but because of the fact that they can be seen as two versions of the same intuition, or as both being a part of the overall story, it is in some cases difficult to do so. In such circumstances, I have tried to make the classification based on the most explicit hypotheses he or she gives concerning mood selection. We will return to the various ways in which the two intuitions might be combined in Section 2.2.2.5.

2.2.2 Semantic theories of verbal mood in complement clauses

In this section, we will discuss theories of verbal mood based on the distribution of indicative and subjunctive complement clauses. As mentioned above, such theories typically begin with a classification of predicates in terms of whether they can combine with an indicative complement, a subjunctive complement, or both. They then develop some principle which aims to explain the choice of indicative or subjunctive as the complements of particular predicates in terms of the lexical semantics of the predicates, possibly in combination with additional pragmatic factors. For some of the theories to be discussed, the entire analysis rests on the lexical semantics of the selecting predicates; in such cases, the idea is that verbal mood simply marks a feature of the clause's semantic context, without contributing any relevant meaning of its own. In contrast, other theories also include claims about the internal semantics of the indicative- or subjunctive-marked clauses themselves (for example, Portner 1997; Schlenker 2005; Villalta 2008), and the distribution of each verbal mood is supposed to follow from interaction between the meaning of the predicate and the meaning of the mood-marked clause itself.

---

[22] The alignment between non-comparative meaning and the entailment of truth throughout the modal base worlds might come apart with negative predicates and predicates with a modal force of possibility. If the assumptions of the standard ordering semantics analysis of propositional attitudes are correct, it is with such predicates that we can try to see whether one of the two leading ideas is more important than the other.

2.2.2.1 Outline of data: complement clauses The empirical basis for this discussion is the patterns of mood selection by semantically defined classes of predicates. I will outline these patterns in terms of the following more-or-less traditional classes:

1. Predicates of knowledge and belief: words with meanings similar to *know* and *believe*.

   These are the classical propositional attitude predicates; they involve an individual's cognitive state which is naturally described in terms of a proposition.

2. Predicates of assertion: words with meanings similar to *say that*.

   These predicates report assertive speech acts of the kind which would be performed with an indicative declarative clause.

3. Interrogative-selecting predicates: words with meanings similar to *wonder* and *ask*.

   These predicates have barely been discussed in the literature on verbal mood. They should be placed into subclasses:

   (a) Predicates of inquisitiveness, such as *wonder*: the interrogative-selecting counterparts of predicates of belief/knowledge (*wonder* means something like 'want to know').

   (b) Predicates of inquiry, such as *ask*: the interrogative-selecting counterparts of verbs of assertion (*ask* means something like 'wants to be told').

4. Predicates of fiction and mental creation: words with meanings similar to *imagine* and *dream*.

5. Commissive predicates: words with meanings similar to *promise*.

6. Perception predicates: words with meanings similar to *see, notice,* and *hear*.

7. Preference predicates: words with meanings similar to *want, like,* and *fear*.

   These report on the individuals' desires, and more broadly their preferences and dispreferences.

8. Directive predicates: words with meanings similar to *order* and *require*.

   These report directive speech acts of the kind which would be performed with imperative clauses.

9. Causative and implicative predicates: words with meanings similar to *make, cause,* and *manage*.

10. Negative counterparts of predicates of knowledge/belief and predicates of assertion: words with meanings similar to *doubt* and *deny*.

    There is a strong intuition that words in this class "contain negation," in some sense.

11. Modal predicates: words with meanings similar to *possible* and *necessary*.

    These are often thought of as the most simple, pure modal words in natural language, with meanings similar to the □ and ◊ of modal logic. Other predicates which are just as surely modal, for example *probable* and *likely*, are less frequently discussed.

12. Factive predicates: words which presuppose the truth of their complement, such as *regret* and *remember*. This class has two important subclasses:

    (a) Neutral factive predicates: factives with meanings lacking a strong evaluative or emotive dimension, such as *remember*. *Know* also falls into this class, though it is more typically discussed together with *believe* as part of a knowledge/belief class. This class is also known as the semi-factives (Karttunen 1971), because they seem not to be factive in certain contexts.

(b) Emotive factive predicates: factives which express an evaluative meaning similar to what would be seen in a preference predicate, e.g. *happy (that)*, *odd (that)*, and *regret*.

The kind of classification given above tends to obscure the issue of how we deal with lexical items which fall into multiple classes and those with multiple meanings or multiple uses. Consider the example of *require*: this verb is listed as directive, because a sentence like *Mary required John to return early* could be true because Mary commanded John to return early through the use of a directive speech act. However, *require* is not limited to such uses—we can also say things like *Mary's health required her to avoid going out in the heat*, which does not depend for its truth on any speech act of the sort which could be performed with an imperative. Should this latter use be considered to exemplify directive meaning? If so, this shows that the description of "directive" under point 8 above is quite rough and far from an adequate definition. Or should it be considered to fall into a distinct class? Or should we not worry about assigning it a second class at all, on the assumption that the core uses of *require* are directive and that this fact determines its relation to verbal mood? Fundamentally, the question is whether we aim to classify lexical items as morphological entities, meanings of lexical items, or uses of them. The answer to this question has both empirical consequences (might we expect *require* to combine with different verbal moods on its different uses?) and theoretical ones (how do we specify the principles which explain the selection of mood, and are these principles syntactic, semantic, or pragmatic?). There may, of course, be no single answer; perhaps in some cases the different meanings of a polysemous predicate are relevant to mood selection, while in others they are not.

With some understanding of these semantic classes of predicates in the background, we can turn to their mood selection properties. While it is well known that the classes are not uniform, both in that there are lexical exceptions to the general patterns of mood selection and in that languages do not all behave alike, many of the classes are generally understood to have default or typical selection properties. The literature tends to identify the defaults with the patterns found in the majority of the most well-known Romance languages. Examples come at the end.

1. Indicative governors
    (a) Predicates of knowledge and belief: normally take indicative, though belief predicates can take subjunctive, as in Italian. The factive 'know' also falls in the neutral factive class (see below), and is perhaps better categorized there. Examples: (44)–(45).
    (b) Predicates of assertion: are usually thought of as taking indicative, because of the fact that they routinely select indicative in Romance languages. They also are seen as selecting indicative in Greek, but notice that what the verb actually selects is a clause introduced by the

complementizer *oti*; it is not entirely clear whether an *oti* clause should be classified as a case of verbal mood, but in any case, it is treated in the semantics literature as falling under the same theory as verbal mood, so we include it here. Example: (46).

German does not follow the same pattern as Romance and Greek; predicates of assertion can take subjunctive or indicative, with no apparent change in meaning. In addition, German can employ the subjunctive with other classes of predicates that normally select indicative with the semantic effect of indicating that someone has said something with the meaning of the embedded clause. Example: (47).

Although predicates of assertion show crosslinguistic variation in mood selection, this fact has not been seen as having deep consequences for the theory of mood. Rather, scholars seem to make an assumption that the German subjunctives illustrated in (47) exemplify a special use, the REPORTATIVE SUBJUNCTIVE, which plays out on top of a more basic indicative–subjunctive contrast. This is the reason I list verbs of assertion under "indicative governors" in this summary; I do not, however, wish to dissuade anyone from an attempt to challenge that assumption.

(c) Predicates of inquiry: have barely been discussed, but initial investigation points to their selecting the indicative. Example: (48).

(d) Neutral factive predicates: normally take indicative. In Greek, they may take the indicative complementizer *oti* used with belief and assertion predicates (cf. (46b)), or another "factive" complementizer, *pu*. Giannakidou (2009) considers them both to mark indicative, but, following Christidis (1981), describes a semantic effect of complementizer choice, with *pu* incorporating a "subjective dimension" of meaning. Example: (49).

(e) Predicates of fiction and mental creation: routinely take indicative. Example: (50).

(f) Commissive predicates: routinely take indicative. Example: (51).

(g) Perception predicates: take the indicative (for example, in Spanish). They take *na* complements in Greek, which would normally indicate subjunctive, but Giannakidou (2009) argues that the *na* clause after perception and aspectual verbs does not mark subjunctive, but rather introduces a "smaller" clause more similar to an infinitive or gerund. Example: (52).

2. Subjunctive governors

(a) Predicates of inquisitiveness: have barely been discussed, but initial investigation points to their selecting the subjunctive. Example: (53).

(b) Preference predicates: 'want' and other predicates of desire and preference typically take subjunctive, though 'hope' can take indicative, for example in French.[23] Examples: (54)–(55).

(c) Directive predicates: routinely take subjunctive. Example: (56).

---

[23] Note that some French speakers prefer the subjunctive (Anand and Hacquard 2013); also note that Spanish *esperar* 'hope' can take indicative when it means 'anticipate/expect', but not when it means 'hope', according to Villalta (2008).

(d) Causative and implicative predicates: typically take subjunctive, but not in Greek. Example: (57).

(e) Negative counterparts of predicates of knowledge/belief and predicates of assertion: routinely take subjunctive. Example: (58).

(f) Modal predicates: The most basic modal predicates, 'necessary' and 'possible', take subjunctive, but others, such as *probable* in French, sometimes take the indicative. Examples: (59)–(60).

3. A class showing crosslinguistic variation

Emotive factive predicates: may take subjunctive (for example, subjunctive is preferred in French) or indicative (for example, in Romanian, Greek). Farkas (1992b, 2003) focuses on the crosslinguistic variation shown by emotive factives. Example: (61).

While there is abundant crosslinguistic variation in mood choice, with the emotive factives we see an entire semantic class showing distinct mood selection properties in otherwise similar languages. For this reason, this case of variation cannot be downplayed as mere idiosyncratic lexical variation, and has received a significant amount of attention within semantic theories of mood.

Examples of mood selection in complement clauses   This data is mainly taken from the semantics literature. Please see the above discussion for an explanation of what each example is meant to show.[24]

(44) (a) *Pierre sait   que Marie est   heureuse. (French)*
         Pierre knows that Marie is.INDIC happy
      (b) *Pietro sa   che Maria è   felice. (Italian)*
         Pietro knows that Maria is.INDIC happy

(45) (a) *Pierre croit   que Marie est   heureuse. (French)*
         Pierre believes that Marie is.INDIC happy
      (b) *Pietro creda   che Maria sia   felice. (Italian)*
         Pietro believes that Maria is.SUBJ happy

(46) (a) *Je dis que le   temps   est   beau. (French)*
         I say that the weather is.INDIC pretty
      (b) *O Pavlos ipe   oti   efije i   Roxani. (Greek)*
         the Paul   said that.INDIC left the Roxani

(47) (a) *Er behauptete, dass jemand   das Auto angefahren habe,*
         he claimed   that somebody the car   on-driven have.SUBJ
         ...(German)

---

[24] Sources are as follows: Portner and Rubinstein (2013): (44a), (45a), (46a), (50), (51), (54a), (55a). Raffaella Zanuttini, p.c.: (48), (53). Giannakidou (2009): (46b), (54c), (61c). Farkas (2003): (49b), (61a,b). Fabricius-Hansen and Saebø (2004): (47). Villalta (2008): (52a), (54b), (55b). Giannakidou (1998): (52b). Mulder (2010): (56), (58). Blanco (2011): (57a). Quer (2001): (57b). Quer (2010): (59b). Proust, *Le Coté de Guermantes*, 1920/1921: (60a). Laca (2010): (60b).

(b) *Ich bat   Dr Stroncickij, er möge   doch kurz   in mein*
    I   begged Dr Stroncickij he may.SUBJ PART briefly in my
    Büro   kommen. (German)
    office come

(c) *Der Minister war überrascht, dass die EG nicht informiert*
    the Minister was surprised   that the EC not informed
    worden sei.   (German)
    become be.SUBJ

(48) *Gli avevo   chiesto se ci   sono   corsi   d'inglese. (Italian)*
     him have-1sg asked if there be.3PL.INDIC courses of English
     'I asked him whether there are English courses.'

(49) (a) *Je me   souviens   que le temps   est   beau. (French)*
         I myself remember that the weather is.INDIC pretty

     (b) *Thimame   pu/oti   ton sinandisa sto Parisi.*
         remember.1SG that.FACT/that.INDIC him met.1SG in Paris
         (Greek)

(50) *J'ai rêvé   qu'il   était   président. (French)*
     I dreamed that he was.INDIC president

(51) *Marie a   promis   à Bill qu'elle   amènerait   le dessert à la*
     Marie has promised to Bill that she bring.COND the dessert to the
     fête.   (French)
     party

(52) (a) *Siento   que va   a haber un problema. (Spanish)*
         sense.1SG that go.INDIC to have a   problem.

     (b) *Vlepo   tin Ariadne na kolymbai. (Greek)*
         see.NONPAST1SG the Ariadne NA swam

(53) *Mi chiedo   se ci   siano   corsi   d'inglese. (Italian)*
     me wonder-1SG if there be.3PL.SUBJ courses of English
     'I wonder whether there are English courses.'

(54) (a) *Pierre veut que Marie soit   heureuse. (French)*
         Pierre wants that Marie is.SUBJ happy

     (b) *Victoria quiere que Marcela venga   al   picnic. (Spanish)*
         Victoria wants that Marcela come.SUBJ to-the picnic

     (c) *Thelo   na kerdisi o Janis (Greek)*
         want.1SG SUBJ win   the John

(55) (a) *J'espère que tu fais   toujours l'effort   d'écouter tes*
         I hope that you make.INDIC always the-effort to listen your
         parents. (French)
         parents

(b) *Espero   enormemente que venga   mi hermano. (Spanish)*
hope.1SG enormously   that come.SUBJ my brother

(56) *Il exige   que tu partes   maintenant. (French)*
he demand that you leave.SUBJ now

(57) (a) *Juan hizo   que María comiera lentejas. (Spanish)*
Juan made that Maria eat.SUBJ lentils

(b) *Fas   que marxi   abans d'hora. (Catalan)*
make.2SG that leave.SUBJ before of time

(58) *Paul doute   que tout le monde soit   venu. (French)*
Paul doubts that everybody   be.SUBJ come

(59) (a) *Il est possible que cet échantillon soit   dissolu   dans*
it is possible that this sample   be.SUBJ dissolved in
l'eau.   (French)
the water

(b) *És possible que dimiteixi.   (Catalan)*
Is possible that resign.SUBJ

(60) (a) *Saint-Loup a   raison et   il est probable que le   prochain*
Saint-Loup has reason and it is probable that the next
Service en Campagne portera   la   trace de cette évolution, dit
Service en Campagne carry.INDIC the trace of the   evolution said
mon voisin.   (French)
my   neighbor

(b) *Es probable que surjan   conflictos. (Spanish)*
is probable that arise.SUBJ conflicts

(61) (a) *Marie regrette que Paul soit   mal. (French)*
Marie regrets that Paul be.SUBJ badly

(b) *Ion e trist că   Maria e   bolnavă. (Romanian)*
Ion is sad that Maria is.INDIC sick

(c) *O Pavlos lipate pu   efije i   Roxani. (Greek)*
the Paul   is sad that.FACT left the Roxani

2.2.2.2 The link between selecting predicate and complement clause In order to construct a theory of verbal mood in complement clauses, one needs
to understand the relation between a sentence-embedding predicate (such as
'believe' or 'want') and the clause with which it combines. In simple standard
versions of formal semantics, this relation is just that the predicate denotes a
function which takes the proposition denoted by the clause as its argument. On
this view, the meanings of the predicate and clause are independent, just as the
meanings of the verb and object are in a simple VP like *saw Mary*. However,
the contrast between indicative and subjunctive clauses shows at least that the

form of a complement clause can depend on the predicate which combines with it, and within a semantic theory of verbal mood, this dependency needs to be encoded somehow in the meanings of the predicate and clause.[25] It would perhaps be ideal if this dependency could be captured by independently needed differences in meaning between indicative and subjunctive clauses and between those verbs which combine with one or the other. For example, a theory in which subjunctive clauses have a type of meaning which can be naturally combined with 'want', but not with 'believe', would certainly be attractive.[26] However, most semantic theories of verbal mood propose that the contribution of mood is only to indicate whether the embedding predicate is appropriate for that particular mood. From this point of view, mood is a kind of dependent modal element, similar to agreement—we could say that subjunctive "agrees with" 'want' but not 'believe'. In order to carry this idea out in a formal semantic theory, we need a way for the mood marker within the complement clause to connect to or "see" the relevant features of meaning of the embedding predicate. This implies that the relation between predicate and complement is not simply that of a function and argument.

In the literature on verbal mood, we see two ideas about the relation between a predicate and its complement clause which help to solve the problem of how indicatives and subjunctives relate to a higher predicate. Because these ideas are important in themselves, and because different analyses carry them out in slightly different ways, it will be useful to discuss them in a general way before we dive into the details of specific analyses. The ideas are as follows:

1. The choice of verbal mood in a complement clause is determined by the modal parameters of interpretation of the matrix predicate. Within an approach based on classical modal logic, the relevant parameter is the accessibility relation. Within one based on Kratzer's version of ordering semantics, several parameters might be relevant: the modal base, ordering source, and the modal force.
2. The relation between the complement clause and those modal parameters of interpretation is analogous to the relation between a root clause and the conversational context in which it is used. For example, suppose we accept the dynamic semantics/pragmatics idea that the primary function of a root declarative sentence is to update the common ground. The analogy states that certain embedded clauses relate to the modal parameters (the accessibility relation or modal base) associated with their embedding predicate in a way similar to assertion.

As we will see in the remainder of this section, scholars have given various technical implementations to these two ideas. Two strategies are fairly perspicuous, and so

---

[25] A purely syntactic theory of mood selection would not have this problem. The fact that some verbs combine with indicative and others with subjunctive would be analogous to the fact that some prepositions take accusative objects while others take ablative.

[26] The analyses of Portner (1997), Schlenker (2005), and Villalta (2008) have the ambition to provide explanations of this kind. However, none of them fully manages to analyze verbal mood in terms of independent semantic values for the predicate and complement clause, and in the end they all implement one of the methods discussed below.

that it will be clear what is going on when we encounter them below, I would like to briefly introduce them here. I label the two strategies the **method of shifting parameters** and the **method of derived contexts**.

We will discuss these strategies using a simple sentence with the matrix verb *think*, (62):

(62)   Ben thinks that the peach is ripe.

The method of shifting parameters proposes that the modal parameters of interpretation for *think* are available when semantic interpretation applies to the complement clause *that the peach is ripe*.[27] The modal parameters for a complement clause are determined by the matrix verb.

(63) $[\![\, A \text{ thinks that } \phi \,]\!]^{P_0} = [\![\, \text{thinks} \,]\!]^{P_0}([\![\, \text{that } \phi \,]\!]^{P_\Theta})([\![\, A \,]\!]^{P_0})$

The whole sentence is interpreted with respect to some default or discourse-level parameter P_0. In a basic modal logic, the important parameter is the accessibility relation; in Kratzer's system, the relevant parameters include a modal base and ordering source. Note that both the subject A and the verb *think* are interpreted with respect to the same parameters (i.e., we have $[\![\, A \,]\!]^{P_0}$ and $[\![\, \text{thinks} \,]\!]^{P_0}$). However, in the piece of (63) which references the compositional interpretation of the complement clause, $[\![\, \text{that } \phi \,]\!]^{P_\Theta}$, we have a different set of parameters P_Θ. P_Θ indicates that, as the complement clause is interpreted, some or all of the parameters in P_0 have been replaced by others which come from the matrix verb *think*. Roughly speaking, the contextual parameters P_0 are replaced by parameters which stand for A's thoughts, such as a doxastic accessibility relation or modal base. We see this parameter-shifting technique in many analyses of mood, including Farkas (1992b), Portner (1997), Giannakidou (1997), Quer (2001), Schlenker (2005), and Anand and Hacquard (2013).

The second strategy for implementing the intuitions listed above, the method of derived contexts, argues that we should incorporate the update functions of dynamic semantics/pragmatics into the compositional rules applied to sentences like (62). Suppose we employ the familiar $+$ notation for contextual update (see Section 1.4.1). Then, the meaning of a declarative sentence ϕ is implicitly defined in the formula $c + \phi = c'$. Assuming that the "context" here is merely a set of worlds (the context set) and that assertive update is merely intersection, we can say that the assertive meaning of ϕ is given by $c + \phi = c \cap [\![\, \phi \,]\!]$. The strategy for building a theory of verbal mood based on the dynamic approach incorporates '$+\phi$' (or something similar) into the compositional meaning of sentences like (62). This might work roughly as follows:

(64) $c + A \text{ thinks that } \phi = c \cap \{w : \Theta_w + \phi = c'\}$

---

[27] Formally, we can achieve this by treating the modal parameters as parameters of the interpretation function $[\![\ \,]\!]$ in a way parallel to how the possible world and model are parameters of interpretation for formulas of modal logic.

Once again, Θ is derived from *thinks*, but in this formula, those parameters are understood as a "context" which is updated by $+\phi$: $\Theta_w + \phi$. Since we are thinking of a context as a context set, a set of worlds, Θ_w must be a set of worlds and hence Θ itself is a function from worlds to sets of worlds. We already have a name for this kind of function: Θ is an accessibility relation, the very prototype of a modal parameter. In particular, in this case with the verb *think*, it is a doxastic accessibility relation: Θ_w is the set of worlds in which everything A thinks in w is true.

Formula (64) is not complete because it does not say what c' is. Heim (1992) points out that setting c' to be Θ_w itself yields a meaning very close to the standard treatment of propositional attitudes as strong modals. That is, with the meaning (65), we have an analysis almost equivalent to (7), except that it is built using $+\phi$.

(65) $c + A$ *thinks that* $\phi = c \cap \{w : \Theta_w + \phi = \Theta_w\}$

Heim seeks to explain the behavior of presuppositions triggered within ϕ in terms of the idea that Θ_w counts as a DERIVED CONTEXT in the sense of Stalnaker (1988, 2014). The guiding intuition of this analysis is that Θ_w counts as the "context" for purposes of satisfying the presuppositions of ϕ. (The theory of presupposition projection is complex, and we cannot go further into Heim's theory here. See her paper for details.)

In the remainder of this chapter, we will repeatedly encounter the idea that verbal mood is determined by the "context" with respect to which it is interpreted. Although the intuition will be presented in various ways, in many cases one of the two strategies identified here—the method of shifting parameters or the method of derived contexts—will be discernable. It is not yet clear exactly what is at stake in choosing one or the other of these strategies. In my opinion, they might turn out to be interchangeable as far as the theory of verbal mood goes, and the choice between them will probably come down to how well each fits into a broader theory of context dependency, presupposition, and the relation between verbal mood and sentence mood.

2.2.2.3 Theories based on comparison

Portner and Rubinstein (2013) describe the claim that mood selection is based on the principle that predicates with a comparative semantics select subjunctive as the "proto-standard analysis of mood." They point out that a majority of recent semantically oriented analyses of mood selection depend on the assumption that mood-selecting predicates have a modal semantics which is to be given in terms of some version of ordering semantics, and in particular the idea that we should explain the truth conditions of subjunctive-selectors by saying that they use an ordering source to rank the proposition expressed by the complement clause with respect to alternatives. We will label this approach the COMPARISON-BASED ANALYSIS OF VERBAL MOOD.

(66)   **The comparison-based analysis of verbal mood:** A predicate P selects the subjunctive iff its ordering source, g_P, is not empty, leading to a comparative semantics. It selects indicative otherwise. (Portner and Rubinstein 2013, p. 464)

We will begin by going through how the comparative analysis deals with the most well-studied data. Then, we will examine specific proposals in the literature which can be counted under this analysis, to see why their proposals should be seen as versions of the comparison-based theory. I think that doing things this way (rather than explaining each proposal in its own terms, and then deriving the statement in (66) from them) will make it easier to see how each specific version works, and will better allow us to identify the most important strengths and weaknesses of this group of theories.

We can expect a comparison-based theory to make correct predictions on some of the most well-known patterns:

- Indicative governors with non-comparative meaning
  1. Predicates of knowledge and belief: Standardly analyzed as involving universal quantification over accessible worlds.
  2. Predicates of assertion: Standardly analyzed as involving universal quantification over accessible worlds.
  3. Neutral factive predicates: No standard analysis, but there is no obvious sense in which these predicates compare alternatives.
  4. Predicates of fiction and mental creation: No standard analysis, but there is no obvious sense in which these predicates compare alternatives.
- Subjunctive governors with comparative meaning
  1. Preference predicates: Standardly analyzed as involving preference-based comparison of alternatives.
  2. Directive predicates: No standard analysis, but naturally analyzed as involving rule-based comparison of alternatives.

However, there are several classes of predicates which do not, at first glance, fit the predictions of (66), and others for which it is hard to say whether they should get a comparative semantics:

- Problematical types
  1. Commissive predicates: Naturally analyzed as involving a comparison between worlds in which the promise is fulfilled and those in which it is not; the former are ranked higher, according to a deontic ordering, than the latter. Yet this class normally takes the indicative.
  2. Negative counterparts of indicative-selecting predicates: Negation does not affect the non-comparative semantics associated with the corresponding positive predicates, yet this class normally takes the subjunctive.
  3. Emotive factive predicates: Naturally analyzed as involving comparison based on the subject argument's subjective evaluation of alternatives, but this class shows crosslinguistic variation.
  4. 'Believe' when it takes the subjunctive, as in Italian: There is no reason that 'believe' should be comparative in Italian but non-comparative in other languages.

- Types about which the approach does not make clear predictions
  1. Perception predicates: Standardly assumed to involve a relation to an event or situation, not a proposition (Barwise 1981).
  2. Causative and implicative predicates: The semantics of causatives is highly controversial, and we would have to accept one analysis in order to identify predictions.
  3. Modal predicates: If they use a non-null ordering source, these are comparative and are expected to take the subjunctive. However, weak modal predicates like 'possible' sometimes express simple possibility, and in such cases would be expected to select the indicative. It is also unexpected that 'probable' would ever take the indicative, since within the ordering semantics framework, it is standardly assumed to require a non-null ordering source.

In the remainder of this subsection, we will see how several authors have understood and tried to formalize the concept of comparison. Among the works we will discuss, only Giorgi and Pianesi's (1997) directly addresses any of the problems identified here, but even they do not attempt to challenge any standard assumptions concerning which predicates have a comparative or non-comparative semantics. Instead, they suggest that other factors (such as factivity) can play a role in addition to comparison. Thus, I think it's fair to say that the above points enumerate the empirical strengths and weaknesses of the comparison-based analysis.

Giorgi and Pianesi.   Giorgi and Pianesi (1997) come very close to giving the comparison-based theory in the form we have done, as seen in the following:

(67)   "…whenever the ordering source is non-null the context of evaluation is non-realistic, and the subjunctive is consistently selected across languages." (Giorgi and Pianesi 1997, p.17)

Though this statement is quite clear, the details of Giorgi and Pianesi's analysis make their position a bit less so. The statement above targets all languages, but they also propose that in some languages a weaker condition governs the choice of subjunctive. Recall that 'believe' in Italian selects the subjunctive. Because they assume that 'believe' has a null ordering source (thereby explaining why it takes indicative in French), other factors must be in play in Italian. So, to understand Giorgi and Pianesi's analysis fully, we first must understand what these other factors are and how they are integrated into the comparison-based analysis.

Giorgi and Pianesi's theory is based on classifying predicates in terms of a Kratzer-style modal semantics. They assume that modal accessibility relations are defined from conversational backgrounds which function as modal bases and ordering sources. For example, 'want' is treated as a strong modal utilizing a doxastic modal base and buletic ordering source. They define a series of properties which conversational backgrounds can have, using these to classify predicates. Here are the key definitions, derived from Giorgi and Pianesi (1997):

(68)   Given a common ground cg and a conversational background h:
  (a) h is *realistic* if h is a subset of the common ground: $h(w) \subseteq cg$, for all $w \in \bigcap cg$.
  (b) h is *non-realistic* if it is not realistic.
  (c) h is *totally realistic* if h is identical to the common ground: $h(w) = cg$, for all $w \in \bigcap cg$.
  (d) h is *weakly realistic* if h overlaps the common ground: $h(w) \cap cg \neq \emptyset$, for all $w \in \bigcap cg$.

(It is actually somewhat unclear in their discussion whether 'non-realistic' is meant to be the complement of 'realistic', or the complement of 'weakly realistic'. I understand it as the complement of 'realistic', and so a single background can be both non-realistic and weakly realistic.) A deontic conversational background is typically non-realistic, since normally not all rules in a system of rules are presupposed to be always followed. (Otherwise, why would we need the rules?) Indeed, a deontic background might not be even weakly realistic, if it is assumed to be possible that none of the rules would be followed. A doxastic conversational background is normally non-realistic, because sometimes we talk about people whose beliefs are incompatible with the information in the common ground. Giorgi and Pianesi make a number of other specific proposals about the conversational backgrounds for particular lexical items and constructions; for example, they say that the modal base for an indicative conditional and the ordering source of the adjective *odd* are both totally realistic.

Giorgi and Pianesi's theory also makes use of a concept of the CONTEXT OF EVALUATION (or DOMAIN OF EVALUATION) for a complement clause, but it is not clear in their discussion how the context of evaluation is to be defined. In some places, they seem to assume that the context of evaluation is simply the set of accessible worlds, analyzed as in standard ordering semantics. In this sense, the context of evaluation is the subset of the worlds compatible with the modal base which are best-ranked by the ordering source (see Section 1.3.2). In other places, they appear to understand the context of evaluation as a set of propositions somehow derived from the modal base and ordering source (e.g. Giorgi and Pianesi 1997, ch. 5, fn. 21, 26). Given this equivocation, and the absence of official definitions, it is quite hard to trace the predictions of their analysis in detail. Crucially, though, they explicitly state that, whenever a predicate uses a non-null ordering source, it creates a non-realistic context of evaluation. We can see this assumption being made explicitly in (67). They also state that, when a predicate has a non-realistic modal base, its context of evaluation is non-realistic.

Giorgi and Pianesi propose that in French the subjunctive is sensitive to the presence of a non-null ordering source; that is, French exemplifies the comparison-based theory in its pure form. In Italian, in contrast, the subjunctive is chosen whenever the context of evaluation is non-realistic, but not weakly realistic. Based on this, they predict that any predicate which selects subjunctive in French will do so in Italian as well, since a non-null ordering source is assumed to imply a non-realistic context of evaluation; and in addition, Italian will select subjunctive in other cases as well, specifically when the modal base is independently non-realistic (but not weakly realistic). 'Believe' is the key case here: they claim that it has a null ordering source and a non-realistic (doxastic) modal base, and for this reason that it selects the subjunctive in Italian.

When Giorgi and Pianesi assume that the doxastic modal base is not weakly realistic, they are saying that it is not presupposed to overlap the common ground. This is a crucial point of contrast with 'say': they claim that 'say' takes a weakly realistic modal base representing the content of the reported conversation (and null ordering source), explaining why it takes the indicative in Italian. But this way of explaining the difference between 'say' and 'believe' is a weak point in Giorgi and Pianesi's theory. There is no clear motivation for proposing that beliefs are more likely to be disjoint from the common ground than reported conversations. We sometimes report on the conversation of people we believe to be misinformed, and conversely we sometimes report on the beliefs of individuals whom we believe to be well-informed.[28]

There are a number of other points to discuss with respect to Giorgi and Pianesi's analysis. They assume that a non-null ordering source always leads to a non-realistic context of evaluation, but this is only the case if the ordering source is itself non-realistic, and while they discuss a number of cases where the ordering source is indeed non-realistic, nothing requires it to be so. With some verbs, it is plausible that the ordering source would be realistic in some cases. For example, with 'regret' it could be that the ordering source (a set of propositions the subject disprefers) could all be presupposed to be true in the conversation.

(69)   [In light of my dispreference for being so dirty and for being so tired:]
        I regret going camping.

In this example, the ordering source of *regret* is at least weakly realistic. Indeed, it's likely that the "dispreference" ordering source is always weakly realistic, since nearly everybody disprefers some of the things we all know to be true.

Like most theorists of mood, Giorgi and Pianesi do not merely wish to describe the difference between contexts in which indicative is selected and those in which subjunctive is selected, but they also want to explain why these two classes align with the moods they do. And like most theorists, the central idea for explaining this is that there is something in common between the indicative-selecting contexts and the use of a root declarative sentence in conversation. Given the tools of modal semantics which are central to their theory, Giorgi and Pianesi aim to do this by drawing an analogy between the modal parameters of evaluation for a complement clause and the context set of an actual conversation. The idea here is that, from the perspective of the local evaluation of the clause, the two kinds of context play the same or similar roles, and the indicative mood can be seen as indicating the

---

[28] Although Giorgi and Pianesi make a reasonable case that the modal base of 'say' would have to share some propositions with a typical common ground, it seems just as reasonable to assume that everyone believes some of the propositions in a typical common ground (for example, that itches feel better if scratched or that the world changes from time to time). Giorgi and Pianesi suggest several motivations for making the distinction between 'believe' and 'say' in the way they do.

same property in both types of cases. However, there is a problem with simply grouping context sets with contexts of evaluation and calling them all "contexts." The context set is defined as the intersection of a single set of propositions (the common ground), while the context of evaluation is defined in terms of two functions from worlds to sets of propositions (the modal base and ordering source). Thus, the analogy is only approximate.[29]

It would be natural for Giorgi and Pianesi's theory to be presented using the strategy of shifting parameters outlined earlier in the section, but they do not do so. Instead, they propose that simple root sentences involve an implicit modal operator. Specifically, they propose that the act of asserting a root declarative should be modeled using a modal operator M with a modal base m defined to link the modal to the context set in the following way: $m(w) = cg$, for every world w (and a null ordering source). Root assertions would then involve a strongly realistic context of evaluation, explaining the use of indicative mood for assertion. However, although their idea is interesting, the particular model of assertion they propose does not work; note the following derivation, which follows Giorgi and Pianesi (1997, p.209):

(70)   1. Assertion of $S = cg + [\![\ M(S)\ ]\!]^{m} =$
         2. $cg \cap \{w : \forall v \in \bigcap m(w), v \in [\![\ S\ ]\!]\ \} =$
         3. $cg \cap \{w : \forall v \in \bigcap cg, v \in [\![\ S\ ]\!]\ \} =$
         4. • $cg \cap \emptyset$, if $\bigcap cg \not\subseteq [\![\ S\ ]\!]$;
            • $cg \cap$ the set of all worlds, if $\bigcap cg \subseteq [\![\ S\ ]\!]$.

The problem is clearly seen between steps 2 and 3: because m does not depend on w, but just returns cg no matter which world we consider, the proposition added to the common ground in the end is either the set of all worlds or the empty set. (In the terminology of dynamic semantics, assertion implements a test on the common ground.) Now it is of course possible that a different definition of M would work within Giorgi and Pianesi's system, but we will not pursue alternatives here.

In addition to the issues raised so far, Giorgi and Pianesi's analysis has the problems which we identified earlier which hold generally for the comparison-based theory, but they make interesting comments on some of the difficult cases. One important discussion concerns 'dream' and other fiction predicates. They note that these predicates are correctly predicted to select indicative in French, in which subjunctive is associated with a non-null ordering source, but they see a problem for Italian, which chooses subjunctive if the context of evaluation is not weakly realistic, and German, which chooses subjunctive if it is not totally realistic. I am actually not sure that Giorgi and Pianesi are correct to worry about Italian; although the context of evaluation for 'dream' is non-realistic, it is also weakly realistic since it is hard to imagine a dream where absolutely no facts in a typical common ground hold. 'Dream' in a language like German poses a more significant problem, and they say something quite interesting about it. They point out that its

---

[29] In addition, as noted above, it's not clear whether contexts of evaluation are to be defined as sets of worlds or sets of propositions.

context of evaluation can persist in discourse in a way that many others do not (based on Giorgi and Pianesi 1997, p.221; see also Portner 1997):

(71)   (a) Mario dreamed that Carlo bought a house.
       (b) It was beautiful and spacious.

Notice the anaphora between (71a–b). Even though *dream* is not repeated in (b), it is possible for *it* to pick up the house which Mario dreamed about as its referent. It seems that (71b) is implicitly modalized, with the same context of evaluation as (a), and so means 'Mario dreamed that it was beautiful and spacious.' The fact that the context of evaluation for 'dream' can be used by a root indicative in place of the context set suggests that this context of evaluation is in some sense "similar to" the common ground. It is for this reason, they suggest, that 'dream' licenses indicative across all of the relevant languages.

Giorgi and Pianesi also have an interesting discussion of emotive and evaluative factives. Recall that items like 'regret' and 'be sad' vary in mood selection properties, taking indicative in Romanian but preferring subjunctive in Italian and French. (Indicative with these predicates is also possible in French, and marginally so in Italian as well, according to Giorgi and Pianesi.) While Giorgi and Pianesi's discussion of these items is not integrated into their explicit theory of mood selection outlined above, it is clear that Italian and Romanian are problematical. On the one hand, Romanian is said to select subjunctive whenever there is a non-null ordering source, and Giorgi and Pianesi explicitly assume that these predicates do have non-null ordering sources. (For example, they take the ordering source with 'odd' to be totally realistic and the modal base to be a subset of the common ground expressing "what is strange.") Thus, they should take subjunctive in Romanian, contrary to fact. On the other hand, Italian is claimed to require indicative whenever the context of evaluation is weakly realistic, and both the modal base and ordering source here are weakly realistic—indeed, the ordering source is realistic and the modal base totally realistic. Thus, in Italian these predicates ought to take indicative.[30]

Implicitly acknowledging these difficulties, Giorgi and Pianesi mention two other factors which might explain these cases: The first factor is that these predicates are factive, presupposing their complements to be true relative to the common ground; for example, (72) presupposes that John wrote a letter to Mary. The second factor is that the predicates can be seen as having a causative or conditional semantics, so that (72) means something like 'John writing the letter made me surprised' or 'If John had not written the letter, I would not have been surprised' (Giorgi and Pianesi 1997, p. 219).

---

[30] Though Giorgi and Pianesi describe Italian as if it falls under the pure comparison-based theory ("the presence of a modal component with an ordering source forces the subjunctive in such a language", p. 219), in the previous discussion they had made clear that Italian takes subjunctive when the predicate uses a non-realistic, but not weakly realistic context of evaluation. The presence of a (non-null) ordering source by itself triggers subjunctive in French and Romanian, according to their proposal, but not in Italian.

(72)   It surprises me that John wrote that letter to Mary.

The intuitive idea is that the factivity of 'surprise' leads to its selecting indicative in Romanian, while its causative meaning leads to its selecting subjunctive in Italian. It seems to me that the first half of this could reasonably be incorporated into Giorgi and Pianesi's theory; factivity would be an additional factor, on top of the core comparison-based theory, which affects mood choice. Later in this section, we will see Farkas's (1992b) more explicit attempt to build a theory of mood selection based on multiple factors.

It seems less likely that factivity will solve the problem of Italian, and so Giorgi and Pianesi point to the causative or conditional semantics to motivate the idea that the relevant class of predicates has a non-null ordering source. However, as we've seen, this would not be enough to lead a predicate to select subjunctive in Italian, according to their analysis. The ordering source would have to be one which gives rise to a non-realistic context of evaluation. Despite this issue, it is worth keeping in mind the intuition that a causative or conditional meaning triggers the choice of subjunctive in some cases, even though we do not yet understand how this feature of meaning relates to others which contribute to mood selection.

Villalta.   Villalta (2000, 2006, 2008) has two important ideas concerning the analysis of the subjunctive mood. First, she proposes that the type of modal comparison represented by Heim's conditional semantics for desire predicates, discussed in Section 2.1 above, is necessary for explaining why certain predicates select the subjunctive mood in Spanish complement clauses. Specifically, we can focus on the relation $<$ in (73): Villalta thinks that this operator is in the semantic representation for all subjunctive-selecting predicates (and no indicative-selecting ones) and that its presence is why subjunctive is used in the predicate's argument. And second, she argues that Heim's analysis must be modified because predicates which select subjunctive mood in Spanish are focus-sensitive and compare multiple alternatives. She is motivated to modify Heim's semantics by a problem with the truth conditions Heim assigns to *want*. In order to understand how her analysis develops, it is necessary to examine this problem in detail.

We begin with Heim's analysis as represented in (73):

(73) $[\![$ *want* $]\!]$ = $[\lambda p \lambda a \lambda s$. a is the thinking participant in s and for every $w \in R_{dox}(s)$: $Sim_w(p) <_s Sim_w(\neg p)]$

This definition implies that 'a wants p' is true in w_* if and only if, for every one of a's belief worlds w (with respect to some situation s in w_* in which a is the thinking paricipant), the worlds most like w in which p is true are preferable to the worlds most like w in which p is false. Notice that according to this analysis, the compared worlds (namely the worlds in $Sim_w(p)$ and $Sim_w(\neg p)$) need not be belief worlds. And this is good, because it is possible to want things one believes certain or impossible (Heim's 1992 examples).

(74)   (a) (John hired a babysitter because) he wants to go to the movies tonight.
       (b) I want this weekend to last forever.

Despite the fact that the analysis (73) makes the correct predictions for (74), Heim rejects it because it fails to explain some other facts having to do with presupposition projection. In its place, she proposes another analysis, (75) (see also Villalta 2008; Rubinstein 2012).

(75) $[\![$ want $]\!]$ = $[\lambda p \lambda a \lambda s$. a is the thinking participant in s and
for every $w \in R_{dox}(s)$: $Sim_w(R_{dox}(s) \cap p) <_s Sim_w(R_{dox}(s) \cap \neg p)]$

In this definition, Sim_w applies not to p and $\neg p$, but rather p and $\neg p$ restricted to belief worlds (i.e., $R_{dox}(s) \cap p$). This restriction is useful for explaining certain examples involving presupposition, but it does not capture the data in (74). To account for those examples, we need the set of compared worlds to extend beyond the subject's belief worlds.[31]

Villalta takes up the challenge which this set of problems poses for the comparative analysis of *want*. Her assumption is that using the set of belief worlds or any other set to restrict the compared worlds in the semantics, as Heim does, is a mistake. Rather, she thinks that context provides the compared alternatives, subject only to the weak constraint that each such alternative be believed possible. In order to see how this works, we will examine Villalta's key example. Here is the background scenario:

Sofía has promised to bring a dessert to the picnic. Victoria believes that there are three possibilities for what she may actually do. She could prepare a chocolate cake, even though Victoria considers that extremely unlikely because it represents far too much work. She might bring an apple pie, which Victoria considers very likely since she can just buy it at the bakery nearby. Or Sofía might bring ice-cream, which seems most likely to Victoria, since she usually has some in her freezer. Victoria prefers the chocolate cake over the apple pie and the apple pie over the ice-cream.   (Villalta 2008, p. 476)

In this setting, (76a) is false and (76b) true. But although the example does not seem to really be a counterexample to Heim's analysis, it does provide a situation in which we can clearly see how Villalta's own analysis works.[32]

(76)   (a) Victoria wants Sofía to bring apple pie.
        (b) Victoria wants Sofía to bring chocolate cake.

Villalta's semantics for *want* is based on there being a contextually relevant set of alternatives to the propositional argument of the verb; in the scenario, the alternatives are Sofía bringing cake, apple pie, or ice cream. To be more precise, the first alternative is not the simple proposition that Sofía brings chocolate cake, but rather whatever is the contextually relevant version of this—presumably Victoria

---

[31] Heim suggests that we do this by using a different set than $R_{dox}(s)$ in the slot X of $Sim_w(X \cap p)$.

[32] Villalta makes her argument at this point with *wish* rather than *want*, but the arguments are just as applicable to *want*. Importantly, she argues that the falsity of (76a) is incompatible with Heim's analysis, but as Rubinstein (2012) shows, this is not the case.

is not thinking about the possibility that Sofía brings a cake on a magic sleigh. Rather, it is something like the proposition that Sofía brings in the expected way a cake baked by her in the expected way.

The entry in (77) gives Villalta's semantics (adjusted for our other assumptions), where C is the contextually provided set of alternatives:[33]

(77) ⟦ *want* ⟧ = [λpλaλs . a is the thinking participant in s and for all $q \in C$: $q \neq p \rightarrow p <_s q$]

Given the definition of $<$, (77) amounts to saying that the best worlds among all of the alternatives are all ones in which p is true; more precisely, for every world in any alternative ($=\bigcup C$), it's either a p world, or there's a p world better than it. In this entry, a's belief alternatives play no role. The range of worlds we look at in the semantics of *want* is not delimited by a semantic component involving R_{dox}, but rather a contextual component, namely the range of worlds in the contextually relevant alternatives.

Because Villalta's analysis boils down to saying that p worlds are best within $\bigcup C$, we can reformulate (77) as a standard necessity modal:

(78) ⟦ *want* ⟧ = [λpλaλs . a is the thinking participant in s and p is a necessity with respect to m_C and $R_{want}(s)$]

Here, m_C is a contextually provided modal base which picks out $\bigcup C$ and $R_{want}(s)$ is an ordering source representing a's desires in s. According to (78), *a wants p* is true iff all of the "best" (most highly-ranked by the buletic ordering source) worlds in $\bigcup C$ are ones in which p is true. This is identical to (77), and we see that C defines the space of relevant possibilities in a way which can be encoded by a modal base.

Villalta has another reason for formulating the semantics as in (77), namely her hypothesis that 'want' is focus sensitive. Building on Rooth's (1992) theory of focus, she proposes that the identity of C is constrained by focus, and hence that the relevance of contextual alternatives to the semantics of 'want' is connected to its being focus sensitive. From there, she argues all subjunctive-selecting predicates are focus sensitive. Based on this collection of hypotheses, Villalta then proposes that the subjunctive encodes focus sensitivity, and that this fact explains why subjunctive clauses are properly used with the particular class of predicates they are. Essentially, subjunctive is used with comparative, focus-sensitive predicates. Moreover, she claims that non-focus-sensitive predicates are strictly incompatible with the kind of focus encoded by the subjunctive, and so they cannot take subjunctive complements. It is important to see that, although Villalta adopts a theory of verbal mood based on comparison, she does not take the common route of trying to explain the distribution of mood forms in terms of concepts from modal semantics (like "realistic modal base") or discourse semantics (like "assertion"). Rather, the key semantic property has to do with focus.

---

[33] Villalta defines the desirability relation $<$ differently from Heim. For Villalta, $p <_s q$ means that p is a better possibility than q, in Kratzer's sense of 'better possibility.'

Villalta's treatment of focus in subjunctive clauses has some technical problems relating to the fact that focus can in general be interpreted in a wide variety of ways, and it is difficult to set up a system in which the focus marked by a subjunctive complement clause can only be interpreted by the embedding verb. For example, why can't the subjunctive mood be interpreted in connection with a different focus-sensitive operator, like *only*, leaving the subjunctive-marked clause as a whole free to embed under an indicative selector? Her analysis also faces a problem with its prediction that all and only subjunctive-selecting predicates are focus sensitive. Portner (2011c) and Harner (2016) raise questions about whether directive predicates are focus sensitive in the way predicted by her theory, and Harner additionally suggests that desire predicates are more complex than Villalta accounts for.

Anand and Hacquard.   Anand and Hacquard (2013) study the distribution of modals in the complements of attitude verbs with the goal of explaining contrasts such as the one observed in (79) (their (1a), (2a)):

(79)   (a) John thinks that Paul has to be innocent. (epistemic reading ok)
　　　(b) John wishes that Paul had to be innocent. (no epistemic reading)

As we see in (79a), when the modal *has to* is embedded under *think*, it can get an epistemic interpretation; on that reading, the sentence means that it is certain, given John's beliefs, that Paul is innocent. In contrast, when embedded under *wish* as in (79b), *had to* does not readily have a similar interpretation. As they develop a theory of this contrast, Anand and Hacquard make use of close connections between the distribution of epistemic readings of modals and the distribution of indicative clauses in Romance languages, and so their analysis can be seen as giving a partial theory of verbal mood. We will review their work with the goal of understanding what it contributes to the development of the comparison-based approach to the indicative/subjunctive contrast.

Anand and Hacquard's analysis of (79) is based on the difference between two classes of predicates which are closely linked to the selection of indicative and subjunctive clauses in Romance. On the one hand, they describe the set of predicates which express REPRESENTATIONAL attitudes as "those which 'convey a mental picture'; that is, those that describe the content of a propositionally consistent attitudinal state." The category of representational attitudes was first proposed by Bolinger (1968) to characterize the class of indicative-selecting predicates, and while Anand and Hacquard agree with Farkas (1985, 1992b) that it does not accurately do so, they argue that it is in fact the class which allows embedded modals to receive an epistemic reading. On the other hand, they endorse a comparison-based approach to the semantics of those predicates which select the subjunctive as part of their explanation for why such predicates do not favor epistemic readings for modals embedded in their complements. To be more precise, they describe the complements of preference predicates (specifically desideratives except for 'hope', because it can take indicative in French) and directives as "core subjunctives." (They do not talk about other predicate classes which tend to select subjunctive across the languages they discuss.) Anand and Hacquard's goal is to show that those predicates which select subjunctive have a property which makes it very difficult for an embedded epistemic modal to be interpreted. That property is, essentially, a modal semantics based on comparison.

Anand and Hacquard adopt Villalta's (2008) preference-based analysis of the subjunctive, although they are not committed to the role Villalta assigns to focus. Acknowledging that there are some problems with the preference-based analysis (they mention Italian *pensare* 'think,' which selects subjunctive, and 'promise' across Romance, which selects indicative), they end up saying that "subjunctive is an imperfect indicator of preferences." Despite this imperfection, they use the subjunctive to argue that desideratives and directives have a comparative semantics.

Assuming that preference predicates and directives have a semantics based on comparison, why would this disallow an embedded epistemic? As we noted in Section 1.3.2, an embedded modal often has its modal parameters controlled by the higher predicate. For example, in (21c), *Ryan said it might be a salamander*, Ryan is the thinking participant in the situation which determines the set of accessible worlds for *might*. What Anand and Hacquard are trying to do is explain why the subject of some verbs ('say,' 'think') is able to be the thinking participant which determines a set of accessible worlds for an embedded epistemic modal, while the subject of other verbs ('want,' 'order') cannot. This is clearly a difficult problem, since the subject of 'want' clearly is a thinking agent, and so this subject's beliefs could define a set of accessible worlds; yet *had to* in (79b) cannot receive the same kind of epistemic interpretation.[34]

Because of this problem, Anand and Hacquard develop a more sophisticated theory which employs the method of shifting parameters outlined earlier in this section to link the embedded modal to the propositional attitude verb in the matrix clause. We have already sketched how this strategy works above; citing in particular Veltman (1996) and Yalcin (2007), they propose the following meanings for 'imagine' and 'might' (modified to fit our formalism):

(80) (a) $[\![\ imagine\ \phi\ ]\!]^S = [\lambda a \lambda s\ .\ a$ is the thinking participant of s and for all worlds $w \in \text{IMG}(s)$, $[\![\ \phi\ ]\!]^{\text{IMG}(s)} = 1]$
      (b) $[\![\ might\ ]\!]^S = [\lambda p\ .\ \exists w \in S[w \in p]]$

The parameter S in $[\![\ ]\!]^S$ is a contextually provided set of possible worlds used in the interpretation of epistemic modals. We can think of it as the context set or as

---

[34] The problem is only present, of course, on the assumption that (79b) does not have the interpretation described. Anand and Hacquard acknowledge that it is not altogether impossible for (79b)'s *had to* to receive an epistemic reading, but they use survey results to show that there is a real difference, and claim that the epistemic reading in this case is not based on the subject argument's beliefs/knowledge. I do not fully agree that *had to* in (79b) can only be epistemic when it targets some body of knowledge other than John's. It can mean that John, the investigator, knows that he cannot rule Paul out as a suspect, but wishes that he could. Anand and Hacquard might say that *had to* targets the evidence already discovered by John in the investigation as the conversational background, and not John's knowledge, but that is a rather fine line to draw.

the set of worlds epistemically accessible from w_*. What should be noted is that the semantic entry for *imagine* replaces S with a different set of possible worlds, $\text{IMG}(s)$, the set of worlds compatible with what a imagines in s. Put together, (80a–b) imply that *might* in the complement of *imagine* will be interpreted relative to $\text{IMG}(s)$. Thus, the complement of (81) means 'it is compatible with John's past imaginings that Paul is innocent.'

(81)   John imagined that Paul might be innocent.

Anand and Hacquard assign semantic entries like (80a) to such verbs as 'say' and 'think.' These are the representational attitudes.

    Non-representational predicates have a comparative semantics and combine with their complements in a different way. Anand and Hacquard's semantics for *want* comes from Villalta, (77), repeated here:

(82) $[\![\ want\ ]\!]^S = [\lambda p \lambda a \lambda s\ .\ a$ is the thinking participant of s and for all $q \in C$: $q \neq p \rightarrow p <_s q]$.

In (82), we don't see the complement clause within semantic value brackets. There is nothing like $[\![\ \phi\ ]\!]^{\text{IMG}(s)}$ from (80a) in (82). Instead, (82) just works with the proposition expressed by the complement, p, comparing it to the alternatives. This means that an epistemic modal embedded in the complement of *want* can only have access to the original, contextually provided accessibility relation S. Crucially, it does not have access to an accessibility relation derived from the matrix predicate. This fact is what makes it difficult to assign an epistemic interpretation to a modal in the complement of *want*. (I'm not sure why it should be difficult to assign embedded *might* an epistemic interpretation relative to the contextually provided set S, but Anand and Hacquard assume that it is. They do agree that it has this meaning, though.)

    The lexical entries for 'imagine' and 'want' establish a correlation between two properties: a comparative semantics, and a contextual shift for the complement. As far as I can see, there's no deep reason in the theory why these two things are connected. It would be simple to write an entry which allows a verb like 'want,' with a comparative semantics, to perform a context shift. Consider the entry in (83), which shifts the context for the embedded clause to $\text{R}(s)$:

(83) $[\![\ want\ \phi\ ]\!]^S = [\lambda p \lambda a \lambda s\ .\ a$ is the thinking participant of s and for all $q \in C$: $q \neq [\![\ \phi\ ]\!]^{\text{R}(s)} \rightarrow [\![\ \phi\ ]\!]^{\text{R}(s)} <_s q]$.

One plausible candidate for R here would be a doxastic accessibility relation, what the subject believes, and in that case *might* under *want* would mean "compatible with the subject's beliefs." Of course, we have no reason to include R here, but the context shift to IMG with 'imagine' is not motivated by any deep considerations either; it is simply stipulated to account for the interpretation of an embedded modal. A more explanatory theory would explain why a non-comparative semantics goes along with the shifting of the modal background, while a comparative semantics does not.[35,36]

Despite these problems, it is important to see the fundamental intuition of Anand and Hacquard's analysis. The idea is that one class of predicates utilizes a set of possible worlds as part of its semantics, and that this set is provided to the complement clause as a modal parameter. In contrast, another class compares alternative possibilities and does nothing special to affect the way in which its complement is interpreted. Although Anand and Hacquard do not propose their theory as an analysis of verbal mood, to my mind it is among the most well-worked-out versions of the comparison-based semantics of "non-representational" attitudes in the semantics literature. For this reason, it gives an important perspective on the comparison-based approach to verbal mood.

2.2.2.4 Theories based on truth in a designated set of worlds The second main idea which semanticists have worked with in an attempt to characterize the distinction between indicative and subjunctive is that indicative clauses are associated with grammatical contexts which guarantee the truth of the clause in some relevant world or set of worlds. This intuition springs from the idea that indicatives are somehow used with the goal of being true, while subjunctives are used for some other sort of goal. This approach to verbal mood is closely connected to the traditional idea that propositions may be distinguished as *realis* or *irrealis*, with the indicative a marker of realis status.

Huntley and Farkas.   The truth-based approach to verbal mood is nicely presented by Huntley (1984, p. 109):

there is intuitively a semantic difference between the indicative and non-indicative clauses. Where the indicative is used a situation is represented as actual in a way that it is not where the non-indicative is used, but it proves difficult to make the contrast more precise. One way of putting it which I will elaborate on shortly is that an indicative clause, even in the future tense, represents a situation (truly or falsely) as obtaining in the actual world (thought of as historically extended), whereas the non-indicative clauses represent it as being merely envisaged as a possibility, with no commitment as to whether it obtains, in past, present or future, in the actual world.

Farkas (1992b) outlines two problems faced by a truth-based approach. First, the factive emotives presuppose the truth of their complement, yet select the

---

[35] Anand and Hacquard argue that 'hope' has a comparative semantics but also makes the subject's belief set available to an embedded epistemic. It is thus somewhat like *want* but licenses embedded epistemics.

[36] Anand and Hacquard point out various other constructions which correlate more or less with the ability to embed epistemics, such as verb second in German and complement preposing in English. Some of these might be used to argue for a difference in compositional mechanism between the two classes of verbs, and moreover might allow a connection to the theory of clause types and sentence mood.

subjunctive in some languages, and second, predicates of fiction and mental creation do not imply in any sense the truth of their complements, which nevertheless take the indicative form. To these points, we should add that belief predicates, assertion predicates, and commissive predicates fail to imply the truth of their complements in the actual world. The main effort in developing a truth-based theory of mood is applied to addressing issues such as these.

Huntley and Farkas propose different approaches to solving these problems. Huntley's is presented in a rather sketchy way, but has an interesting intuition: He proposes that indicative clauses involve indexical reference to a single world of evaluation, identified as the actual world in root indicatives, and that because of this reference to a particular world of evaluation, it makes sense to talk about indicatives as being true or false. In contrast, non-indicatives do not make reference to a world of evaluation; as a result, even though they technically do have truth conditions, they cannot normally be said to be true or false.

It is not clear to me exactly how to understand Huntley's ideas, and it is for this reason that his analysis has not been very influential in subsequent theories of verbal mood. It would fit with his explicit discussion to conclude that the indicative mood is a possibility modal $\Diamond_{indic}$ which uses the totally realistic accessibility relation which makes accessible, for any world w, only w itself ($\{\langle w, \{w\}\rangle : w \in W\}$). However, this analysis would not lead to a semantic difference between ϕ and $\Diamond_{indic}(\phi)$, and so it cannot be right. At this point we might be justified in moving on, but I believe that there is an interesting way to reconceptualize Huntley's ideas. We can understand much of what he writes in terms of the idea that non-indicative clauses, but not indicative clauses, express a DIAGONAL PROPOSITION. Let me briefly explain what diagonalization is and how it relates to Huntley's comments about verbal mood.

We ordinarily understand the proposition expressed by a sentence to be the set of worlds at which it is true, given that it is interpreted in a context tied to the world of evaluation w_*. This conception of sentence meaning can be represented as in (84a). Crucially, in (84a) the truth conditions are represented by the set of worlds w, while the context parameter $c(w_*)$ remains fixed. In contrast to this, the proposition expressed by diagonalized clauses loses the separation between the context $c(w_*)$ and world of evaluation w. Instead, it uses an alternate context $c(w)$ linked to w. The diagonal proposition can be represented as in (84b).[37]

(84)   a. Ordinary proposition expressed by ϕ in $c(w_*)$: $\{w : [\![\phi]\!]^{c(w_*),w} = 1\}$
      b. Diagonal proposition expressed by $D\phi$ in $c(w_*)$: $\{w : [\![\phi]\!]^{c(w),w} = 1\}$

---

[37] See Stalnaker (1978, 2014) and Brown (2011) for broader discussion of the significance of diagonalization. The definition in (84b) leaves open what type of thing a "context" $c(w_*)$ or $c(w)$ is. If a context is simply a world, then $c(w_*) = w_*$ and $c(w) = w$, and (84b) is a proper definition of diagonalization. But if a context is something richer, for example a sequence of indices $\langle world, time, speaker, \ldots \rangle$, we face the issue of how the other parameters are affected. These issues become crucial in theories which use diagonalization to analyze *de se* readings and shiftable indexicality (Anand and Nevins 2004; Schlenker 2011).

Under this interpretation of Huntley's ideas, the indicative indicates that the context parameter is fixed (as c_*) to a particular world, and this (for some reason) represents the idea that the sentence expresses a proposition which is being used to say something true or false about that world. In contrast, a non-indicative is interpreted relative to a context parameter ($c(w)$) which varies along with the world of evaluation w, and this plausibly represents Huntley's idea that the proposition is not being used to say something true or false about a particular world. This way of explaining Huntley's ideas is certainly very sketchy, and in any case it goes well beyond what he explicitly says. I mention it here only because it strikes me as a reasonable and interesting way to understand his informal intuitions. See Section 3.1.3 for comments on Huntley's main concern, the semantics of imperatives.

Farkas's early work on verbal mood focuses on explaining the patterns of mood selection in Romance, especially Romanian and French. She proposes that those predicates which select the indicative introduce a single world at which their complement is entailed to be true, while those which select the subjunctive introduce a set of worlds (or futures of a world) for this function. When a single world is introduced, it is called an EXTENSIONAL ANCHOR for the embedded proposition; when a set of worlds in introduced, it is an INTENSIONAL ANCHOR. The proposal about verbal mood is that indicative is used whenever the sentence expresses a proposition with an extensional anchor.

It is not very clear how to understand Farkas's ideas in formal terms. One might think that the anchors should be identified with the set of accessible worlds provided by the matrix predicate, but this cannot be correct. The semantics of 'believe' cannot be given as in (85), since A's beliefs could never be specific enough to pick out a particular world:[38]

(85) $[\![A \; believes \; \phi \;]\!]^{w_*} = 1$ iff $[\![\; \phi \;]\!]^{w} = 1$ in the world w picked out by A's beliefs.

Rather, as we know from the standard semantics of propositional attitude verbs as strong modals, 'believe' quantifies over a set of possible worlds compatible with the subject's beliefs.

Later research in the tradition of Farkas, in particular Giannakidou (1997, 1999, 2009) and Quer (1998, 2001), aims to solve this problem. We will look at Giannakidou's and Quer's work below. However, before getting to that, I would like to sketch another way of making Farkas's ideas precise, which may be more fruitful. It seems to me that Farkas's idea that indicatives have an extensional anchor is actually quite similar to Huntley's proposal that indicatives involve indexical reference to a particular world at which their truth or falsity can be evaluated. In combination with the suggestion made above that Huntley's non-indicatives denote a diagonal proposition, we reach the following thoughts:

---

[38] In previous overviews of Farkas's ideas, I have understood her proposal in the way given by (85), and have therefore concluded that it cannot be correct as it stands (e.g. Portner 2011c). Here, however, I will consider another way of interpreting her proposals.

- Indicatives
  1. An indicative clause denotes the proposition corresponding to the set of worlds at which it is true, given a particular context of evaluation $c(w_*)$.
  2. Predicates which select the indicative anchor the context parameter for their complement clause to the world which contains the situation described by the predicate.
- Subjunctives
  1. A subjunctive clause denotes the proposition corresponding to the set of worlds at which it is true, given that the context of evaluation is anchored to the same world (the diagonal proposition).
  2. Predicates which select the subjunctive do not anchor the context parameter for their complement clause. Instead, the context parameter is linked to the world of evaluation by a diagonalization operator.

It seems to me that an analysis of this kind would to some extent capture Farkas's ideas about extensional and intensional anchoring.[39]

An important worry about Huntley's and Farkas's proposals is that they do not make deep predictions about which predicates govern indicative and which govern subjunctive. Although Farkas goes through various classes of predicates and says what the anchor for each should be (including whether the anchoring is extensional or intensional), the identity of the anchor does not follow from any analysis of the lexical semantics of the different classes. It is not at all clear why 'believe' has an extensional anchor but 'want' an intensional anchor. Nor is there a fact about the meaning of 'dream' or 'order' which would lead to their complements having the particular type of anchoring they do.

Overall, then, we see in Huntley's and especially Farkas's work two points which are, in fact, endemic to the truth-based approach to verbal mood. On the one hand, this type of theory has insightful things to say about the meanings of the clauses marked with indicative and subjunctive themselves. But on the other, they do not have enough to say about why meanings of those types are used in the particular semantic contexts that they are. In this way, its strengths and weaknesses are, from a high-level perspective, the inverse of the strengths and weaknesses of the comparison-based approach—comparison-based theories offer insightful ideas about the lexical semantics of predicates which embed indicatives or subjunctives, but say less about the mood-marked clauses themselves.

Giannakidou and Quer. Giannakidou (1997, 1999, 2009, 2011, 2016), Giannakidou and Mari (2015), and Quer (1998, 2001) develop Farkas's notion of an "anchor" in an attempt to make Farkas's ideas more precise and to apply them to a wider range of data. The concept of anchor used by Giannakidou is that of an INDIVIDUAL MODEL, a set of worlds provided by applying a special accessibility

---

[39] Brasoveanu (2006) proposes that a specific Romanian verbal mood form, referred to as the conditional-optative or Subjunctive B, encodes both temporal *de se* and "propositional *de se*" when embedded under *crede* ('believe'). See Section 2.3.1.1 for discussion. Though he does not describe it in this way, perhaps the propositional *de se* component could be analyzed in terms of diagonalization.

relation to an individual. The idea can be expressed in terms of the method of shifting parameters outlined earlier in Section 2.2.2. Suppose that the semantics of a simple sentence with 'think' is computed as in (63), repeated here:

(86) $[\![\,A\ thinks\ that\ \phi\,]\!]^{P_O} = [\![\,thinks\,]\!]^{P_O}([\![\,that\ \phi\,]\!]^{P_\Theta})([\![\,A\,]\!]^{P_O})$

Assuming that P_Θ is the set of worlds accessible by the doxastic accessibility relation used by 'think', the meaning of (87) is the following:

(87) $[\![\,Alice\ thinks\ that\ it\ is\ raining\,]\!]^{P_O} =$
 • $\{w :$ for some situation $s < w$: Alice is the thinking participant in s and $\forall w'[w' \in R_{dox}(s) \rightarrow w' \in [\![\,that\ it\ is\ raining\,]\!]^{R_{dox}(s)}]\}$

Giannakidou observes that, according to (87), 'think' is VERIDICAL:

(88)   **Veridicality:** Suppose O is a propositional operator associated with individual model P_Θ. Then:
    O is VERIDICAL iff, for every argument ϕ, $O(\phi)$ entails that $P_\Theta \subseteq [\![\,\phi\,]\!]$.

'Think' is veridical because 'A thinks that S' entails that S is true in every world compatible with what A thinks.

   In contrast to 'think', Giannakidou gives a semantics for the verb 'want' which makes it non-veridical. Its semantics is given by (89):

(89) $[\![\,Alice\ wants\ that\ it\ be\ raining\,]\!]^{P_O} =$
 • $\{w :$ for some situation $s < w$: Alice is the thinking participant of s and $\forall w'[w' \in R_{want}(s) \rightarrow w' \in [\![\,that\ it\ is\ raining\,]\!]^{R_{Fdox}(s)}]\}$

Note the individual model which serves as the shifted context for the complement clause in (89). I call it R_{Fdox} and, according to Giannakidou, it represents the future realizations of the actual world according to the subject. Of course 'A wants that S' does not entail that S is true in every world which is a possible future according to A, and so Giannakidou classifies 'want' as non-veridical. Based on this understanding of the semantic difference between belief-type verbs and desire-verbs, Giannakidou proposes that the indicative is associated with veridicality and the subjunctive with non-veridicality. We can express this proposal in terms of licensing conditions on indicative and subjunctive mood:

(90)   a. A subjunctive clause S_{subj} is licensed as the argument of a non-veridical operator.
    b. An indicative clause S_{indic} is licensed as the argument of a veridical operator.

Giannakidou's explanation of the difference between 'think' and 'want' relies on their both anchoring their complements to the doxastic accessibility relation (or something closely related, like R_{Fdox}), and so, in order to extend this analysis to other predicates, Giannakidou must specify, for each matrix predicate, what individual model it assigns to its complement. Because 'dream' selects the indicative, she cannot say that it assigns the doxastic or future-possibility accessibility relation. (If it did, veridicality would not hold, since 'A dreams S' does not entail that A believes S.) Instead, 'dream' assigns the "dreams" accessibility relation R_{dream}. Similarly, 'say' assigns the "says" accessibility relation. But a subjunctive-selector like 'order' does not assign an "orders" relation R_{order}, because if it did, it would be veridical. Rather, as with 'want', Giannakidou says that 'order' uses the future-possibility relation R_{Fdox}.

Giannakidou's theory ultimately suffers from the same explanatory gap as Farkas's. Although veridicality captures in an interesting way the intuition behind the truth-based approach to verbal mood, the fact that it is relativized to a lexically specified parameter, the individual model, means that the theory does not explain mood selection unless the particular individual model assigned by a given verb is motivated by some deeper syntactic, semantic, or pragmatic factor. For example, if we had a verb with the same core semantics as 'dream' but which assigned R_{dox}, it would take subjunctive; if we had a verb like 'want' which assigned R_{want}, it would take the indicative. The analysis as given so far cannot explain why such verbs do not exist.[40] As we will see in Section 2.2.2.5, it may be possible to address this issue by combining the truth-based approach to verbal mood with the comparison-based approach. Indeed, some comments by Giannakidou point in this direction.

Quer (2001) uses Giannakidou's concepts of the individual model and anchoring in a slightly different way which avoids the problem of determining what the individual model will be for a given predicate. According to Quer, all sentence-embedding predicates provide their complement with an individual model based on the predicate's accessibility relation. The model for the complement of 'dream' is R_{dream}, the model for 'want' is R_{want}, and so forth. But unlike Giannakidou's theory, which says that verbal mood is determined by veridicality assessed relative to the individual model, Quer proposes that mood is determined based on whether there is a MODEL SHIFT: subjunctive is chosen when the individual model for a clause S is sufficiently different from the model of its matrix clause S'. We can see how this works by looking at (87). Quer assumes that the initial, contextually provided parameter P_0 with respect to which the whole sentence is interpreted is the speaker's belief model at the utterance time, $R_{dox}(u)$.[41] As we see, this parameter has shifted to $R_{dox}(s)$ in the embedded clause. The idea of the analysis is that this shift from $R_{dox}(u)$ to $R_{dox}(s)$ does not amount to a significant change, because both are based on R_{dox} (Quer 2001, p. 88).

---

[40] The way Giannakidou's theory is presented, it might appear that she has a partial explanation. It is certainly natural that 'dream' would use R_{dream} to derive the individual model—but the question is why R_{dream} can be an individual model in the first place. In contrast, she assumes that R_{want} is never the basis for an individual model. In the end, it is just a premise of the theory that the only accessibility relations which can be turned into an individual model are those for predicates of knowledge and belief, predicates of assertion, and predicates of fiction and mental creation.

[41] Giannakidou and Quer call the sets of worlds accessible by a doxastic accessibility relation "epistemic models," but I find this choice potentially confusing given that "epistemic" modality is normally understood to imply not just belief, but actual knowledge.

Now consider sentences with 'dream' and 'want':

(91)   a. $\llbracket$ *a dreams that it be raining* $\rrbracket^{R_{dox}(u)} =$
- $\{w :$ for some situation $s < w$: a is the thinking participant of s and $\forall w'[w' \in R_{dream}(s) \rightarrow w' \in \llbracket$ *that it is raining* $\rrbracket^{R_{dream}(s)}]\}$

   b. $\llbracket$ *a wants that it be raining* $\rrbracket^{R_{dox}(u)} =$
- $\{w :$ for some situation $s < w$: a is the thinking participant of s and $\forall w'[w' \in R_{want}(s) \rightarrow w' \in \llbracket$ *that it is raining* $\rrbracket^{R_{want}(s)}]\}$

Quer assumes that the shift from $R_{dox}(u)$ to $R_{dream}(s)$ is not a significant model shift, so indicative is used in the complement of 'dream.' In contrast, he takes the shift from $R_{dox}(u)$ to $R_{want}(s)$ to be significant, and as a result 'want' selects subjunctive. In essence, Quer proposes to group the accessibility relations of all sentence-embedding predicates into two classes, those which count as similar to the speaker's belief model $R_{dox}(u)$, and those which are different. Subjunctive is chosen whenever a predicate brings about a shift from the first class to the second.

I think that the most insightful way to look at Quer's theory is not to focus on the issue of model shift, but rather on this grouping of accessibility relations into two sets, those which are similar to $R_{dox}(u)$, and those which are different from it. The function of verbal mood is to mark into which group the parameter falls. Quer (2001) explores some interesting further extensions of his approach to verbal mood choice in non-complement clauses, a topic we will touch on in Section 2.2.3.

Portner. Portner (1997) develops a theory of verbal mood which, like that of Quer (2001), assigns to the indicative and subjunctive the function of marking the modal parameters of interpretation used by a clause. He assigns explicit meanings to complementizers and attitude verbs which shift the modal parameters for a complement clause based on the meaning of the matrix predicate. Unlike Farkas, Giannakidou, and Quer, however, he argues that the parameter is not just a set of accessible worlds, but rather a pair consisting of an accessibility relation and a modal force. Adjusting our current notation, meanings for 'think and 'want' would be as follows:

(92)   a. $\llbracket$ *a thinks that it be raining* $\rrbracket^{P_0} =$
- $\{w :$ for some situation $s < w$: a is the thinking participant of s and $\forall w'[w' \in R_{dox}(s) \rightarrow w' \in \llbracket$ *that it is raining* $\rrbracket^{R_{dox},F_{\forall}}]\}$

   b. $\llbracket$ *a wants that it be raining* $\rrbracket^{P_0} =$
- $\{w :$ for some situation $s < w$: a is the thinking participant of s and $\forall w'[w' \in R_{want}(s) \rightarrow w' \in \llbracket$ *that it is raining* $\rrbracket^{R_{want},F_{\forall}}]\}$

I have notated the force parameter in (92) as $F_{\forall}$. It matches the universal quantification over worlds which takes place within the lexical semantics of 'think' and 'want'; another way to put the same point would be to say that the verbs are necessity modals and to refer to the force as '$\Box$'.

It is also worth noting that, according to Portner, the quantification over possible worlds in (92a)–(92b) is not introduced directly by the propositional attitude verb.

Instead, he proposes that the complementizer of the complement clause triggers quantification using the modal parameters (accessibility relation and force). That is, the verb *think* in (92a) sets the contextual parameters to R_{dox} and $F_\forall$, and then the complementizer *that* introduces an appropriate modal operator C with universal quantification over belief worlds. To put the idea differently, in Portner's formalization the CP complement is a modal functor whose arguments are provided by the matrix verb (Portner 1997, p. 195). This system for introducing modal quantification allows us to understand why parameter-shifting occurs: parameters are the "pipe" through with the modal force and accessibility relation are transferred to the modal operator in C.[42]

Given lexical meanings like those given in (92), Portner proposes that verbal mood is sensitive to the modal parameters of interpretation. In the case of Italian, he proposes that indicative mood is only possible if the accessibility relation parameter is classified as REALISTIC (what he calls "factive"):

(93)   An accessibility relation R is **realistic** iff, for every situation s in its domain, $w_s \in R(s)$.

(The subjunctive mood is taken to be unmarked, and so it is licensed if the indicative is not.) Portner's analysis is similar to Quer's in proposing that verbal mood marks features of the modal parameters of the clause, but the two theories are different in several important respects: First, Portner proposes that verbal mood marks intrinsic properties of these modal parameters, such as realism, rather than a "shift" of parameters, as on Quer's theory. Second, the two scholars offer quite different treatments of negation; we will return to this point in Section 2.2.3 below. And third, Portner invokes an analogy between verbal mood and nominal gender (or noun class marking). He sees the class of accessibility relations which trigger the indicative (i.e. R_{dox}, R_{dream}, R_{say}, etc.) as having a status similar to the set of things referred to by nouns of a given noun class. The parallel is supposed to go as follows: In some languages, noun classes have a strong semantic basis but allow for exceptions (he mentions the fact that Yidiny *birriny* 'salt water' falls into the class for drinkable liquids; Dixon 1982). In other languages, noun class is much more arbitrary (for example, gender in Indo-European languages which extend natural genders to non-gendered objects). If verbal moods are like nominal genders, we therefore expect that mood selection will show prototype effects and some degree of lexical idiosyncrasy, and he claims to find such effects in several places. One such case is the selection of indicative by 'say'; he proposes that while 'say' does not literally have the property of realism which licenses the subjunctive, in "prototypical" contexts it does. Essentially, 'say' takes the indicative because, in the prototypical case, what people say is true. Portner's theory runs into serious problems with predicates of imagination like 'dream', however. Although it is reasonable to assume that what people say is prototypically true, it would not be reasonable to think the same about what people dream (unless, that is, seers

---

[42] This treatment of modal quantification is similar to some other proposals based on parameter-shifting, such as Yalcin (2007) and especially Kratzer (2013).

are the prototypical dreamers). While Portner might counter that the selection of indicative by 'dream' is a case of pure idiosyncrasy, such a response would not be plausible if its mood selection is consistent across languages.[43]

Schlenker. In a series of papers investigating the analysis of indexicality, logo-phoricity, and *de se* interpretation, Schlenker (2003, 2005, 2011) makes several interesting proposals concerning the semantics of verbal mood in French and German. To understand his ideas, we have to begin with the phenomenon of shiftable indexicality. Consider the following example from Amharic (Schlenker 2003):

(94)   *jon jəgna nə-ññ   yil-all.*   (Amharic)
       Jon hero be.PF-1SO 3M.say-AUX.3M
       'John says that he is a hero.'

A morpheme-by-morpheme calque of (94) would be 'John said that I be a hero.' In English the *I* would have to refer to the person who spoke the sentence, but in Amharic and other "shifting" languages, the first person pronoun can, in certain circumstances, shift its reference to another individual. In Amharic, the verb 'say' allows the first person pronoun in its complement to shift to the referent of the matrix subject. The intuition about what's going on here is simple: 'I' refers to the individual who utters a sentence; in English, only the actual utterance counts, but in Amharic, the reported utterance (in this case, what John said) counts, and the first person pronoun can thus refer to John.

Schlenker argues that the semantics of a shifted indexical is more subtle than is captured by this simple description. Most importantly, the shifted indexical inevitably receives a *de se* interpretation: For (94) to be true, John had to say something like "I am a hero"; it would not be enough for him to have said "the man who shot the General is a hero," not knowing that he himself was the one who shot the General. In light of the analysis of *de se* attitudes (see Section 2.1 above), this fact implies that the embedded subject of (94) is treated more like a bound variable than a referential expression.

Schlenker proposes that the shiftable indexical is bound by a special shifting operator in the complementizer position of the embedded clause.[44] He explores several ideas for how best to formalize this operator, and while it is not worthwhile to discuss them in any detail here, it is quite interesting to note that one option is that the complementizer hosts a version of the diagonalization operator discussed earlier in this section. We see two options in (95):

(95)   a. John say $\lambda \langle i, w, t \rangle$ I_i be(w, t) hero
       b. John say $D\, I_c$ be(w_c, t_c) hero

---

[43] I now believe that Portner's (1997) proposal that indicative marks prototypical factivity in Italian is incorrect. The analysis of 'dream' in English, based on "prototypical expandability," is probably closer to the mark for Italian as well.

[44] Other theories propose that the shiftable subject is bound by the verb (von Stechow 2003, 2004) or a special context-shifting operator (Anand and Nevins 2004).

In (95a), the shifting operator is an ordinary λ which binds the subject, world, and time variables in the complement clause. In (95b) we have a diagonalization operator, and these same arguments are represented as context-dependent elements. Since D shifts the context c of the complement clause, these elements are, in effect, bound by it. It seems to me that there is a potentially productive connection to be drawn between Schlenker's analysis and the version of Farkas's and Huntley's ideas reconceptualized in terms of diagonalization.

With this background, we are now ready to see what Schlenker says about verbal mood. In his body of work, he makes two distinct proposals. The first, applied to French, is that the indicative marks a clause whose world argument can be presupposed to be in some accessible context, either the actual utterance context or a reported context. The following condition on the indicative is slightly different from Schlenker's proposal, but captures the essential idea:

(96) For any world w, $[\![\phi_{indic}]\!]^{P_\Theta} (w)$ is only defined $w \in P_\Theta$.

The subjunctive is the default form which emerges when the presupposition of the indicative is not met.[45] This analysis is clearly a version of the family of theories which associate indicative with truth in a designated set of worlds, and is in fact quite similar to Giannakidou's system. Schlenker's second proposal, applied mainly to German, is that the subjunctive marks a clause whose world argument is obligatorily shifted (in other words, "logophoric"). Given the significant differences between the French and German mood systems, these two proposals are not in conflict.

Schlenker's proposal for French is similar to Giannakidou's analysis. Schlenker identifies the accessible context used to check the presupposition of the indicative, P_Θ above, with the "context set" of some event in the logical form. Consider the following semantics for a sentence with 'think':

(97) $[\![a \text{ } thinks \text{ } that \text{ } it \text{ } is \text{ } raining]\!]^{cs_*} =$
  - $\{w : \text{for some situation } s < w\text{: } a \text{ is the thinking participant of } s \text{ and } \forall w'[w' \in R_{dox}(s) \rightarrow w' \in [\![that \text{ } it \text{ } is \text{ } raining]\!]^{cs(s)}]\}$

The root clause is interpreted with respect to the context set of the conversation, cs_*. Using the method of shifting parameters, in the complement clause cs_* has been replaced by $cs(s)$, the "context set" of the thinking situation s. Because of the indicative mood, the condition $w' \in [\![that \text{ } it \text{ } is \text{ } raining]\!]^{cs(s)}$ is only defined if w' is in $cs(s)$. Schlenker assumes that in this case, where s is a belief situation, the context set is the set of doxastically accessible worlds. In an obvious way, Schlenker's $cs(s)$ plays the same role as R_{dox} in Giannakidou's and Portner's theories. Similarly, if the matrix verb is 'dream,' s is a dreaming situation, and the context set $cs(s)$ is the set of worlds in which the dream actually happens (i.e. $cs(s)$ in this case is R_{dream}). But

---

[45] In reality, Schlenker assumes that the subjunctive competes against both the indicative and infinitive; this allows him to capture the fact that subjunctive subjects normally cannot corefer with the matrix subject (the obviation effect; see e.g. Farkas 1992a; Kempchinsky 2009 and Section 2.3.1.1 below). He notes that Portner (1997) and Siegel (2009) also treat the subjunctive as the default form.

if s is a wanting situation, $cs(s)$ is identified with the set of doxastically accessible worlds, and crucially not with a's buletically accessible worlds; hence, the condition in (96) is not met. In this way, Schlenker's analysis manipulates the context set in a way very similar to what Giannakidou's does with the individual model.

One way in which Schlenker's proposal differs from Giannakidou's is that his theory is set up to suggest that cs is a linguistically natural function which assigns accessibility relations to situations, with the context set of the conversation cs_* as a prototypical case. Whether this feature of the proposal contributes to a real explanation depends, in large measure, on our assumptions about what situations are like. Why does cs return a doxastically accessible set of worlds both when its argument is a thinking situation and when its argument is a wanting situation—but not when its argument is a dreaming or promising situation? The idea seems to be that a wanting situation should be closely connected to a set of beliefs, so that it can identify the same set of belief worlds, but a dreaming or a promising situation is not related to a set of belief worlds in the same way. This idea may well be plausible, but it relies on some assumptions which are not fully clear about the nature of mental states of various kinds.

2.2.2.5 Further issues for theories based on comparison or truth in a designated set We have organized the discussion of theories of verbal mood in terms of two main approaches: theories based on comparison and theories based on truth in a designated world or set of worlds. In this section, we will consider three challenges to this way of dividing up the field. In turn, we discuss the following points:

1. There is reason to think that the two approaches might be **non-distinct**. Some proposals which explicitly fall under the truth-based approach make reference to the comparative semantics of predicates like 'want,' suggesting that these fail to entail the complement's truth in the designated set because they are comparative. On this way of looking at things, a predicate fails the truth-based condition for indicative mood if it meets the comparison-based condition for subjunctive mood.
2. Farkas's (2003) proposal that **both** comparativity and truth in a designated set of worlds are relevant to mood selection; they are independent factors which in combination explain the mood selection properties of a given language.
3. Portner and Rubinstein (2013) argue that **neither** comparativity nor truth in a designated set is responsible for mood selection. Instead, they argue for the importance of CONTEXTUAL COMMITMENT.

The possibility that the two approaches are not distinct is suggested by a close reading of the proposals of authors like Farkas (1992b), Giannakidou (1997, 1999), Quer (2001), and Smirnova (2011, 2012). As has been mentioned several times, the main problem which faces theories based on the truth of the complement clause is that it is difficult to independently motivate the choice of a particular world or set of worlds against which to check the truth of the complement. The choice of this set (which goes by such names as "anchor," "individual model," "modal context," and "context set (of a situation)") is typically just stipulated as part of the meaning of the matrix predicate. However, comments like the following (Giannakidou 1999) suggest a connection to the comparison-based theory:

The semantics of *want*-type attitudes proposed here presumes that what one desires is connected with what one believes, a connection prevailing in the classical treatments of desire reports, see Stalnaker (1984), Asher (1987), Heim (1992). The connection is done in terms of preference.   (Giannakidou 1999, p.391)

Giannakidou is pointing out here that the only set of accessible worlds mentioned in Heim's (1992) analysis of desire predicates is the subject's belief worlds. The desirability ordering $<_s$ used in giving the meaning of 'want' in (14), earlier in the chapter, is not an accessibility relation, and so according to Giannakidou it is not the right sort of thing to serve as our P_Θ. As a result, non-comparative predicates will select the indicative, because they quantify over P_Θ, while comparative predicates typically will not, because they are not simple universal quantifiers over P_Θ.

Smirnova (2012) gives an analysis of mood selection in Bulgarian which most clearly combines the comparison-based and truth-based approaches. Her reasoning is not quite the same as that sketched above because of the way she integrates comparativity into the semantics of predicates like 'want,' but the key insight is the same: a comparative semantics breaks the truth-based property which triggers the indicative. Smirnova's analysis is interesting from a technical point of view because she models comparativity using a standard Kratzerian ordering semantics, rather than the combination of similarity and preference used by Stalnaker and Heim or the comparison of contextual alternatives proposed by Villalta. Though it is not quite stated that way, Smirnova's analysis boils down to the claim that the indicative is chosen when the ordering source is empty (or entirely absent), because when it is empty the sentence entails that the complement is true throughout the modal base. In giving crucial importance to whether the ordering source is empty or not, her theory is quite similar to that of Giorgi and Pianesi (1997).

Next we turn to the idea that comparison and truth in a designated set are both relevant to verbal mood. Farkas (2003) develops the truth-based analysis of verbal mood in a way that makes clear that the importance of comparativity is explaining why certain predicates do not select the indicative, but in addition she makes two important innovations. The first is that she adopts the method of derived contexts. Thus, the meaning of 'think' is represented roughly as in (65), repeated here:

(98) $c+A$ *thinks that* $\phi = c \cap \{w : \Theta_w + \phi = \Theta_w\}$

(Recall that Θ_w is the modal parameters associated with 'think,' and for our purposes can be thought of as $R_{dox}(w)$, but it is being treated internally to the semantics as a derived context.) Farkas's claim is that 'think' selects the indicative because its complement ϕ updates Θ_w using '+' ($\Theta_w + \phi$), just as a root declarative S is indicative because it updates the discourse context c ($c + S$). Farkas describes this situation by saying that the complement of 'think' has an ASSERTIVE CONTEXT CHANGE POTENTIAL, and she believes that most classes which select indicative, including predicates of assertion, fiction, and mental creation, have meanings given in this same assertion-like update.

Farkas proposes that desire predicates and other subjunctive-selecting predicates do not perform an assertive context change, but rather an "evaluative" one. She does not define this type of context change; the idea seems to be that the meaning of 'want' should look something like the following:

(99) $c + A$ wants $\phi = c \cap \{w : \ldots \Omega_w \star \phi \ldots\}$

That is, somewhere in the semantics for 'want', the complement ϕ will be used to update in the evaluative way a derived context Ω_w. We use $\star$ to indicate evaluative update, and compared to (98), the key point is that $\star$ replaces $+$. The evaluative update $\star$ triggers the choice of subjunctive mood.

Although her intuitions are intriguing (and I will try to build on them further in Chapter 4), in fact Farkas does not give a meaning for 'want' which fits the pattern (99). Farkas refers to Heim's (1992) analysis in which 'want' has the meaning that does not fit well with her proposal (100):

(100) $c + A$ wants that $\phi = c \cap$
$$\{w : \forall w' \in \Theta_w[Sim_{w'}(\Theta_w + \phi) <_{A,w} Sim_{w'}(\Theta_w + \neg\phi)]\}$$

Within (100), ϕ performs an assertive update ($\Theta_w + \phi$), and it seems to me this would be expected to trigger the indicative. I think the following definitions better capture Farkas's ideas:

(101)   a. A context c is a pair $\langle cs_c, <_c \rangle$ of a context set cs_c and an ordering relation $<_c$.
b. • For any context c and atomic sentence ϕ, $c + \phi =$
$\langle cs_c \cap [\![\phi]\!], <_c \rangle$
• For any context c and sentence ϕ, $c \star \phi =$
$\langle \{w \in cs_c : Sim_w(c + \phi) <_c Sim_w(c + \neg\phi)\}, <_c \rangle$
c. $c + A$ wants $\phi = \langle cs_c \cap \{w : \Omega_w \star \phi = \Omega_w\}, <_c \rangle$

We assume that a context involves both a set of worlds and an ordering relation and then define an evaluative update $\star$.[46] In the complement of 'want', $\star\phi$ evaluates ϕ relative to the derived context Ω_w. This derived context must give a set of worlds cs_{Ω_w} and an ordering $<_{\Omega_w}$. The set of worlds should be the subject's doxastically accessible worlds and the ordering should represent the subject's desires. With all of this in place, the 'want' sentence means that the subject prefers ϕ to $\neg\phi$, given her beliefs.

---

[46] There are probably better ways to define $\star$, but this one reflects Farkas's reliance on Heim's (1992) paper. I believe that one of the dynamic updates proposed for imperatives and deontics by the likes of van der Torre and Tan (1998), Portner (2004), or Starr (2013) would work better. See Sections 3.3.3 and 4.1 for detailed discussion.

The second main contribution of Farkas (2003) is her proposal that verbal mood is not only sensitive to whether the update is assertive or evaluative, but also to another factor, DECIDEDNESS. As we have seen, the assertive/evaluative contrast corresponds to the difference between non-comparative and comparative meanings, and so that factor falls under the comparison-based approach to verbal mood. Decidedness, in contrast, reflects the intuition that the indicative marks the truth of a clause in a designated set of worlds. We can see the two factors at play in the mood-selection facts relating to emotive factives like *regret* and *odd (that)*. Emotive factives are clearly evaluative, but their complement is true in the derived context. In the case of 'regret' (102), the derived context for ϕ would be doxastic, as with 'want', and the ordering relation $<$ would encode dispreference.

(102)   *A regrets that ϕ.*

'Regret' performs an evaluative update, but because of factivity, the sentence as a whole guarantees that ϕ is true throughout the doxastically accessible worlds. This means that the complement of 'regret' counts as decided.

With emotive factives, the comparison-based component (evaluativity) suggests that the complement should be subjunctive, but the truth-based component (decidedness) suggests indicative. Farkas proposes that, when the two factors are in conflict, languages may differ in which one takes precedence. In Romanian, we find that emotive factives select subjunctive; in this language, evaluativity wins out. But in French, they select indicative, indicating the opposite ranking.

Finally we turn to the skeptical note raised by Portner and Rubinstein (2013). Based on a study of several less-studied classes of predicates in French, they argue that neither comparison nor truth in a designated set is sufficient to explain verbal mood selection. To begin with, they point out that the classic modal adjectives 'possible' and 'necessary' typically select the subjunctive, but it is not clear that they always involve ordering in their meanings.

(103)   *Il est possible   que cet échantillon soit   dissout   dans l'eau.*
         It is possible   that this sample   be-SUBJ dissolved in   the water
         'It is possible that this sample dissolves in water.'

Here, 'possible' seems to indicate nothing more than that there is some circumstantially accessible world where the sample dissolves in water. There is no obvious sense in which the meaning is comparative or evaluative.

Several other predicates raise the opposite issue. Portner and Rubinstein point out that 'promise', 'hope', and in some cases 'probable' take indicative complements, though their meanings certainly involve comparison or an ordering of worlds.[47] With none of them is their complement decided, so Farkas's analysis of emotive factives does not seem applicable. One option for dealing with these cases is to consider them as providing examples of prototype effects, as assumed by

---

[47] Some French speakers prefer subjunctive with *espérer* 'hope', but many only allow indicative. See Schlenker (2005) and Anand and Hacquard (2013) for other ideas about 'hope.'

Portner (1997). We could say that, while people don't always keep their promises, in prototypical cases they do, and this is good enough to make the complement or 'promise' count as decided. Portner and Rubinstein pursue a different idea, though: they propose that the indicative mood indicates CONTEXTUAL COMMITMENT on the part of the arguments of the matrix predicate.

As defined by Portner and Rubinstein, an individual is contextually committed to a modal background (a modal base or ordering source) if he is prepared to defend it, in context, as a good basis for action. The concept is easy to see with 'promise': If I promise to do P, I imply that P, together with my other promises, is a contextually defensible priority. Portner and Rubinstein argue that the difference between 'hope' and 'want' is that hopes must be based on preferences to which one is contextually committed, but 'want' need not be. They say that 'want' expresses a "visceral" desire and 'hope' an "intellectual" one.[48] With regard to the modal adjectives, they argue that there are two versions of 'probable,' a normal subjunctive-selecting variant and an indicative-selecting one that requires the speaker's contextual commitment towards its ordering source. With 'possible,' whether or not it has an ordering source is unimportant, since it never implies contextual commitment on the part of the speaker. Their analysis receives some support from the fact that the indicative-marking version of 'probable,' for speakers that allow it, seems to imply a more "objective," less "subjective," judgment.

2.2.3 Clauses which are not complements to a selecting predicate

Semantic theories of verbal mood have been developed with the primary aim of explaining the selection of indicative and subjunctive complement clauses by a matrix predicate, but at times semanticists have paid attention to verbal mood in other contexts, and in this section we will outline some of their main ideas and findings. We will not, however, be able to give anything like an overview of the distribution of verbal mood forms in non-complement positions, for the simple reason that the field of semantics has not attempted to produce a general theory of mood which encompasses all such contexts, or even a significant range of them. Rather, within the semantics literature we only find sporadic discussions of specific constructions. In this section, we will consider work on purpose clauses, relative clauses, *if* clauses (conditional antecedents), and root clauses. The field could certainly benefit from more rigorous attempts to extend theories of verbal mood to a wider range of adjuncts, and in this connection I can point out that Thieroff and Rothstein (2010), a collection of overview articles on the mood systems of European languages, includes a great deal of useful information on mood choice in non-complement clauses.

Adjunct purpose clauses.   In a brief discussion, Quer (2001) notes that purpose clauses select subjunctive in Catalan and aims to explain this fact in terms of his theory of model shift (Section 2.2.2.4; example Quer 2001, (14)).

---

[48] Their idea is closely related to Bolinger's (1974) claim that 'want' expresses a "glandular" preference.

(104) *L'ha   convidada perquè no s'enfadi/*enfada.*
       her-have.3SG invited   so that not SE-get.angry.SUBJ/INDIC.3SG
       'S/he has invited her so that she will not get angry.'

According to Quer, the purpose clause 'so that she will not get angry' must
be subjunctive because it is interpreted relative to a buletic individual model,
specifically here a model representing the desires of the individual referred to by
the matrix subject. In Quer's theory, the subjunctive is chosen because this buletic
individual model is different from the speaker's doxastic model $R_{dox}(u)$ in which
the entire sentence is interpreted. In his theory, the subjunctive is chosen for the
same reason that it would be required in the scope of 'want.'

Quer is not explicit about how the buletic individual model enters the sentence's
logical form or what role it plays in the compositional semantics. In the case of
(104), we can speculate that it is contributed by *perquè* 'so that.' We might associate
'so that' with a meaning like 'because x wants and intends p,' with x bound by the
matrix subject. Given such a logical form, it seems that Quer's explanation of mood
selection by 'want' can indeed be extended to (104).

Relative clauses.   In many languages, both indicative and subjunctive verbal
mood occur in relative clauses, and in contexts in which both forms are possible,
the choice between them relates to a difference in meaning. Work by such scholars
as Farkas (1985), Quer (1998, 2001), and Giannakidou (2014) reveals that relative
clauses have subjunctive mood when they are interpreted in the immediate scope of
an attitude verb or other operator which would trigger subjunctive in its argument.
Since relative clauses typically take the same scope as the noun phrase whose head
noun they modify, this pattern can often be described in terms of quantifier scope:
the use of a subjunctive relative indicates that the noun phrase of which it forms a
part is given narrow scope relative to a subjunctive-selecting, intensional operator,
and the use of an indicative relative as part of a noun phrase which appears to be
within the scope of such an operator indicates that it is to be assigned wide scope in
logical form. These generalizations can be illustrated with the following (examples
from Quer 1998, pp. 105, 108):

(105) a. *Vull   enviar-li   regals   que el   facin*
          want.1SG send.INF-him presents that him make.SUBJ
          content. (Catalan)
          happy
          'I want to send him presents that make him happy.'
       b. *Vull   enviar-li   regals   que el   fa   content.*
          want.1SG send.INF-him presents that him make.INDIC happy
          'I want to send him presents that make him happy.'

In example (105a), the phrase *regals que el facin content* ('presents that make him
happy'), with subjunctive mood, is interpreted within the scope of 'want,' and as a
result it means roughly that, if the speaker's desires are satisfied in world *w*, then

he gives the recipient presents in *w* which make the recipient happy in *w*. In (105b) the corresponding phrase *regals que el fa content*, with indicative mood, receives wide scope, and so means that there are some presents that make this individual happy in the actual world, and if the speaker's desires are satisfied in world *w*, the speaker gives him those presents in *w*.

It is also common to describe the contrast between (105a) and (105b) in terms of specificity rather than scope, saying that the indefinite 'gifts that make him happy' is non-specific when it contains the subjunctive and specific when it contains the indicative.[49] Such terminology is even more natural in examples like (106a)–(106b) (Quer 1998, p. 121):

(106) a. *Estem buscant una intèrprete   que sap   oromo.*
          be.1PL seeking an   interpreter that know.INDIC.3SG Oromo
          'We are looking for an interpreter who knows Oromo.'

       b. *Estem buscant una intèrprete   que sàpiga   oromo.*
          be.1PL seeking an   interpreter that know.SUBJ.3SG Oromo
          'We are looking for an interpreter who knows Oromo.'

Intuitively, (106a) says that our search will only be satisfied by a specific interpreter, while (106b) means that it can be satisfied by any interpreter who meets our criteria. In light of this way of thinking about these examples, subjunctive relatives are sometimes described as triggering a non-specific interpretation. As Quer points out, the subjunctive is only determined when the relative clause is in the scope of an operator with the type of meaning that governs subjunctive. The relative clause on the definite in (107a) must have indicative mood, because it is in the complement of the indicative-selecting 'say' (Quer 1998, p. 116):

(107) a. *El Pau diu que el noi que va   trucar ahir*
          the Pau says that the guy that AUX.INDIC.3SG called yesterday
          era   grec.
          be.INDIC.3SG Greek
          'Pau says that the guy that called yesterday was Greek.'

       b. **El Pau diu que el noi que truqués   ahir*
          the Pau says that the guy that call.PST.SUBJ.3SG yesterday
          era   grec.
          be.INDIC.3SG Greek
          'Pau says that the guy that called yesterday was Greek.'

The concept of specificity is especially salient when the noun phrase containing the relative clause is an argument of the matrix predicate, as in the following (Quer 1998, p. 119):

---

[49] In a very different way, Baker and Travis (1997) propose that verbal mood in Mohawk encodes definiteness.

(108)   *El que hagi   assassinat tants   d'algerians   és*
        the that have.SUBJ.3SG murdered so many of Algerians be.INDIC.3SG
        una bèstia infame.
        a   beast infamous
        'The one that murdered so many Algerians is an infamous monster.'

With the subjunctive relative, the phrase *El que hagi assassinat tants d'algerians* ('the one who murdered so many Algerians') is not understood to refer to a particular individual whom the speaker has in mind; rather, the sentence can be paraphrased as something like "the person who murdered so many Algerians, whoever he may be, is an infamous monster." Following Farkas, Quer connects this semantic effect to Donnellan's (1966) attributive reading and proposes that the sentence contains an operator (in this case, a covert modal 'must') to produce the intensional context which licenses the subjunctive. He thus takes the sentence to be equivalent to "the person who murdered so many Algerians must be an infamous monster," with 'must' having wider scope than the subject.

  Among the theoretical tools designed for the analysis of verbal mood which have been discussed in this chapter, the method of shifting parameters appears to be well-suited to developing an analysis of mood choice in relative clauses. Consider the meaning 'want' in (92b) above:

(109)   a. Paul wants to find an interpreter who knows Oromo.
        b. $[\![$ *Paul wants (Paul) find an interpreter who knows Oromo* $]\!]^{P_0} =$
            - $\{w :$ for some situation $s < w$:
              Paul is the thinking participant in s and
              $\forall w'[w' \in R_{want}(s) \rightarrow w' \in [\![$ *Paul finds ...* $]\!]^{R_{want}, F_\forall}]\}$

In (109b), the relative clause *(an interpreter) who knows Oromo* is interpreted within the scope of 'want,' and as a result its modal parameter of interpretation has shifted from the original P_0 to R_{want}. If we understand the mood of the relative clause to be sensitive to this modal parameter (as it is according to several of the theories discussed in Section 2.2.2), it is correctly predicted to be subjunctive in Catalan and other languages with similar patterns of mood choice in relative clauses. However, if the phrase *an interpreter who knows Oromo* were assigned wider scope than 'want,' its modal parameter would be P_0, and indicative would be the correct verbal mood for the relative clause. It seems likely that the examples in (105)–(107) could be explained by a theory along these lines. It is much trickier to explain the use of the subjunctive in the root subject position, (108). Just saying that it contains an unpronounced 'must' is not sufficient; the modal would have to shift the modal parameter to one which triggers subjunctive.

Negation.   Subjunctive mood often appears in subordinate clauses when the matrix is non-affirmative, for example when it is negated or interrogative. The following examples show the subjunctive as the complement of verbs which would select indicative in an affirmative sentence (from Mulder 2010, p.170; Quer 2010, p.227):

(110)   a. *Pierre ne   croit   pas   que   tout le monde soit   venu. (French)*
                Peter NEG believe NEG that everybody   be.SUBJ come
                'Peter does not believe that everybody has come.'
         b. *Recordes   que els   hagin   donat mai   un premi? (Catalan)*
                remember that them have.SUBJ given never a   prize
                'Do you remember if they have ever given them a prize?'

Quer (1998, 2010) classifies these cases as examples of the POLARITY subjunctive (or "dubitative" subjunctive), which he also identifies as occurring under predicates like 'doubt.' He argues that they have very different properties from the INTENSIONAL or "volitional" subjunctive selected by 'want' and 'order.' In particular, Quer points out that the dubitative contexts license subjunctive in multiple levels of embedding, as in (111), and that they do not show the same sequence of tense and subject disjoint reference properties as volitional subjunctives (Catalan example from Quer 2010, p. 228):[50]

(111)   *Dubto   que creguin   que ens hagin   convençut amb això.*
             Doubt.1SG that believe.SUBJ that us   have.SUBJ convinced with this
             'I doubt that they believe that they have convinced us with this.'

We should not, however, understand Quer to be proposing that there are two distinct but homophonous subjunctive forms, since in his work on model shift he tries to explain cases like (110a) using the same theory as he applies to subjunctives selected by a volitional predicate. This analysis is problematical, however. Quer (2001, p. 91) proposes that subjunctive is triggered under negation because the individual component of the model shifts; in the case of (110a), it shifts from the speaker to Pierre. I do not see how this proposal can fit into his overall theory, though, since even in the non-negative version of this example, the same model shift would occur.

   Giannakidou offers a straightforward analysis of the subjunctive under negation. Recall that her theory is based on the idea that the subjunctive is sensitive to non-veridical contexts, and negation is clearly a non-veridical operator. Thus it appears easy to explain (112) by saying that *dhen* licenses the subjunctive (from Giannakidou (2011, (39))):

(112)   *Dhen pistevo   na   irthe o   Janis. (Greek)*
             NEG   believe.1SG SUBJ came the John
             'I don't believe that John came.'

It remains unclear, however, why negation cannot trigger the subjunctive in its own clause. Perhaps negation is not in the right structural position to do so.

---

[50] See Quer's work for additional examples of these properties. Note that subjunctive relatives do not consistently show the properties which Quer associates with either type of subjunctive, and so it is difficult to assign them to either class (Quer 1998).

Portner (1997) treats cases like (110a) and (112) in a way which explains the fact that negation only leads to the subjunctive in a subordinate clause. In intuitive terms, he proposes that negation and the verb it negates combine to yield a complex modal meaning, and that the resulting modality licenses the subjunctive. Recall that Portner follows the method of shifting parameters, but he utilizes two such parameters: an accessibility relation and a modal force. In the affirmative sentence *I believe that John came*, the modal parameters for the embedded clause are the doxastic accessibility relation R_{dox} and the force of necessity $F_\forall$. But when the matrix clause is negated, as in (112), he argues that negation is integrated into the modal force, resulting in the force of non-necessity $F_{\neg\forall}$. (The sentence is therefore true if not all of the speaker's belief worlds are ones in which John came.) Portner proposes that the indicative is incompatible with the force of non-necessity, and so the subjunctive is selected in the negative environment.

Conditionals.   In many languages, conditional 'if' clauses can have the subjunctive mood. Consider the following examples from Catalan (Quer 2010, p.232):

(113) a. *Si té   gana,   agafarà   una galeta.*
          if have.PRS.INDIC hunger, take.INDIC a   cookie
          'If s/he is hungry, s/he will take a cookie.'

       b. *Si tingués   gana,   agafaria   una galeta.*
          if have.PST.SUBJ hunger, take.COND a   cookie
          'If s/he were hungry, s/he would take a cookie.'

       c. *Si hagués   tingut gana,   hauria   agafat una galeta.*
          if have.PST.SUBJ had   hunger, have.COND taken a   cookie
          'If s/he had been hungry, s/he would have taken a cookie.'

       d. *Si tenia   gana,   agafaria   una galeta.*
          if have.PST.INDIC hunger, take.COND a   cookie
          'If s/he were hungry, s/he would take a cookie.'

Following Quer, we can describe the differences in meaning among these examples in terms of tense and the contrast between **real** and **unreal** conditionals. With the present indicative *if* clause, (113a) is a real conditional: it leaves open whether the referent of the subject will, in fact, be hungry. The past subjunctive (113b) is an unreal conditional about the present: it suggests that this individual is not in fact hungry.[51] Example (113c), with the past perfect subjunctive, is an unreal conditional about the past: it suggests that he or she was not hungry.

In philosophical work on conditionals, it is common for unreal conditionals to be described as "subjunctive conditionals," and this terminology makes sense given the correlation between subjunctive mood and the unreal interpretation in (113a–c). However, as pointed out by Iatridou (2000), crosslinguistic investigation reveals that the unreal interpretation actually depends on the past marking of the

---

[51] Such examples are often called "counterfactuals," but as pointed out by Anderson (1951) and many subsequent authors, they are compatible with certain contexts in which the antecedent clause is true. For this reason, the term "unreal" is preferable. See Portner (2009, ch. 5) for further discussion.

if clause.[52] Subjunctive form may be (and sometimes must be) used if the language has an appropriate past subjunctive form, but it seems better to understand the subjunctive as licensed by the unreal interpretation, rather than triggering it. In this context, note that Quer's example (113d), with the past (imperfect) indicative, has a meaning very close to (113b); this fact further suggests that the subjunctive mood has only a marginal role in deriving the unreal interpretations.

Looking beyond the *if* conditionals, mood choice seems to play a role in less well-studied types of adverbial clauses with conditional-like meaning. For example, French employs subjunctive in clauses introduced by *à condition que* ('on condition that'), *avant que* ('before'), *de sorte que* ('so that'), *quoique* ('although') (see Mulder 2010 for examples). Quer (1998, 2001) examines mood choice in concessive clauses. He points out that a clause introduced by *encara que* ('although') in Catalan means 'although' with indicative mood, but 'even if' with subjunctive. This variation seems similar to that observed with German *wenn* ('when/if') clauses, where indicative marking tends to lead to the meaning 'when' and subjunctive to 'if' (Thieroff 2010, pp.141–4). In many of these cases, it is natural to think of the role of subjunctive as reflecting or contributing some kind of modal meaning and, in his study of concessives, Quer (1998, 2001) develops this intuition in a plausible but relatively informal way. The field could certainly benefit from more precise and compositionally detailed theories of verbal mood in conditionals and other adverbial clauses.

Root clauses.   The canonical verbal mood of root declaratives and interrogatives is, of course, the indicative. Certain theories of sentence mood assign a crucial role to the indicative verbal mood (for example Truckenbrodt 2006a, Lohnstein 2007; see Chapter 3). Still, we do find root subjunctive clauses with various non-declarative, non-interrogative discourse functions. Portner (1997, pp.192–3) gives examples of the Italian subjunctive expressing an order, wish, supposition, and astonishment:[53]

(114)   a. *Tenga   le   mani a   posto.*
           hold.SUBJ.3SG the hand in place
           'Keep your hands in place!'

      b. *Il   Signore ci protegga.*
           the Lord   us protect.SUBJ.3SG
           'May the Lord protect us!'

      c. *L'avesse   anche detto lui.*
           it-have.SUBJ also   said him
           'Suppose he had said it too.'

      d. *Che sia   nel   bagno?*
           that be.SUBJ in-the bath
           'She is in the bath?!'

---

[52] See the works cited by Iatridou for many important points on this issue, especially Steele (1975).

[53] Examples are from Moretti and Orvieto (1981). Examples (114a,b,d) are literary examples; the original sources are C. Cassola, *La ragazza di Bube*; G.T. di Lampedusa, *Il Gattopardo*; C. Cassola, *Una relazione*.

The first example can be considered a subtype of the imperative sentence mood in which the subjunctive is used in place of the imperative form. This so-called suppletive imperative results from the choice of third person morphology to express the lack of familiarity between the speaker and the addressee (informally, "politeness," though that term is particularly inappropriate for this example).[54] Example (114b) has a similar meaning, and can be described as an optative or third person imperative.

There has been very little research in semantic theory on these root uses of the subjunctive. Han (1998) explains the choice of subjunctive in suppletive imperatives by proposing that they have an [irrealis] feature appropriate to the imperative sentence mood (see Section 3.1.3 for discussion). Grosz (2011, 2014) develops a detailed analysis of German optatives in which subjunctive mood plays a critical role. (It is interesting that Grosz's analysis of optatives ties them closely to conditionals; see Section 3.3.4 for some more discussion of Grosz's ideas.) Portner (1997) proposes that the modal parameters of a root clause can sometimes be shifted to ones which would trigger the subjunctive. His idea is that an example like (114d) can be interpreted relative to the same modal parameters which would be introduced by 'be surprised that,' and therefore mean that the speaker is surprised that she is in the bath. Ambar (2016) discusses root uses of the Portuguese subjunctive in some detail and relates them to a broader theory based on the idea that subjunctive marks evaluation and indicative marks assertion.

2.3 Beyond verbal core mood

As has been mentioned above, the most influential semantically-based theories of verbal mood focus on explaining the selection of indicative and subjunctive forms by a matrix predicate. In Section 2.2, I hope to have given both a useful presentation of those theories and some insights into the valuable intuitions which drive them. But the discussion has not yet touched on a number of areas of research which are deeply relevant to the study of verbal mood. In this section, I would like to give some pointers into the body of work on those topics.

2.3.1 Other mood-indicating forms

Thus far, we have focused on the contrast between the core verbal moods, indicative and subjunctive. Many languages have distinct types of clauses which, in addition to or instead of these, seem to meet the criteria for being considered verbal moods. The most obvious and well-studied examples of such forms are infinitives and dependent modals.

2.3.1.1 Infinitives   The study of infinitives is closely connected to the analysis of verbal mood. In many languages, we find infinitives in contexts which are very

---

[54] The use of the term "suppletive" here is not meant to imply that *tenga* is to be analyzed as a form based in one paradigm (the subjunctive) replacing a form within another (the imperative).

similar to those in which the subjunctive is used. We see this point in English with the fact that infinitives are typically used in the complement of desiderative and directive verbs, as in (115), and can also be used to express meanings similar to root subjunctives, (116):

(115)   a. Ben wants for John to be successful.
        b. She ordered me to leave.

(116)   Oh, to some day live in Paris!

Not all infinitives in English are associated with subjunctive-like contexts. For example, 'know' and 'believe' do not typically have an affinity for the subjunctive, yet we use infinitives in examples like the following:

(117)   Ben knows/believes John to be hiding in the basement.

There is a crucial difference in temporal interpretation between the infinitives in (115) and (117). The former examples—that is, the ones which appear in subjunctive-like contexts—are future-oriented, while the latter ones describe a situation which overlaps temporally with the time of Ben's knowing/believing. Bresnan (1972), Stowell (1982), Pesetsky (1992), and Portner (1992) argue that there is a semantically distinct subclass of future-oriented infinitives, sometimes known as "*for*-infinitives" due to the fact that the presence of the complementizer *for*, as in (115a), signals future orientation. Portner (1997) discusses *for*-infinitives from the point of view of the theory of mood.

   In languages which make robust use of the subjunctive, infinitives and subjunctives occur in similar contexts. In the complement of verbs like 'want' and 'order,' the infinitive is typically required when the subject of the embedded clause is semantically bound by (and hence, in an intuitive sense, coreferential with) the matrix subject (from Quer 2009, p.1789).

(118)   a. *No vull que saludis   absolutament ningú.* (Catalan)
           NEG want that say.hello.SUBJ absolutely   anyone
           'I don't want you to say hello to anyone at all.'
        b. *No vull saludar   absolutament ningú.*
           NEG want say.hello.INF absolutely   anyone
           'I don't want to say hello to anyone at all.'

See Ruwet (1984), Kempchinsky (1985, 2009), Picallo (1985), Raposo (1986a), Suñer (1986), Farkas (1992a), Tsoulas (1996), Avrutin and Babyonyshev (1997), Quer (1998), Dobrovie-Sorin (2001), Schlenker (2005, 2011), Costantini (2006), Ambar (2016), and Zu (2016) for some of the many analyses of this OBVIATION EFFECT. Farkas (1992a) proposes that the infinitive represents both "world-dependency" and "subject-dependency," while the subjunctive marks only world-dependency, and the former blocks the latter when the subject is responsible for the action described by the clause (the "canonical control relation"). Schlenker, Costantini, and Zu relate the obviation effect to a preference for a *de se* reading to be expressed in an unambiguous way if possible. (Zu also takes into account Farkas's canonical control relation.) Pearson (2013) is an important recent study of *de se* interpretation which incorporates a theory of control of infinitival subjects.

The temporal interpretation of subjunctives and infinitives. The close connection between infinitives and subjunctives highlights some important features of the temporal interpretation of subjunctive clauses. As illustrated in (115), the complements of desiderative and directive predicates are future-oriented. When these predicates take a subjunctive complement, there are severe restrictions on the tense morphology in the subordinate clause. For example, the following contrast shows that the past subjunctive is not allowed under matrix 'want' in the present tense (from Quer 1998, p.33):

(119) a. *Vull   que acabi   la   tesi.   (Catalan)*
          want.PRES.1SG that finish.SUBJ.PRES.3SG the dissertation
          'I want her/him to finish the dissertation.'

       b. **Vull   que acabés   la   tesi.*
          want.PRES.1SG that finish.SUBJ.PST.3SG the dissertation
          'I want her/him to finish the dissertation.'

Facts like this have led to the idea that the tense of subjunctives is dependent on that of the matrix clause. This dependency can be understood in different ways. The subjunctive tense is sometimes analyzed as anaphoric (Picallo 1984, 1985; Luján 1979, 1980; Pica 1984, among others) or as a semantically vacuous copy of the matrix tense (Progovac 1993; von Stechow 1995). Such analyses minimize the distinction in temporal interpretation between infinitives and subjunctives, and therefore lead naturally to the view that the two types of clauses differ mainly in whether the subject is controlled by the matrix subject or not (as seen above in (118)). Related ideas about the temporal dependency of subjunctives and infinitives are pursued by Ambar (2016) and Wiltschko (2016).

While these intuitions are important and probably provide essential clues to the full analysis of verbal mood, their applicability is limited by the fact that subjunctives in adjunct clauses and those triggered by negation are freer in their temporal interpretation (Raposo 1986b; Suñer and Padilla-Rivera 1987; Suñer 1986; Quer 1998). Moreover, as pointed out by Portner (2011c), merely identifying the temporal properties of (selected) subjunctives does not explain why clauses with those properties occur in precisely the contexts they do. Does the ungrammaticality of (119b), for instance, follow from some incoherence in the meaning which would be expressed if its complement had an independent past tense, or is it fundamentally a syntactic fact?

In order to properly analyze the temporal dependency of subjunctives and their relation to infinitives, it will be necessary to have a better understanding of the temporal semantics of subjunctives and infinitives than we currently do. The semantics literature on these topics is quite fragmentary, and so while there are important insights, they are difficult to combine into a single coherent theory. It may prove useful to point out a few key observations:

1. Von Stechow (1995, 2004) and Giannakidou (2009) propose that the temporal argument of a subjunctive clause is bound by a λ-operator in C, creating a phrase which denotes a property of times. We might then assume that verbs which select for the subjunctive take a temporal property as their semantic argument, while those which select for indicatives take temporally saturated propositions. However, this would probably not be correct, as standard theories of tense treat all embedded clauses as denoting temporal abstracts (e.g. Ogihara 1996, 2007; Abusch 1997).

2. Portner (1992) points out the following contrast (examples from Portner 1992, pp.260–1):

    (120)   a. Jackie remembers reading *Jude the Obscure*.
            b. Jackie remembers that she read *Jude the Obscure*.

    In order for (120a) to be true, Jackie has to be able to place herself in the moment of reading *Jude the Obscure*; in contrast (120b) only requires that she be able to recall a fact. Portner says that (120a) describes Jackie as having "internal perspective" on the event she remembers, while (120b) describes an "external perspective." Higginbotham (2003) proposes that (120a) represents a *de se* attitude towards the event of reading, and Schlenker (2011) suggests infinitival complements are also used to express event-related *de se* attitudes.

3. Portner (1997) and Abusch (2004) provide explicit semantic theories of the future-orientation of *for*-infinitives. Both postulate an operator which introduces futurity in a way that is very different from standard tenses. (In other respects their analyses are quite different. Portner uses a situation semantics and introduces futurity within the infinitival clause, while Abusch employs a more standard tense semantics, and introduces futurity in the matrix VP.)

4. Schlenker (2005) notes that some temporal expressions can receive a *de se* interpretation, and Brasoveanu (2006) argues that a particular Romanian verbal mood form (the conditional-optative or Subjunctive B) directly encodes a temporal *de se* meaning (Brasoveanu 2006, (1)):

    (121)   *Maria crede   că   ar   fi în pericol. (Romanian)*
            Mary believes that SUBJ.3SG be in danger
            'Maria believes that she is in danger.'

Putting these points together, it seems plausible to assume that the temporal properties of temporally-dependent subjunctives and infinitives should be explained on the basis of the particular varieties of *de se* meaning which they encode. We might guess that 'want' expresses an attitude which is always *de se* with respect to the complement's time or event argument, and that the only way to produce a time- or event-based property which can serve as its argument is to use a subjunctive or infinitival clause. This way of viewing things connects nicely to the idea that the obviation contrast between infinitives and subjunctives has to do with the preference to express subject *de se* with an infinitive. Against this approach, though, is the fact that indicative clauses can also have *de se* meanings, both in their subject position and their temporal argument. It is thus unclear why indicatives cannot be used in place of subjunctives and infinitives (under their *de se* logical forms) and why subjunctives and infinitives cannot be used in place of indicatives (in contexts where a *de se* reading is to be derived).

2.3.1.2 Mood-indicating modals Building on the presentation by Palmer (1990), Portner (1997) proposes that the modal auxiliaries *may* and *would* are "mood-indicators" in sentences like the following (his (42c,d) and fn. 11; (a) is from Palmer):[55]

(122)   a. I pray that God may bless you.
         b. It is possible that Sue may win the race.

(123)   If you would come, I would be happy.

The clauses in which *may* occurs in (122) would be subjunctive in many languages. Moreover, the meanings of the sentences do not seem to involve two separate modal operators; for example, (122b) does not mean 'It is possible that it is possible that Sue wins the race.' Given these facts, Portner proposes that *may* in the subordinate clause is dependent on the modality of the matrix predicate, and is therefore a mood-indicator within his theory. Similarly, he suggests that the first *would* in (123) is a mood-indicator, though he does not give a detailed analysis of this case.

Other linguists have not pursued Portner's idea, but several have pointed out the similarity between examples like (122) and MODAL CONCORD. Modal concord is the phenomenon whereby a modal adverb and a modal auxiliary or verb in the same clause seem to represent a single modal element at logical form (example from Zeijlstra 2008, (3)):

(124)   You may possibly have read my little monograph upon the subject.

Zeijlstra (2008) in fact classifies patterns like (122), in which a modal can be thought of as in concord with a matrix predicate, as modal concord, although the analysis he proposes focuses on the clause-mate cases.

There is a small but interesting body of research on modal concord, including work by Geurts and Huitink (2006), Zeijlstra (2008), Huitink (2012), Grosz (2010), and Anand and Brasoveanu (2010). Cui (2015) presents a detailed corpus investigation of combinations like (122) in Mandarin and applies rigorous criteria to determine in which cases the embedded modal makes no detectable contribution to

---

[55] The term "mood-indicator" suggests that there is an inventory of moods on which languages draw, and that they may be indicated or marked by various grammatical means. In the terminology of this book, Portner's idea might be better expressed by saying that these modals are verbal moods or components of verbal moods.

the overall sentence's meaning. She identifies a significant number of verb–modal combinations which can be said to be in a concord relation, such as *huaiyi ... keneng* ('suspect ... might') in examples like the following (based on Cui 2015, 4.11, 4.26):

(125)   a. *Lao Li huaiyi xiongshou keneng shi Xiao Wang. (Mandarin)*
         Lao Li suspect culprit   might   be Xiao Wang
         'Lao Li suspects that the culprit might be Xiao Wang.'

      b. *Lao Li pizhun   Xiao Wang keyi likai.*
         Lao Li approve Xiao Wang may leave
         'Lao Li approved Xiao Wang's optional departure.'

Cui's theory of these combinations of modal concord builds on Yalcin's (2007) and Anand and Hacquard's (2013) method of shifting parameters (see Section 2.2.2). Her analysis of epistemic examples like (125a) ends up being similar to Yalcin's proposal about English *might*, but her treatment of examples with priority modality, like (125b), is novel and based on a proposal involving reported speech acts.

2.3.2 The roles of semantics, syntax, and non-grammatical factors

The goal of this book is to introduce and evaluate semantic theories of mood, and we have accordingly focused on proposals which use the tools of semantic theory. As we have seen, the best such theories are quite successful in explaining certain properties of verbal mood systems, in particular the distribution of indicative and subjunctive in complement clauses. In this section, however, I would like to briefly consider to what extent we should expect to fully explain the distribution and linguistically-relevant properties of verbal mood forms solely within a semantic analysis. Do other components of linguistic theory, such as syntax and morphology, play independent roles? And beyond grammar, what are the contributions of usage-based, social, psychological, and historical factors?

We should certainly expect syntax to make an important contribution to an overall theory of verbal mood. In order to explain the patterns of indicative and subjunctive in a given language, we will have to take into account what logical forms can be syntactically derived; we would not expect a subjunctive relative in a nominal phrase which obligatorily takes widest scope, for example. Similarly, morphology will certainly play an important role, since a language may simply not allow for a choice of verbal mood forms under certain conditions. The relevance of these components of the grammatical system follows from the architectural relationship between morphosyntax and semantics more generally.

The issues are less clear when we consider the role of non-grammatical factors. As mentioned in Section 2.2.2, Portner (1997) proposes that verbal mood systems are similar to gender systems, and that as a result we should expect a certain amount of idiosyncrasy in the distribution of verbal mood forms. He suggests that semantic properties are the basis for mood choice (as biological sex might be for gender systems), but that in specific cases the choice of verbal mood might be made on the basis of similarity to a prototype; for example, if 'want' is the prototypical subjunctive-selector, another verb might also trigger subjunctive if it is similar to 'want', even if it does not have the key property which makes 'want' itself such a strong trigger for subjunctive. A theory which allows mood choice to be determined on this basis will clearly incorporate a strong psychological component.

It is also important to address the role of sociolinguistic factors. It is easily imaginable that a particular verbal form could take on associations with a salient aspect of social identity, for example a form which is understood as indicating that a speaker is highly educated. Based on this, speakers might use it to index that social identity, resulting in a disconnect from its semantic basis. Usage-based factors could have a similar effect. We can imagine a particular pairing of matrix verb and mood form coming to be so highly associated in usage that the form is used in the presence of that verb, even if the verb is used in a meaning or structural position which would not be expected to trigger the mood form by semantic criteria.

Much of the discussion points to the need for semanticists to be attentive to historical developments as they study verbal mood. As a language's mood system changes over time, there may be points at which it cannot be fully understood in terms of any single, coherent analysis. There may be stages in the historical development at which the semantics of mood is in flux, with two or more systems in play. The morphological and syntactic systems might likewise not be entirely complete or consistent. The effects of psychological, social, and usage-based factors may lead to further complexity. In this type of situation, the essential goal from a semanticist's point of view is to understand all of the complexities sufficiently well to continue the pursuit of a better understanding of the semantic factors which, it seems, are the most powerful in explaining the properties of verbal mood in the long run.

3

Sentence mood

In syntax, speech act theory, dynamic semantics, and other areas of linguistics and philosophy which study how functions of language like asserting a fact or asking a question are achieved using language, one idea often comes up: that one can read off from the form of a sentence which of these important functions it has, or at least gain information which will probably tell, in combination with other things you know, which it has. The sentence moods of a language are the particular forms which carry information of this kind. Our goal in this chapter is to develop a better understanding of how sentence moods fit into theoretical conceptions of the basic functions of language and the architecture of grammatical theory.

This chapter will begin in Section 3.1 with an examination of some fundamental topics, both foundational and empirical, related to sentence mood. We will try to situate the phenomenon of sentence mood properly within syntax, semantics, and pragmatics, and we will especially try to understand the relation between sentence mood and the concepts of clause type and force. Then we will survey some work within the two main theoretical approaches to sentence mood, those embedded within speech act theory (Section 3.2) and the dynamic approach to meaning (Section 3.3). These surveys form the core of the chapter, as it is there that I will explain and evaluate some of the important recent research on particular sentence moods. Finally, in Section 3.4 I will take the discussion into a broader perspective by asking what insights each major theory can offer concerning the overall systems of clause types and sentence mood in natural language. As we will see, although linguists have yet to develop a grand theory of sentence mood which explains all relevant syntactic, semantic, pragmatic, and typological facts, the recent literature does offer a great many insights that should be maintained and developed as the field works towards such a theory.

3.1 Sentence mood, clause type, and sentential force

The term "mood" is not always employed in the same way in discussions of the relation between the syntactic/semantic forms of sentences and their conversational functions. It is sometimes used as a semantic or pragmatic category, for example by Wilson and Sperber (1988). In this sense, we often hear of some particular grammatical feature being a "mood-indicator" or "mood-indicating device," and in such cases it is not clear whether mood itself is understood to be a semantic category or an abstract grammatical category which groups together sentences which do not share any specific element in common. "Mood" is also used

Mood. First edition. Paul Portner.
© Paul Portner 2018. First published 2018 by Oxford University Press.

to pick out a particular paradigm of linguistic form; this use is more in parallel with that of "verbal mood," and because a broad goal of this book is to better understand how different notions of mood are related, we will use it in this way here. This usage fits with the working definition of mood from Chapter 1, Section 1.1.2: Mood is an aspect of linguistic form which indicates how a proposition is used in the expression of modal meaning. Building on this, I would like to define sentence mood as follows:

(1)   SENTENCE MOOD is an aspect of linguistic form conventionally linked to the fundamental conversational functions within semantic/pragmatic theory.

Sometimes we will use the term "sentence mood" in a slightly sloppy way to refer to a set of sentences which share the same sentence mood in the sense of (1).

The aspects of linguistic form which define sentence mood could be as simple as a single piece of morphology or as complex as a combination of several constructional patterns of lexical choice and word order. This definition leaves open several crucial matters at the very foundation of the concept of sentence mood:

1. It does not say what "the fundamental conversational functions" are. We cannot decide in advance what those conversational functions are, as different theories will identify them differently. These functions are given a label, "sentential forces," just below.
2. It leaves open how to identify the linguistic forms which get linked to the functions; different approaches to morphology and syntax can motivate different ideas about sentence mood; conversely, different assumptions about how to classify conversational functions into fundamental classes can motivate different models of morphology and syntax.
3. It presupposes that there is a set of linguistic forms conventionally linked to these functions, but it leaves open how this conventional link between form and function is established.[1] We will consider several approaches to the issue of how this form–function relation is established in Section 3.1.3.

As we will see, different theories settle these points in different ways.

It will also be helpful to define two other terms, CLAUSE TYPE and SENTENTIAL FORCE.

(2)   CLAUSE TYPES are grammatically defined classes of sentences which correspond closely with sentence moods.

---

[1] Note that the use of the term "conventional" is not meant to imply that the relation is a matter of social convention. Davidson (1979) and Harnish (1994), among others, critique the idea that sentence mood is a matter of convention. It could be a matter of literal meaning produced by innate brain circuits. Nor does it imply that any social convention which associates a form with a function would count as a sentence mood; a code which uses *Are you thirsty?* to mean 'I am going outside to smoke a cigarette' does not establish a new sentence mood.

The difference between the concepts of clause type and sentence mood is that the former are primarily identified in terms of grammatical form, while the latter are primarily identified in terms of meaning. Traditional grammatical descriptions make use of such clause types as declarative, interrogative, and imperative. In many languages, sets of sentences can be associated with these types strictly in terms of their morphosyntactic properties; for example, the clause types of Korean can be defined in terms of sets of sentence-final particles, while the clause types of English can be defined in terms of matters like the form of the verb, the position of the verb, the presence or absence of wh-phrases in clause-initial position, and the choice of complementizers. Such differences are thought of as central matters for syntactic theory to explain.

A good example of the difference between sentence mood and clause type concerns subordinate clauses. The embedded clause in (3) is an interrogative in terms of its clause type, but may not have a sentence mood at all, since it does not perform the function of asking a question.[2]

(3)   Everybody knows **who won the race**.

It can be confusing that clause types often go by the same names as the sentence moods, including the names 'declarative,' 'interrogative,' and 'imperative.' Many discussions use the term SENTENCE TYPES to think about the systems that I am describing as clause types and sentence moods (e.g. Sadock and Zwicky 1985; Reis 1999). The notion of sentence type has the syntactic orientation of clause type but it is typically not applied to subordinate clauses on the grounds that they do not have an independent conversational function. In a terminology like this, 'sentence type' is very similar to 'sentence mood' as used here; specifically, a sentence type is a set of sentences of the same clause type which share the same sentence mood.

Next we define the concept of sentential force:

(4)   SENTENTIAL FORCES are the fundamental conversational functions with which sentence moods are associated.

There are many different views on the nature of sentential forces. They might be many and specific or few and general. According to the literal meaning hypothesis (as discussed in Section 1.4.2), the sentential forces are the illocutionary forces of classical speech act theory. According to dynamic semantics and pragmatics, there might be as few as two or three sentential forces (distinct ones for declarative, interrogative, and possibly also imperative sentences; see Section 1.4.1). The version of speech act theory which invokes the notion of illocutionary point puts the number at five (Searle 1975b; Searle and Vanderveken 1985; Vanderveken 1990; see Sections 1.4.2 and 3.2.2). In our reading of some scholars, we will have to determine

---

[2] One could propose that the embedded clause in (3) is associated with the function of asking, but that the association does not lead to its actually asking a question in this case. (Using the terminology about to be introduced we might say that it has the sentential force of asking which is somehow neutralized.) But the very fact that we can ask whether it has a sentence mood, while still being clear that it is an interrogative, shows the difference between the two concepts.

TABLE 3.1   Terminology for sentence moods

	Our terms	Alternative terminology
Forms associated with functions	sentence mood	sentence type
Those functions	sentential force	mood (or sentence mood)
Related clauses containing those forms	clause type	(none)

the best way to align their understanding of conversational function with our concept of sentential force.[3]

Our notion of sentential force covers the semantic use of the term "mood" in theories which might say that clause type is a "mood-indicating device." Table 3.1 lays out correspondences between the terminology used in this book and other ways scholars talk about similar categories. Though the alternative terms can be used in a clear and precise way, I believe it is important to have a name for the aspects of form which are linked to fundamental conversational functions (= the sentence moods) as distinct from the syntactically defined types which incorporate those aspects of form (= clause types). This allows us to talk, for instance, about the subordinate clause in (3) being of the interrogative clause type and having many of the grammatical features which comprise the interrogative sentence mood; from such a vantage point, we can then ask in a clear way how it is different from root examples of the same clause type and why these differences lead to it not having a sentential force.

Theories of sentence mood focus on a number of basic questions:

1. What grammatical properties constitute sentence moods, and how do they relate to the syntax of clause types?
2. What are sentential forces?
3. How are sentential forces linked to sentence moods?

We will investigate how they are answered by approaches based on speech act theory in Section 3.2 and by theories which follow the dynamic approach in Section 3.3. In the remainder of this section, we will discuss some important background concerning clause types, sentential forces, and sentence mood. First we will describe the basic properties of clause type systems (Section 3.1.1), then review the intuitive functions of the most widely discussed sentential forces (Section 3.1.2), and finally categorize at a general level the approaches to sentence mood within syntax (Section 3.1.3).

3.1.1 Clause types as grammatical categories

The concepts of clause type and sentence type are used to take a syntactic, or more generally a structural, approach to understanding the relation between grammar

---

[3] This determination is sometimes difficult. For example, Gazdar (1981) and Kaufmann (2012) assume an austere version of dynamic pragmatics while also accepting the notion of illocutionary force from classical speech act theory. See Section 3.2.3 for discussion.

and sentential force. As I use the terms, clause types are categories defined properly within syntax which are observed to have a close relation to sentential forces, but they are distinct from sentence moods because they do not have to align precisely with sentential forces. We have already seen in the opening part of this section that an embedded interrogative clause may be seen as lacking sentence mood, even though it is a member of the interrogative clause type. Similarly, there is a case to be made that sentence moods sometimes do not have simple definitions in terms of syntactic properties, even if we restrict ourselves to unembedded clauses. For example, Zanuttini and Portner (2003) argue that there is no natural syntactic property which groups together the following three subtypes of exclamatives in Paduan (data from Zanuttini and Portner 2003):

(5)   a. *Che   roba   che   l   magna! (Paduan)*
         what stuff that he eat
         'The things he eats!'

      b. *Quanto   è alto!*
         how much is tall
         'How tall s/he is!'

      c. *No   ga-lo   magnà tuto!*
         NEG has-SG.CL eaten   everything
         'He ate everything!'

The wh-phrase *che roba* in (5a) cannot occur in interrogatives, and it occupies a different position in the clausal structure than the *quanto* in (5b), which can occur in an interrogative. The exclamative in (5c) does not seem to have a wh-phrase at all, and its verb is in a higher position than the subjects of (5a–b). If Portner and Zanuttini are correct that sentences showing exclamative sentence mood in Paduan do not share any single syntactic property, it might still be possible to group them into a single clause type with a disjunctive definition which references the two types of wh-phrase and the position of the verb, but this ersatz clause type would not be a natural object for syntactic analysis. Nevertheless, because they all share the same sentential force, they would constitute a natural sentence mood, and be a proper subject for study at the syntax/semantics/pragmatics interface.

The traditional conception of sentence types.   Sentence types are syntactically defined classes of sentences which are of interest because they are associated in a regular way with specific conversational functions. For example, (5a) can be seen as a representative of a sentence type defined by the association between the pattern of structure in (6a) and the function (6b):

(6)   a. Special wh-phrase in initial position (*che*+N), followed by the comple-
         mentizer *che*; verb in post-subject position
      b. Exclamation about a property of an object or group of objects

The concept of sentence type is most often used in linguistics research where the primary goal is to provide systematic descriptions of the variety of sentences in a language and to identify the specific conversational functions which a given sentence could be associated with. The descriptions are typically pattern-oriented, based on surface properties, and non-generative. Research of this kind represents what I call the "traditional conception of sentence types."

We can get a sense of the range of research which builds on the traditional conception of sentence types by considering two important (and otherwise very different) works: Sadock and Zwicky (1985) and Altmann (1987).[4] Sadock and Zwicky define the concept of sentence types with the goal of creating a single conceptual framework which can be applied across a range of typologically different languages. Their work makes a contribution by emphasizing the fact that sentence types form a CLOSED SYSTEM, in the following sense:

(1) "The sentence types of a language form a *system*, in at least two senses:
   (a) there are sets of corresponding sentences, the members of which differ only in belonging to different types, and . . .
   (b) the types are mutually exclusive, no sentence being simultaneously of two different types."
(2) "Sentence types show certain *characteristic forms* across languages."

This definition of a system of sentence types implies that certain syntax–pragmatics correspondences should not be understood as sentence types. For example, the cleft structure, while it is syntactically definable and has a characteristic discourse function, is not a sentence type because it cross-cuts the classes of declaratives and interrogatives.

In a comprehensive study of sentence types in German, Altmann (1987) gives a fine-grained and precise description of many specific pairings between grammatical patterns and conversational use. His work shows how much valuable knowledge about a language's grammar can be uncovered and systematized using the traditional concept of sentence type. But as shown by Reis (1999), his work also makes apparent the conception's weaknesses. As Reis argues, because sentence types are understood as specific pairings of form and function, it forces us to subdivide some of the most intuitively important categories. For example, the three kinds of exclamatives seen in (5) would not count as a sentence type, beause they do not share a single grammatical form. Similarly, Reis argues that Altmann's theory does not allow for a single broad category of imperative sentences in German. In addition, Reis highlights the tendency of work which uses the concept of sentence types to assume a view of grammatical description based on surface patterns. These "form types" (as Reis calls them) are defined as collective patterns, with no individual compositional contribution made by the component features. For example, when we talk about the form type (6a) and its function (6b), we do not assign any particular significance to the presence of *che+N* or the position of the verb.

These two problems for the traditional conception of sentence types are quite critical, and they lead me to avoid using the term in this work. However, it is likely

---

[4] Other useful discussions are found in Palmer (2001), Allan (2006), and König and Siemund (2007).

that they are really due not to the concept of sentence types itself, but rather to the simple pattern-based method of defining form types. As we will see in Section 3.1.3, a more flexible pattern-based syntactic theory like Construction Grammar may be able to solve these problems. But even if this is the case, the concept of sentence types still suffers from the fact that it does not allow us to separate clearly when we are talking about syntactic categories and when we are talking about semantic/pragmatic categories. It forces us to treat all syntactic categories as semantic categories, and vice versa, and so it may be misleading in cases when they do not align in a simple way.

Basic properties of clause type systems.   Although it is important to distinguish the concepts of sentence mood and clause type, it is impossible to develop a theory of sentence moods which does not pay close attention to the syntax of individual clause types and to the structure of clause type systems. By studying the syntax of a clause type or a set of clause types whose sentences all have the same sentence mood, we learn a great deal about semantics and ultimately the discourse function of that sentence mood. For example, it is obvious that clauses introduced by wh-words can have interrogative or exclamative sentence mood, but not declarative sentence mood. In order to explain this fact, we will need to understand the kinds of contribution which wh-words can make to the meaning of a clause and the relation between those meanings and sentential force.

In the remainder of this section, I will outline some of the most important properties of clause type systems. Our perspective here will be that of identifying some important properties of clause type systems as a whole, rather than studying each clause type in detail. We will discuss individual clause types in Sections 3.2–3.3, as part of a detailed survey of semantic theories of individual sentence moods. We will then return to a system-oriented view in Section 3.4.

Basic and minor clause types.   Linguists often assume that the declarative, interrogative, and imperative clause types can be recognized in all languages, and that this is so because the sentential forces which these types realize are somehow fundamental to the communicative function of human language. Sadock and Zwicky (1985) refer to these three as the basic types in recognition of both their ubiquity and function. In addition, linguists commonly recognize minor types, including exclamatives, optatives, and prohibitives.

Various traditions within linguistics come with different, and often unexamined, assumptions concerning the right way to identify types and describe the relations among them. We can understand the issues involved by examining some of the types which may be related to imperatives: prohibitives, hortatives/exhortatives, promissives, jussives, and optatives.

Many linguists would describe the English examples in (7a) and (7b) as positive and negative imperatives, respectively:

(7)   a. Open the window!
      b. Don't open the window!

Calling both of these "imperative" implies that they are members of a single type, differing only in the presence or absence of sentential negation. In contrast, in her discussion of realis marking in Teiwa, Klamer (2012) treats the sentences in (8) as exemplifying two different types. She calls (8a) an imperative, but (8b) a PROHIBITIVE (her (2b), (19)).

(8)   a. *yo, iqaan ba   tewar*
          yes dark SEQ walk
          'Yes [it's getting] dark so go!'
       b. *wat   wrer gaxai!*
          coconut climb do.not
          'Don't climb the coconut [tree]!'

Klamer's perspective on (8b) is motivated by the fact that prohibitives are marked by the negative verb *gaxai* rather than a general-purpose negative marker. Van der Auwera and Devos (2012) label the English (7b) a prohibitive, and while they are clear that this term is equivalent to "negative imperative," they are not explicit whether positive imperatives and prohibitives are separate types, with imperative a higher-level grouping of similar types, or whether the more general imperative is the sentence type, with positive and negative imperatives being variants that do not count as types on their own.

In this way, discussions of clause types (and sentence types) are not often particularly explicit on how basic and minor types relate to one another within the overall system of types. They could be members of the same type or members of distinct (but pragmatically similar) types. The distinction matters as we try to analyze the sentence moods, because (for example) if one decides to treat prohibitives as a separate type, there will be the possibility—and in practice, the tendency—to treat their function, "prohibition," as a sentential force distinct from that of imperatives. Thus, in the context of developing and evaluating theories of sentence mood, the decision about classification will have consequences for our theories of semantics and pragmatics.

Similar points can be made about the other clause types related to imperatives. EXHORTATIVES and PROMISSIVES are illustrated with data from Korean in (9), from Zanuttini et al. (2012, (2)):

(9)   a. *Cemsim-ul sa-la.*   *(imperative)*
          lunch-ACC buy-IMP
          'Buy lunch!'

       b. *Cemsim-ul sa-ma.*   *(promissive)*
          lunch-ACC buy-PRM
          'I will buy lunch.'

       c. *Cemsim-ul sa-ca.*   *(exhortative)*
          lunch-ACC buy-EXH
          'Let's buy lunch.'

The imperative type is marked in this example by the sentence-final particle -*la*. The promissive type, marked by -*ma*, is used to make a promise; the exhortative, marked by *-ca*, is used to urge a joint action by the speaker and addressee. The differences between telling someone to do something, promising to do it, and urging to do it together might suggest that these three comprise distinct clause types. However, according to Portner (2004) and Zanuttini et al. (2012), these three types actually share a common function: they are all used to create a commitment on the part of one or more discourse participants to take a certain action. For this reason they can be thought of as members of a broader class, JUSSIVES (e.g. Pak et al. 2008a,b). The idea that they belong to a common, general type implies that they differ only in grammatical features not directly tied to sentential force. (For Pak et al., this feature is grammatical person.[5])

OPTATIVE sentences like (10) are used to express a wish of the speaker (from Grosz 2014, (2)):

(10)   If I'd only listened to my parents!

As with promissives and exhortatives, the status of optatives as a clause type is not clear. The normal use of an optative implies that the speaker prefers one alternative to another, and in this way it is similar to an imperative. On this basis it is reasonable to think of some optatives as third person imperatives (or third person members of a jussive type including imperatives), as suggested by König and Siemund (2007). Grosz (2011, 2014), however, relates optatives to exclamatives rather than imperatives and Biezma (2011) treats them as conditional antecedents with elided (declarative) consequents; thus, it remains unclear whether optatives and imperatives share any property as fundamental as their sentential force.

The other basic clause types have subtypes as well. Among interrogatives, we can distinguish yes/no (or polar), information (or wh-), alternative, biased, confirmative, echo, and rhetorical interrogatives. There is little question that all of these show the same interrogative clause type. On our view here, they belong to a common clause type because they can be described as forming a class in syntactic terms which is, as a whole, associated with one sentential force. By these criteria, certain rhetorical questions might have a kind of split status: interrogative in clause type but not sentence mood. For example, an utterance of (11) is typically associated with the suggestion that no answer exists (Obenauer 2004, (37)):

(11)   Who can you trust, nowadays?

On the assumption that (11) does not have the sentential force of asking, it would not have the interrogative sentence mood. Nevertheless, it would be a member of the interrogative clause type. The interrogative clause type, in other words, could not be seen as an unambiguous exponent of interrogative sentence mood, though

---

[5] Note that there is an important distinction to be made between promissives and first person imperatives (cf. Aikhenvald 2010; König and Siemund 2007), in that promissives lead to the speaker's commitment to do something, while first person imperatives aim to get the addressee to allow or make the speaker to do something.

we would of course want to explain why interrogative clause type almost always leads to the sentential force of asking a question.[6]

Linguists do not normally talk about subtypes of declarative clauses from the perspective of sentence mood or clause type. They are used to considering differences in function among declaratives as arising from independent factors like negation, information structure, modality, and evidentiality. Sadock and Zwicky (1985, p. 170) briefly mention the non-affirmative mode of Blackfoot as likely representing a separate dubitative sentence type which is used both for expressing uncertainty and asking yes/no questions. They treat it as a type separate from that of other declarative-like sentences, the affirmative.

Gunlogson (2001) discusses the examples in (12a–b), distinguished by rising vs. falling intonation, as members of the declarative clause type (her (1)–(2)):[7]

(12)   a. It's raining?
       b. It's raining.
       c. Is it raining?

In her analysis, clause type and intonation contribute compositionally to the discourse function of the sentence, and so we cannot say whether (12a–b) have the same sentence mood without determining which levels of function count as fundamental for the purposes of identifying sentential force. It is possible to understand her as suggesting that (12a) and (12b) each have two sentence moods: (12a) would have the declarative sentence mood (marked by clause type) and "addressee-oriented" sentence mood (marked by rising intonation); (12b) would have the declarative sentence mood and the "speaker-oriented" sentence mood (marked by falling intonation). Such a classification would be quite novel, and though we cannot confidently attribute this perspective to Gunlogson herself, it is worthwhile to bring it out as an innovative possibility. We will discuss Gunlogson's ideas in more detail in Section 3.3.1.

There is one minor clause type with a fairly uncertain status, exclamatives.

(13)   a. What a nice guy he is!
       b. How very tall you are!
       c. He is such a nice guy!
       d. You are so very tall!

Unlike the other minor types discussed above, the sentential force of exclamatives is not in any obvious way related to that of a major type. As a result, exclamatives are normally considered as forming their own type. In terms of syntax, they show obvious connections to interrogatives (and sometimes declaratives) across languages. For example, (13a–b) are similar to interrogatives in including

---

[6] It is also possible that rhetorical questions do have the sentential force of asking (which is somehow neutralized), and so have interrogative sentence mood. The interpretation of their status given in the text is raised at this point only for illustration.

[7] Gunlogson uses the term "sentence type," but her usage is close enough to our "clause type."

a wh-movement structure (also (5a–b) above). In terms of semantics, some have argued that exclamatives have a type of meaning closely related to that of in-terrogatives as well, with the difference between interrogatives and exclamatives residing in pragmatic factors (Zanuttini and Portner 2003). Of course, there are syntactic differences as well, such as the particular forms of the wh-phrases in (13a) and (5a). The uncertain status of exclamatives deepens further if one also considers the sentence in (13c) to be an exclamative; the only visible aspect of syntax which indicates that this sentence is exclamative is the correspondence between *what an X* and *such an X*. Overall, exclamatives seem to represent a case where a clearly distinct sentential force goes along with a messy characterization in terms of clause type. This makes the type quite important for evaluating theories of sentence mood at the syntax/semantics interface.

Marking of clause types.   In discussions of clause type, sentence type, and sen-tence mood, linguists often talk about some grammatical element or combination of grammatical features as "marking" a sentence as belonging to a particular category. The idea behind this way of speaking seems to be that the range of possible types (or moods) is known in advance, and the task of the speaker is to indicate—and the task of the hearer to determine—the type of each sentence uttered. As we have seen, I think this way of thinking runs together a grammatical issue, what the forms of the clause types are, with an interface issue, how the relationship is established between sentences with a particular sentence mood and their sentential force. Still, setting aside the nature of the relation between clause type and sentence mood for discussion later (Section 3.1.3), it is useful to describe some patterns of clausal syntax associated with sentence mood. In other words, we will review the most common ways in which clause types are marked across languages.

I would like to make a distinction between clause types which are explicitly marked (in a particular language) and ones which are inexplicitly marked. In not very precise terms, we can say that a clause type is explicitly marked when there is a grammatical feature or set of features which unambiguously identifies the type. It is inexplicitly marked when there is no such form. As an example, we can point to the uses of *how* and *how very* seen in (14)–(15). Clauses of the form (14a) cannot be anything but an exclamative, as we see in their root and embedded occurrences in (14b)–(14d). *How very* explicitly marks an English clause as exclamative. In contrast, we might think of the form in (15a) as inexplicitly marked, since it can serve as an exclamative or as an embedded interrogative.

(14)   a.   how very tall she is
       b.   How very tall she is!
       c.   I'm amazed how very tall she is.
       d.   *I wonder how very tall she is.

(15)   a.   how tall she is
       b.   How tall she is!
       c.   I'm amazed how tall she is.
       d.   I wonder how tall she is.

The contrast between explicit and inexplicit marking is of course theory-bound, since one might argue that (15a) is structurally ambiguous and that the type is always explicitly marked (though the marking may be covert, in the sense of not being reflected in the phonological output). Cheng (1991), for example, proposes the Clause Typing Hypothesis, which states that all clauses must be syntactically typed.[8] Be that as it may, we need the concept of inexplicit marking so as to be able to talk about cases where there is an issue of whether the types are marked explicitly or not.

Clause types can be explicitly marked by grammatical structure, by the morphological form of the verb, and by independent particles. I will briefly illustrate each of these possibilities. When we say that clause type can be marked by grammatical structure, this is meant to encompass differences in word order, the absence of elements which are normally obligatory, or the presence of elements which are normally absent. For example, English interrogatives require either the fronting of the auxiliary (in most root questions) or an interrogative word of some sort. In (16a) the auxiliary is at a position before the subject; in the subordinate clause of (16b) there is a wh-word in clause-initial position, and in the subordinate clause of (16c) there is an interrogative complementizer:

(16)   a. Is it raining?
       b. I wonder who that is.
       c. I wonder if/whether it is raining.

Looking back at (15a), it is reasonable to say that, as an interrogative, its type is marked by the presence of a wh-word, in the same way as (16b). But of course, given the ambiguity of (15a), this would be a case of inexplicit marking. In order to maintain the idea that all clause marking is explicit, one would have to claim that the wh-element does not mark the type on its own; rather it would be marked by some other grammatical property (such as a particular syntactic structure or abstract element), possibly in combination with the wh-element. It is for reasons like this that most linguists who aim to develop a syntactic and semantic theory of clause types would rather think of this case as one where the type is marked by grammatical structure, and would call the wh-word a "marker" only in an informal sense.

Clause type can be marked by the morphological form of the verb in various ways. The verb may have a special affix, as in the Panyjima imperative (Dench 1991, cited in Aikhenvald 2010):

(17)   *minyma panti-ma*
       still   sit-IMP
       'Sit still!'

---

[8] In fact, her claim is stronger than merely that all clauses are explicitly marked. The hypothesis states that all clauses are marked by S-structure, implying that marking is always accomplished by syntactic means.

The verb might employ a particular verbal mood form. Here the terminology gets a little bit tricky. In (18a), we see that a basic imperative in Italian uses a reduced form of the verb (compared to root declaratives and interrogatives). This canonical form is used when the subject is second person singular familiar and the clause is non-negative. In other cases, the verb takes a different form. When negative, it is the infinitive; when the subject is plural, it is indicative; and when the subject refers to an addressee towards whom the speaker marks politeness, it is subjunctive.

(18)   a. *Siediti!*
          Sit.IMP-you
          'Sit!'
       b. *Non sedersi!*
          NEG sit.INF-self
          'Don't sit!'
       c. *Sedetevi!*
          sit.INDIC-you.PL
          'Sit!' (plural)
       d. *Si   sieda!*
          self sit.SUBJ
          'Have a seat!' (polite)

Once again, the verb forms in (18b)–(18d) are not in themselves explicit markers; infinitive, indicative, and subjunctive verbs have other uses. If we believe in explicit marking of clause type, the marker must be a feature of the abstract syntactic representation. In many cases, there is good evidence that they do have a distinct syntax from other uses of infinitives and subjunctives. For example, the verb precedes the object clitic in (18b) and (18c), whereas infinitives and indicatives would normally follow the clitic. But in (18d), there is no direct evidence for a syntax distinct from other subjunctives. If we wish to maintain the idea that (18d) is explicitly marked as an imperative, we would need to seek indirect arguments or just take it on faith. The alternatives are to consider it to be inexplicitly marked or to decline to categorize it as imperative clause type at all.

   As mentioned above, Korean marks clause types through the use of sentence-final particles. The following illustrate the simplest forms of the declarative, interrogative, and imperative types (from Pak 2008).

(19)   a. *Cemsim-ul mek-ess-ta*
          lunch-ACC eat-PAST-DECL
          'I ate lunch.'
       b. *Cemsim-ul mek-ess-ni*
          lunch-ACC eat-PAST-INT
          'Did you eat lunch?'
       c. *Cemsim-ul mek-e-la*
          lunch-ACC eat-IMP
          'Eat lunch!'

The particles in (19) are unambiguous and occur in both root and embedded clauses. They can be seen as fully explicit markers of clause type. But other sentence-final particles which express gradations of formality and speech style are not in themselves explicit markers of clause type. For example, the marker of intimate style *-e* is compatible with both declarative and interrogative functions in root clauses.

(20)   *Cemsim-ul mek-ess-e*
      lunch-ACC eat-PAST-INTIMATE
      'I ate lunch.'/'Did you eat lunch?'

We might categorize *-e* as an inexplicit marker of clause type, or we might assume there are abstract (explicit) markers of type which determine whether (20) is declarative or interrogative.

Korean illustrates another point which is important when describing how languages mark their clause types. Although across languages clause types are marked in a variety of ways, there are patterns to the combinations of ways which a particular language will employ. For example, Korean is consistent in using the sentence-final particles to mark type; it does not use particles for some types and word order for others. This fact suggests that the differences among types can be condensed into the choice of a single morpheme. But in contrast, many languages will use grammatical properties such as word order to mark the distinction between declaratives and interrogatives, but a form of the verb (perhaps together with word order, as in Italian (18a)) for imperatives. This fact suggests that declaratives and interrogatives share something which separates them from imperatives. Then again, in many languages, imperatives (at least in specific cases) have a form more similar to declaratives than to interrogatives (for example, Italian polite imperatives, (18d)), suggesting that interrogatives have some property which distinguishes them from imperatives and declaratives. Furthermore, as mentioned above, minor types tend to be more closely allied with some basic types than others. A theory of clause types should seek to explain not only how individual types are marked within and across languages, but also what patterns of marking are used for entire clause type systems.

Next we turn to some more cases in which the type of a clause might be seen as inexplicitly marked. Scholars who are pursuing a syntactic or semantic analysis of clause types or sentence types are generally unwilling to treat any case as truly involving the inexplicit marking of the type. Rather, they propose some covert explicit marking. A relatively simple case for discussion purposes concerns the ways of expressing a directive speech act in Hebrew (from Sadock 1974, pp. 92–3):

(21)   a. *šev*
         sit.2M.SG
         'Sit!'

      b. *tišev*
         FUT-sit.2M.SG
         'Sit!' or 'You will sit.'

The form in (21a) can only be used with an imperative-type meaning, but (21b) is a more common way to issue a directive and is the normal future declarative form as well. Based on several factors, Sadock argues that the directive meaning is not pragmatically derived, but rather that the sentence has two distinct Logical Forms (realized within the Generative Semantics framework at deep structure).

While linguists are often quite willing to propose a covert explicit marking of clause type in cases where there is no marking visible on the surface, they are sometimes puzzled by cases in which a clause type seems to be marked in a descriptive sense, but not in a way which makes sense according to the syntactic or semantic theory being developed. We can describe the situation by saying that the type is indicated or determined, but not necessarily "marked."

One relatively well-studied case where type is indicated but maybe not marked involves sentences with declarative word order but rising interrogative intonation, as in (12). Clearly (12c) is an interrogative and (12b) is a declarative. But what about (12a), with the word order of (12b), the intonation of (12c), and a discourse function which seeks a response from the addressee? Given its function, it is very natural to classify (12a) as an interrogative, and in that case, the only visible marking of its interrogative status is the intonation. This fact leads us to the following possibilities:

1. Sentences like (12a) are explicitly marked as interrogatives by rising intonation.
2. Sentences like (12a) are explicitly marked as interrogatives by some hidden grammatical structure which correlates with rising intonation.
3. Sentences like (12a) are inexplicitly marked as interrogatives; rising intonation is merely a clue to their type.
4. Sentences like (12a) are explicitly marked as declaratives by their word order. Their function, which involves seeking a response from the addressee, is atypical for declaratives. We account for this atypicality by saying one of the following things:
   (a) The sentence has the clause type of declarative, but the sentence mood of interrogative.
   (b) The sentence has both the clause type and sentence mood of declarative, and its function is compatible with declarative sentence mood.

Option 1 requires a framework of grammatical analysis in which intonation, morphology, and syntax all contribute to defining grammatical categories like clause type. Option 2 requires some abstract syntax and a grammatical framework in which syntax can determine intonation. Option 3 requires that we give up on thinking of clause types as grammatical categories which can be defined in terms of more primitive grammatical properties. And option 4 requires us to think more carefully about the way in which clause types are associated with conversational functions.

Gunlogson (2001) in fact argues for option 4. While (12a) seeks a response, it is biased towards the response being "yes, it's raining." Building on this point, Gunlogson argues that the declarative clause type conveys a commitment towards the propositional content of the clause (here, that it's raining). The difference between falling and rising intonation is that, in the former cases, the speaker indicates her own commitment, while in the latter, she indicates the addressee's commitment.

As pointed out earlier in this section, Gunlogson's analysis raises some difficult questions for our overall understanding of clause types. The role she assigns to rising and falling intonation is so central to the discourse model that it is difficult to see the traditional declarative/interrogative opposition as more relevant to sentence mood than the opposition between rising and falling intonation. This may mean, on the one hand, that clause type systems are more complex than we traditionally assume, or, on the other, that we have failed to identify the fundamental contribution of the declarative clause type. As we will see in Section 3.3.1, I believe the latter to be the case; Gunlogson's analysis of rising and falling intonation is essential, but more must be added to her analysis of declarative type in order to give a proper account of the sentential forces of these examples.

3.1.2 Sentential forces as pragmatic categories

The sentential forces are the fundamental conversational functions within semantic/pragmatic theory. As such, we cannot identify them *a priori*, but rather must determine what they are through empirical investigation and a scientific process of theory-building. Within linguistics and philosophy, there are two main theoretical approaches to conversational function which have served as a basis for thinking about sentence mood: speech act theory and the dynamic approach to meaning. Our goal in this subsection is to understand the range of sentential forces which scholars assume as the basis for the analysis of sentence mood and how different theoretical perspectives influence their understanding of which conversational functions count as sentential forces.

Within speech act theory, the most obvious set of functions to stand in the role of sentential forces are the illocutionary forces. We have seen in Section 1.4.2 that the existence of indirect speech acts leads to serious problems for the simple idea that sentence moods can be defined in terms of illocutionary force and that one would at least have to say that sentential forces are the illocutionary forces conventionally associated with utterances of a sentence. In other words, we would identify sentential force with the illocutionary force of a sentence used in a direct speech act. If one adopts such an approach, one is committed to the claim that the distinction between direct and indirect speech acts (in particular, the distinction between conventional and inferred illocutionary forces) makes sense within the overall understanding of communication within speech act theory.

Let us assume that one can identify direct speech acts and, based on this, define the conventionally determined illocutionary forces. Even so, since its earliest stages speech act theory has identified the illocutionary force of an explicit performative with the act-type named by its main verb. For example, (22a) has the force of claiming and (22b) has the force of apologizing:

(22)   a. I claim that Bill will win the election.
        b. I apologize for ruining the stew.

Obviously, the idea that performative verbs identify the illocutionary forces of their sentences leads to a theory with a huge number of illocutionary forces—all of which are conventionally associated with the performative sentences in question. So, we end up with a huge number of sentential forces. But normally we think of (22a)–(22b) as declaratives (both in clause type and sentence mood). This route towards defining sentential force will lead to the conclusion that declarative sentences, at least, are associated with a great number of sentential forces and so either (i) the sentence mood–sentential force relation is not one-to-one, or (ii) the declarative clause type actually participates in a large number of different sentence moods. As discussed in Section 1.4.2, this problem has led many scholars of speech act theory to assume that the sentential force of an explicit performative is not to be identified with the illocutionary force it seems to have; rather, they claim that the examples in (22) have the same sentential force, either assertion (the force of non-performative declaratives) or declaration (the special force of performatives), with the specific, intended illocutionary forces of claiming or apologizing derived from the sentential force.

Setting aside explicit performatives, we also find variation in sentential force within the classes of sentences we normally assume to comprise a sentence mood. For example, (23a) and (23b) are both imperative, but one is naturally thought of as having the same force as an explicit performative with *order*, while the other is naturally thought of as having the same force as an explicit performative with *invite*.

(23)   a. Don't you move!
        b. Please have a glass of wine!

In fact, all clause types can be used in diverse ways paraphrasable by a variety of performative verbs. If we apply speech act theory to the analysis of sentence mood by identifying illocutionary force with sentential force, examples like those in (22)–(23) suggest that all clause types will be associated with very many sentential forces.

There are two main strategies available for developing a concept of sentential force within speech act theory. One of them identifies sentential force with a set of illocutionary forces. According to Harnish (1994), an ILLOCUTIONARY FORCE POTENTIAL is the set of illocutionary forces with which a particular clause type is compatible. For example, sentences of the declarative clause type are compatible with any illocutionary force which presupposes the speaker's belief in the propositional content of the sentence.[9] The set of such forces thus constitutes the illocutionary force potential of each declarative clause, and we can generalize to the thesis that they constitute the illocutionary force potential of the declarative sentence mood.

Another strategy for creating a concept of sentential force within speech act theory is to group the illocutionary forces in terms of some more fundamental

[9] It is difficult to express the relation between clause type and illocutionary force with complete accuracy without laying out the entire framework of Bach and Harnish (1979) and Harnish (1994). See the works cited for details.

property that they share and identify this common property as the sentential force. As discussed in Section 1.4.2, this is the approach of Searle and Vanderveken (1985) and related work. Searle and Vanderveken propose five illocutionary points, the assertive, directive, commissive, declaratory, and expressive points, which combine with other factors including degree of strength and felicity conditions of various sorts to produce fully realized illocutionary forces. Within this framework, sentential forces are naturally identified with the illocutionary points, yielding a much simpler relation between clause types and sentential forces. However, as pointed out in Section 1.4.2, this perspective still does not lead to a theory of sentence mood which treats the basic clause types as fundamental in the way that linguists traditionally assume that they are. Notably, it groups interrogatives (which have the directive point—specifically, they direct the addressee to answer) with imperatives, even though in grammatical terms interrogatives and imperatives each share more with declaratives than they do with each other. It also fails to explain why promissives (with the commissive point) are so much rarer than imperatives (with the closely related directive point) and how exclamatives (which presumably have the expressive point) are related to interrogatives.[10] The version of speech act theory which uses the concept of illocutionary point contains an interesting intuition about the relation between explicit performatives and other declaratives (see Vanderveken 1991, pp. 140–1), namely that the declarative point entails the assertive point and therefore assertion is marked by adding something onto the basic declarative sentence mood, but it is still not clear why declarations across languages are never realized with a distinct clause type of their own.

There have been other attempts to reconcile speech act theory with a linguistically informed notion of sentence mood, including Zaefferer (1986, 2001, 2007) and work which follows the dynamic force hypothesis (Section 1.4.3). We will discuss the analysis of sentence mood in speech act theory in more detail in Section 3.2 below.

In comparison with speech act theory, the dynamic approach appears to be much more readily suited to play a role in the theory of sentence mood. The reason for this advantage is simply that it developed in its earliest stages with the goal of giving an idealized model of conversation which emphasizes those functions, like assertion and asking, which are needed for the analysis of sentence mood (for example, Hamblin 1971); it has downplayed highly specific functions like urging or warning, which have been of interest to speech act theory. It is not clear whether this focus on fewer, more general conversational functions initially resulted from an unarticulated goal of explaining the pragmatics of clause types, or whether it is the result of an intuition which sees as fundamental the same functions which are fortuitously also treated as important by grammar. Eventually, many scholars working within the dynamic approach have taken on the explicit goal of explaining sentential force within a theory of sentence mood which focuses on

---

[10] Perhaps exclamatives are related to interrogatives because the two share certain propositional content conditions. That is, perhaps the interrogative-like structures which we often see with exclamatives are due to the fact that the expressive point needs to operate on a semantic meaning which is similar to that which the directive forces related to asking do.

the basic clause types (e.g. Portner 2004; Roberts 2004; Mastop 2005; Starr 2013). These scholars try to provide a theory of update potentials which treats asserting a proposition, asking a question, and directing someone to do something as simple and fundamental because of the fact that they seem fundamental when we look at clause type systems. The challenge for the dynamic approach is more in explaining the functions of language other than these basic sentential forces. We will return to the analysis of sentence mood within the dynamic approach in Section 3.3.

Although the dynamic approach may provide a more natural basis for developing a theory of sentence mood than classical speech act theory, we should not overstate the importance of this advantage. It is quite possible that a version of speech act theory could be developed which better matches basic illocutionary forces or illocutionary points with clause types. What is not clear, though, is whether the goal of contributing to the theory of sentence mood is sufficiently compelling to justify adjusting the classification of communicative acts embedded in classical speech act theory. It might just be, for example, that there is a truth to the idea that the function of interrogatives and the function of imperatives are closely related which needs to be incorporated into the philosophy of language even at the cost of not participating in the explanation of empirical patterns related to sentence mood.

3.1.3 The syntax/sentence mood interface

Sentence moods are conventionally linked to conversational functions. Either speech act theory or the dynamic approach would lead us to say that the declarative in (24a) is linked to the function of assertion, specifically the speaker asserting that Ben played horn in the concert. Likewise, (24b) is linked to asking (whether he played horn) and (24c) to directing (the addressee to play horn).

(24)   a. Ben played horn in the concert.
        b. Did Ben play horn in the concert?
        c. Ben, play horn in the concert!

Because of obvious associations like these, we conclude that the declarative form of (24a) is linked to the function of asserting, and so on for the other types. Since each of the sentences in (24) can be used for other functions, though, we think of sentence mood in terms of some kind of special, **conventional** association between form and conversational functions. We have called the function with which a sentence mood is associated (in the right, "conventional" way) its sentential force. Scholars of pragmatics have long struggled with the issue of how to define the sentential force of a sentence. Although we have an intuition that (24a), used in its most "basic" way, is used to make an assertion, we have no simple way of identifying basic uses from non-basic uses, and, as pointed out in discussion of the literal force hypothesis in Section 1.4.2, there are sentences which are not so naturally used with the force which we wish to specify as their sentential force.[11] It seems that, if we

---

[11] A good example is Levinson's (1981) *May I remind you that your account is overdue.* Because this sentence accomplishes the reminder, it cannot possibly be asking permission to remind.

believe in sentential force, we must give up on defining the force of a sentence based on its basic use, considered in isolation from the rest of the language. We must, rather, identify the sentential forces of sentences through a more holistic process of theory-building, whereby sentence moods and sentential forces are linked even though some sentences may not as a practical matter ever have the exact function afforded by their sentential force.

Besides the descriptive question of how to identify the sentential force of a particular sentence, linguists have addressed an important issue concerning the syntax/meaning interface: How does the grammatical form of a sentence contribute to its sentential force? That is, starting with a grammatical structure assigned to a sequence of morphemes (and maybe other meaningful components, like intonation), what semantic and pragmatic processes apply and how do they determine, constrain, or influence the sentential force which is eventually associated with the sentence? We find three main types of response to this question in the literature:

1. **The operator approach.** A distinct element in the sentence's representation determines its sentential force. This operator might be identified as a morpheme in the grammatical representation or be treated as a more abstract element of logical form, and it might determine the sentential force either through its semantics or by triggering an interpretive rule at the discourse level. In canonical cases like (24), we can say that the operator marks the clause type and encodes the sentential force.
2. **The construction-based approach.** Sentence moods are patterns of grammatical form, or CONSTRUCTIONS, which are translated into sentential force by (often implicit) interpretive rules. Looking at the standard paradigm (24), we can say that the construction as a whole marks the clause type and encodes the sentential force.
3. **The compositional approach.** Sentential force is not itself encoded in the grammatical form at all; rather, the grammatical form is compositionally interpreted, with the force arising from the combination or interplay of all of the particular meaning-components which are derived through the compositional processes. The analysis might also involve a model of the discourse context and a pragmatic theory of how sentence-meanings interact with that context. From this point of view, sentence moods are epiphenomenal patterns which arise from more fundamental processes.

These three approaches are not entirely distinct. For example, the first can be combined with either of the other two. We might say, in accordance with the second approach, that the construction includes an operator as part of the pattern. Or we might say, in connection with the third, that while there is no force-encoding operator in the grammatical form, there is an operator with a more standard semantics which effectively (though indirectly) determines the sentential force.[12]

---

[12] For example, Rawlins (2013) defines two operators Q and A which have no meaning except to place restrictions on the denotations of their arguments. He assumes that they should also "capture" the speech acts of asking and assertion (presumably by encoding force), but he leaves this out of his

Before going through these approaches, it might be helpful to point out a pair of ideas which are present in many analyses across all three. The first of these is that an important role is played by the position (or set of positions) in which we find complementizers like *that* and *whether* and to which the tensed verb moves in languages which show verb-second order in root declaratives. This position is labeled C in many generative systems and the phrase it heads is CP. We will repeatedly find versions of the intuition that the root CP is associated with a sentential force on the basis of the material in C. The same fundamental intuition can be seen in theories which do not have a single CP, but rather "split" it into a larger functional field (e.g. Rizzi 1997), and in construction-based theories (such as Ginzburg and Sag 2001). The second theme which will emerge is the idea that sentence mood is fundamentally a matter of which syntactic features a clause has. For example, we see features like [+wh] and [imp(erative)]. Since syntactic features have syntactic effects, like driving movement or requiring the insertion of phonological material, these features give rise to the overt patterns which we typically think of as marking clause types. In addition, these syntactic features have meanings which influence or determine the sentential force of the clauses in which they occur. The generalization that the C position is relevant to sentence mood and the strategy of marking clause type through the use of syntactic features go together in a natural way: many analyses place some kind of syntactic feature relevant to sentence mood in C.

The importance of the C position (or more generally, the syntax involving complementizers and verbs at the periphery of the clause) leads to another way in which we may classify approaches to the type/force relation. Do they use the syntax of CP primarily to explain clause type, sentential force, or some other syntactic generalization? We see three approaches. For a given clause type, it is possible that:

1. All members of the clause type share a crucial property of CP syntax. For example, if we assume that clause type is marked by the presence of a particular syntactic feature in C, this approach would claim that all members of the clause type—whether root or embedded—have the feature. We would then probably say that, depending on the syntactic context, the feature can either determine a sentential force or contribute to the semantic processes involved in subordination.

2. Only members of the clause type with independent force share the crucial property of CP syntax. Again, on the assumption that this property is the presence of a specific feature in C, this way of thinking would say that members of that clause type which lack force (for example, complement clauses) lack the feature. The clause type itself would then need to be defined by other syntactic properties.

3. Members of the clause type with independent force, as well as sentences lacking independent force but with a CP-level syntax like those which do,

analysis because it is not crucial to the points he wants to make. However, within the compositional approach, an operator which restricts the sentence's compositional semantic value could be sufficient to determine its sentential force.

have the crucial property. In terms of syntactic features, we would say that a specific feature in C is shared by all root clauses with independent force as well as some subordinate, non-force-bearing clauses.

A prime empirical domain for observing these three approaches concerns Germanic V2 declarative clauses. For the most part, root declarative clauses have the tensed verb in C, while embedded declarative clauses have the verb in a lower position. However, it has long been noted that certain subordinate clauses allow the verb in C. We exemplify this with Swedish examples based on Wechsler (1991).

(25) a. *Hon* **köpte** *inte en ny bil idag.* (Swedish)
      she bought not a new car today

    b. *Johan vet att [hon inte* **köpte** *en ny bil].*
      John knows that she not bought a new car

    c. *Hugo påstod att [hon* **köpte** *inte en ny bil].*
      Hugo claimed that she bought not a new car

In these examples, the verb is understood to be in C when it precedes the negation *inte*. A theory focused on clause-typing would place a declarative feature in C in (25a–c), and the feature would mark clause type. A theory focused on force would have the feature in C for (25a) only, and it would be understood to encode or otherwise determine force. And one which aims to explain the behavior of the tensed verb would have it in C for (25a,c) but not (25b); in this case, the feature would then be seen as representing something which root sentences and sentences embedded under 'claim' have in common, but which is not shared by sentences embedded under 'know.'

The operator approach.   We can begin this discussion with the concept of a force-indicating operator. The idea that something like force is represented via a primitive operator has its origins at least as far back as Frege's judgment stroke, long before linguistic theory had advanced to a point which would allow syntacticians and semanticists to formulate precise theories of sentence mood. Building on a long-standing tradition,[13] Stenius (1967) gives a very influential version of the idea at just about the point in time when speech act theory was becoming the dominant perspective on how linguistic meaning is used for communication. According to Stenius, the logical form of a sentence is $M(p)$, with a MODAL ELEMENT M as the force indicator and SENTENCE RADICAL (p) expressing the descriptive content.[14] Stenius specifically identifies three force indicators, I, O, and $?$, for the indicative, imperative, and interrogative mood, respectively. Each is associated with specific

---

[13] See Huntley (1980) for a brief summary, including an interesting discussion of Frege's ambiguous position. Dudman (1970, 1972) also provides helpful background on Frege.

[14] Note that the parentheses are part of the notation for the sentence radical. Stenius actually says that M signifies the sentence's mood, but this clashes with our terminology. We would say it is the mood (in the logical language) and therefore signifies the sentential force.

rules which determine how the descriptive content can be used in a conversation. (Stenius's broadly Wittgensteinian ideas cannot be readily classified within either speech act theory or the dynamic approach.) Thus, Stenius builds into his proposal the suggestion that the conversational functions which he discusses should be understood as associated with the major clause types. In this way, I think, he implies that they are in fact the most fundamental conversational functions, that is sentential forces. What he does not do, though, is address the interface question of how a logical form with I, O, or $?$ is derived.

Many linguists and philosophers have followed Stenius in taking on an implicit goal of explaining sentence mood without being completely explicit about how grammar and force are related. For example, Bierwisch (1980) proposes that declaratives, imperatives, and interrogatives have logical forms (or "semantic structures") $\langle p \rangle$, $\langle Imp, p \rangle$, and $\langle Qu, p \rangle$, respectively. The logical form of a sentence determines its utterance meaning in the context in which it is used; an utterance meaning is a pair of an attitude and a propositional content. Attitudes are "pre-reflexive," fundamental stances which one can take towards a proposition, and among the attitudes are three crucial ones D, I, and Q (roughly 'taking it to be the case that,' 'intending that,' and 'intending to know'). Specifically, the utterance meaning of a declarative is $\langle D, [\![p]\!] \rangle$,[15] that of an imperative $\langle I, [\![p]\!] \rangle$, and that of an interrogative $\langle Q, [\![p]\!] \rangle$. These utterance meanings then influence the determination of which speech act is ultimately performed by the use of the sentence in context.

Bierwisch's paper elegantly distinguishes the syntax/semantics notion of a force-marker (Imp, Qu, and the absence of either in declaratives) from the components of utterance meaning (I, Q, and D) which help determine the type of speech act performed. Bierwisch does not, however, help us understand what Imp and Qu precisely are. What kind of thing could Imp be which "determines" the attitude I but which is distinct from I? Moreover, he does not present an analysis of how the syntactic structure of each clause type leads to the right force-marker being present in logical form.

Another operator-based analysis which proceeds at a similar level of abstraction is given by Krifka (2001). He uses the "illocutionary operators" ASSERT, COMMAND, and QUEST for declaratives, imperatives, and interrogatives, and he means to imply, I think, that the speech acts these define are sentential forces—fundamental conversational functions linked to particular grammatical forms. In Krifka (2001) he does not develop a theory of the forces themselves, instead referring to Wittgenstein (1953), Stalnaker (1974), Heim (1982), and Merin (1991). (In later work, such as Krifka 2014 discussed later in this section, he develops a dynamic semantics system with illocutionary operators.) In (26), for example, Krifka (2001, p. 21) assigns types to ASSERT (type pa, functions from propositions to speech acts) and ˆRAINING (type p), composing them by function application.

(26)   a. It is raining.
        b. ASSERT(ˆRAINING)

---

[15] Bierwisch actually allows the utterance meaning of a declarative to include an attitude other than D, though D is the unmarked case.

Yet, while Krifka gives derivations of speech act-type meanings, he does not describe a morpheme or propose a semantic rule which introduces the crucial operators like ASSERT.

Stenius, Bierwisch, Krifka, and others following them do not make any specific claims about the grammar/sentential force relation; as Reis (1999, pp. 198–9) says, works of this kind presuppose a notion of sentence types, but "skirt the crucial *grammar-internal* issue, which should be uppermost in a linguist's mind." Other linguists have, however, proposed that similar force-indicating operators are directly represented in syntax. An important early analysis along these lines is given by Rivero and Terzi (1995). They propose that the syntactic C position "preferably" hosts the sentence's modal element, "the formal ingredient that contributes to the determination of illocutionary force" (p. 305; they also call this element "logical mood"). Specifically citing Stenius (1967) as explanation for how they intend for this element to be interpreted, they then propose that, in the case of Modern Greek imperatives, the modal element should be understood as having the syntactic status of a grammatical feature which drives verb movement to C. The result of verb movement is a structure which represents sentential force in C. Rivero and Terzi are not, however, clear about the syntax of the force-marking element in imperatives in those other languages, like Ancient Greek, in which the imperative modal element is not in C, nor is it clear how sentential force is represented in other clause types.

Rizzi (1997) goes a step further than Rivero and Terzi and proposes a functional projection ForceP which identifies the sentence's clause type and serves as its interface with higher grammatical structure or the discourse context. While Rizzi's proposal is focused on the syntax, and so does not incorporate any specific idea about the nature of sentential force, it is natural to interpret his analysis as representing in the ForceP an element which (in addition to identifying its clause type directly) determines the sentence's sentential force, if it has one (e.g. if it is not embedded). In this way, we can see Rizzi placing into syntax a version of the force-indicating operator.[16] One thing that is left mysterious by Rizzi and his followers, however, is exactly what Force does in an embedded clause and how this is related to the assignment of illocutionary force in root contexts.

The idea of a force-indicating operator heading a syntactic phrase has become quite common. Platzack and Rosengren (1994) offer a brief but interesting discussion of clause type and sentential force using the ForceP. According to them, clause typing is accomplished through the presence of syntactic features in ForceP; specifically [−wh] in Force° (the head of ForceP) marks declarative, [+wh] marks interrogative,[17] and [imp] marks imperative. These features do not, however, introduce the characteristic meanings of the clause types. In addition to the features, interrogatives contain a Q operator and imperatives an N operator (for "necessity"). Declaratives contain no extra operator. In their analysis, it is not entirely clear what

---

[16] Within syntax, 'operator' sometimes has a technical meaning which we should set aside here. The point is that we see strong similarities between the kind of element which we are calling the force-indicating operator and the material in ForceP in Rizzi's syntactic theory.

[17] Note that a [+wh] feature can be present without a wh-word, and a wh-word can co-occur with a [−wh] feature. See Platzack and Rosengren (1994, pp. 182–4).

aspects of meaning are accounted for by the features and which by the operators. In the discussion of Q, they refer to "the rather complicated semantics of interrogative clauses" and say that it "signalizes" slightly different things in yes/no and wh-interrogative clauses. In the case of imperatives, it is more clear that N introduces a sentential force: "The operator so to speak directly sets or creates what we may call a norm" (Platzack and Rosengren 1994, p. 188). The operators Q and N are associated with the features [+wh] and [imp] in ForceP, but Platzack and Rosengren are not explicit about the syntactic relation between them, nor do they delve into other important issues like whether the operators are present only in clauses with independent force.

Another influential version of the idea that force is encoded in an operator is developed by Han (1998). Han proposes that imperative clauses contain an imperative operator consisting of two features, [directive] and [irrealis], the former of which encodes directive illocutionary force. Han clearly identifies illocutionary force with sentential force here (adopting the literal force hypothesis for imperatives), so her account is that imperatives contain a clause-typing operator which includes, as one component, a feature which encodes sentential force. (The feature [irrealis] also occurs in subjunctives and infinitives.) Han differs from many proponents of the force-indicating operator, however, in that she does not apply it uniformly across the grammar. She allows that in many cases, sentential force is not directly encoded. She briefly indicates that declarative and interrogative clauses receive their illocutionary force by pragmatic reasoning. More importantly, she argues that imperatives which are not expressed with the canonical imperative morphosyntax receive their force by pragmatic inference as well. In other words, she divides the clause type of imperative sentences into those in which force is encoded and others for which it is inferred. Because Han develops in an explicit way a line of reasoning which many linguists seem to assume implicitly, we will briefly review her reasons for dividing up the clause type of imperatives in this way.

In both Platzack and Rosengren's and Han's analyses, the crucial feature (i.e. [imp] or [directive]) not only encodes sentential force; it also serves the purely syntactic function, in many of the languages they discuss, of driving verb-movement to the left periphery of the clause. We can see this in Rivero and Terzi's (1995) example cited by Han, (27):

(27) *Lée   lo! (Spanish)*
      read.IMP it
      'Read it!'

However, in certain cases imperative meaning cannot be expressed with the verb form and syntactic construction seen in simple imperatives like (27). Han focuses on one very common type of such case, negative imperatives. In Spanish, negative imperatives are expressed with a verb form from a different paradigm, such as subjunctive or infinitival. We see this in Han's examples (28):[18]

---

[18] The subjunctive is the normal way of expressing the negative imperative meaning in Spanish, but the infinitive is standard in other languages like Italian.

(28) a. *No   lée   lo! (Spanish)
         NEG   read-2SG.IMP it
         'Don't read it!'

      b. No   lo leas!
         NEG it read-2SG.SUBJ
         'Don't read it!'

      c. No   leer   lo!
         NEG read-INF   it
         'Don't read it!'

Notice that the verb follows the object in (28b), indicating that [directive] is not present. As a result, according to Han force is not encoded and therefore must be determined pragmatically. Han argues that subjunctives contain [irrealis] and that its meaning is sufficient to allow hearers to identify the sentence's directive force. Han gives the same explanation to the infinitival negative imperative (28c), even though the verb precedes the object clitic in this case. We therefore see in Han's theory a combination of the first (force-indicating operator) and third (compositional determination of force) approaches outlined earlier in this section. It is worth asking whether there is any reason to accept that [directive] encodes force, if [irrealis] by itself is enough to guarantee that (27) is associated with directive force. (There is in fact a reason within Han's theory; on the assumption that force cannot be encoded within the scope of another operator, the idea that [directive] encodes force explains why (27) cannot be negated or embedded.)

Another theory which straddles the line between the operator approach and the compositional approach is due to Truckenbrodt (2006a), and his theory also has some properties which are worth discussing here. Building on the important tradition of research on the interaction between verbal mood and verb movement in Germanic,[19] he proposes that C contains a "context index" which determines sentential force. The context index is a rather complex object, with the form $\langle DEONT_S(, x)_1(, \langle EPIST \rangle)_2\rangle$. The details of the theory are complex, but it is built from three basic ideas:

1. All speech acts can be paraphrased as "so-and-so wants p." The attitude of wanting is represented by *DEONT*.
2. With speech acts of assertion and asking, what is wanted can be paraphrased as "so-and-so knows p." The attitude of knowing is represented by *EPIST*.
3. Sometimes the speech act involves the speaker wanting someone else to be responsible for bringing about what he wants. This situation is represented by including the variable x and setting its reference to that individual.

---

[19] We encounter this tradition throughout this chapter. Representative works include Altmann 1987; Meibauer 1989; Wechsler 1991; Platzack and Rosengren 1994; Brandt et al. 1992; Reis 1999, 2003; Lohnstein 2000, 2007; Gärtner 2002; Brandner 2004; Meinunger 2004; and the papers in Rosengren 1992a,b.

Truckenbrodt describes syntactic principles which determine the form of the context index. The first concerns *DEONT*: root C contains *DEONT* but embedded C does not. The second concerns *EPIST*: *EPIST* is present when either indicative mood or [+wh] is in C. This leads, roughly, to the following possibilities:

(29)   a. Imperatives have *DEONT* but not *EPIST*, and only occur as root clauses. They express the meaning that the speaker wants x (= the addressee) to do something.

b. Root declaratives and interrogatives have *DEONT* and *EPIST*. They mean that the speaker wants p to be common ground, either on the basis of the speaker's contribution (declaratives, where x = the speaker) or the addressee's (interrogatives, where x = the addressee).

c. Embedded clauses lack *DEONT*, but with V2 contain *EPIST*. Embedded V2 is only possible when *EPIST* is compatible with the semantics of the embedding predicate.

Truckenbrodt (2006a, p. 267) introduces a rule which assigns a context change potential to any CP with a context index containing *DEONT*. In this way, *DEONT* makes the whole index into a force-indicating operator.

Although Truckenbrodt's article proposes a version of the operator-based approach, it should be noted that in a response to commentaries on his ideas (Truckenbrodt 2006b) he revises the analysis just outlined. Specifically, he removes *DEONT* from the context indices and achieves the same effect by means of a pragmatic rule which applies to root clauses. This revised theory no longer explicitly represents sentential force and is more in line with the compositional approach to the relation between clause type and sentential force.

All of the operator-based approaches we have discussed so far have an important assumption in common. If they take a clear stand on the issue at all, they assume that their operator only introduces sentential or illocutionary force into the clause's meaning when the clause is unembedded. This assumption is not accepted by one recent analysis, however. Building on his earlier work discussed above, Krifka (2014) proposes that illocutionary operators can be present in the logical forms of both root and embedded clauses. A sentence-embedding verb will only be able to combine with a clause whose meaning is built with such an operator if it has a meaning which can take a speech act (a meaning built from a force and a content) as argument.

In order to see the issues at play, it is worthwhile to compare Truckenbrodt's and Krifka's analyses of embedded V2 clauses in German. The pattern in German is very similar to the Swedish one outlined in (25).[20] In (30), we see that embedded

---

[20] Embedded V2 is one example of what are often called MAIN CLAUSE PHENOMENA, morphemes or constructional patterns which for the most part occur only in root clauses. Emonds' (1969) root transformations are classical examples: negative inversion, topicalization, VP-preposing, and others. Hooper and Thompson (1973) critique Emonds' classification, showing that many root constructions can occur in embedded clauses, and argue that they are actually restricted to "asserted" environments,

V2 clauses naturally occur in German as the complement of 'say' and 'believe,' but not 'want' (examples from Truckenbrodt 2006a):

(30) a. *Maria glaubt [Peter **geht** nach Hause].*
         Maria believes Peter goes to   home

      b. *Maria sagt [Peter **geht** nach Hause].*
         Maria says Peter goes to   home.

      c. **Maria will,   [sie **ist** in diesem Fall in Berlin].*
         Maria wants she is in that   case in Berlin.

The explanation of embedded V2 should aim to relate V2 to a property shared by both root assertions and the meaning of verbs like 'say' and 'believe,' as opposed to 'want.' Building on Hooper and Thompson (1973), Meinunger (2004) says that V2 clauses have "assertive potential" and that only predicates which are compatible with this meaning may embed them.[21]

Meinunger's semantic analysis is sketchy, but Truckenbrodt and Krifka give more content to the notion of "assertive potential." According to Truckenbrodt, embedded CPs with a verb in C contain *EPIST*, the semantics of which implies that the referent of the matrix subject believes the content of the V2 clause. According to Truckenbrodt, this implication is compatible with 'believes' but not 'wants' (he says that 'believe' "absorbs" the entailment of *EPIST*), so the sentence is acceptable. The idea of absorption is intriguing, but we would want to operationalize it more precisely before judging whether it captures a useful notion of "assertive potential."

Krifka (2014) is not explicit in the same way as Truckenbrodt concerning his assumptions about the interface between clause type and sentential force, but he does think about the pattern in ways which are crucially different from Meinunger and Truckenbrodt. He argues that V2 introduces assertive force (not merely assertive potential) even in some embedded clauses. So, for example, in (30b) the embedded clause would have the logical form ASSERT(p), just as the same structure would as a root clause. In this case, the predicate 'say' would not have a meaning which takes a proposition as argument, but rather it would be a function which takes an act-type argument, together with its individual arguments, and expresses the proposition that a speech act of the kind denoted by the complement took place. Though Krifka does not take a stand on the full range of embedded V2 cases, in order to extend his analysis to (30a,c), one would have to say that 'believe' can embed an assertive act, but 'want' cannot.

The construction-based approach.   As we saw in Section 3.1.1, the traditional conception of sentence types incorporates a broadly construction-oriented perspective on the status of clause types in grammar. This conception leads to two

whether syntactically root or embedded. For more on the syntactic perspective on main clause phenomena, see Haegeman (2006) and the papers in Aelbrecht et al. (2012).

[21] See Wiklund et al. (2009) and references therein for more on the semantic distinction between predicates which allow embedded V2 and those which do not.

serious problems: first, the classes of sentences we intuitively think of as clause types can be non-uniform in their morphology and syntax, and these differences typically correspond to differences in meaning. For example, as we saw in our discussion of Italian, Spanish, and Greek imperatives, different subtypes of imperatives are often expressed with different grammatical patterns. This situation pushes one towards the view that there are actually two or more distinct clause types (positive imperatives, prohibitives, polite imperatives), and unfortunately this leads, within the traditional view, to the conclusion that imperatives as a group have no theoretical status at all.

The second problem concerns the arbitrariness of the mapping between form and sentential force. The traditional conception assigns sentential force holistically. For example, it would map the Spanish negative imperative pattern seen in (28b) (negation plus clitic preceding the subjunctive verb) to the force of prohibition. The approach does not offer an explanation for why a particular combination of grammatical properties is associated with a particular force. But clearly (28b) has the meaning it does largely in virtue of the meanings of its characteristic parts, such as the negation *no* and the subjunctive verbal mood.

One way of addressing these problems is to define the relevant patterns only in terms of a very restricted set of grammatical properties.[22] For example, Wechsler (1991) proposes that the Swedish CP is assigned sentential force (what he calls "illocutionary potential") if it contains a finite verb in C, with the particular force determined by two simple properties: whether it is root or embedded and whether the verb is preceded by another element in CP. (Technically, the second property is whether the maximal projection of CP is C' or C''.) For example, a verb-initial root CP will be assigned the force of a polarity question, while an embedded verb-second clause with the tensed verb in C is assigned the force of (in)direct assertion.[23] In Wechsler's system, we do not have to worry about distinguishing sentence moods too finely, since the system can only define a small number of them. And on the assumption that such elements as negation and subjunctive have their normal semantic contribution, it also reduces the problem of arbitrariness greatly. We can see Wechsler as proposing a very modest version of constructionism which focuses only on sentence mood. More recent work within the construction grammar approach has not been so modest, though, and seeks to solve the problems in a different way. The key idea of such work is that constructions form an **inheritance network.**

---

[22] We should not assume that Wechsler (1991) would see himself as advocating a construction-based approach. Perhaps certain details of the analysis were not essential to his thinking. However, because it is given in precise terms, we can see that it does in fact have the characteristics of that approach.

[23] The specification "(in)direct" apparently indicates two alternatives: either direct assertion for examples like (i) or indirect assertion for ones like (ii) (his (24b), (14a)):

(i) ... *eftersom Johan har inte kommit*
    since   John   has   not   come

(ii) *Hugo påstod   att   du   kommer aldrig att läsa den här boken.*
     Hugo claimed that you will   never read this   book

Indirect assertion is the illocutionary potential of embedded V2 clauses.

In construction grammar, sentences instantiate abstract grammatical patterns, or CONSTRUCTIONS, which include specifications of both form and meaning. A construction can be understood as an abstract type and particular phrases and sentences as tokens of the types. The constructions form a hierarchy in which pairs of constructions stand in inheritance relations: If construction c_1 inherits from c_2, then c_1 has all of the properties of type c_2, plus some more. For example, specific constructions like 'polar interrogative', 'fronted-wh interrogative', and 'in-situ-wh interrogative' could all inherit from a general 'interrogative' construction; meanwhile, the two wh-interrogative constructions could inherit from a general 'wh-clause' construction. A particular sentence like *Who left?* would then instantiate a specific construction ('fronted-wh-interrogative') and thereby have the properties specified by both of the constructions from which that one inherits (interrogative and wh-clause).

The constructional framework has promise for solving the problems of the traditional approach to clause types. The first problem, that of overly specific clause types, will be solved by having both specific and general constructions. In the case of interrogatives, for example, the goal would be to group all members of the clause type under 'interrogative' even while assigning specific sentences to constructions which inherit from it. Each sentence will involve a more specific form–force pairing, but will share those aspects of the pairing specified by the overall type. The second problem, the arbitrariness of the form–function pairing, might also be solvable. Certainly a simple association like that between a negative morpheme and sentential negation could be captured using inheritance (from a 'sentential negation' construction).

Michaelis and Lambrecht (1996) give one of the first construction-based analyses of a clause type. They focus on a sentence pattern which they label the NOMINAL EXTRAPOSITION construction illustrated in (31) (from Michaelis and Lambrecht 1996, (1)):

(31)   It's AMAZING the people you SEE here.

They propose that the nominal extraposition construction inherits from a general ABSTRACT EXCLAMATIVE CONSTRUCTION which brings in several semantic/pragmatic components. They are not very specific about how this construction should be related to the concepts of sentence mood and clause type. It seems that they treat exclamation as a type of assertion, namely "assertion that something manifests a property to an unusually high extent" (Michaelis and Lambrecht 1996, p. 238). It's not clear, however, whether they would consider this type of assertion to be a sentential force in a sense which would qualify it as a sentence mood. While their article gives a good idea of how construction-based theories approach the analysis of clause types, it does not go into enough detail to allow us to discern a theory of sentence mood.

The most fully developed theory of sentence mood based on the constructional approach is given by Ginzburg and Sag (2001). They present a precisely formalized analysis of constructions corresponding to the traditional clause types declarative, interrogative, imperative, and exclamative. They discuss the semantic values of each type as well as the mechanisms by which each is assigned a sentential force when unembedded. It is worthwhile to study their theory with the goal of understanding the potential of the construction-based approach.

Ginzburg and Sag's theory of sentence mood is based on two central claims:

1. Each clause type is associated with a distinct type of semantic value:
    (a) The declarative construction specifies a semantic type of proposition.
    (b) The interrogative construction specifies a semantic type of question.
    (c) The imperative construction specifies a semantic type of outcome.
    (d) The exclamative construction specifies a semantic type of fact.
2. The ROOT construction is associated with the semantic type of proposition together with an appropriate illocutionary relation towards the semantic value of the clause it embeds:
    (a) When the root construction embeds a declarative clause, the illocution-ary relation is assertion.
    (b) When the root construction embeds an interrogative clause, the illocu-tionary relation is asking.
    (c) When the root construction embeds an imperative clause, the illocution-ary relation is ordering.
    (d) When the root construction embeds an exclamative clause, the illocu-tionary relation is exclaiming.

According to this view, the root interrogative in (32a) has the semantic value (32b):

(32)   a. Who left?
        b. the proposition that the speaker asks the addressee the question who left.

This semantic value is derived by combining the interrogative construction, which gives a semantic value of question (namely, the question who left), with the root construction, which causes the sentence as a whole to denote the proposition that the speaker asks the addressee this question.

Ginzburg and Sag do not make clear how making an utterance with the meaning (32b) amounts to asking who left. As they formalize it, the root construction denotes a proposition built with a performative modal operator, and thus in its understanding of semantics and pragmatics, their theory seems little different from the performative hypothesis together with the assertion-based theory of performatives (see Section 1.4.2).[24] Apart from this important issue, Ginzburg and Sag's work shows that a construction-based theory can be very effective at

---

[24] Ginzburg and Sag (2001, p. 266) argue that their analysis does not suffer from certain problems which affect the performative hypothesis, but I do not understand their claims. First, they state that information about illocutionary force is not syntactically represented, but it does occur within the feature structures which are the syntactic representations within the HPSG theory. And second, they state that "the way in which CMT [conversational move type] information enters into the content of a sign does not affect the assignment of (non-illocutionary) content." However, simply labeling the illocutionary relation an "illocutionary relation" does not make it special, and since the content of the root clause is a proposition, it seems that the illocutionary relation is nothing but a modal operator.

making precise the concept of clause type and defining the clause types in a particular grammar. It improves upon the traditional conception of sentence types by allowing for types to be defined at multiple levels, including at the high level of the common-sense declarative, interrogative, imperative, and exclamative types.

Though Ginzburg and Sag develop a traditional theory of clause types and sentential force based on the performative hypothesis, their system does open up some other possibilities which are worth remarking on. The way they assign distinct semantic values to the clause types actually lends itself naturally to the compositional approach to the assignment of sentential force. They might have said something like this: the root construction does nothing but add a [*root*] feature to the clause. Principles of pragmatics assign a dynamic update function (a context change potential) to root clauses, selecting the appropriate update type based on the clause's content (proposition, question, outcome, or fact). For example, the natural update type for propositions is assertion, while the natural update type for questions is asking, so declaratives are assigned an assertive update while interrogatives are assigned an asking update. Such an analysis would be developed within a construction-based theory of grammar, but it would not be a constructional analysis of how sentential force is assigned. I am not certain, however, whether such an approach would have been compatible with Ginzburg and Sag's broader views on semantics and pragmatics.

The compositional approach.   Under both the operator-based approach and the construction-based approach, some grammatical element or pattern represents a sentence's sentential force. This force then influences or determines the ultimate communicative effect of the utterance. For example, in Stenius's (1967) theory, grammatical form determines whether the modal operator is I, O, or $?$, and then this operator determines which rules of use apply. When a sentence $M(p)$ is actually used, we implicitly invoke a principle like this: "when someone utters a sentence with logical form $M(p)$, apply the instructions associated with M to p in order to determine what counts as rule-abiding behavior going forward." In contrast, the compositional approach to sentential force recommends that we take the instructions for how p is used out of the logical form, and instead derive the instructions from p itself. We invoke a principle like this:

(33)   Someone who utters a sentence with meaning p uses p according to the rules which are appropriate given the semantic properties of p, under such-and-such normal conditions.

An analogy goes as follows. Suppose you work in a metal shop with two big machines. One takes a bar of metal and turns it into a blade, and the other takes a bar of metal and turns it into a frying pan. From time to time I send you some metal to work with. Stenius's theory is like a situation where I attach a red or blue label; the

---

It might be possible to solve the second problem by taking a dynamic approach and interpreting the illocutionary relation as a context change potential.

red label indicates that you're to make a blade while a blue one indicates that you're to make a frying pan. By contrast, the compositional approach is like the scenario in which the metal is either steel, appropriate for making a blade, or aluminum, appropriate for making a frying pan, and you are expected to use your judgment to put it into the right machine. Continuing the analogy (and perhaps overdoing it), a theory in which sentence meanings are full speech acts, like Krifka's, is like my loading the bar into one or the other machine for you, and only expecting you to turn it on. A theory in which sentence meanings are modal propositions based on distinct semantic types at the content level, like Ginzburg and Sag's, is like the situation where the blade might be steel or aluminum, and I attach a note telling you which machine to put it in, since you can't be trusted to figure it out on your own.

The compositional approach is immediately ruled out by certain standard ways of presenting the theory of speech acts. For example, Searle (1965) states that all of the following have the same semantic content, the proposition that John will leave the room (his (1)–(5)):

(34)   a. Will John leave the room?
       b. John will leave the room.
       c. John, leave the room!
       d. Would that John left the room.
       e. If [John will leave the room], I will leave also.

Anyone who wishes to pursue the compositional approach will have to deny Searle's assumption that all of the sentences in (34) have the same content; most likely, she will say at least that (34a–c) differ in their narrow semantics.

Two early proponents of the compositional approach are Hausser (1980) and Pendlebury (1986). Their proposals are somewhat similar, and we will illustrate their potential by examining Hausser's. He proposes that declaratives, imperatives, and interrogatives have distinct semantic types: declaratives denote propositions, imperatives properties of the hearer, and interrogatives properties of possible answers, and he hypothesizes that this is all there is to the semantics of clause types. From one side, he argues that there are no grammatical features which could be interpreted as force-indicating operators, and so it would be unduly abstract to introduce them. From the other, he argues that it suffices to differentiate sentence moods by their semantic types. He then makes the proposal that the conversational uses of each sentence can be determined on the basis of its semantics. The implication seems to be that the semantic type of each clause type strongly influences the uses to which sentences of that type can be put, and in this way he raises the idea that the contribution of grammatical structure to conversational function is exhausted by its contribution to narrow semantic content of the kind he proposes for each clause type. A sentence's clause type (and more generally, its syntactic form) only affects its conversational use indirectly, through the mediation of semantics. There are no force-indicating operators or constructions which introduce force into sentences' meanings.

Although Hausser thinks that semantic type can explain the conversational uses to which declarative, interrogative, and imperative clauses are put, he does not present a theory of how it does so. What is lacking in his version of the compositional approach is a specification of what conversational uses are and what principles lead from denotations in the types mentioned above to the uses that we see. In particular, we would want an explanation of sentential force: why declaratives are characteristically used to assert the proposition they denote, why imperatives are characteristically used to direct the addressee to have the property they denote, and why interrogatives are characteristically used to ask for an assertion of the true answer. Later work in the compositional approach attempts to answer these questions.

Two other early advocates of the compositional approach are Huntley (1984) and Wilson and Sperber (1988). Focusing on the analysis of imperatives and the ways they differ from declaratives, Huntley argues that both types have propositions as their denotations, but that these propositions have different characteristics. The propositions denoted by declaratives (and other indicatives) involve indexical reference to the actual world (or another world of evaluation), while those denoted by imperatives (and other non-indicatives, in particular infinitives) do not. His intuition is that both declaratives and imperatives are evaluated as true or false at a world, but only declaratives indexically identify the world at which they are to be evaluated. Imperatives lack indexical reference to a world of evaluation. See Section 2.2.2 for some discussion of Huntley's ideas about the semantic difference between indicatives and non-indicatives.

However we evaluate Huntley's ideas about that contrast, he does not present any concrete ideas about how the difference in indexicality between declaratives and imperatives explains their difference in conversational function. In fact, it may be reading a bit too much into his discussion to see it as advocating the compositional approach as I've defined it here. Still, comments like the following suggest that he favors the compositional approach:

I have identified a minimal respect in which declaratives and imperatives differ semantically, but it remains to be seen if the particular proposal I have offered is compatible with an adequate pragmatic theory of the use in context of these different sentence types.

(Huntley 1984, p. 131)

Wilson and Sperber (1988) understand Huntley's proposal as following what we have called the compositional approach but argue that the semantic values he proposes for declaratives and imperatives cannot explain their conversational functions. They focus in particular on the fact that Huntley assigns the same non-deictic denotation to infinitives as he does to imperatives, pointing out that infinitives are not as tightly tied to directive uses as imperatives are:[25]

---

[25] Infinitives often do receive a directive, imperative-like force, as noted by Palmer (2001), for example. Sperber and Wilson's argument is weakened by the fact that the infinitive and imperative have subjects with different properties; the directive meaning of the imperative might also be connected to its second person subject.

(35)   a. To meet the president of the United States. Hmm! (Wilson and Sperber 1988, (9b))
        b. Meet the president of the United States!

Sperber and Wilson argue that imperatives describe worlds not merely as possible, but as achievable and desirable. More precisely, imperatives describe states of affairs in worlds which the speaker regards both as achievable and as desirable to some individual z. (Different uses of imperatives are distinguished by the identity of z. In requests, orders, and other cases, $z =$ the speaker, while in advice and permission, $z =$ the addressee.) On the basis of this meaning, the force of an imperative should be pragmatically derived "by manifest contextual assumptions" using the ideas of Relevance Theory (Sperber and Wilson 1986). Unfortunately, they do not give a detailed account of this derivation or the semantics of imperatives which underlies it.[26]

The compositional approach has been taken up again in recent years by such authors as Portner (2004) and Lohnstein (2007). Portner makes a set of semantic assumptions very similar to Hausser's (1980), but pairs it with a dynamic pragmatics model of conversational update. He proposes an articulated model of the discourse context which extends Stalnaker's common ground with two additional components, the question set (based on Roberts 2012) and the to-do list function:

1. Common ground: a set of propositions
2. Question set: a set of questions
3. To-do list function: a function from participants in the conversation to to-do lists. The to-do list of an individual a is a set of properties restricted to a.

We will examine this type of model of context in more detail in Section 3.3. For now it is enough to see how he uses the framework to give an explanation for the assignment of sentential force. Because declaratives denote propositions, they are naturally used to update the common ground. This makes the operation of adding to the common ground, assertion, the sentential force of declaratives. Likewise, questions are naturally used to update the question set and imperatives are naturally used to update the to-do list of the addressee. Generally, the sentential force of a sentence S is the update operation $C_x \cup \{ [\![S]\!] \}$, for that component C_x of the context which is a set of semantic values matching $[\![S]\!]$ in type (and in the case of imperatives, domain-restriction). Portner's analysis shows that the compositional approach can assign appropriate sentential forces to root occurrences of the basic clause types; he does not, however, consider Wilson and Sperber's puzzle with (35) or the considerations which led other scholars (like Wechsler 1991;

---

[26] Recently, Jary and Kissine (2016) have presented a DRT analysis of the semantics of imperatives closely related to Sperber and Wilson's view. On their theory, imperatives introduce "potentialities" which cannot be evaluated for truth in the main DRS, and directive force results "from pragmatic considerations: the hearer seeks to identify the point of a nonassertoric utterance which presents him as the agent of an action, and a reasonable hypothesis is that the utterance is offered as a reason for him to take that action."

Gärtner 2002; Truckenbrodt 2006a) to propose that certain embedded clauses are assigned sentential force.[27]

Lohnstein (2007) addresses some of these issues left open by Portner while developing the compositional approach in a slightly different direction. Building on the tradition of research on German V2, he assigns importance to several grammatical factors: the presence or absence of a [+wh] or [−wh] element in CP, the presence or absence of a tensed verb in C, and the mood of the tensed verb. The role of [±wh] is to differentiate declarative and interrogative clauses. Lohnstein proposes that the denotation of a yes/no question is the semantic core for both of these clause types. A yes/no question is a bipartition of the context set C, as in (36):[28]

(36) a. Is it raining?
      b. $\{C \cap \{w : \text{it's raining in } w\}, C \cap \{w : \text{it's not raining in } w\}\}$

From (36), a [−wh] element reduces the bipartition to a singleton, so that declaratives denote propositions, while a [+wh] word differentiates the partition, so that each possible answer to the question is represented by a separate element of the partition.

Lohnstein's ideas about the imperative are not as fully developed. He proposes that there are two "conversational backgrounds," the factive and the epistemic. Indicatives and some subjunctives are restricted to the epistemic background, while imperatives and other subjunctives are restricted to the factive background. It is not clear, though, what role this distinction plays in explaining the conversational functions of the clause types.

The position of the finite verb also plays an important role in Lohnstein's theory. Only when the finite verb is in C should the semantic object denoted by the clause be "anchored" to the discourse context; otherwise it should be anchored to the grammatical context. This is a way of addressing the issue raised by Wilson and Sperber (1988) with regard to (35)—infinitives would not be anchored to the discourse context, and so would not have a sentential force.[29]

It is my judgment that the compositional approach is best suited to explaining the relation between syntax and sentential force. Theories based on a force-indicating operator find it difficult to explain the diversity of structures which constitute some sentence moods. Operators and features in C may be important in the analysis of clause types, because clause types are syntactically coherent, but

---

[27] In Portner (2017), I present a theory which aims to explain the connections between infinitives and imperatives, but not the absence of directive meaning in examples like (35a).

[28] More precisely, Lohnstein builds on Groenendijk and Stokhof (1982) and treats the partition as index-dependent: $\{C \cap \{w : \text{the fact about whether it's raining in } w \text{ is the same as it is in } v\}, C \cap \{w : \text{the fact about whether it's raining in } w \text{ is not the same as it is in } v\}\}$.

[29] Of course, other principles might determine a function for phrases which would not get a sentential force in the normal way. For example, Lohnstein might say that root V-final clauses in German cannot have a sentential force, since the principles of sentential force assignment do not apply, but nevertheless can be used to perform an illocutionary act with the help of Gricean reasoning or language-specific convention. Portner might say something similar about root infinitives in English.

a good analysis of a clause type does not amount to a full analysis of sentence mood except in very simple cases. The construction-based approach also seems unable to explain why particular constructional patterns are associated with the sentential forces they are (unless it is combined with the operator or compositional approach). The compositional approach explains a sentence's force in terms of its semantic content, and its semantic content in terms of standard compositional principles. In this way, it promises to explain why a given range of sentences have the same force: they have the same force if they derive meanings which are similar in the relevant ways.[30]

3.2 Sentence mood in speech act theory

In Section 1.4.2, we reviewed some of the ideas in speech act theory which have allowed it to serve as an important basis for thinking about the nature of sentence mood. As we now trace some of the more linguistically informed uses of speech act theory in the analysis of sentence mood, we will notice that there is no one simple and direct way to apply even the most basic tenets of speech act theory to the grammatical categories of clause types and sentence moods or the semantic/pragmatic notion of sentential force. And, it must be said, the literature on the relation between speech acts and grammar is quite extensive, going far beyond what I can review in a book of this one's scope; if we were to attempt a more thorough study of sentence mood in speech act theory, we would find even more diversity in approaches, hypotheses, and assumptions. My goal in this section is to highlight some of the ideas which are most important for understanding recent research with the aim of developing a better understanding of sentence mood.

As we saw in Chapter 1, the ideas of speech act theory have become so fundamental to thinking about information flow in discourse that it is almost impossible to talk about sentence mood without invoking at least its most basic concepts like "speech act" and "illocutionary force." In the interests of keeping the discussion organized, however, we need to have a somewhat narrow definition of what it means to use speech act theory as the basis for an analysis of sentence mood. In this section, we are going to discuss approaches to sentence mood which endorse the following claims:

1. The logical form of a root sentence used to perform a speech act is $F(c)$, with F the illocutionary force and c the propositional content.
2. Except possibly in the case of explicit performatives, the identity of F is constrained by the sentence's clause type.

---

[30] As this book was being completed, I became aware of some new papers advocating the compositional approach (Farkas and Roelofsen 2017; Roberts, to appear). Farkas and Roelofsen's work is developed in an inquisitive semantics framework. Roberts' adopts the property-based analysis of imperatives originating with Hausser and Portner. Their ideas about the relation between clause type and sentential force appear to be quite similar to those of the authors discussed above.

3. The nature of illocutionary force is to be explained in terms of conventions which allow speakers to perform social acts when the felicity conditions for those acts are met.

Notice the first point concerns the logical form; it says that the fully specified meaning of a root clause should be decomposed into a force and a content. It does not necessarily imply that these two components are independently represented in the syntax, even at an abstract level like deep structure or Logical Form. The second point is meant to exclude work on speech act theory which does not hold enough concern for its relation to grammar to be considered a theory of sentence mood. The third point serves to distinguish analyses based on speech act theory from certain closely related dynamic theories of sentence mood. Specifically, a dynamic semantics or dynamic pragmatics theory which analyses sentential force as an update function defined in terms of a formal model of discourse will not count as being based on speech act theory (though it might owe much to speech act theory), because the update functions are treated primarily as formally defined meanings, rather than as social acts. Many analyses are close to the line between speech act theories and dynamic theories, for example Charlow (2011), Starr (2013), and Krifka (2014).[31] We should not see this line as a border, but rather as an organizational principle.

3.2.1 The performative hypothesis

The first attempt to use speech act theory as the basis for a linguistically-oriented theory of sentence mood was based on the idea that the underlying syntactic form of root sentences contains a marker of illocutionary force. This underlying marker would both encode the illocutionary force of the sentence and drive the transformational processes which lead to declaratives, interrogatives, and imperatives having distinct surface forms. An early statement of this idea, from which much generative work on the topic was derived, is due to Katz and Postal (1964). Katz and Postal propose that interrogative and imperative sentences contain the abstract markers Q and I in deep structure. In meaning, these markers are meant to correspond closely to the highest clause of explicit performatives, *I ask* and *I request*. We can thus say that, according to this theory, the sentential forces of interrogatives and imperatives are represented in logical form and encoded in syntax (in this framework, deep structure). In contrast to interrogatives and imperatives, declaratives do not contain an "assertion" prefix, and it is not clear how their sentential force is derived.

Katz and Postal's ideas developed into an important approach to sentence mood. The PERFORMATIVE HYPOTHESIS states that the deep structures of root sentences contain, as their highest clause, material very close in syntax and semantics to the

---

[31] Based on their professed allegiances, I treat Charlow (2011) and Krifka (2014) as followers of speech act theory, but Starr (2013) as an adherent of the dynamic approach.

highest clauses of explicit performatives. Thus, (37) illustrates the deep structures of declarative, interrogative, and imperative sentences according to Sadock (1974).[32]

(37)   a. You will sing.
             [$_S$ I [DECLARE YOU [you will sing]]]

       b. Will you sing?
             [$_S$ I [ASK YOU [you will sing]]]

       c. Sing!
             [$_S$ I [REQUEST YOU [you will sing]]]

Compared to Katz and Postal's analysis, what's crucially new in (37) is that the force markers are built from a performative verb and its arguments, rather than each being an atomic mood marker, operator, or syntactic feature.

The performative hypothesis has been criticized on various grounds, but for our purposes it is most important to recognize two. First, the hypothesis accepts the claim of classical speech act theory that an explicit performative has the force indicated by its highest clause and the content denoted by the complement of the performative verb. As a result, it must either treat the performative verb and its arguments as contributing to regular semantics (and then derive the division between the force and content of the speech act from additional principles) or treat that material as having a special, force-indicating meaning. Neither alternative turns out to be easy to defend. And second, it identifies the meanings (at both the semantic and speech act levels) of simple declaratives, interrogatives, and imperatives with the meanings of their performative paraphrases (perhaps adjusting slightly for the difference in meaning between DECLARE and *declare*). But the two do show differences in meaning. For example, (38a) is true if and only if it is raining, but its performative paraphrase (38b) is true iff the speaker declares that it rains. (Sadock 2004 discusses this example.)

(38)   a. It is raining.
       b. I declare that it is raining.

The performative hypothesis does not make it easier to solve these problems. See Boër and Lycan (1980), Levinson (1980, 1983), and Sadock (1985, 2004) and references therein for detailed discussion of these and many other important issues regarding the performative hypothesis.

The performative hypothesis is certainly no longer pursued as actively as it once was. As a syntactic hypothesis, it is associated with the now-abandoned Generative Semantics model. However, some of the main ideas of the hypothesis continue to be pursued. For example, Condoravdi and Lauer (2011) aim to develop an analysis of explicit performative sentences like (38b) which treats them as normal

---

[32] These trees are Sadock's initial presentation of his ideas; the analysis becomes more sophisticated later on. Sadock's proposal is used here to represent a range of Generative Semantics theories which endorse the performative hypothesis.

declaratives. Based on this, Condoravdi and Lauer (2012) propose a semantics for imperatives which they present in terms of an operator IMP with the same basic features as performative verbs like *order* and *request*. This analysis can be seen as an updated performative hypothesis. (It is important to be aware, though, that at the end of their paper Condoravdi and Lauer (2012) suggest a different account which would be better classified as a version of the dynamic force hypothesis (see Section 3.2.3 below). It seems that Condoravdi and Lauer are not committed to a particular approach to sentence mood, and consider the performative operator IMP to merely provide a convenient way to state some other ideas about imperatives.)

Whether honestly defeated or simply superseded, scholars no longer treat the performative hypothesis as an important position on the nature of sentence mood. We do often see, however, remarks that a particular theory is reminiscent of the performative hypothesis. Scholars today look back on the performative hypothesis as an admirably explicit presentation, within the syntactic theory of its day, of three key claims which are still very much with us today. Specifically, we should keep in mind that the following ideas were introduced or developed to new levels of explicitness as parts of the overarching performative hypothesis: (i) the claim that the logical forms of speech act theory are in fact explicit at some level of syntax, (ii) the assumption that the major clause types have characteristic underlying syntactic structures and logical forms, and (iii) the hypothesis that the force-indicating component of the grammatical representation may be articulated into a predicate–argument structure with distinct parts corresponding to the speaker, the addressee, and the force itself. The fact that these ideas are still being pursued within linguistics thirty years after the last days of the performative hypothesis shows how important a project it was in the history of syntactic and semantic theory.

3.2.2 Adjustments to classical speech act theory

These days, it is a common assumption among linguists that speech act theory offers support for a view of sentence mood according to which the grammatical forms of root sentences contain a marker of illocutionary force which combines with a phrase denoting the propositional content to which it applies, but in fact during the period when speech acts were a topic of active collaboration among linguists and philosophers, it was not taken for granted that there was such a simple relation between the force-content logical form of an illocutionary act and the syntactic structure. Rather, alongside the analysis of Katz and Postal (1964) and the performative hypothesis, which did roughly put the $F(c)$ logical form into syntax, we see many scholars whose thinking is more closely connected to the traditional view of sentence types. These scholars, prominently including Searle, understand the logical form's force-marker to be represented in the grammatical structure in diverse ways, sometimes explicitly (as with explicit performatives) and sometimes inexplicitly through a pattern of grammatical properties. This understanding of the relation between form and force is captured quite well by Searle's term "function indicating device":

Function indicating devices in English include word order, stress, intonation contour, punctuation, the mood of the verb, and finally a set of so-called performative verbs: I may indicate the kind of illocutionary act I am performing by beginning the sentence with 'I apologize', 'I warn', 'I state', etc. Often in actual speech situations the context will make it clear what the illocutionary force of the utterance is, without its being necessary to invoke the appropriate function indicating device.   (Searle 1965, p.6)

Searle's understanding of the grammar of function indicating devices has much in common with the traditional conception of sentence types. A wide range of morphological, syntactic, phonological, and orthographic properties can serve as function indicating devices, and no theory is given for why particular properties mark the particular functions they do.

The central problem which arises as one tries to develop a theory of sentence mood in speech act theory is to resolve the tension between two facts: (i) There are very many illocutionary forces; and (ii) there is a small set of grammatical patterns, namely the clause types, which should surely qualify as function indicating devices. It is impossible to say that each clause type indicates just one illocutionary force, so how can we define their force-indicating function? There are two ways to answer this question.

1. Illocutionary forces are decomposed into more primitive components of meaning, and the clause type indicates one of these more primitive components. This would imply, in our terminology, that sentential forces are not to be identified with illocutionary forces, but rather with components of illocutionary forces.
2. Illocutionary forces are grouped into natural classes, and the clause types indicate a class rather than a specific force. On this view, a sentential force is a partial specification of an illocutionary force.

In the remainder of this section, we will look at some of the important work which follows one or the other of these strategies.

Searle and Vanderveken's compositional analysis of illocutionary acts.   We have already discussed the theory of Searle and Vanderveken (Searle 1975b; Searle and Vanderveken 1985; Vanderveken 1990, 1991) in Section 1.4.2, but it may be helpful to review the main points relevant to sentence mood here. They develop a compositional analysis of illocutionary force according to which the overall force is built from six properties: illocutionary point, mode of achievement, degree of strength, propositional content conditions, preparatory conditions, and sincerity conditions. Each of these can be determined by different properties of the sentence, or may even be unspecified, in which case they will receive a default or inferred value. For example, (39b) is associated with the illocutionary force of answering-and-lamenting, with *alas* introducing the sincerity conditions of a lamentation and *yes* the preparatory conditions of an answer (see Vanderveken 1990, pp. 16–17):

(39) a. Are you quitting?

b. Alas, yes, I'm quitting.

Thus, this analysis assumes that the relation between grammatical form and sentential force is complex and often inexplicit.

Searle and Vanderveken have more to say about sentence mood. The compositional analysis of force allows them to identify simpler components of force which can be associated with grammatical form. From the perspective of this framework, the clause types look like this:[33]

1. Basic types
   (a) Declaratives have the assertive point, except for explicit performatives, which have the declarative point.
   (b) Imperatives have the directive point.
   (c) Interrogatives have the directive point plus special propositional content conditions.
2. Minor types
   (a) Exclamatives have the expressive point.
   (b) Promissives have the commissive point.

What exactly are the principles which give rise to these associations? Vanderveken (1990, p. 108) states that the declarative, imperative, and exclamative sentence moods "express" the assertive, directive, and expressive illocutionary points, respectively. He argues that in explicit performatives, the combination of declarative sentence type and additional markers (such as *hereby*) expresses the declarative point. While it might seem strange that the grammatical pattern which expresses one point is contained within the pattern which expresses another, he justifies this unusual situation by claiming that declarations "contain" assertions with the same propositional content. Interrogatives are an even more difficult case. As in classical speech act theory, asking a question is assumed to be a type of directive act, and one might expect that the two clause types which express directive acts, imperatives and interrogatives, would have some morphosyntactic similarity. Yet interrogatives and imperatives each have more in common with declaratives than they do with each other. I do not know of any specific statement within this framework about which grammatical features express the directive point of interrogatives or the other components of interrogative force.

Zaefferer (1983, 2001) argues that the classification of asking acts as directive poses a serious problem for the theory of speech acts developed by Searle and Vanderveken. In addition, he points out several other similar discrepancies between the typology of speech acts assumed by this framework and

---

[33] A similar perspective is developed by Allan (2006). Allan proposes that each clause type is associated with a particular **primary illocution** as part of its semantics, and that the primary illocution serves as a force-indicating device. It seems that Allan in effect accepts the literal force hypothesis, but it remains somewhat unclear what the relation is between primary illocution and illocutionary force. Allan's theory also has some commonalities with that of Bach and Harnish (1979).

grammatically defined classes of sentences.[34] An important one concerns the status of commissives. Even though commissives form a basic category in Searle and Vanderveken's framework (as they do in classical speech act theory), very few languages have promissives, the clause type specialized for the commissive point. If the illocutionary points are really the most fundamental classification of conversational functions relevant to grammar, we might expect that each such point would normally (or at least often) have its own, equally fundamental grammatical form. Zaefferer argues that commissive declaratives should be classified fundamentally as assertions, while true commissive promissives are distinct.

Vanderveken (1990, p. 109) addresses the issue of why promissives are rare by boldly stating that the commissive point "is less important than the other points for the purpose of linguistic communication." He suggests that our inexplicit way of normally marking commissives may actually be an advantage for speakers, since they can then more easily manipulate their interlocutors by pretending not to have actually made a promise when convenient. What this diagnosis leaves out, of course, is that for every promiser, there is a promisee, who is also a participant in the linguistic community; it can be very important for one who needs a commitment from another to know that the commitment is without a doubt on the record. Similarly, Searle (2001, p. 287) states without qualification that "commissives are rather uncommon in ordinary speech."[35] In any case, Searle's and Vanderveken's counterarguments here are really no more than speculation. We are not given any social theory or empirical data supporting their claims about the importance or frequency of commissives compared to other illocutionary acts.

I think we can evaluate this exchange between Zaefferer and Searle and Vanderveken as follows. The grammatical evidence from interrogatives and commissives suggests that, if speech act theory is to be the basis of a theory of sentence mood, we will need a different classification of act types from the one provided by Searle and Vanderveken. Zaefferer thinks that speech act theory should serve as the basis for the theory of sentence mood, and so he sets out to change it; we will look briefly at his proposals below. Searle and Vanderveken think that speech act theory provides the background for the theory of sentence mood, but that the typology of sentence moods is not derived from the typology of illocutionary acts in a very direct way. For them, illocutionary point is sometimes central to explaining sentence mood and sometimes not. A third response, of course, is to look for a theory of information flow in discourse which allows us to better explain the properties of sentence mood and clause types. We will see how this perspective plays out in Section 3.3.

---

[34] He also makes some philosophical objections to criteria by which Searle and Vanderveken classify illocutionary acts, but Searle counters these (Searle 2001), and in any case, Zaefferer's comments are too brief to be evaluated effectively.

[35] He also says that "it is a rather big deal to make a promise, and consequently you do not have common separate devices for making promises." I do not understand why more important acts would be less likely to be explicitly marked.

Rett on exclamative force.   Rett (2011) presents an analysis of exclamations based on assumptions about illocutionary force which could easily be integrated with Vanderveken's views.[36] It is useful to study her proposal with the goal of understanding how recent versions of speech act theory can be used as part of the analysis of sentence mood. Rett discusses the similarities and differences between sentence exclamations and exclamatives (her (40)):

(40)   a. (Wow), John arrived early!
      b. How (very) early John arrived!

Exclamations like (40a), in Rett's terminology, are sentences with the morphosyntax of a declarative but special intonation associated with the illocutionary force of exclamation. Exclamatives like (40b), in contrast, form a separate clause type from declaratives and interrogatives and have an illocutionary force very similar to exclamations. The essence of Rett's analysis is that exclamations and exclamatives share the same illocutionary force, represented by the illocutionary operator E-FORCE, but that they differ in the details of the propositional content which the operator takes as its argument. She argues that exclamatives introduce a predication involving degrees, while exclamations do not. In the case of (40), the difference is that (40a) expresses that John wasn't expected to arrive early (but asserts that he did), while (40b) expresses that the degree of earliness of John's arrival exceeds the speaker's expectation (and asserts nothing).

For the purposes of understanding Rett's views about sentence mood, what's important are her comments on E-force. The first thing to note is that it is not quite clear whether exclamations and exclamatives constitute a single sentence mood. We have defined sentence mood in terms of the association between grammatical form and sentential force, and (40a,b) share the illocutionary force introduced by E-force. So, in this respect, they have the same sentential force and might be regarded as one sentence mood. But Rett proposes that the exclamation (40a) is also associated with the function of asserting that John arrived early, and so it can be seen as sharing its sentential force with ordinary declaratives. As we will see below, Rett proposes that the assertive force of (40a) follows as a kind of entailment, and so from our perspective, the right conclusion is probably that the examples in (40) belong to the same sentence mood.

A second important point to observe about Rett's theory is that she does not associate the illocutionary force operator E-force with any specific piece of grammatical structure. She only states that this operator "models" the force of exclamation. From the context of her discussion, we can infer that she thinks that the meaning of (40a) involves E-force because of its characteristic intonation (indicated in writing by the exclamation point). With regard to (40b), it is not clear whether Rett associates E-force with its intonation or its grammatical form. Overall, it seems that Rett thinks that illocutionary force is sometimes inexplicitly represented by grammatical form, but her discussion leaves open the possibility

---

[36] Gutiérrez-Rexach (1996) sketches an analysis with many similarities to Rett's. See also Castroviejo (2006b) for discussion of Gutiérrez-Rexach's view.

that syntactically defined clause types play a very important role in the determination of illocutionary force. Such a perspective on the relation between form and force is completely compatible with Searle and Vanderveken's views.

Now we can look at the meaning which Rett assigns to E-force (Rett 2011, p. 429):

(41)   E-FORCE(p), uttered by s_C, is appropriate in a context C if p is salient and true in w_C. When appropriate, E-force(p) counts as an expression that s_C had not expected that p.

The definition (41) begins with an appropriateness condition which could as well have been called a preparatory or sincerity condition. Then, in saying that E-force(p) counts as an expression that s_C had not expected that p, Rett identifies its illocutionary point as Vanderveken's expressive point.[37] Therefore, as far as I can tell, Rett's analysis should be seen as operating within Vanderveken's (1990) theory of speech acts.

Although E-force represents the illocutionary force of both exclamations and exclamatives, it has a somewhat different effect in the two cases, and she traces this difference to a contrast between the semantic values of the two types. With an exclamation, the semantic value of the clause is an ordinary proposition; for example, the propositional content of (40a) is that John arrived early. When E-force takes this proposition as argument, we have a speech act which is only appropriate if John actually arrived early, and which expresses that the speaker did not expect that he would arrive early. The hearer can normally infer that the speaker expected that John would not arrive early (although the theory suggests that a weaker inference would be good enough, that is, that the speaker didn't have any expectation). Rett also states that the appropriateness condition implies that the speech act of exclamation entails a speech act of assertion. In the case of (40a), the point is that E-force(p) illocutionarily entails (in the sense of Vanderveken 1990) an assertion that John arrived early. Therefore, the fact that (40a) asserts that John was early is a byproduct of the felicity condition on exclamations, and not due to its having declarative sentence mood.

Turning to the exclamative (40b), Rett proposes that its content is not fundamentally propositional. Rather, its semantic denotation is a property of degrees: $\lambda d[\text{early}(j, d)]$. As a result of its having this kind of denotation, E-force produces a speech act in which the speaker expresses an attitude towards a degree; in the case of (40b), the speaker's use of the sentence counts as expressing that, for some degree of earliness d, he did not expect that John would be d-early. (See also Katz 2005; Castroviejo 2006b for discussion of attitudes towards a degree.) In my opinion, the steps which lead to this expressive act are not motivated in a clear way: she says that context provides a degree argument for an exclamative's denotation, and that the resulting proposition (e.g. early(j, d')) is the argument of E-force and determines the speech act's appropriateness condition; in turn, because of the unbound degree variable in the argument of E-force (here d'), the precise

---

[37] The inference that Rett uses "expresses" to point to Vanderveken's definition of the expressive point is supported by her discussion of Vanderveken's (1990) treatment of lamentations.

attitude it expresses is adjusted to the one noted above.[38] Rett also suggests that the unbound variable is responsible for the fact that exclamatives, in contrast to declarative-like exclamations, do not assert anything—although she admits that she does not have a clear idea for why this would be ((40b) should illocutionarily entail the assertion that John arrived d'-early).

Summing up, the most important thing to observe about Rett's paper is that she develops a sophisticated analysis of exclamatives and exclamations within the general framework outlined by Searle and Vanderveken. In comparison to Searle and Vanderveken's own discussion, her proposals are grounded more rigorously in linguistic facts and are embedded in a more detailed theory of syntax and semantics. Therefore, Rett's work provides a good illustration of the use to which the notion of illocutionary point could be put within the theory of sentence mood. Conversely, some of the problems we identify with Rett's analysis seem to be derived from the version of speech act theory she adopts. Most significantly from our perspective, Rett does not give principles for deriving logical forms containing E-force from the syntax of exclamatives and exclamations. We do not know, in the end, why the exclamation (40a) is not assigned the force of assertion, normally associated with its declarative clause type, and gets E-force instead. Nor do we see a role for the special syntax of the exclamative (40b) in deriving its logical form with E-force. Of course, one can imagine ways of addressing these issues which are compatible with Rett's analysis, but it is an open question whether any of them could work as a general theory of sentence mood.

Zaefferer's alternative classification of illocutionary acts. Alongside the critique of the versions of speech act theory developed by Searle and Vanderveken mentioned above, Zaefferer (1981, 1983, 1986, 1998, 2001, 2006b,a, 2007) attempts to radically revise the classification of illocutionary acts to meet the concerns he raises. His ideas are worth examining because they give a sense of how a version of speech act theory based more closely on linguistic data would go, but the new classification he proposes is quite complex and not motivated in sufficient detail to be considered a theory of sentence mood. In one paper (Zaefferer 2007), for instance, he classifies acts according to the following criteria, among others: structuredness (whether they have grammatical structure), telicity, epistemicness (whether they have to do with an agent's knowledge of the propositional content), holophoricity (whether the semantics of the sentence refers to the illocutionary act itself), and opacity (whether it aims at a partially specified propositional content). Some of the more important sentence moods are treated as follows:

1. He has a separate category for question acts, the "structured opaque epistemic telic acts." Question acts are distinguished from representatives, commissives, and declarations in virtue of the property of opacity. The idea here seems to be that a question word in an interrogative introduces a variable or

---

[38] One would think that the sentence expresses that the speaker did not expect John to arrive d'-early, rather than what Rett actually proposes, that there is *some* degree such that the speaker didn't expect John to be that early.

placeholder into the semantics, so that the sentence's propositional content is only partially specified.

2. Directives, promissives, and exhortatives form a class of "structured direct telic" acts. The members of this class are distinguished from the other major types (declaratives and interrogatives) by virtue of the property of non-epistemicness (what Zaefferer calls "direct"). The idea is that in an imperative, what is important is that the propositional content of the sentence become true, whereas with a declarative, what is important is that someone believe it to be true.

3. Despite the fact that they seem to perform the same type of illocutionary act, promissives and declarative-like commissives are separated into two categories. The former are grouped with directives (as above), while the latter are grouped with representatives.

4. Expressive acts appear to be split among three categories (Holistic, i.e. non-structured (*Wow!*), Structured-Epistemic-Telic-Holophoric-Social-Intralinguistic-Institutive (*Thanks!*), and Structured-Representative-Atelic-Hybrid (I'm not sure what type of case Zaefferer has in mind)).

There are several serious problems with Zaefferer's ideas, though to some extent these may be due to the fact that they were presented in only a few short papers. As can be observed, speech acts are classified in terms of a great variety of properties, which combine or fail to combine in mysterious ways. (For example, there are no opaque atelic acts, opaque holophoric acts, or atelic epistemic acts.) More importantly, the crucial properties are not clearly defined and are not integrated into a broader theory of communication and meaning.

Zaefferer's alternative classification of speech acts has not had much influence on later research, but it is worth thinking about because it exemplifies one reasonable approach towards developing an explanatory theory of sentence mood. Zaefferer attempts to use the typology of sentence moods and clause types to provide guidance for a new classification of illocutionary acts. A novel classification of illocutionary acts will require, of course, a whole new theory of speech acts. In other words, the advocate of a new typology of illocutionary acts will need to go back to the foundations of speech act theory to see to it that the whole apparatus still functions as well as it does in the classical system systematized by Searle. The essential point of Searle's (2001) response to Zaefferer is that Zaefferer fails to do this and so fails to appreciate the full motivation for the classical typology.

Bach and Harnish.   Searle and Vanderveken's ideas about the relation between grammatical form and sentence mood are naturally linked with either the operator-based or construction-based approaches to the interface between syntax and sentential force. This is so because they seem committed to the idea that the illocutionary force of an utterance is normally represented (even if inexplicitly) in its grammatical form. However, speech act theory is also compatible with the compositional view of the syntax–force interface. Though they may not have thought of their work in quite this way, the theory of Bach and Harnish (e.g. Bach and Harnish 1979; Harnish 1994) is better suited to the compositional view of the mood–force interface. Here I would like to make a few remarks on what their theory—which is quite deep and comprehensive in its re-evaluation of central features of speech act theory, but not at all focused on developing a linguistic theory that can explain how particular sentences are linked with their sentential forces—has to say about the nature of sentence mood.

According to Bach and Harnish, the mapping between sentence moods and illocutionary force happens in two steps. The first concerns a relation between the grammatical forms and propositional attitudes. They say that each basic clause type expresses a characteristic kind of propositional attitude. The second step gives a relation between expressed attitudes and illocutionary forces; they propose that each type of attitude constrains the range of illocutionary forces that the sentence can be assigned. For example, according to Harnish (1994, pp. 433–4), the interfaces work like this:[39]

Step (1): Form–Expressed Attitude
  (a) Declaratives
    - Form: NP+AUX+VP
    - Expressed Attitude: S believes that p.
  (b) Imperatives
    - Form: $(NP)+VP_{[+imp]}$
    - Expressed Attitude: S desires/intends that H make it the case that p.
  (c) Yes/No Interrogatives
    - Form: AUX+NP+VP *or* NP+AUX+VP^{rising}
    - Expressed Attitude: S desires that H tell S whether or not it is the case that p.
  (d) Wh-Interrogatives
    - Form: Wh-x+AUX+(NP)+VP *or* NP+AUX+[. . . Wh-/x/ . . .]VP
    - Expressed Attitude: S desires that H tell S Wh-x such that p(x).
Step (2): Expressed Attitude–Illocutionary Force Potential
  (a) Declaratives
    - Expressed Attitude: S believes that p.
    - Illocutionary Force Potential: Any act with the belief that p as a necessary condition.
  (b) Imperatives
    - Expressed Attitude: S desires/intends that H make it the case that p.
    - Illocutionary Force Potential: Any act with the desire/intention that H make it the case that p as a necessary condition.

---

[39] The earlier but more well-known joint book (Bach and Harnish 1979) is quite similar in its overall perspective on these issues, but not as explicit about its understanding of the nature of clause types. Note that I have adjusted the notation for grammatical patterns to make it more transparent.

    (c) Yes/No Interrogatives
- Expressed Attitude: S desires that H tell S whether or not it is the case that p.
- Illocutionary Force Potential: Any act with the desire that H tell S whether or not it is the case that p as a necessary condition.

    (d) Wh-Interrogatives
- Expressed Attitude: S desires that H tell S Wh-x such that p(x).
- Illocutionary Force Potential: Any act with the desire that H tell S Wh-x such that p(x) as a necessary condition.

Unlike Searle and Vanderveken's, this analysis does not seek to decompose illocutionary force to find some components which can be shared by all members of a sentence mood. Rather, it sees the assignment of illocutionary force as the result of inference, and seeks to identify the constraints which sentence mood places on the assignment of force as part of that inferential process. As Bach and Harnish see it, the sentence moods constrain the force which their sentences can be assigned through the types of attitudes that they express.

Seen this way, Bach and Harnish's approach to sentence mood seems to exemplify the compositional approach to sentence mood. For them, force is not encoded (either through an operator or a grammatical pattern), but rather inferred on the basis of an aspect of meaning which is closer to grammar than speech acts are. However, it is not entirely clear how the expressed attitudes are derived. Looking at the Form–Attitude relation for imperatives, presumably $(NP) + VP_{[+imp]}$ compositionally denotes p, but where does attitude of desire/intention come from? It could arise from an interpretive rule triggered by the structure $(NP) + VP_{[+imp]}$ (a sentence type or construction) or inferred from the precise content p. This second way of thinking would represent a doubling-down on the compositional approach to sentence mood.

3.2.3 The dynamic force hypothesis in speech act theory

Since the 1980s, the dynamic approach to meaning has increasingly become the mainstream way of thinking about information flow in discourse within formal semantics and pragmatics. As a result, it is not surprising that scholars have sought to combine the insights of that approach with the framework of speech act theory. As discussed in Section 1.4.3, Gazdar (1981) was a pioneer in this way of thinking; more recently, we see such authors as Charlow (2011), Kaufmann (2012), and Krifka (2014) pursuing the idea in different ways. In this section, we will review their proposals about the nature of sentence mood.

Kaufmann: Illocutionary force potential under the dynamic force hypothesis. Kaufmann's discussion builds on the most basic concepts of the dynamic approach already introduced in Chapter 1, and we begin with it. She suggests we define illocutionary acts as sequences of contexts. Intuitively, for example, we can think of a successful act of assertion as a move from a context in which the propositional content of the act is unsettled, through one in which a speaker says something appropriate, to an ending context in which the speaker and addressee agree that the propositional content is true. More formally, we have the following:

1. Contexts
   (a) A context c has four components $\langle c_S, c_A, c_T, c_W \rangle$, where c_S is the speaker, c_A is the addressee, c_T is the time, and c_W is the world of c.
   (b) From c we can specify various additional parameters, including crucially:
       - c_E is the "disambiguated LF of the linguistic object uttered" in c (if there is one).
       - $CS(c)$ is the context set of c.
       - $\Delta(c)$ is the salient decision problem in c, if there is one.
2. Speech acts
   (a) A speech act is a description of a sequence of contexts $\langle c', c, c'' \rangle$, where:
       - Felicity conditions of the act are conditions on c'.
       - The speaker c_S utters some linguistic object c_E in c. In effect, the locutionary act happens in c.
       - The essential effect of the speech act obtains in c''.
   (b) Example: ASSERT(ϕ)
       - Both ϕ and $\neg\phi$ are compatible with $CS(c')$.
       - The assumption that c'_S has reasons to believe ϕ is compatible with $CS(c')$.
       - c_S says c_E in c.
       - $CS(c'')$ entails that c_s believes ϕ.

Notice that, in the definition of assertion, no link is drawn between the asserted proposition ϕ and the linguistic expression c_E which the speaker utters in c. Clearly, and as Kaufmann notes, we need to incorporate a semantic or pragmatic relation between c_E and ϕ and to explain the role c_E plays in deriving an output context where the speaker is entailed to believe ϕ.

Later on in her discussion Kaufmann makes the connections among c_E, ϕ, and c'' more explicit in a way very similar to Gazdar's (1981) proposal. She assumes a basic force function $\mathcal{J}$ which applies to propositions or questions to yield an update function, that is a function from contexts to contexts. This $\mathcal{J}$ is sensitive to the semantic type of its content argument m, that is, whether it is a proposition or a question.[40]

1. If m is a proposition, $\mathcal{J}(m)$ is an assertive update, mapping c to a c'' where m is entailed by the context set of c''.
2. If m is a question, $\mathcal{J}(m)$ is a partitioning update, mapping c to a c'' where m partitions the context set of c''.

---

[40] Kaufmann gives these definitions in terms of the common ground, rather than the context set, but I state them in terms of the context set in order to be consistent with portions of her theory presented above. In her terminology, $\mathcal{J}$ is called the "update function," but in our terminology, it is better referred to as a force.

Let us leave aside the nature of the partitioning update. It is derived from the dynamic approach to questions discussed below (Section 3.3.2). What's crucial here is that $\mathcal{J}$ is defined in overtly dynamic terms and does its job on the basis of the semantic type of its argument.

Finally, Kaufmann uses this apparatus to explain what a "theory of speech acts" consists in. A theory of speech acts is essentially a specification, for every triple of contexts $\langle c', c, c'' \rangle$, of one of the speech acts like ASSERT (defined above), COMMAND, PERMIT, REQUEST, MARRY, and so forth. A proper speech act assignment must respect $\mathcal{J}$ in the sense of relating c and c'' in the way that $\mathcal{J}$ says: $\mathcal{J}(\llbracket c_E \rrbracket^c)(c) = c''$. This description of speech act assignment implies that a sentence which denotes a proposition can only receive an illocutionary force which involves an assertion-like update, while a sentence which denotes a question can only receive an illocutionary force which involves an asking-like update. (For example, though the act performed by *I now pronounce you husband and wife* is not an act of assertion, it should be assertion-like in that it results in a common ground which entails that the speaker did pronounce them husband and wife.) I think it also implies (whether intentionally or not) that phrases which do not denote propositions or questions cannot receive any speech act assignment at all.

Kaufmann's ideas here suggest quite a few consequences for the theory of sentence mood. As noted, the dynamic update determined by $\mathcal{J}$ is fully determined by the semantic type of c_E, and hence strongly influenced by (maybe even determined by) the grammar of c_E. In contrast to this specificity, Kaufmann does not present any comprehensive theory of speech acts. We do not know how diverse she takes the set of illocutionary acts to be—is it very fine-grained as in classical speech act theory, or a smaller set? However, she does make heavy use of the acts like assertion, commanding, and permitting in the analysis of imperatives, and they allow us to understand further her view of sentence mood.

Kaufmann treats imperatives as semantically equivalent to declarative sentences with *should*, for example:

(42)   a. Sit down!
       b. You should sit down.

While there is a close relation between these forms, they are obviously not semantically identical, and so the puzzle for Kaufmann is to explain how they differ. Her approach to this puzzle begins with the distinction between the performative and descriptive uses of (42b). The performative use can be exemplified by a parent speaking to a child, uttering (42b) with the intention of telling her to sit down. On this use, it is not naturally described as true or false and is much closer to the imperative (42a). On the descriptive use, in contrast, (42b) can readily be judged true or false and can be used to make an assertion about what is in the best interests of the addressee. The descriptive use is obvious when the subject is third person (*That guy over there should sit down because it looks like he might pass out*).

According to Kaufmann, the performative and descriptive uses of the modal sentence differ in speech act assignment: the performative use might involve an assignment of COMMAND, while the descriptive use might involve ASSERT. What makes for the choice between these two are the preconditions of the respective act types. An act of the COMMAND type requires that the speaker c_S is an authority on the truth of the propositional content $[\![\, c_E \,]\!]$ and that $[\![\, c_E \,]\!]$ provides an answer to some salient open issue about what to do, the "decision problem" $\Delta(c)$. For example, (42a) would answer the child's decision problem "Do I stand or sit now?" And, according to Kaufmann, imperatives presuppose that these same conditions hold. Since an imperative presupposes that the speaker is an authority and that the imperative answers a decision problem, it is compatible with being assigned the speech act COMMAND. But in contrast, she assumes that the presuppositions of the imperative make it incompatible with ASSERT as its speech act type. As a result, imperatives have the pragmatic properties of performative deontic sentences, such as the property of not being naturally described as true or false.

A worrisome gap in Kaufmann's analysis is that she does not explain precisely what condition on assertion is incompatible with the presupposition of imperatives. The framework states that an act of assertion ASSERT(ϕ) places a condition on c' or c which cannot be met when ϕ is an imperative. It appears that Kaufmann takes as crucial the authority condition and the condition that ϕ must answer $\Delta(c)$. But I do not know why these conditions would rule out assertion. In the case of the child who needs to decide whether to sit or stand, I see no reason why the existence of this decision problem, together with the assumption that I will definitely be correct in my assessment of what she should do, would make it impossible to assert that she should sit down. This would amount to pointing out the right decision without imposing it. More generally, the crucial assumption for Kaufmann is that there is some property P of contexts which allows only a performative use of deontic modals; she proposes that imperatives presuppose P. But we are not given any positive argument that there really is any such property.[41]

The issue just raised for Kaufmann's theory has been presented in a somewhat abstract way, but we can see its concrete consequences in the following contrast, from Portner (to appear):

(43)　You should not park in the dry cleaner's lot, because you'll get a ticket if you do. So, ...
　　　a. do not park in the dry cleaner's lot!
　　　b. ??you should not park in the dry cleaner's lot!

What is crucial here is that the imperative is felicitous in a context in which a declarative with *should* is not. This fact contradicts the proposal that imperatives essentially are *should* sentences, just restricted to contexts in which the *should* is performative. In (43a), the imperative has a normal imperative function, namely urging the addressee not to park in the lot, which the modal sentence cannot have in the same context.

Similarly, von Fintel and Iatridou (2015) point out a related problem for Kaufmann's theory. In certain contexts, imperatives can readily be used to give

---

[41] Jary and Kissine (2016) critique Kaufmann's analysis for similar reasons.

permission or express acquiescence, but the deontic modals lack these uses (von Fintel and Iatridou 2015, p. 6):

(44)   A: May I open the door?
        B: Sure, go ahead, open it!
        B′: Sure, go ahead, #you must open it.
        B″: Yes, in fact: you must open it!
        C: Sure, go ahead, you should open it.

They point out that B can be understood as giving permission without endorsing the choice to open the door at all, whereas B′ and C imply that the speaker requires or endorses the action. If imperatives are equivalent to sentences with *must* or *should* in any context in which they are felicitous, the difference is unexpected.

What does all of this tell us about sentence mood? Within Kaufmann's theory, there are three candidates for the status of sentential force: (i) the type of update potential assigned by $\mathcal{J}$, (ii) a specific force which is most prototypically associated with $\mathcal{J}$, or (iii) the set of forces compatible with a given sentence mood. If we think of sentential force as (i), there are only two sentential forces correlating with the two semantic types of root sentences: the intersective update of propositions and the partitioning update of questions. From this perspective, imperatives and declaratives would have the same sentential force, and so belong to the same sentence mood. The second view (ii) implies that there is some distinguished subset of triples $\langle c', c, c'' \rangle$ which are related by a particular force; much of Kaufmann's discussion suggests that the sentential force of imperatives is ORDER because ordering is compatible with all "unmarked" contexts.[42] If sentential force is (iii), we are treating sentential force as an illocutionary force potential in a sense similar to Bach and Harnish (1979). It seems to me that (iii) fits best with her overall approach.

I believe that Kaufmann accepts the standard moods of declarative, interrogative, and imperative, and we can infer the following illocutionary force potentials from her discussion:

1. The sentential force of declaratives: the potential to be assigned any speech act which involves adding propositional content to the context set.
2. The sentential force of interrogatives: the potential to be assigned any speech act which involves partitioning the context set.
3. The sentential force of imperatives: the potential to be assigned any speech act which involves adding propositional content to the context set and answering a salient decision problem.

Kaufmann's approach seems to fit readily with the compositional approach to the assignment of sentential force. The update potential $\mathcal{J}(S)$ is assigned based on S's semantic type, while its illocutionary force potential is constrained by both $\mathcal{J}(S)$ and other presuppositions of S. Specifically in the case of greatest interest to

---

[42] See especially the discussion in her Sections 1.1–1.4 and 4.2.4.

Kaufmann, she hypothesizes that the illocutionary force potential of imperatives is limited to appropriate options like ordering, permitting, advising, and the like by its semantic type (proposition) and its presuppositions.

Krifka: The operator-based view under the dynamic force hypothesis.   Whereas Kaufmann develops a theory of sentence mood which relies on an understanding of sentential force as the class of illocutionary acts which a sentence type can perform, Krifka (2014) takes up the view that sentential force is explicitly expressed within syntax. Building on the syntactic analysis of Rizzi (1997), he proposes that operators such as ASSERT and PERFORM occupy the head of a ForceP projection. (PERFORM is for explicit performatives. He suggests that there would be additional operators for questions and commands.) It thus seems that Krifka assumes a taxonomy of force operators which would identify the three basic sentence moods, plus one more to account for performatives. Krifka does not provide any new syntactic arguments which would support the idea that all sentences of a given sentence mood share a particular syntactic operator, and so would have difficulty explaining the diverse range of syntactic structures which can realize a single sentence mood (Section 3.1.3).

Although it takes a familiar approach to sentence mood, Krifka's analysis is innovative when it comes to its implementation of the dynamic force hypothesis. He describes the standard dynamic approach of Stalnaker as giving a picture of "a dynamic conversation and static world: a sentence changes the common ground and the set of available discourse referents, but the world and time of the utterance stays the same" (Krifka 2014, p. 5). In contrast, he wants to develop a theory in which speech acts change worlds and times: they map indices (world–time pairs) onto other indices. Krifka believes that such a picture better captures the true nature of speech acts.

To give an example of how Krifka sees speech acts, we can consider his treatment of the ASSERT operator. The idea is that ASSERT maps indices in which the speaker lacks a commitment to the asserted content onto ones in which she has such a commitment. We begin with a predicate COMMITTED which describes an individual as liable towards another individual for the truth of a proposition.[43]

(45)   COMMITTED$(i, p, x, y) = x$ is liable toward y for the truth of p at i.

Given (45), the operator ASSERT takes a propositional content p and a context c and maps indices onto indices. (The following definition simplifies at several points. As in the discussion of Kaufmann's theory, c_S is the speaker of context c and c_A the addressee; c_I is the world–time index.)

(46)   ⟦ ASSERT ⟧ $(p) =$
$\lambda c \lambda i' \iota i [i' = c_I$ and i differs from c_I in that COMMITTED$(i, p, c_S, c_A)]$

---

[43] Krifka calls this predicate ASSERT and the speech act operator ASSERT.

With regards to an example like *It's raining*, the operator (46) assigns a function which maps a context c onto a function which maps c_I onto the index which results from it when the speaker c_S becomes liable towards the addressee c_A for the truth of p. It "changes the index" from the existing one to one in which the speaker is committed to p in conversation with the addressee.

Krifka calls assertion defined in this way "an index changing device," but by itself, a function from indices to indices does not change any indices. We need some additional principle to account for what happens when an assertion is made in a particular discourse context. Krifka discusses several options for how to integrate (46) into a model of conversational update, each cast in terms of an update operator $+$. The most interesting attempt looks like this:

(47)   For any context $C = \langle C_S, C_A, C_{cs} \rangle$: $C + A =$
$$\langle C_S, C_A, \{A(C)(i) : i \in C_{cs}\} \rangle$$

This definition is a bit subtle, because we have two notions of context in play. In the previous definition of ASSERT, a context is a triple of a speaker, an addressee, and an index. We use lower-case c for this type of context. The update function (47) treats a context as a triple of a speaker C_S, an addressee C_A, and a context set C_{cs}. (Recall that a context set is a set of indices.) I use upper-case C for this new notion of context. Upper-case contexts differ from lower-case ones in that their third component is a set of indices, rather than an index.

What definition (47) says is that, when you update a context with A, you adjust the context set of the context by replacing each index in it with one in which the commitments specified by A are in place. Notice that the definition does not say that the propositional content of A is added to the context set. That is, in the case of ASSERT, the proposition asserted does not automatically become common ground—only the proposition that the speaker is liable for its truth. In this way, it is different from most dynamic theories derived from Stalnaker's work.[44]

As mentioned above, Krifka views his proposal as capturing the idea that speech acts, as "index-changing devices," do more than change the state of the conversation in the way which is standard in Stalnakerian dynamic pragmatics. Krifka's assertion operator derives a function (46) which modifies each world–time pair in the context set C_{cs}, thereby creating the new context set, rather than by eliminating indices through an intersective update, as happens in theories more closely based on Stalnaker's treatment of assertion. It is useful to ask, though, whether Krifka's theory really gives us more than a different implementation of the same procedure of update. One difference between Krifka's theory and Stalnaker's is that Krifka assumes that the primary effect of assertion is to adjust the speaker's commitments. The same update can certainly be expressed in an intersective theory. Suppose that the context set cs is a set of world–time pairs $\langle t, w \rangle$ where the speaker is not committed to p (at t in w), and that, at time $t + 1$, the speaker may or may not be committed to p (that is, there is at least one $\langle t, w' \rangle \in cs$ where the speaker is

---

[44] The contextual update recorded by ASSERT is essentially the secondary effect of assertion in a theory such as Stalnaker's. Thanks to Malte Willer for pointing out this way of understanding ASSERT.

committed to p at $t + 1$ in w' and at least one $\langle t, w'' \rangle \in cs$ where the speaker is not committed to p at $t+1$ in w''). The speaker then takes one second to utter a sentence asserting p. The time index is now $t + 1$ and the context set only contains pairs $\langle t + 1, w \rangle$ where the speaker is committed to p. The world w'' has been eliminated from cs.

It seems that Krifka assumes that the context set does not contain indices which differ in the way we have described $\langle t, w \rangle$ and $\langle t, w'' \rangle$ in this discussion. The index-to-index mapping (46) would not be different from intersective update if the worlds where the speaker comes to have a commitment to p are already present in cs. Instead, Krifka implies a view of the context set on which indices do not represent the presence or absence of discourse commitments unless the commitment is explicitly introduced by a speech act. In this respect, Krifka's ideas require a philosophical understanding of possible worlds different from Stalnaker's. Indeed, I am not confident that it would even be possible to develop a coherent concept of possible worlds which does the job Krifka's analysis needs it to do. It certainly seems that the context set can contain worlds in which a commitment may or may not be taken on in the future, since a sentence like (48) can be true:

(48)   You may be about to commit yourself to the claim that it's snowing.

The central idea of Krifka's analysis could be maintained, however, by enriching the notion of context or index to contain more than just individuals, worlds, and times. It should contain some component in addition to the context set which ASSERT changes to record a discourse commitment. If modified in this way, Krifka's analysis would be quite similar to dynamic theories which propose individual commitment slates in the context (see Section 3.3).

Charlow: Update potential as sentential force under the dynamic force hypothesis.   Charlow (2011) shows another way of using the tools of the dynamic approach to analyze sentential force within speech act theory. In its broad outlines, his theory is extremely similar to the pioneering ideas of Gazdar (1981) discussed in Section 1.4.3. Charlow proposes (2011, p. 80) that:

1. "A force—the semantic denotation of a force operator—is represented as a function from propositions into functions from states into states."
2. "A speech act is represented as the result of applying a force to a proposition."

These definitions imply that a speech act is a function from states into states, and except for its use of (cognitive) states in the definition, rather than contexts, these definitions match Gazdar's. Moreover, Charlow understands states in a way derived, ultimately, from Hamblin's (1971) commitment slates, one inspiration for Gazdar's conception of context. Therefore, we can see Charlow's work as representing the approach to speech acts originally sketched by Gazdar.[45]

---

[45] We also see Gazdar's ideas reflected in much work which we will classify under the dynamic approach, in particular Roberts (2004, 2012); Portner (2004, 2007); Starr (2013). However, Charlow presents his ideas as a form of speech act theory.

Charlow has a traditional, operator-based view of sentence mood which identifies sentence moods closely with clause types. He assumes that a root clause's grammatical form can be factored into a type-indicator and a clausal radical, giving its "clause type representation" (2011, p. 71):

(49)   a. dec(the window is shut)
      b. int(the window is shut)
      c. imp(the window is shut)

The clause types are conventionally associated with logical forms representing the illocutionary act they will perform, but this relation is based on the speaker's goals in the the context and hence defeasible.[46] The basic clause types of (49) are conventionally but defeasibly associated with familiar-looking logical forms:

(50)   a. ▷(the window is shut)
      b. ?(the window is shut)
      c. !(the window is shut)

Each speech act operator determines a characteristic update on the cognitive state. Charlow assumes that the cognitive state is structured to allow an explanatory theory of speech acts of assertion, asking, and "necessitation" (the act conventionally performed by imperatives). Each speech act operator updates a characteristic component of the discourse context based on its propositional content: $▷(\phi)$ modifies the informational component so that ϕ is included in the information in the state, and $!(\phi)$ modifies an action-guiding component so that ϕ is necessary in view of the state.[47] (He is uncertain whether interrogatives should be thought of as updating the informational component or a third component of their own.)

To summarize, in Charlow's theory sentence moods are identified with clause types, and sentential forces are the functions designated by the speech act operators ▷, ?, !. The relation between moods and forces is given by an inferential component of the theory which incorporates defeasible rules linking each clause type with its sentential force. The overall structure of the theory implies that the range of sentential forces is itself explained by the range of natural updates which can be performed on a cognitive state, and so the model of the cognitive state is itself quite crucial. Overall, Charlow offers a coherent theory addressing many of the issues which are central to the analysis of sentence mood. As has been mentioned, the picture he offers is similar to several theories within the dynamic approach. What's unique, apart from details we have set aside here concerning the specific update performed by imperatives, is the fact that Charlow integrates his ideas into speech act theory—albeit a "Gazdarian," not a "Searlean," version of it.

---

[46] Compare Charlow's ideas on this relation to earlier work by Bierwisch (1980); see Section 3.1.3.

[47] In its use of the structure of the context to provide the basis for an explanatory theory of sentence mood, Charlow follows closely previous and contemporary work in the dynamic approach. We will return to this idea below (see especially Section 3.3). Note that the actual updates which Charlow proposes are fairly complex, but the details are not important to our goals here.

3.3 Sentence mood in the dynamic approach

Since the 1980s, dynamic semantics and pragmatics have come to be the basis for much important research on the nature of sentence mood. As we see from its early incarnations, such as Hamblin's (1971) commitment slates and Stalnaker's (1978) common ground, the dynamic approach seeks to model a body of information and how that information is affected through communication. Sentence moods can then be understood as indicating the linguistically basic ways in which that body of information is affected by utterances of full sentences.

In order to understand how different versions of the dynamic approach work, we have to focus on the vague phrase "body of information." In its narrowest sense, the body of information is specifically a model of what the world is like. In simple cases, we often think of the common ground as a repository of factual presuppositions: as the participants in a conversation share knowledge with one another, the common ground grows to include more and more facts. You say "It's cold" and I say "It's raining," so now we both know it's cold and raining. This pooling of knowledge can obviously be of great benefit to those who share access to the pool.

This view of information flow in discourse as only the sharing of factual nuggets is too simple, and so we can map out how various versions of the dynamic approach work by tracking how their conception of discourse information differs from it. There are three main issues on which approaches differ.

1. How do we understand the "body of information"? It could represent:
   (a) A state of a conversation, for example Stalnaker's view of the common ground as mutual presuppositions.
   (b) A cognitive state, for example an individual's beliefs.
   (c) Any type of hypothetical scenario, such as a story, a dream, or the consequences of a hypothesis.
2. What goes into the "body of information"? It could contain information about:
   (a) How things are, for example the common ground.
   (b) What further information is relevant, needed, or expected.
   (c) What priorities are operative for judging situations as more or less preferred.
   (d) What entities are available to be referred to.
3. How the theory models changes to the "body of information" over time. It could represent:
   (a) Information at a particular point in time. A theory which takes this approach would then associate each sentence with a context change potential or update potential, a model of how the sentence affects the body of information.
   (b) The history of information states through an entire conversation, with rules governing which sequences constitute a proper conversation.

Because dynamic theories differ on a variety of fundamental philosophical para-meters, the list above can only be expressed accurately in a fairly abstract way. For example, the exact interpretation of "how things are" in point 2 depends on the answer to question 1. When a dynamic theory models how things are, this might concern how things are according to the presuppositions of a conversation, or someone's beliefs, or some hypothetical scenario. But in actual practice, the various dynamic approaches aren't so difficult to understand, and they are not as different from one another as their philosophical differences might lead one to expect. Let us look briefly at a few early dynamic approaches, to see how they stand on the issues above:

1. Stalnaker's common ground model understands the body of information it represents to be the shared presuppositions of the participants in a conversation at a given point in time (Stalnaker 1974, 1978). It is only concerned with how things are (according to those presuppositions). Therefore, the model is simply a set of propositions. It contains a pragmatic mechanism (assertion) for changing the body of information.

2. Hamblin's commitment slate model understands the body of information to represent the commitments of the participants in a conversation as they change through the course of a conversation (Hamblin 1971). It represents each participant's commitments pertaining to how things are (factual commitments) and to a limited extent expectations about what information will be added next (inquiries). In order to model the ways in which commitment slates change through a conversation, it defines a dialogue as a legal sequence of locutions and commitment slates. (We will discuss Hamblin's paper in more detail in Section 3.3.1 below.)

3. Kamp's Discourse Representation Theory understands the body of information to be the semantic content and pragmatic context of what has been said in a conversation at a given point in time (Kamp 1981). It represents both how things are and the discourse referents which are available for subsequent reference. It understands the discourse representation to be a mental model and precisely defines mechanisms for changing the mental model as new utterances are interpreted.

The differences among these approaches are significant, and we have only summarized three early papers. But at a practical level, we can describe them as all sharing a model of factual information (the common ground, factual component of the commitment slate, and discourse representation). To this core, Hamblin adds ideas to deal with questions and answers, while Kamp adds mechanisms to deal with discourse referents. As we consider various theories within the dynamic approach, I will aim to emphasize their commonalities. I will treat as less important those differences among theories which do not seem likely to play a role in explaining the nature of sentence mood. In particular, I'll de-emphasize differences which have to do with whether the factual information they represent should be thought of as the common ground, interlocutors' beliefs, or some other sense of communicated meaning. Instead, I'll focus on the formal structure of the model and the use to which it can be put as we aim to develop a better understanding of sentence mood.

The structured context.   As discussed just above, different dynamic theories think of the body of information which is changed through communication in different ways. Among those which attempt to address the properties and nature of sentence mood, however, they virtually all think of that body of information as the discourse context in the following specific sense:

(51)   The DISCOURSE CONTEXT is constituted by all of the features of a conversation which are essential to linguistic communication.

Stalnaker's common ground is understood as a partial model of the discourse context because the theory seeks to explain the important linguistic concepts of assertion and presupposition in terms of it. For the remainder of this section, we will use this notion of the conversational context to explain, compare, and further articulate what the various dynamic semantics and pragmatics theories have to say about sentence mood. We will do this even though, admittedly, some of the authors might not describe their own ideas using the term "discourse context."

The central idea of the dynamic approach is that each sentence is associated with a context change potential (see Section 1.4.1). This context change potential is meant to explain how the sentence contributes to the flow of information in discourse. Within this tradition, it is natural to think of different sentence moods as contributing differently to the flow of information, and hence many scholars have pursued the idea that each sentence mood has its own characteristic kind of context change potential. From this perspective, Stalnaker's definition of assertion is just the beginning. Assertion, so the thought goes, is the force of declaratives (or maybe of just some declaratives); we need an analysis like that of assertion for the forces of interrogatives, imperatives, and sentences exemplifying other sentence moods. So the question becomes: what other kinds of updates can there be, beyond updates of assertion?

In the remainder of this section, we will see various answers to this question, but as we set out, it is important to note a theme common to many of them. This is the idea that, if we are to define more sentential forces, there must be more structure in the discourse context. We will call a model of the conversational context which is structured so as to allow an explanation of the properties and nature of sentence mood the "structured discourse context":

(52)   A STRUCTURED DISCOURSE CONTEXT is a model of the discourse context which has internal structure allowing an explanatory theory of sentence mood.

A simple example of a theory like this is due to Portner (2004). Portner defines a context as a triple consisting of the common ground, the question set, and a function assigning a to-do list to each participant in the conversation.

(53)   A PORTNER CONTEXT is a triple $\langle cg, qs, tdl \rangle$:
       a. The common ground cg, a set of propositions.

    b. The question set qs, a set of question-denotations.

    c. The to-do list function tdl, assigning a set of properties to each participant p.

Portner uses the structure of (53) to define the sentential forces as in Table 3.2. We will see how Portner's model works in detail in Section 3.3.3 (and by that point we will have discussed the previous work on which it builds). The key point for now is to see it as an example of the structured discourse context.

TABLE 3.2   Structured discourse context of Portner (2004)

Sentence mood	Force	Component of context
declaratives	assertion	updates cg
interrogatives	asking	updates qs
imperatives	requiring	updates tdl

    Dynamic theories which employ a version of the structured discourse context do not necessarily think of that structure in terms of a list of simple components. For example, Inquisitive Semantics proposes that a single component can have enough structure to model the functions of both declaratives and interrogatives (see Section 3.3.2). In evaluating a theory of sentence mood within the dynamic approach, the main question often becomes whether the particular version of the structured discourse context which it proposes allows an analysis of all of the sentential forces of the sentence moods it attends to, and more generally whether it serves as the basis for an explanation of important properties of sentence mood systems in natural language.

Dynamic semantics vs. dynamic pragmatics.   Before we go on to discuss what theories have been developed of the sentence moods in the dynamic approach, I want to briefly highlight several ways in which these theories differ that may not be so easy to see as the discussion proceeds. The first of these has to do with the difference between dynamic pragmatics and dynamic semantics. As we've defined it in Section 1.4.1, dynamic pragmatics is a dynamic theory in which the semantic content of a sentence is not inherently dynamic; it is a traditional, static semantics value like a proposition or a property. Within this approach, sentences or utterances are assigned an update potential based on their static semantic values according to some pragmatic principles. For example, within Stalnaker's theory, sentences denote propositions which can be asserted. The assertion of a proposition updates the common ground, and so we can think of assertion as a pragmatic tool associating a proposition with an update potential. Heim's File Change Semantics (Heim 1982, 1983) is even more explicit about the relation between the content of a sentence (a satisfaction set $Sat(S)$) and its update potential (the context change potential defined implicitly as $F + Sat(S)$).

    In dynamic semantics, the meaning of a sentence is identified with its update potential. In fact, as mentioned in Section 1.4.1, Heim ultimately endorses dynamic semantics as she says that the meaning of S is its context change potential. Dynamic semantics is often associated with the Amsterdam school of logic (e.g. Groenendijk and Stokhof 1990, 1991; Groenendijk et al. 1997; Aloni and van Rooy 2002; Groenendijk and Roelofsen 2009). It is not clear how important the difference between dynamic pragmatics and dynamic semantics is when it comes to evaluating theories of sentence mood. We see, for example, very similar theories about sentence mood in the dynamic pragmatics analysis of Portner (2004), the speech act analysis of Charlow (2011), and the dynamic semantics analysis of Starr (2013). All of these treatments pursue the hypothesis that we have three basic sentence moods—declaratives, interrogatives, and imperatives—because there are three natural ways to update the structured discourse context; these three ways of updating the context serve as the sentential forces of the basic sentence moods. Nevertheless, there are important differences of detail among the proposals. All three authors focus on imperatives and yet they treat the update potential of imperatives in different ways and have different proposals about how the syntax of imperatives determines their update potential. For the most part, these differences simply represent different ideas about the semantic/pragmatic system, and cannot be attributed to the deeper differences among speech act theory, dynamic pragmatics, and dynamic semantics.

As we go forward, we will also see differences among dynamic theories in how they view the interface between grammar and update potential. In Section 3.1.3, we identified three approaches to this interface: the operator-based approach, the construction-based approach, and the compositional approach. In dynamic semantics and pragmatics, scholars often assume an operator-based explanation of the relation between sentence mood and sentential force. We also find examples of the compositional approach (Portner 2004; Farkas and Roelofsen 2017; Roberts to appear). I do not know of any explicitly construction-based dynamic theories of sentence mood, but there is no reason one could not exist.[48]

A third difference among the theories discussed in this section concerns whether they formulate their ideas in terms of the discourse context which is changed by the update potentials of sentences, or whether they aim to given an overall "grammar" of discourse. Most dynamic theories take the first shape, and I will typically discuss all of them in that way. But we see another way in the work of Hamblin (1971) and Roberts (1996/2012, 2004). These authors aim to define a well-formed dialogue as a sequence of sentences which conforms to a set of rules; these rules can be seen as defining a generative grammar for dialogues. However, as we will see, in practice the latter type of theory can always be recast in the more typical context-and-update format, and I will do so in order to ease explanations and comparison with other theories.[49]

---

[48] As noted in Section 3.1.3, it would be quite feasible to marry Ginzburg and Sag's (2001) construction-based view of syntax and semantics with a dynamic analysis of sentential force. It is also reasonable to view Lauer's (2013) theory as implicitly assuming a construction-based view.

[49] See also Portner (to appear) for additional discussion of the variants of the dynamic approach.

3.3.1 Declaratives in the dynamic approach

For most work in dynamic semantics and pragmatics, the analysis of the sentential force of declaratives is obvious. Following Stalnaker, the discourse context is represented by (or contains as a part) the common ground or a closely related construct. Propositions can be asserted, and the essential effect of a successful assertion is to add the proposition to the common ground (Section 1.4.1). If the discourse context is modeled as a context set rather than a common ground, the essential effect of assertion is to intersect the proposition with the context set. In File Change Semantics (Heim 1982, 1983) and classical dynamic semantics (Groenendijk and Stokhof 1990, 1991; Groenendijk et al. 1996), the discourse context is a context set augmented to represent discourse referents, and the dynamic meaning of a sentence is a function updating this augmented context set.

Hamblin (1971) presented a framework for analyzing dialogue which preceded Stalnaker's papers by a few years and which contains very similar ideas. His approach is to define a grammar of dialogues—that is, a set of rules which define as well-formed certain sequences of "locutions." He defines a number of systems within this general framework, several of which concern dialogues involving assertions and retractions. Intuitively, these would be dialogues in which all of the sentences uttered are declarative. These systems can be summarized as follows:

1. There are two types of LOCUTIONS: assertions and retractions.
2. A DIALOGUE is a sequence of locutions $\langle l_0, l_1, \ldots, l_i \rangle$. Each locution is associated with a speaker.
3. A COMMITMENT SLATE is a set of assertions.
4. The relation between locutions and commitment slates: For each locution in a dialogue $D = \langle l_0, l_1, \ldots, l_i \rangle$, $CS_j(p)$ is a commitment slate representing participant p's commitments in D after locution j.
5. RULES define possible sequences of locutions.

The rules mentioned in point 5 say what locution i can be, given the preceding commitment slates $CS_{i-1}(p)$, and what $CS_i(p)$ can be, given locution i and $CS_{i-1}(p)$. For example, Hamblin proposes the following rules:[50]

(54)   a. Following an assertion, everyone's commitment slate includes that assertion.

   b. Following a retraction by participant p, p's commitment slate does not include the retracted assertion, but the other participants' commitment slates remain unaltered.

Hamblin's various systems differ in interesting ways, and overall the paper is an exploration of various models of dialogue. For example, systems differ in whether commitment slates are sets of locutions (as in the presentation above)

---

[50] Hamblin's theory, including the rules, is given in a dense set-theoretic notation. I present the rules in non-formal language so that we can focus on their role in his theory of sentence mood.

or sets of propositions (i.e. the denotations of locutions). Another difference concerns whether a commitment brings with it commitment to other propositions, in particular logical consequences of it. The relation between assertions and their consequences becomes difficult when the dialogue contains retractions (as well as when it contains questions and answers, discussed in Section 3.3.2), and his discussion of these problems is interesting, but not very relevant to sentence mood.

Because the rules which define possible sequences of locutions involve the relation between locution l_i and the commitment slates of the participants at $i - 1$, Hamblin's systems can be translated into rules for contextual update along the lines familiar from Stalnaker's work. In fact, as discussed in Section 1.4.3, Gazdar presciently pointed out how well Hamblin's model fits with the dynamic force hypothesis in which "an assertion that ϕ is a function that changes a context in which the speaker is not committed to justifiable true belief in ϕ into a context in which he is so committed" and moreover "the familiar 'common ground' view of the context can be defined on the basis of the set-of-commitment-slates view" (Gazdar 1981, p. 69). From this perspective, Hamblin's notion of assertion is quite close to Stalnaker's.

Although there is widespread agreement within the dynamic approach that an assertion results in either the addition of a proposition to the common ground (or the speaker's commitment slate) or the intersection of a proposition with the context set (or file, or information state), scholars are for the most part not explicit about how assertion relates to the declarative sentence mood. Scholars in this tradition use the word "assertion" in slightly different ways. Stalnaker talks of assertions as acts: "assertions are made in a context" (Stalnaker 1974, p. 315). Hamblin treats them as a variety of "locution." Roberts describes them as "moves," writing: "Note that moves, on the interpretation I will give them, are not speech acts, but the semantic objects which are used in speech acts: A speech act is the act of proffering a move" (Roberts 2012, p. 5). In contrast, Portner uses "assertion" primarily to name a sentential force, specifically the force of declaratives. I do not think it's possible to paper over these differences. Stalnaker's conception of assertions as acts seems quite different from Roberts' idea that they are semantic objects used in speech acts.

Despite these differences, it probably is reasonable to assume a common perspective on the sentential force of declaratives among all followers of the dynamic approach. Using the terminology favored in this book, the canonical view includes the following tenets:

(55) The sentential force of declaratives is ASSERTION, understood as either (a) or (b):
   a. The addition of the proposition denoted by the sentence to a component of the structured discourse context representing either
      (i) the mutually presupposed information, i.e. the common ground, or
      (ii) the speaker's commitments, i.e. the speaker's commitment slate.
   b. The operation of intersecting the proposition denoted by the sentence with a proposition representing (i) or (ii), i.e. the context set.

(Perhaps Hamblin would disagree with (55), since retractions presumably take the form of declaratives in most cases; if so, this fact would leave Hamblin without a good candidate for the sentential force of declaratives.)

Although (55) is widely accepted within the dynamic approach, only a few scholars present explicit ideas about how declaratives are associated with the force of assertion. Portner (2004) follows the compositional approach; he assumes that declaratives, but not interrogatives or imperatives, have propositions as their denotations, and proposes that a pragmatic principle assigns assertion as the force of declaratives on the basis of their propositional type. In contrast, Lauer (2013) argues against a compositional approach based on semantic type and proposes a normative "declarative convention." While he does not address the grammatical status of clause types in detail, it seems that he treats declarative as an unanalyzed construction to which sentential force is associated holistically by the declarative convention. The operator-based view is represented by Starr (2013) and Charlow (2011), both of whom assume an assertion operator.[51]

The relation between assertion and asking.   In a number of dynamic theories, the analysis of assertion cannot be understood simply by thinking about the function of declaratives. Rather, they develop, in one way or another, ideas about assertion which are closely related to the analysis of questions. A clear example of this perspective comes from dynamic semantics and early forms of inquisitive semantics. In these frameworks, several scholars have proposed that the discourse context is a relation over a set of possible worlds, that is, a set of pairs of worlds (Jäger 1996; Hulstijn 1997; Aloni and van Rooy 2002; Aloni et al. 2007; Mascarenhas 2009; Groenendijk 2009). Assertion affects the domain of the relation, that is, the set of worlds which participate in the pairs. This view of assertion is not fundamentally different from the standard one, since it amounts to intersection. For example, if we assume that S denotes proposition p, to assert S in context C amounts to the following:

(56) Assertion in dynamic semantics for questions: The result of asserting S in context c is $c \cap (p \times p)$.
 • In the notation of dynamic semantics: $c[S] = c \cap (p \times p)$.

The motivation for treating the context as a relation (rather than a simple set of worlds) comes from the dynamic approach to questions. A question affects the set of pairs in a different way from assertion. We will see how dynamic theories of questions work in the next subsection.

Other theories which closely relate assertions and questions are more radical. As discussed above (Section 3.1.1), Gunlogson (2001) does not clearly distinguish the sentential force of declaratives from that of interrogatives. In her view, declaratives always involve postulating that some participant in the conversation is committed

---

[51] Note that Starr's theory draws on Inquisitive Semantics, and so involves a more complex view of the discourse context than assumed so far. We will discuss it below. Charlow's theory is a version of speech act theory which accepts the dynamic force hypothesis.

to their propositional content, but when this participant is the addressee (the case of rising declaratives), Gunlogson describes the result as a question. An example of a declarative question is (57a) (=(12a) above). In contrast, when the declarative postulates that the speaker is committed to the propositional content (as with the falling declarative (57b)), the sentence functions as an assertion. (An interrogative (57c) always functions as a question.)

(57)   a. It's raining? (rising intonation, declarative)
        b. It's raining. (falling intonation, declarative)
        c. Is it raining? (rising intonation, interrogative)

It is not precisely clear in Gunlogson's dissertation exactly how the meaning associated with the declarative clause type works. With rising intonation, a declarative seeks confirmation that the proposition is in the addressee's commitment set, but with falling intonation, it adds the proposition to the speaker's commitment set. This difference between seeking confirmation and adding a proposition is never fully explained, but the theory is nevertheless interesting because of the way it attempts to treat assertion and some cases of asking a question as subvarieties of a single discourse function, differing only in which participant's commitment slate is targeted for the postulation of a commitment.[52, 53]

It is difficult to say what Gunlogson's theory implies for the broader theory of sentence mood. She does not give an explicit analysis of interrogatives, so we cannot determine whether they have a sentential force which is significantly different from rising declaratives. Nevertheless, she describes both rising declaratives and interrogatives as questions, suggesting that rising declaratives have more in common with interrogatives in terms of their pragmatic function. If this is right, Gunlogson's ideas seemingly would imply that interrogatives and some declaratives constitute one sentence mood, and the other declaratives another. This conclusion would imply that declarative is not a clause type in the sense we use the term here.

Some of the unclarities that we find in Gunlogson's theory are addressed in later work by Farkas and Bruce (2010). They define the structured discourse context as follows:

(58)   A FARKAS/BRUCE CONTEXT is a tuple $\langle CS, cg, qs, ps \rangle$, where:
        a. CS is a function from discourse participants p to p's discourse commitments.
        b. cg is a common ground.
        c. qs, or the 'table', is a stack of questions under discussion.
        d. ps is a set of projected extensions of cg.

---

[52] For other important work on rising declaratives, see Pierrehumbert and Hirschberg (1990), Šafářová and Swerts (2004), Šafářová (2005, 2007), Truckenbrodt (2006a), and Trinh and Crnič (2011).

[53] In recent work, I have also argued that the difference between strong imperatives like orders and weak ones like those which offer advice or permission can be explained in a version of Gunlogson's system (Portner, to appear).

The component *CS* associates each participant with a commitment slate, as in Hamblin's and Gunlogson's work; *cg* is the common ground, and *cg* is defined to be the commitments shared by all participants. We will set aside discussion of *qs* for now; Farkas and Bruce call it the "table," and it is equivalent to Roberts' (2012) question under discussion stack. The final component *ps* is essential to clarifying some of the issues raised about Gunlogson's system above, since it links a current discourse move like making an assertion or asking a question with conventional expectations about what effects that move will have.

Suppose the speaker asserts (59):

(59)   I am hungry.

According to Farkas and Bruce, an assertion operator **A** applies to the sentence and context, yielding a new context in which the proposition that the speaker is hungry has been added to the speaker's commitment slate. So far, this is similar to Gunlogson's and Hamblin's systems (though Hamblin would immediately add it to all participants' commitment slates). But crucially, in addition the proposition is simultaneously added to the projected extensions of *cg* in *ps*. This can be seen as representing the idea that the speaker expects his commitment to become a shared commitment. At the next stage of the discourse, the addressee can either agree (or fail to object), in which case the projected extension of the common ground will take effect (the proposition that the speaker is hungry is added to the common ground *cg*), or dissent.[54]

Farkas and Bruce (2010) do not discuss rising declaratives, and so their analysis does not lead to any cloudiness concerning the difference between declaratives and interrogatives. In fact, they assume that the two types are distinguished by "sentential features" [D] and [I] and that different force operators apply to sentences marked by [D] and [I]. Their ideas about clause types and sentence mood thus seem similar to the views of Stenius (1967) and Krifka (2001, 2014). Some recent work has built on Farkas and Bruce's model to incorporate analyses of the pragmatic effects of rising and falling intonation (Malamud and Stephenson 2015; Roelofsen and Farkas 2015; Farkas and Roelofsen 2017).

Another theory which diminishes the difference between assertion and asking a question is the later form of inquisitive semantics (Ciardelli et al. 2013). As this is primarily an analysis of questions, we will discuss it just below in Section 3.3.2. For our purposes here, I only want to point out that in inquisitive semantics, the updates associated with statements and questions are both intersective, and there are hybrid sentences as well (sentences with both assertion-like and question-like effects).

Declaratives in a probability-based discourse semantics.   As discussed in Section 2.1, a number of probability-based theories of sentential and subsentential

---

[54] A similar sequence occurs when a question is added to *qs*, except that, because a question projects multiple extensions of the common ground in *ps*, an answer is required to determine which proposition is to be added to *cg*.

modality have been developed in recent years, and in some of them the compositional meaning of a sentence is not a possible worlds proposition but rather something which encodes information about probabilities. In the particular version of the idea which was sketched above, the denotation of a sentence is a set of credal information states as defined in (38) in Chapter 2. In this section, we will consider the consequences of such theories for the analysis of sentence mood.

Yalcin (2012) and Swanson (2015) give the most linguistically sophisticated versions of the view according to which sentence meanings are credal information states.[55] Swanson defines assertion as follows:

(60)   Assertion of credal information: In asserting that ϕ, a speaker advises her addressees to conform their credences to the semantic value of 'ϕ'. Holding all other factors fixed, the advice associated with 'ϕ' is stronger than the advice associated with 'ψ' iff 'ϕ' is more informative than 'ψ'. (Swanson 2015)

Swanson's definition here captures the essential intuition of the credal information semantics: People have credences, sentences express credal information, and the function of assertion is to guide one's interlocutors in adjusting their credences. Swanson's proposal is not explicit about the status of "advice" in the theory of sentential force.

Yalcin (2012, p. 6) proposes a dynamic semantics in which the common ground is reanalyzed in terms of probabilities.

(61)   A CREDAL CONTEXT is a set of credal information states.

(Yalcin uses the term "blunt information state" for what is labeled "credal context" here.) Given this definition of the conversational context, together with the proposal that sentence meanings are also sets of credal information states, the sentential force of declaratives can be represented as intersection:

(62)   Assertion in the probability-based semantics: The result of asserting S in context $c = c \cap [\![\, S \,]\!]$.

Statement (62) conforms to the standard analysis of assertion within the dynamic approach, and for this reason it does not have any unique implications for the theory of sentence mood. As far as can be determined on the basis of existing proposals, the probability-based approach is compatible with the same theories of sentence mood as other dynamic approaches are. Of course, since the probability-based approach has not been extended to other sentence moods, we cannot say that it is as well-supported as other, non-probabilistic dynamic approaches. It may

---

[55] Yalcin discusses the choice between a dynamic semantics treatment, on which sentence meanings are update potentials, and a dynamic pragmatics version, on which they are sets of credal information states. Swanson follows the latter approach.

or may not be able to incorporate adequate theories of interrogatives, imperatives, and minor clause types.

3.3.2 Interrogatives in the dynamic approach

Background on the semantics of questions. In order to understand what dynamic theories have to say about the sentence mood of interrogatives, we must build on some basic knowledge concerning the semantics of interrogatives. We refer to the semantic values of interrogatives as QUESTIONS. (As with 'assertion', the term 'question' is used in several ways: for a type of utterance, sentence, act, or semantic value. Here we use it only for denotations of the kind assigned to interrogatives.) In some of the earliest work on the topic in a modern semantic framework, Hamblin (1958, 1971, 1973) develops both an analysis of questions as semantic objects and a dynamic model of how questions and answers function in dialogue, and as might be expected, the analysis of dialogue draws naturally on his ideas about questions.[56] Subsequent work in the dynamic tradition has followed the same pattern, incorporating specific ideas about what a question is into analyses of what asking a question does. As we will see, to some extent advances and disagreements in the literature on the semantics of interrogatives can be ignored as we look at their function in discourse, but it will be necessary to have a basic understanding of semantic developments, if only to allow a useful statement of each scholar's views.

We can begin with Hamblin's semantics for questions. He treats questions as sets of propositions, where each proposition is understood to be a possible answer to the question. This idea is developed into a compositional analysis of interrogatives in Hamblin (1973); there he treats (63a) as denoting the answer-set (63b), and likewise for (64):

(63) a. Is it raining?
   b. $\{\{w: \text{it is raining in } w\}, W - \{w : \text{it is raining in } w\}\}$

(64) a. Who cried?
   b. $\{\{w : a \text{ cried in } w\} : a \text{ is an individual}\} =$
   $\{p : \text{for some individual } a, p = \{w : a \text{ cried in } w\}\}$

The hypothesis that the semantics of interrogatives is something like a set of answers is motivated by an intuition about the discourse function of questions, namely that to ask a question involves changing the context in such a way that some party to the conversation will be motivated to answer it. (Obviously this intuition is not unique to the dynamic approach; speech act theory develops it in a different way.) Since we observe that people do in fact often provide answers to our questions, it seems that knowing what constitutes an answer is at least part of knowing the meaning of a question.

---

[56] Another well-known early theory of questions is due to Karttunen (1977).

The idea that a question denotes a set of possible answers will be mostly sufficient for our purposes, but as discussed by Cross and Roelofsen (2014), it is not derived from a detailed study of which kinds of responses to a question should count as an answer. As they point out, Hamblin's formal theory treats (65a) as an answer to (64a), but not (65b) or (65c):

(65)   a. Beatrice cried.
         b. Beatrice alone cried.
         c. A girl cried.

Groenendijk and Stokhof (1982, 1984, 1997) develop a theory which conforms to Hamblin's and Karttunen's general approach but which is more specific about the notion of answerhood which underlies it. They argue that certain semantic and logical issues can be solved by building the semantics of questions specifically on one distinguished type of answer, the true, exhaustive answer. More precisely, they take the meaning of an interrogative to be a function from worlds to propositions, where the proposition represents the true, exhaustive answer to the question in that world. As an example, assume that in the actual world, Beatrice was the only individual who cried. Then, the question denoted by (64a) would assign the proposition expressed by (65b) to the actual world.

Because it isolates the true, exhaustive answer to a question as the basis for the semantics, Groenendijk and Stokhof's theory can be neatly expressed in another way. Notice that, if a question Q maps a given world w to proposition p (thus, p is the true exhaustive answer to Q in w), Q will also map any world in p to p. This is so because the true, exhaustive answer to Q is the same for every world in p. In terms of our example, $[\![(64a)]\!] (w_{actual})$ = the set of worlds in which Beatrice alone cried, and in any of those worlds, the true exhaustive answer to (64a) is also that Beatrice alone cried. In symbols:

(66)   For every world $w \in p$, $Q(w) = p$.

Generalizing this reasoning, the semantics of a question divides up the set of possible worlds into subsets corresponding to the true, exhaustive answer, and assigns each of these subsets to every world in it. The result can be visualized as in Figure 3.1. Another way to represent the same fundamental information would be to treat the question as a relation holding between any two worlds in the same answer, as in Figure 3.2. (Note that each world is also paired with itself, but this is left out of the figure for simplicity.) This structure is a partition of the set of possible worlds, and Groenendijk and Stokhof's analysis is often referred to as the PARTITION THEORY.

There are many places for readers interested in learning more about the semantics of questions to look. The handbook articles Groenendijk and Stokhof (1997) and Krifka (2011) are good places to start, covering a range of issues and theories. Dayal (2016) is more comprehensive, especially on issues related to the syntax/semantics interface.

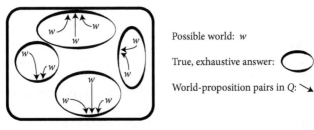

FIGURE 3.1   The question as function from worlds to answers

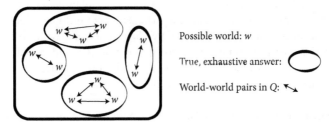

FIGURE 3.2   The question as a partition

Dynamic theories of asking a question.   Above in Section 3.3.1, I presented a summary of one of Hamblin's (1971) systems of dialogue. That system was designed to account for assertions by proposing that the discourse effect of an assertion was to add it to the commitment slates of all participants in the conversation. In the same paper, he presents more elaborate systems which also cover questions. The following is a partial description which aims to give the basic idea of how his rather complex system works:[57]

1. There are five types of LOCUTIONS: assertions, retractions, inquiries, retraction-demands, and *I don't know*.
   In symbols: The set L consists of five non-overlapping subsets $\lambda, \mu, \xi, \eta, L_0$.
2. A DIALOGUE is a sequence of locutions $\langle l_0, l_1, \ldots, l_i \rangle$.
3. A COMMITMENT SLATE is a set of assertions.
4. The relation between locutions and commitment slates: For each locution in a dialogue $D = \langle l_0, l_1, \ldots, l_i \rangle$, $CS_j(p)$ is a commitment slate representing participant p's commitments in D after locution j.

The preceding is the same as the system described earlier, except that there are more kinds of locutions. The rules which define the set of well-formed dialogues are different so as to account for inquiries, retraction-demands, and *I don't know*. Some of the relevant rules are paraphrased below:

[57] I am describing Hamblin's (1971, pp. 146–8) System 7 here.

(67) a. Following an assertion, everyone's commitment slate includes that asser-
          tion.
      b. Following a retraction by participant p, p's commitment slate does not
          include that retraction, but every other participant's commitment slate
          remains unaltered.
      c. An inquiry is not allowed if an answer to it is in anyone's commitment
          slate.
      d. Following an inquiry, the next locution must be an assertion by someone
          other than the speaker of the inquiry and must answer it.

As before, a well-formed dialogue is one in which each locution l_j follows the rules
given the preceding locution l_{j-1} and the participants' commitment slates $CS_{j-1}(p)$.
In turn, each participant's commitment slate $CS_j(p)$ associated with l_j is determined
by that participant's preceding commitment slate $CS_{j-1}(p)$ and the latest locution
l_j. This means we can think of locution l_{j-1} and all of the participants' associated
commitment slates as the discourse context for locution l_j:

(68) A HAMBLIN CONTEXT is a locution and an assignment of commitment slates
      to participants.
      Specifically, the context for locution l_j is:

      $\langle l_{j-1}, CS_{j-1} \rangle$, where $CS_{j-1}(p)$ is defined for each participant p.

This notion of context lets us recast Hamblin's theory of inquiries in the more
familiar context-and-update model of dynamic approaches. Assertions affect the
context in two ways, by becoming the locution component l_{j-1} of the new context
and by being added to each commitment slate. This, as we said above, amounts
to a version of the standard dynamic treatment of assertion. Inquiries affect the
context in only one way, by becoming the locution component of the new context.
Inquiries do not affect anyone's commitment slate, but when the last locution
was an inquiry, discourse rules constrain the choice of the next locution: after
an inquiry must come an assertion which answers it. Hamblin's dynamic theory
of inquiries therefore amounts to saying that the context change potential of an
inquiry is to limit the range of locutions which can come next to a specific set of
assertions. As we noted above, Hamblin does not say enough to allow us to attribute
a specific theory of sentence mood; crucially, it is not clear that the inquiries
correspond exactly to interrogatives. (In fact, Hamblin (1973, p. 52) suggests that
the interrogative *What entity is an entity?* "is really an indicative," because its
denotation contains a single proposition.)[58]
    Roberts (1996, 2004, 2012) formulates a theory of assertions and questions
which is similar to Hamblin's in several ways.[59,60] Like Hamblin's, the theory is

---

[58] This is so because, for each entity x, the proposition that x is an entity is the same proposition, the
tautology W.
[59] Ginzburg (1995a,b, 1996) develops ideas very similar to Hamblin's and Roberts' within a Situation
Semantics framework.
[60] Roberts (2012) is essentially the same paper as Roberts (1996). There are some corrections in the
newer version.

formulated in terms of a grammar of dialogue, though Roberts uses the term INFORMATION STRUCTURE for what Hamblin called the dialogue. The information structure employs a structured discourse context as a key part and the portion of the context which is devoted to questions is more sophisticated than Hamblin's. I will give a partial description of Roberts' notion of information structure here.

(69) An INFORMATION STRUCTURE has seven components:
   1. A set of MOVES M.
   2. A set of questions Q, a subset of M.
   3. A set of assertions A, a subset of M.
   4. The precedence relation < over M, reflecting the order in which the moves are made in the discourse.
   5. The set of accepted moves ACC, a subset of M.
   6. The COMMON GROUND function CG which assigns a common ground cg to each move in M.
   7. The QUESTION UNDER DISCUSSION function QUD which assigns a question set qs to each move in M.

The first four parts of the information structure correspond directly to features of Hamblin's model. The component ACC is an innovation and allows for the possibility that certain moves do not affect the other components because the participants other than the speaker reject them.[61] The common ground is of course familiar. Note that $CG(m)$ is the common ground "just prior to the utterance of m." It will include the effects of all moves preceding m as well as any other information which has become presupposed through other means. The real innovation is in the final component, which assigns to each move a question set.[62] Unlike Hamblin's system, where a question only has an effect on the next locution, in Roberts' theory multiple questions can influence the discourse at a single point in time, and they stand in both semantic and pragmatic relations to assertions and other questions. These relations allow a better explanation of the role which questions play in dialogue.

For a given move m, the appropriateness and effect of m are defined entirely in terms of the common ground and question set associated with m. Some of the important rules relevant to assertions and questions may be paraphrased as follows:

(70) a. An accepted assertion a_i is in $CG(m_j)$ for all subsequent moves m_j.
   b. An accepted question q_i is in qs for all subsequent moves m_j, unless an answer to it is entailed by $CG(m_j)$ or "q_i is determined to be practically unanswerable."
   c. As long as a question is in qs, any new question must be more specific than it.

---

[61] In reality, moves are probably not rejected so completely and abruptly as the model suggests. In Hamblin's system, cases of rejection would be handled through retraction-demands and retractions. Merin (1994) creates a system in which some of the complexity of negotiation can be represented.

[62] Roberts calls the question set a "question under discussion stack" but since the order associated with the stack is just <, we can treat qs as a simple set.

More precisely: For any questions q and q' both in QUD(m), if $q < q'$, then a complete answer to q' entails a partial answer to q.

The fact that the appropriateness and effect of each accepted move may be determined on the basis of its common ground and question set makes it possible to extract a more standard notion of context from Roberts' definition of information structure.

(71)   A ROBERTS CONTEXT is a common ground and a question set.

Definition (71) allows us to restate Roberts' theory in terms of a more standard context-and-update-potential format. Assertion, as usual, is the addition of a proposition to the common ground (assuming the move is accepted). Asking a question is the addition of a question to the question set, subject to the condition that it be more specific than any other question in the set (see Roberts 2012, (17)). There are other interesting aspects of conversational dynamics which can be explored in this framework. For example, Rule (70b) implies that a question is removed from the question set as soon as the common ground entails an answer to it; this could happen because an assertion provides the answer. Roberts also defines a notion of Relevance for moves:[63]

(72)   The question under discussion for move m is the most recent member of QUD(m).

(73)   A move is RELEVANT to the question under discussion Q if and only if:
a. m is an assertion, and it provides at least a partial answer to Q, or
b. m is a question and a complete answer to m entails at least a partial answer to Q.

After presenting her basic theory of information structure, Roberts goes on to investigate the role of focus in discourse.

Roberts' theory represents a milestone in the development of dynamic pragmatics theories of questions in discourse, and has been the basis for much continuing work (e.g. Büring 2003; Beaver and Clark 2008; Biezma and Rawlins 2012). But she does not quite set things up in a way which provides a clear notion of sentential force or a theory of sentence mood. Her discussion is not explicit about the relation among interrogative sentences, utterances of them, question denotations, the "proffer" of a question denotation, and speech acts. As we are looking for ideas about the nature of sentence mood, however, I think it's reasonable to associate with Roberts' theory the following claim, even if it may not be a hypothesis she has explicitly endorsed:

---

[63] Roberts' version of (73b) employs a notion of a "strategy" to answer a question, but from what I can tell, rule (70b) guarantees that it is part of a strategy in the relevant sense.

(74)   The sentential force of interrogatives is ASKING, understood as the addition of the question denoted by the interrogative to a component of the structured discourse context representing the mutual commitment to add to the common ground information which answers the question.

In Roberts' approach, the question set encodes even more than this, in particular a commitment to answer the questions in a certain last-to-first order, but I think she intends for the issue of how the interlocutors should address the questions in the question set to be a matter of Gricean cooperativeness rather than an aspect of their sentential force.

The relation between asking and assertion.   In Section 3.3.1, we began an overview of one important approach to questions in dynamic semantics. This work treats the context as a relation over a set of worlds, with assertion equivalent to the operation of restricting the domain of that relation (Jäger 1996; Hulstijn 1997; Aloni and van Rooy 2002; Aloni et al. 2007; Mascarenhas 2009; Groenendijk 2009). Now we are ready to see how the update potential of interrogatives is explained in this approach, and in order to do this, we have to understand precisely what type of relation the context is and what it represents. The dynamic semantics analysis of questions is built on two principles:

1.   Questions are analyzed following the partition theory.
2.   The context is a big question.

Let us begin with the second point. Since questions are understood as partitions, to say that the context is a question is to analyze it as a partition. Specifically, each cell in the partition represents a complete answer to all open questions. See Figure 3.3. (Note that the worlds in each cell of the partition are also related to themselves— that is, the relation is reflexive—but the reflexive pairs are left out of the diagram for simplicity.) Intuitively, the partition represents a conversation which will reach its resolution as soon as the domain of the context is a subset of one of the cells in the partition. An assertion of proposition p in the context illustrated would answer all of the open questions, leading to a new context with a single cell consisting of those two worlds.

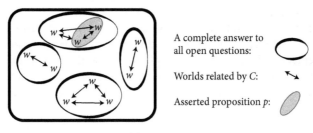

FIGURE 3.3   The context as a partition

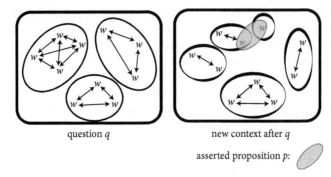

question q new context after q

asserted proposition p:

FIGURE 3.4   Asking a question in the partition context

If the context is a partition and a question is likewise a partition, the effect of asking a new question can be modeled as dividing the cells in the context along the lines between the cells of the question. Figure 3.4 is an example. The new context represents the result of incorporating question q into the context of Figure 3.3. In order to answer all of the questions in the new context, p is no longer informative enough, because it overlaps two cells in the partition. The reason for this is that p provides only a partial answer to q (it overlaps two cells in q). The result of asserting p in the context illustrated will be a new context with two disconnected worlds, each constituting its own cell in the partition.

As we have described the dynamic semantics analysis of questions so far, assertion and asking a question are closely related operations on the context.[64]

(75)   Assertion and asking in dynamic semantics for questions:
    a. if S denotes a proposition p, $C + S = C \cap (p \times p)$
    b. if S denotes a partition q, $C + S = C \cap q$

Though it has not previously been identified in the literature on dynamic semantics, so far as I am aware, an interesting intuition about sentence mood can be found in (75). This intuition is that sentences which denote propositions and those which denote questions have almost the same sentential force. Unlike Roberts' theory, where assertion and asking a question update different components of the discourse context in the same way, in the version of dynamic semantics we are considering, they update the same component of the discourse context in different (though similar) ways.

It is possible to extend the dynamic framework so that there is no force-like difference between assertion and asking. Suppose that we no longer assume that any sentences denote sets of possible worlds. Rather, we assume that even declaratives denote partitions, but that their partitions are so rudimentary that they do not introduce any new questions into the context. It is easy to do this within the

---

[64] The conceptualization of assertion and asking in (75) can readily be represented as proper dynamic semantic values. The meaning of sentence S would simply be the function $\lambda c[c + S]$.

framework of dynamic semantics. Suppose that we would normally assume that S denotes some proposition p. Now we take it to denote $p \times p$. Then the same update can be applied using both rudimentary and articulated partitions:

(76)   Unification of assertion and asking in dynamic semantics:

For any sentence S denoting partition p, $C + S = C \cap p$

This type of unification of assertion and asking is found in inquisitive semantics (see especially Ciardelli et al. 2013).

Now we have three intuitions about the relation between assertion and asking in the dynamic approach:

1. Assertion and asking update different components of the structured discourse context in the same way (Roberts).
2. Assertion and asking update the same component of the structured discourse context in similar ways (first version of dynamic semantics for questions).
3. Assertion and asking update the same component of the structured discourse context in the same way (second version of dynamic semantics, inquisitive semantics).

Though, as far as I know, no scholars working in the dynamic tradition have done so, these three intuitions can be seen as representing three ideas about sentence mood. The first says roughly that declaratives and interrogatives have different sentential forces. This view coincides with the traditional conception of sentence mood, according to which declaratives and interrogatives are basic and not related to one another in an especially close way. The second says that declaratives and interrogatives have different sentential forces, but that these forces are closely related. This view fits well with the idea that the force of declaratives and interrogatives share something important, as proposed in very different ways by such authors as Truckenbrodt (2006a) and Lohnstein (2007). The third intuition says that the difference between declaratives and interrogatives is entirely a matter of their compositional semantic values, and that at the most fundamental level, they have the same conversational function. In a sense, the third approach implies that declaratives and interrogatives constitute a single sentence mood.

Now we turn to the most recent incarnation of dynamic semantics for questions, INQUISITIVE SEMANTICS.[65] Inquisitive semantics differs from earlier dynamic theories mainly in how it represents the meanings of questions (including the "big question," the structured context). In order to see this point in detail, we want to focus on how inquisitive semantics diverges from the partition theory of questions

---

[65] Some but not all proposals within the inquisitive semantics tradition technically fall within dynamic semantics, as we are defining that category here. I think it's correct to understand all work labeled "inquisitive semantics" as following the dynamic approach, but some of it probably assumes a dynamic pragmatics conception of the relationship between semantic content and discourse meaning. I will present it using the techniques of dynamic semantics, however, because that allows us to see more clearly the links to earlier theories. Thanks to Malte Willer for drawing my attention to this issue.

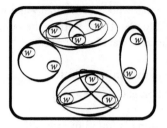

A possible assertion which
would completely settle all
open questions:

FIGURE 3.5   The inquisitive context

assumed by earlier versions of dynamic semantics. For technical reasons that
need not concern us here, inquisitive semantics replaces the view of questions
as partitions with the closely related hypothesis that a question is a downward-
closed set of propositions based on an equivalence relation. (A context is still a
big question, and so a context is also a downward-closed set of propositions based
on an equivalence relation.) The context previously represented as in Figure 3.3
corresponds to the one in Figure 3.5; the context is the set of all of the sets of
worlds represented by ellipses in the figure. Each of these sets can be thought of
as a proposition which, if asserted, would completely settle all open questions.

As with the version of dynamic semantics which unifies assertion and asking (i.e.
(76)), in the inquisitive approach all sentences denote semantic objects of the same
sort, in this case downward-closed sets of propositions,[66] and when a sentence
updates the context, the context is reduced through intersection. The contents
of some sentences are so rudimentary that they only reduce the domain, and do
not split any cells of the context; these have "informative content." Others split
cells in essentially the same way as illustrated in Figure 3.4; they have "inquisitive
content." (The theory also allows "hybrids," contents which both reduce the domain
and split cells.) Given this nice distinction between informative and inquisitive
content, as we seek to apply the methods of inquisitive semantics to natural
language, it is natural to ask: which sentences have informative content, and which
have inquisitive content? One might think that the answer is that declaratives
have informative content and interrogatives inquisitive content, but as it has been
developed, inquisitive semantics does not postulate such a neat correspondence
with clause types.

Disjunction provides the noteworthy exception to the attractive idea that we
can link declaratives with informative content and interrogatives with inquisitive
content. Within inquisitive semantics, disjunction creates a semantic value with
inquisitive content in just the same way that an interrogative operator does. And
this is not just a matter of mismatch between the logical formalism in which
inquisitive semantics is normally pursued and natural language. Roelofsen and
Farkas (2015) propose rules for interpreting Logical Forms of English according to
which (77a) and (77b), both uttered with rising intonation on the disjuncts, have
the same meaning:

---

[66] Or, more accurately, an update potential based on such a set, but we are simplifying here.

(77) a. Igor speaks English or French.
      b. Does Igor speak English or French?

In fact, Roelofsen and Farkas (2015) treat rising declaratives as equivalent to rising interrogatives quite generally, in this respect both agreeing with and clarifying the perspective of Gunlogson (2001). As mentioned in Section 3.3.1, recent work by Farkas and Roelofsen (2017) develops the line of research on declaratives and interrogatives which began with Gunlogson's work within an inquisitive semantics framework.

3.3.3 Imperatives in the dynamic approach

Background on the semantics of imperatives.   As with interrogatives, theories of the sentential force of imperatives are based on a variety of different assumptions about their semantics. We find scholars who assume that imperatives denote propositions, properties, and actions (as well as the dynamic semantics versions of some of these things). These differences are not primarily motivated by the need to analyze sentence mood, but rather by a number of syntactic and semantic properties of imperative clauses. In this section, I will summarize these properties and highlight the ones which are most significant as we evaluate theories of sentence mood.[67]

The following properties have been important in the literature on imperatives:

1. Imperatives cannot be naturally described as true or false.
2. In some languages, imperatives cannot be embedded; in others, they can be embedded only in a limited range of contexts (Han 1998; Pak 2008; Crnič and Trinh 2009; Kaufmann 2012; Kaufmann and Poschmann 2013).
3. In many languages, the imperative subject must refer to the addressee, refer to a set containing the addressee, or quantify over a set of addressees (Downing 1969; Schmerling 1982; Platzack and Rosengren 1994; Potsdam 1996; Jensen 2003; Rupp 2003; Zanuttini 2008; Kaufmann 2012; Zanuttini et al. 2012).
4. Even when the imperative subject is not associated with the addressee as in point 3, the imperative is normally used to tell the addressee what to do. Some languages have minor clause types (promissives and exhortatives) which are similar to imperatives in discourse function, but which target an individual other than the addressee (Pak et al. 2008a,b; Zanuttini et al. 2012).
5. Imperatives are normally future-oriented, but past-oriented types may exist in some languages (Palmer 1986; Mastop 2005, 2011).

---

[67] Some important work on the semantics of imperatives will not be discussed because it does not address to a sufficient extent the nature of sentential force and sentence mood. This includes much of the tradition of imperative logic (for example, Ross 1944; Geach 1958; Lemmon 1965; Åqvist 1967; Chellas 1969, 1971; Kanger 1971; Segerberg 1990; Vranas 2008, 2011). Some linguistically-oriented work discusses imperatives in semantic terms without introducing any distinctive component of force (for example, the modal analysis of Aloni 2007).

6. In many languages, imperatives take on a different morphosyntactic form when negated or when they express pragmatic features of speech style and politeness (Rivero and Terzi 1995; Zanuttini 1997; Han 1998; Zanuttini and Portner 2003; Han and Lee 2007; Kaufmann 2012).

7. Imperatives can be conjoined and disjoined with one another and with declaratives and interrogatives. When they are conjoined or disjoined with other clause types, interesting semantic effects arise; for example, *Touch me again and you're in big trouble!* implies that the addressee should not touch the speaker again. Imperatives can also serve as the main clause of a conditional sentence (Bolinger 1967; Davies 1986; Clark 1993; Han 1998; Franke 2005; Russell 2007; Kaufmann 2012; Starr 2013; von Fintel and Iatridou 2015).

8. Imperatives have a different logic than declaratives. As a result, they show the **free choice inference** and give rise to **Ross's paradox** (some significant references, among many others, are Ross 1944; Kamp 1973; Han 1998; Van Rooij 2000; Asher and Bonevac 2005; Aloni 2007; Barker 2010; Mastop 2011; Portner 2011b; Aloni and Ciardelli 2013; Fine 2016; Kaufmann 2016).

9. Imperatives are functionally diverse. They can be used to give orders, make requests, offer suggestions, give permission, record instructions, and express wishes, among other functions (Wilson and Sperber 1988; Portner 2004, 2007; Charlow 2011; Condoravdi and Lauer 2012; Kaufmann 2012).

The references listed above are only representative. There is extensive literature on several of these properties, and I also note the handbook articles by Han (2011) and Portner (2016).

For our purposes, the only properties which require further explanation are points 8–9. Free choice refers to the observation that (78a) implies the truth of (78b). Not only imperatives, but many modal sentences as well, show the free choice inference.

(78)   a. Have an apple or a pear!
       b. You may have an apple, and you may have a pear.

(79)   a. You must/may talk to John or Mary.
       b. You may talk to John and you may talk to Mary.

Free choice is not explained by standard theories of modal semantics derived from modal logic. For example, $\Box(p \lor q)$, interpreted as "every accessible world is in the union of the p worlds with the q worlds," does not entail $\Diamond p \land \Diamond q$, "there is at least one accessible p world and at least one accessible q world," because (for example) the former would be true if all accessible worlds were p worlds.

Ross's paradox (Ross 1944) is the closely related pattern whereby (80a) does not imply (80b), in that you can give the former as an order without agreeing that the latter would be a good order to give.

(80)   a. Have an apple!
       b. Have an apple or a pear!

(81)   a. Noah ate an apple.
        b. Noah ate an apple or a pear.

The lack of inference in (80) is different from the pattern seen with declaratives, where (81a) entails (81b).

The other important property of imperatives is their functional diversity, some of which can be observed in the following:

(82)   a. March! (order)
        b. Please don't tell mom about this. (request)
        c. Take the 3A bus. (suggestion)
        d. Have some wine! (invitation)
        e. Add the wet ingredients to the dry. (instruction)
        f. Stop raining! (wish)

Though the differences among some or all of these types of uses may be semantic in nature, as on Kaufmann's (2012) modal analysis, within the dynamic approach, they have not been seen that way. Instead, these differences are understood as reflecting either the social basis justifying the use of the imperative or the speaker's reasons for issuing it. For example, an imperative cannot be called an order unless it is backed by the right kind of social authority, and suggestions differ from orders and requests in that the speaker thinks the action mentioned would serve the addressee's interests or goals, and leaves it to the addressee whether to commit to the action.

All of the properties mentioned in this section are important for theories of imperative meaning and discourse function, but we will for the most part not explore what the various dynamic analyses discussed in this section have to say about them. Rather, our goal is to bring out the consequences of each version of the dynamic approach for our understanding of sentence mood, and I will present the various scholars' work in ways which make it easier to do so. It should be kept in mind that different theories may be more or less adequate to account for these other properties; readers who wish for a more complete understanding of imperative semantics should study the literature cited. I would also note that readers interested in the force of imperatives generally should compare the theories discussed in this section with Kaufmann's and Charlow's analyses embedded in the speech act theory framework (Section 3.2.3).

Dynamic theories of imperatives and directive meaning: early work.   David Lewis (1979b) initiated research on imperatives within the dynamic approach as he described a language game involving three participants: the master, the slave, and the kibbitzer.[68] He analyzes imperatives as having a nearly standard modal semantics of the kind familiar from modal logic (see Section 1.3.2). Specifically,

---

[68] We could alternatively see Lewis's paper as falling within speech act theory and so as being an early representative of the dynamic force hypothesis. However, in his only reference to speech acts he calls himself an "Old Harry" with respect to the performative/constative distinction and does not make

he proposes that imperatives are interpreted with respect to two accessibility functions: One of these, f_{sp}, defines the SPHERE OF PERMISSIBILITY, the set of worlds representing the requirements governing the slave's actions at w and t; the other, f_{sa}, is a historical accessibility relation defining the SPHERE OF ACCESSIBILITY, the set of worlds compatible with the actual history of w up to time t. An order-type imperative has the logical form $!\phi$, with $!$ understood as a modal logic $\square$ interpreted with respect to the intersection of these two relations.

(83)   a. $!\phi$ is true with respect to $\langle w, t \rangle$ iff ϕ is true at every world both permissible and accessible from w and t.

b. Formally: $[\![\, !\phi \,]\!]^{\langle w,t \rangle} = 1$ iff
$$f_{sp}(\langle w, t \rangle) \cap f_{sa}(\langle w, t \rangle) \subseteq \{ \langle w', t' \rangle : [\![\, \phi \,]\!]^{\langle w',t' \rangle} = 1 \}.$$

To this standard modal semantics, Lewis adds a pragmatic component to his analysis which ties it closely to dynamic pragmatics. In a context where the speaker has authority over the addressee (in Lewis's language game, the master is speaking to the slave), the contextual parameters which influence the truth conditions of the imperative must be understood in such a way that what the speaker says is true. Given that the two relevant parameters are f_{sp} and f_{sa}, and that the latter is an objective circumstance of the world, this means that f_{sp} must be understood (if possible) in such a way that the imperative is true. If $!\phi$ is used in a context in which it is not true, f_{sp} must be adjusted so as to make it true. Lewis (1979c) sees this adjustment as an example of a general rule of ACCOMMODATION, of a kind with other cases of accommodation involving presuppositions, indexicality, vagueness, and other pragmatic features of meaning.

Lewis points out that with command-type imperatives, it is easy to describe how the sphere of permissibility adjusts to make an imperative sentence true. In general, $f_{sp}(\langle w, t \rangle)$ adjusts to $f_{sp}(\langle w, t \rangle) \cap [\![\, \phi \,]\!]$. This intersective effect of an imperative on the sphere of permissibilty is analogous to assertion (relative to the context set) on Stalnaker's analysis, but as mentioned above, it differs in that Lewis sees it as due to a general principle of accommodation. That is, the dynamic pragmatic effect of an imperative is not, for Lewis, a basic matter of updating the sphere of permissibility by the imperative's content, but rather derived indirectly from its modal semantics, and the principle of accommodation.

Lewis's theory is able to partially unify the analyses of deontic modal sentences and imperatives. When used in a situation in which accommodation is not applicable, sentences of the logical form $!\phi$ are simply understood as deontic modal assertions; this would be the case when the speaker is the slave or kibbitzer, or when the speaker is the master but the requirement is already understood in the context. For example, (84), spoken by the master to the slave (in a context in which it is not understood that the slave has to carry rocks), means "Carry rocks!," but spoken by the kibbitzer to the master, it means "The slave has to carry rocks."

---

any reference to illocutionary acts or force. Hence, I think it's more reasonable to see his ideas as falling within the dynamic approach.

(84)   !*The slave carries rocks*
    a. Master to slave: *Carry rocks!*
    b. Kibbitzer to master: *The slave has to carry rocks.*

But this unification of modal and imperative meanings is also a major weakness of Lewis's analysis, if it is seen as a linguistic theory of imperatives. It is not, in fact, possible for the slave to use an imperative sentence to assert that he has to carry rocks, or for the master or kibbitzer to use one to assert that the slave has to carry rocks, but they can certainly use a deontic modal sentence this way. The master can well say (85a) to gloat about the awful day the slave has ahead of him, but (85b) cannot have this use.

(85)   a. You have to carry rocks.
    b. Carry rocks!

We see, then, that imperatives (at least, order-type imperatives) have a key property distinguishing them from modal necessity statements: there are contexts in which a deontic modal statement can be used to make an assertion about what is required, while the imperative cannot. This points to a problem in Lewis's use of accommodation to derive the context change effect of imperatives. As is understood elsewhere in Lewis's writings and in the subsequent literature, accommodation occurs to bring a context into alignment with what it needs to be for an utterance to be "correct." (In the case of imperatives, the idea would be that they are not correct unless they are true.) But when the context is one in which the utterance would already be correct, accommodation is unnecessary. But, it seems, Lewis would need to say that imperatives can only be used in contexts where they would trigger accommodation. This amounts to saying they can only be correctly used in contexts in which they are not correct. The preceding discussion suggests that Lewis's analysis would be more accurately applied to explicit modal sentences, which can be used both descriptively (to make an assertion about what's permissible) and performatively (to create a change in what's permissible).

It is worth noting at this point the relevance of Kaufmann's (2012) analysis of imperatives as obligatorily performative deontic modal sentences. As discussed in Section 3.2.3, Kaufmann argues that imperatives are associated with a set of presuppositions which ensure that they are only properly used in contexts in which a modal sentence would be performative. Suppose we incorporate this idea into Lewis's theory; that is, we add to the meaning of imperatives a presupposition that they only occur in contexts in which they are not true. Then the rule of accommodation would have to be defined in such a way that it adjusts the sphere of permissibility to make the imperative true while ignoring the fact that this will cause its presupposition to be no longer satisfied. It seems quite difficult to understand accommodation in a way that would give this result, and this fact points out the problem which afflicts Lewis's use of accommodation.

We can now see the way in which Lewis's theory contributes to the dynamic approach. Setting aside the precise mechanisms involved, Lewis proposes that order-type imperatives normally have the contextual effect of shrinking a component of the discourse context, namely the sphere of permissibility. The sphere of permissibility can therefore be seen as analogous to the common ground/context set and the question set. The sphere of permissibility is the "target" for update by imperative sentences, just as on the dynamic approach the common ground is the target for update by declaratives and the question set is the target for update by interrogatives. Though Lewis did not make this move himself, we can build on his idea and elaborate our theory of the structured discourse context to include a component or feature (like the sphere of permissibility) which is characteristically targeted by imperatives. Subsequent work on imperatives in the dynamic approach has in fact built on Lewis's ideas in this way.

The preceding discussion has focused on Lewis's analysis of order-type imperatives, but the main focus of Lewis (1979b) concerns a problem which arises when he tries to extend it to permission sentences. He assumes that permission sentences have the logical form ¡ϕ and that ¡ has the semantics of a possibility modal. Just as with sentences of the form !ϕ, when a sentence ¡ϕ is uttered by the master to the slave in a context in which ¡ϕ is not true given the current sphere of permissibility, the sphere of permissibility must be adjusted so as to make it true. Given the possibility semantics of ¡ϕ, this requires that the sphere of permissibility be expanded. However—and this is the key point—unlike in the case of order-type imperatives, there is no simple recipe for expanding the sphere of permissibility. Crucially, adjusting $f_{sp}(\langle w, t \rangle)$ to $f_{sp}(\langle w, t \rangle) \cup p$ will not work, because it would permit every way of bringing about ϕ. For example, if the master permits the slave to take the day off, he would thereby permit the slave to take the day off and kill the master. But this is clearly not what the master would intend.

Lewis considers various responses to this problem of permission, and one of them foreshadows subsequent developments in the dynamic approach to imperatives. He observes that the expansion of the sphere of permissibility dealt by a permission sentence should be "minimal," in that it should bring into permissibility those impermissible worlds which are, prior to the permission sentence being uttered, the "least impermissible" (Lewis 1979b, p. 171). In our example, taking the day off and killing the master is highly impermissible, while taking the day off and resting is as minimally impermissible as a world can be in which the slave takes the day off. Thus, when the master utters *Take the day off!*, only worlds of the latter type should be added to the sphere of permissibility. Though he thinks this idea is a step in the right direction, he notes that we critically would need a principle governing how the comparative permissibility relation itself evolves over time. As we will see, later work in the dynamic approach solves the problem by replacing the sphere of permissibility with something that models the relative permissibility of worlds (see in particular the discussion of Van der Torre and Tan 1998; Van Rooij 2000; Mastop 2005; Portner 2004, 2011b).

Two important works published prior to Lewis's (1979b) foreshadow later developments among dynamic theories of imperatives, and I will mention each briefly. First, van Fraassen (1973) develops an analysis of *ought* statements based on the premise that there is, at each point in time, a set of imperatives "in force."[69] These

---

[69] Lemmon (1965) also uses this notion.

imperatives can be seen as very similar to a conversational background in the ordering semantics theory of modality. He defines the SCORE of a state of affairs as the set of imperatives in force which it satisfies, and then gives a semantics to modal sentences very similar to Kratzer's analysis of weak necessity. Treating states of affairs as possible worlds and imperatives as sets of possible worlds, his semantics amounts to:

(86) $[\![$ ought ϕ $]\!]$ = 1 iff for some possible world $w \in [\![\phi]\!]$, there is no $w' \in$ $[\![\neg\phi]\!]$ such that score$(w) \subseteq$ score(w').

What is interesting for us about the paper is not the precise semantics for *ought*, but the function of imperatives. Concerning the question of how we know what imperatives are in force, he writes:

... First, there are many conceivable imperatives, but only some are in force. The problem of the ontogenesis of moral imperatives is the problem of what brings imperatives in force. I assume their sources are legion: conscience, ideals, values, duties, commitments, and so on. The process must be complicated, because one imperative may be overridden by another (under given circumstances); this means presumably that one imperative's being in force may prevent another's being in force. In this way, direct orders may cancel standing orders, and circumstances may take away the authority under which a standing order is the reason that a certain imperative is in force.   (van Fraassen 1973, p. 15)

It seems that van Fraassen uses the term "imperative" to refer to a fundamental object of the moral universe, and not a type of sentence. He does, however, imply that members of the imperative clause type can express imperatives. Specifically, he assumes that *Honor thy father or thy mother!* can express an imperative (p. 18), suggesting that the imperatives in force can sometimes be identified with the semantic values of sentences of the imperative clause type. From van Fraassen's paper, we can draw the idea that imperative sentences can contribute to a component of the discourse context (for van Fraassen, the set of imperatives in force) which affects the semantics of modal sentences with *ought*. This idea will be developed further within the dynamic approach.

Kamp (1973) develops an idea very similar to van Fraassen's as part of a discussion of free choice permission. Kamp's theory begins with a "set of social, legal and moral prohibitions to which B is subject" and then analyzes an act of permitting as the lifting by an agent A of some prohibition (or prohibitions) to which B is subject under the authority of A. For example, if P_0 is a set of prohibitions to which B is subject under the authority of A, and A uses (88), B's new prohibition-set will be P_1:

(87) a. $P_0 = \{$'You don't go to the beach', 'You don't go to the cinema'$\}$
      b. $P_1 = \{$'You don't go to the cinema'$\}$

(88) You may go to the beach!

This change in prohibition-set gives rise to an expansion in the set of worlds permissible for B. With respect to P_0, no worlds in which B goes to the beach are permissible, while with respect to P_1, worlds in which he goes to the beach but not the cinema are. We see in this way that Kamp gives an analysis of permission which fits the essential characteristics of the dynamic approach.

From this point, Kamp goes on to discuss sentences with free choice disjunction. He proposes that (89) lifts both prohibitions in P_0, thus explaining why it leads to a situation where both going to the beach and going to the cinema are permitted.

(89)   You may go to the beach or the cinema.

On the assumption that a disjunctive permission sentence like (89) lifts two prohibitions, Kamp is able to explain certain cases of the free choice inference. He offers a definition of entailment under which (89) entails (88) (Kamp 1973, p. 66):

(90)   For any sentences s and s', s P-ENTAILS s' iff in any situation in which both
        s and s' can be used to grant permissions, the class of actions which would
        be moved by a permission statement involving s would include the class of
        actions moved by a permission statement involving s'.

Kamp's notion of p-entailment is novel and influential because it explicitly relies on a dynamic conception of meaning.

Although Kamp's idea that permission amounts to the lifting of a prohibition is important, he does not develop a complete analysis of permission sentences. He seems to assume that a standard analysis of disjunction as set-theoretic union by itself predicts that (89) removes both prohibitions from P_0, but I do not see how this is the case, since we can render P_0 consistent with (89) by lifting either one (or both) of the prohibitions. Thus, Kamp cannot be seen as having already provided a solution to the problem of permission subsequently discussed by Lewis. For our purposes, the importance of Kamp's theory is in the way it builds an analysis of permission sentences based on the effect they have on a feature of the discourse context. The set of prohibitions in place at a given point in time can be compared to the set of imperatives in force within van Fraassen's theory (each prohibition is an imperative which requires someone not to do something). From this perspective, van Fraassen's and Kamp's ideas foreshadow modern versions of dynamic semantics and pragmatics in which imperative sentences contribute to the set of requirements and prohibitions in force at a given point in time.

Dynamic theories of imperatives: the development of contemporary theories.
Ideas about the semantics of imperatives and other directive sentences within the dynamic approach began to take their contemporary shape at the very end of the 1990s. Building on the earlier work just discussed, we see two main strands of scholarship. One of these has its origins in dynamic logic. This research has largely been focused on the logical problems associated with imperatives, such as free choice permission and Ross's paradox. The other is more linguistically oriented and gains much of its motivation from a concern for understanding clause types and sentence mood. As we will see, these two strands have slowly converged to the point that they should no longer be seen as separate traditions of research.

We begin with two representative and important works published in the same year, Han (1998) and Van der Torre and Tan (1998). On the one hand, we have Han's dissertation, a study of the syntax and semantics of imperatives focusing on such issues as the relation between imperatives and negation, the nature of suppletive imperatives (imperative sentences with the morphological form of infinitives or subjunctives), embeddability, and the history of the English imperative. On the other, Van der Torre and Tan's paper applies Veltman's (1996) dynamic logic framework to an analysis of prescriptive sentences. Seen from our perspective of seeking an understanding of sentence mood, Han's and Van der Torre and Tan's ideas are complementary: Although she touches on some insights concerning imperatives in dynamic semantics, Han's major contributions concern the nature of sentence mood at the syntax/semantics interface. In contrast, Van der Torre and Tan have an insightful discussion of the type of contextual update which could represent the imposition of new obligations in discourse, but they do not have anything to say about the kinds of natural language sentences which might be associated with those effects. In what follows, we will briefly review both of these works, using each as a basis for discussing other important research on imperatives within the dynamic approach.

Han (1998) begins with the hypothesis that the syntax of imperatives contains a force-indicating operator and a sentence radical expressing a propositional content. The operator consists of two features, [directive] and [irrealis], where the former is unique to the imperative clause type and encodes sentential force. In contrast, an infinitive or subjunctive only has the [irrealis] feature, with no representation of sentential force. As discussed in Section 3.1.3, she proposes that the combination of sentential negation and the [directive] feature is ruled out in certain languages (such as Spanish (28)) because negation would illicitly take scope over the force-encoding feature. (In other languages, such as English, the syntax of negation would give it scope unproblematically below [directive].) When sentences with [directive] cannot be combined with negation, languages employ another form with [irrealis], with the intended directive force derived by pragmatic reasoning.

Han explains the directive force encoded by [directive] as follows:

> ... the directive force of imperatives turns the sentence into a DIRECTIVE ACTION, which we in turn define as an instruction to the hearer to update his/her PLAN SET. A plan set is a set of propositions that specify the hearer's intentions, and it represents the state of affairs that the hearer intends to bring about.   (Han 1998, pp. 149–50)

In an obvious way, Han's perspective on the force of imperatives is similar to Stalnaker's analysis of assertion relative to the common ground. She does not, however, give any more precise semantic/pragmatic content to the notion of plan set. For example, she does not say what exactly is implied about an individual's linguistic or non-linguistic behavior given the fact that some proposition p is in her plan set. Thus, we are left uncertain of basic matters like what goes wrong when someone accepts an imperative and then shows no inclination to do what it says.

We turn now to the contribution of Van der Torre and Tan (1998).[70] Their analysis builds on Veltman's (1996) discussion of defaults in dynamic semantics, and so, in what follows, I will briefly review Veltman's logic, following closely the presentation of Portner (2009, sect. 3.2). As discussed in Chapter 1, the simplest model of context in dynamic semantics is that of an information state s, which may be understood as simply a set of possible worlds. In order to account for expectations, Veltman adds to the information state a second component ε, the EXPECTATION PATTERN, an ordering of worlds. We have an information state $\sigma = \langle \varepsilon, s \rangle$, where s represents the factual information in σ and $w \leq_\varepsilon v$ represents the judgment in σ that w is at least as expected as v.

The following three crucial concepts can be defined in terms of this new version of the information state:

(91) (a) **Absolutely normal worlds:**
           $n\varepsilon = \{w \in W : \text{for all } v \in W, w \leq_\varepsilon v\}$
      (b) **Maximally normal worlds in s:**
           $m_{\langle \varepsilon, s \rangle} = \{w \in s : \text{there is no } v \in s \text{ such that } v <_\varepsilon w\}$
      (c) **Refinement of an expectation pattern ε with p:**
           $\varepsilon \circ p = \{\langle w, v \rangle \in \varepsilon : \text{if } v \in p, \text{then } w \in p\}$

Veltman proposes meanings for two operators within his logic: *presumably*(ϕ) uses (91b) to test whether ϕ is expected (given the information in s), while *normally*(ϕ) uses (91c) to refine the expectation pattern so that ϕ becomes a new expectation. More precisely:

(92) For any information state $\sigma = \langle \varepsilon, s \rangle$,
      1. $\sigma[presumably(\phi)]^M =$
          (a) σ, if $m_\sigma \cap \{w : [\![\phi]\!]^{w,M} = 1\} = m_\sigma$;
          (b) †, otherwise.
      2. $\sigma[normally(\phi)]^M =$
          (a) $\langle \varepsilon \circ \{w : [\![\phi]\!]^{w,M} = 1\}, s \rangle$, if $n\varepsilon \cap \{w : [\![\phi]\!]^{w,M} = 1\} \neq \emptyset$;
          (b) †, otherwise.

Notice that *presumably* is a test: it has no effect on an information state which passes the test, and reduces to absurdity (†) an information state which does not pass. *Normally* refines the expectation pattern, subject to the presupposition that all existing expectations and the new expectation being added could be satisfied together.

To account for obligation sentences, Van der Torre and Tan (1998) propose a DEONTIC STATE with a structure very similar to Veltman's information state. A deontic state δ is a triple $\delta = \langle W, s, \leq_\delta \rangle$, with W the set of possible worlds, s a subset of W representing factual information, and $\leq_\delta$ indicating the deontic relation of comparative "goodness." The reason for including W in the deontic state

---

[70] In Portner (2009, sect. 3.2.5), I sketched an analysis similar to Van der Torre and Tan's of how Veltman's (1996) logic could be applied to imperatives. I was unaware of their work at the time.

arises from the interesting observation that, as part of deontic reasoning, we may need to talk about both the set of possible worlds which are deemed realizable at a point in time, and a wider set of options which might go beyond those ever deemed realizable. In δ, the set s represents the realizable worlds; it is called the CONTEXT OF DELIBERATION and is akin to Lewis's sphere of accessibility. The set W, or CONTEXT OF JUSTIFICATION, represents all of the possible worlds which are relevant more broadly to deontic judgments. The dynamic meaning of a factual sentence affects s and the dynamic effect of a deontic sentence affects $\leq$. The context of justification W is not changed by any updates.

Van der Torre and Tan define four deontic operators, two of which target the context of justification and two of which target the context of deliberation. Among each pair, one is similar to *presumably* in performing a test on the ordering $\leq_\delta$ and the other similar to *normally* in refining the ordering.[71, 72]

(93) For any deontic state $\delta = \langle W, s, \leq_\delta \rangle$,
    1. Operators of the context of justification
        (a) $\delta[ideal(p)] =$
            (i) δ, if $\mathbf{n}_\delta \subseteq p$;
            (ii) $\dagger$, otherwise.
        (b) $\delta[oblige(p)] =$
            (i) $\delta \odot p$, if $\mathbf{n}_{\delta \odot p} \subseteq p$;
            (ii) $\dagger$, otherwise.
    2. Operators of the context of deliberation
        (a) $\delta[ideal^*(p)] =$
            (i) δ, if $\mathbf{m}_\delta \subseteq p$;
            (ii) $\dagger$, otherwise.
        (b) $\delta[oblige^*(p)] =$
            (i) $\delta \circledast p$, if $\mathbf{m}_{\delta \circledast p} \subseteq p$;
            (ii) $\dagger$, otherwise.

The operators *ideal* and *ideal** act as tests on the deontic state (targeting W and s, respectively), while *oblige* and *oblige** refine the ordering (on the worlds in W and s, respectively). This differentiation of the operators of the context of justification

---

[71] In what follows, I simplify by ignoring conditional obligations. In fact, all four operators take conditional form, e.g. $ideal(\alpha|\beta)$. I also note that they give the presupposition of the operators in a more sophisticated way which takes account of the fact that the ordering may have multiple distinct maxima and may include infinite chains of ever-better worlds. In this presentation, I simplify the definitions to the same level as those in (91)–(92).

[72] We need new definitions of $\mathbf{n}_\delta$, $\mathbf{m}_\delta$, $\delta \odot p$, and $\delta \circledast p$:

(i) For any deontic state $\delta = \langle W, s, \leq_\delta \rangle$,
    $\mathbf{n}_\delta = \{w \in W : \text{for all } v \in W, w \leq_\delta v\}$
    $\mathbf{m}_\delta = \{w \in s : \text{there is no } v \in s \text{ such that } v \leq_\delta w\}$
    $\delta \odot p = \langle W, s, \{\langle w, v \rangle : w \leq_\delta v \text{ and if } v \in p, \text{ then } w \in p\} \rangle$
    $\delta \circledast p = \langle W, s, \{\langle w, v \rangle : \langle w, v \rangle \in (s \times s) \cap \leq_\delta \text{ and if } v \in p \cap s, \text{ then } w \in p \cap s\} \rangle$

These formulations are simplified and adjusted from Van der Torre and Tan's to make them more parallel to (92), and as a result are not equivalent to the originals in all settings.

from the operators of the context of deliberation is related to Thomason's important work (Thomason 1981a,b), and it is significant because it allows one to model both deontic language which pertains to what is obliged independently of whether it can obtain and deontic language which is relevant only to what is understood to be a realizable outcome.

Van der Torre and Tan do not make any clear claim that their logic should be used as a direct analysis of the meanings of any linguistic forms, but it is tempting to use *oblige** as a model of the sentential force of imperatives. This amounts to the idea that imperatives function to refine the deontic ordering within the space of actually realizable possibilities, subject to the condition that by doing so they create an ordering in which the ideal worlds (relative to what is considered realizable) are ones in which the imperative's propositional content is true. We could also consider using *oblige* to give a theory of imperatives and imperative-like sentences which seem to affect our assumptions about which worlds are preferable setting aside whether they are realizable. Good examples of this latter type might be absent wishes like (94a) and counterfactual deontic sentences like (94b) (from Kaufmann 2012; Mastop 2011, respectively):

(94)   a. Please, be rich! (on the way to a blind date)

    b. *Was toch lekker thuisgebleven.*   *(Dutch)*
      WAS PRT PRT   at.home.stay-PP
      'You should just have stayed at home.'

Similarly, the *ideal* operators might be understood as models of the meanings of descriptive deontic modals. However, Van der Torre and Tan do not describe how these operators are interpreted in complex sentences, and an analysis based on them would be at best highly incomplete. More recent work in dynamic deontic logic, such as Willer (2014), comes closer to providing a plausible theory of deontic modals.

Following Van der Torre and Tan (1998), there has been other interesting work in dynamic deontic logic, including Žarnić (2003a,b), van Benthem and Liu (2004), Yamada (2007a,b,c), and Willer (2014). However, as our goal is to better understand the significance of this tradition for understanding the nature of sentence mood, we should focus on dynamic semantics research which aims to address linguistic issues. Important works which meet this criterion are Van Rooij (2000), Mastop (2005), and Starr (2013); we will review these authors' ideas briefly before returning to research which builds on Han's more linguistically-oriented ideas.

We begin with Van Rooij (2000). He gives an analysis of imperatives based on the assumption that their meanings can be represented in terms of command and permission logical forms $Must(p)$ and $May(p)$. He accepts a dynamic semantics of command imperatives very close to the *oblige* operator of Van der Torre and Tan (1998), but then turns his attention to incorporating permission imperatives.

Recall that the problem of permission, as outlined by Lewis, is that it is not clear how to express exactly which worlds enter the sphere of permissibility when a permission is granted. As we saw, an appealing intuition is that $May(p)$ adds the

p worlds which are, prior to permission being granted, the least impermissible. The framework developed by Van der Torre and Tan (1998) seems promising for addressing this problem, because the ordering relation $\leq_\delta$ which is used to determine the ideal worlds also expresses which non-ideal worlds are better than others. If we identify the ideal worlds with the sphere of permissibility, permission can then be formulated as adding the highest-ranked p worlds into the permissibility set.[73]

(95)   After permission $May(p)$ is granted in deontic state δ, the permissible worlds are $\mathbf{m}_\delta \cup \{w \in p : \text{for no } v \in p, v \leq_\delta w\}$.

While (95) identifies the expansion of the sphere of permissibility in the way suggested by Lewis, it does not define the deontic state which results from updating δ with $May(p)$. Crucially, it does not say how $\leq_\delta$ itself changes. In order to have a full dynamic analysis, the theory must identify the result of updating δ for a permission sentence, $\delta[May(p)]$.

To make progress on this problem, Van Rooij proposes to make use of an additional set S of propositions "that potentially determine reprehensibility." His idea is that, when permission $May(p)$ is granted, we add p worlds into the ideal set and then order them with respect to one another on the basis of S (using a technique of Harper 1976). The problem, however, is that it is not made clear what it means for a proposition to be in S, and Van Rooij is inconsistent in describing it. At one point, he says that "the simplest way is to let this set of designated propositions be the set of atomic propositions"; at another that it "is contextually determined, and stays constant during the 'discourse' " (Van Rooij 2000, p. 132). However, neither of these choices seems appropriate, since the set of propositions which determine reprehensibility could itself change as a discourse progresses—indeed, imperatives affect the determination of reprehensibility. The analysis of imperatives under the dynamic approach should be expected to explain how they affect the relation of comparative reprehensibility.

Mastop's (2005, 2011) dissertation on imperatives differs from other dynamic semantics work on the topic in several ways. First, he rejects the claim that sentence moods should be understood in terms of logical forms consisting of a force indicator and a propositional content radical. Rather, he proposes that the semantic values of imperatives are "instructions," a basic type of semantic object on a par with propositions. And second, he constructs the states which represent the evolving context from propositions and instructions, rather than in the usual way from possible worlds. Inspired by Hamblin (1971), he labels his notion of a context the "commitment slate" defined as a FACT SHEET and a COMMITMENT FUNCTION.[74] The component relevant for imperatives, the commitment function, is defined as a function from worlds to sets of pairs of the form $\langle i, \text{do} \rangle$ or $\langle i, \text{don't} \rangle$, where i is

[73] I carry out this discussion in the formalism developed during our discussion of Van der Torre and Tan (1998). Van Rooij presents the ideas in a rather different format.

[74] Commitment slates have a third component, the CONSEQUENCE FUNCTION, which we can ignore here.

an instruction. Intuitively, a commitment function gives, for each world, a set of collections of *do*'s and *don't*'s, and an agent acts in *w* in accord with his commitment function if he does all the *do*'s and avoids all the *don't*'s of any one of the collections assigned to *w*.

Mastop's system is rather complex, and interested readers should study the works cited for details. For our purposes, it's important to point out several positive developments. First, Mastop aims to explain a wider range of linguistic phenomena than previous work in dynamic semantics. Second, he aims to give an overall theory of sentence mood based on the idea that imperatives have a unique type of semantic value, what he calls "instructions," and not propositions. This proposal is in accord with the compositional view of sentence mood. Third, he suggests that the definition of commitment slates as assigning sets of collections of *do*'s and *don't*'s to each world provides the basis for an understanding of free choice. And fourth, because within the commitment slate we retain a record of previously accepted instructions, it is possible to model the retraction of a commitment as the removal of pairs $\langle i, \text{do} \rangle$ or $\langle i, \text{don't} \rangle$. This type of retraction might allow an analysis of permission along the lines of Kamp's (1973). Mastop's theory has important weaknesses as well, however. Most notably, by treating instructions as *sui generis* semantic objects, he cannot explain their logical connections to facts and to one another. More generally, since they are not given a deeper foundation in a cognitive or discourse model, I find it difficult to understand exactly what instructions are.[75]

Starr (2010, 2013) develops a dynamic semantics theory of imperatives based on the operator theory of sentence mood, with a force marker attached to a sentence radical !ϕ. Unlike Mastop, he defines his version of the structured discourse context from possible worlds, but in a slightly different way than Van der Torre and Tan (1998). Whereas for Van der Torre and Tan, the deontic state crucially involved an ordering relation over worlds, Starr uses an ordering over propositions. Specifically, a PREFERENCE STATE R is a set of pairs of propositions, where we interpret $\langle p, q \rangle \in R$ to mean that p is preferred to q.

(96)　a. A preference state R is a set of pairs of propositions.
　　　b. The context set of R, c_R, is the union of all of the propositions related by
　　　　R: $c_R = \bigcup \{p : \exists \langle a, b \rangle \in R[p = a \vee p = b]\}$

An imperative !ϕ introduces a preference for the proposition p denoted by ϕ over its negation.[76] In a manner similar to the way assertion works in the dynamic semantics of questions, Starr proposes that a declarative $\rhd\phi$ updates c_R by restricting every proposition in one of the pairs of R and introducing a preference for its propositional content over $\emptyset$.

---

[75] Vranas (2008) and Starr (2013) note other serious issues with Mastop's analysis. Jary and Kissine (2014) criticize analyses like Mastop's and Portner's (discussed in what follows) which assign non-propositional denotations to imperatives.

[76] Technically, the sentence radical is given a dynamic semantics, but its intuitive propositional content can be recovered from its dynamic value.

(97) For any preference state R and sentence radical ϕ with meaning p,

a. $R[!\phi] = R \cup \{\langle c_R[p]c_R[\neg p]\rangle\} \cup \{\langle q[p], q[\neg p]\rangle : \exists\langle a, b\rangle \in R[q = a \vee q = b] \wedge q \cap p \neq \emptyset\}$

b. $R[\triangleright\phi] = \{\langle a[p], b[p]\rangle : \langle a, b\rangle \in R \wedge a[p] \neq \emptyset\} \cup \{\langle c_R[p], \emptyset\rangle\}$

Starr is not clear about the motivation for analyzing imperatives in terms of an ordering of propositions, as opposed to an ordering of worlds (like Van der Torre and Tan) or a set of propositions (like Han and others). He suggests that one reason is the fact that an ordering of propositions allows him to describe a situation where p is preferred to $\neg p$ and q to $\neg q$, even though these two preferences don't add up to an overall preference for $p \wedge q$ over $p \wedge \neg q$ and $\neg p \wedge q$. However, this result is not a matter of including pairs of propositions in the context; we could interpret a Han-type plan set $\{p, q\}$ as not implying a preference for $p \wedge q$. Admittedly, Portner (2004) uses a construct similar to the plan set in such a way as to prefer worlds in which all of the individual preferences are satisfied, but as Starr notes, this could be accounted for by making $p \wedge \neg q$ a preference, not simply p. In any case, Starr's actual proposal for imperatives (97) does imply that updating with $!\phi$ and $!\psi$ does normally result in a context preferring $\phi \wedge \psi$-worlds. So it's not clear what empirical consequences follow from Starr's decision to define R as a set of pairs of propositions. There is a significant technical consequence, however; by treating the preference relation as a set of pairs, the context set can be recovered from the preference relation (as in (96b)). In contrast, with a Han-style plan set $\{p\}$, we cannot tell which not-p worlds are considered relevant.[77] This is why in Portner's treatment which builds on Han's, the common ground is included explicitly as a separate part of the context. Perhaps Starr's main motivation for the way he defines the preference state is that he wishes to integrate the model of preferences and the representation of factual information as seamlessly as possible in a single set-theoretic object.

Finally we turn to Portner's (2004, 2007, 2011b) dynamic pragmatics theory of imperatives. At the most essential level, Portner's analysis is most similar to Han's. Where Han has the plan set, understood in psychological terms, Portner proposes a new component of the discourse context, the TO-DO LIST FUNCTION tdl. For reasons we will discuss below, Portner treats imperatives as denoting properties, and so, for each participant a in a conversation, a's to-do list $tdl(a)$ is a set of properties. The to-do list defines an ordering of worlds, as follows:

(98) For any worlds w and v,

$w <_{tdl(a)} v$ iff $\{P \in tdl(a) : P(a)(v) = 1\} \subset \{P \in tdl(a) : P(a)(w) = 1\}$

---

[77] If the context set were itself included in the plan set, and all of the other propositions in the plan set were required to be a subset of the context set, we could recover the context set as the union of the plan set in a way very similar to Starr's (96b).

A world w is ranked above another v if the agent does a better job of carrying out his to-do list in w, in the standard sense that in w he has every one of the to-do list properties he has in v, plus at least one more.[78]

While we can see Portner's analysis as similar to Han's (as well as Mastop's and Starr's) in that it keeps track of the contribution of each imperative, this use of the ordering relation also makes it similar to Van der Torre and Tan's. Unlike earlier authors (specifically Han and Van der Torre and Tan), he attempts to give a pragmatic interpretation to the to-do list. As discussed at the outset of this section, Portner extends Stalnaker's theory of assertion and Roberts' theory of questions in discourse in the following way (see Portner 2004, 2007):

(99)   A PORTNER CONTEXT is a triple $\langle cg, qs, tdl \rangle$:
    a. The common ground cg, a set of propositions.
    b. The question set qs, a set of question-denotations.
    c. The to-do list function tdl, assigning a set of properties to each participant a.

(100)   Agent's commitment: For any participant i, the participants in the conversation mutually agree to deem i's actions rational and cooperative to the extent that those actions in any world $w \in \cap cg$ tend to make it more likely that there is no $v \in \cap cg$ such that $v <_{tdl(a)} w$.

The basic idea here is that the agent's actions will be judged according to how well they can be expected to make the actual world turn out as highly-ranked as possible, given the factual assumptions in the common ground. For example, if I agree to give you a piece of bread, and then eat it, my actions would not be expected (given the common ground) to maximize the satisfaction of my to-do list, and you are justified in judging me negatively—as one who is either confused or dissimulating.

As discussed in Section 3.1.3, a major goal of Portner's work is to argue in favor of the compositional approach to sentence mood. He assumes that each major clause type has a characteristic semantics. Declaratives denote propositions, interrogatives sets of propositions, and imperatives properties restricted to the addressee. For example, *Leave!* denotes the property of leaving, with the presupposition that its subject argument is the addressee:

(101) $[\![\,Leave!\,]\!]^c = [\lambda x \lambda w : x = addressee(c) \,.\, x \text{ leaves in } w]$

Given his assumptions about the discourse context and the semantics of clause types, Portner hypothesizes that the sentential force of each sentence mood is determined by a pragmatic principle which uses the denotation of sentences with that mood in the simplest, most natural way to update the discourse context. The sentential force of declaratives is assertion (adding to the common ground) because

---

[78] Portner (2004) uses the $<$ relation in the opposite direction, but I reverse it here to make the presentation more similar to other theories discussed in the section.

TABLE 3.3   Main contributions of dynamic theories of imperatives

Han	imperatives add to a set of imperative-meanings; feature-based analysis of imperative operator
Van der Torre and Tan	dynamic semantics framework; imperatives update an ordering relation; context of deliberation vs. context of justification
Portner	dynamic pragmatics framework; pragmatic interpretation of ordering relation; compositional approach to sentence mood
Mastop	multiple action plans represent choice; operation of retraction
Starr	encoding of context set within ordering relation

the denotation of a declarative is a proposition and the most simple and natural way to incorporate a proposition into a context of the form (99) is to add it to *cg*. Similarly, the sentential force of imperatives is "requiring," defined as updating the addressee's to-do list, and the sentential force of interrogatives is asking.

This overview of Portner's theory concludes our discussion of recent theories of imperatives within the dynamic approach. Before moving on to consider some other relevant work, I summarize in Table 3.3 what I take to be the main ideas or contributions which each one first brought into the literature.[79] It should be noted that several of these authors have important ideas about other topics beyond our scope here, such as conditional imperatives, Ross's paradox, and imperatives conjoined or disjoined with declaratives.

Actions.   Building on Segerberg (1990), a few papers in the dynamic tradition propose that imperatives denote ACTIONS, defined as functions from worlds to worlds (e.g. Lascarides and Asher 2003; Barker 2012).[80] The idea is that an imperative tells you ways of making a transition from worlds at which the action has not been performed to other worlds at which it has. Taking an example from Barker, assume that in world w_1, Mary can eat one apple and thereby arrive at w_3, or eat a different apple and arrive at w_4. In world w_2 there is just one apple, and if she eats it she arrives at world w_5. In this context, the action of Mary eating an apple is represented by the following function:[81]

(102)   the action of Mary eating an apple = $\{\langle w_1, w_3\rangle, \langle w_1, w_4\rangle, \langle w_2, w_5\rangle\}$

[79] If the same basic idea was discovered more than once, I attribute it to the author who was, to the best of my knowledge, the first to introduce it.

[80] The notion of action here is similar to speech acts as conceived by Krifka (2014), discussed in Section 3.2.3.

[81] Note that the notion of "possible world" here cannot be the standard one of a complete way things could be. In a standard possible world, Mary either eats the apple or she doesn't, and nothing she does will move her to a different world. Barker must assume a different notion of possible world, for example sets of possible worlds in the standard sense.

The semantic value of the imperative *Eat an apple!*, addressed to Mary, is this action. As Barker points out, the idea that imperatives denote actions has the immediate benefit that it explains why imperatives are not naturally described as true or false. (Of course, all other dynamic theories, with the possible exception of Han's, have the same benefit.)

Action-based analyses of imperatives are not entirely explicit about the nature of directive force. Working within a DRS framework, Lascarides and Asher say "the defining characteristic of a discourse which includes a commanded imperative is that its CCP changes the input world into an output one where the action has been performed" (Lascarides and Asher 2003, p. 6). This makes it sound as if adding the imperative into the DRS amounts to performing the action which it specifies. Barker suggests a version of the compositional approach to sentence mood:

> There is no direct update effect. If uttering an imperative causes the addressee to believe that the speaker desires for an action to be performed, and if the addressee is inclined to fulfill the desires of the speaker, the imperative may influence the behavior of the addressee, not through grammatical regulation, but through simple pragmatical reasoning, very much in the way that thrusting a broom into the hands of an idle person and pointing at some dirt can cause the thrustee to behave as if they were newly under an obligation to begin sweeping.
>
> (Barker 2012, p. 60)

This analogy is not strong enough to explain sentential force, however. I could imply many different things by the act of handing you the broom and pointing at the dirt; maybe I just wish to show you that I have a broom and imply that I will sweep up later. The link between imperative form and the directive function is tighter than this, but one could imagine integrating his ideas into a more complete pragmatic explanation.

The main goal of Barker's analysis is to solve Ross's paradox and the problem of free choice disjunction. He points out that the action expressed by *Eat an apple!* is a subset of that expressed by *Eat an apple or a pear!*, but by itself this does not solve the problem. Of course this subset relation also exists when propositions are disjoined, and Ross's paradox is the fact that a subset does not amount to an entailment.

Barker advocates an analysis of permission which makes (103a) mean (103b):

(103)   a. You may eat an apple.
          b. All worlds which can be reached by your eating an apple are ok.

(104)   You may eat an apple or a pear.

On such a semantics, (103a) does not entail (104), but from what I understand this result does not depend on the action-based semantics. Example (103b) could be stated in terms of propositions as "all accessible worlds in which you eat an apple are ok."

Overall, these works which treat imperatives as denoting actions offer an interesting version of the idea that imperatives differ from declaratives semantically, and not just in terms of their force. This idea fits naturally within the compositional approach to sentence mood. However, they have not yet given a detailed analysis of what that force is, and we have not yet seen an argument that actions will lead to improvements over existing dynamic analysis.

Notes on free choice, permission, and Ross's paradox.   Much research on imperatives takes as a primary goal to explain the free choice permission and Ross's paradox. While modal theories of imperatives, like those of Aloni (2007) and Kaufmann (2012, 2016), aim to reduce free choice in imperatives to a general explanation of free choice in modal sentences, scholars who favor dynamic theories often argue that the specific analysis they propose explains these phenomena. Unfortunately, by and large such arguments are not made in the context of comparing one proposal about free choice to another—that is, we sometimes see such an argument presented without any detailed discussion of how the given explanation differs from and is better than other dynamic theories' explanations. In this section, I will consider how a number of dynamic theories approach the problems of free choice and Ross's paradox, with the goal of understanding what some of the options for developing a theory are in this area.

The earliest works we have discussed in this section, Han (1998) and Van der Torre and Tan (1998), do not address free choice or Ross's paradox. They are major preoccupations of Van Rooij (2000), however. As we saw above, Van Rooij develops Lewis's intuition that permission works by expanding the sphere of permissibility to include the least-reprehensible worlds in which the proposition being permitted is true. He points out that, with a disjunctive permission sentence with logical form $May(p \vee q)$, if p and q are equally reprehensible (more precisely, if the least reprehensible p worlds and the least reprehensible q worlds are equally reprehensible), then expanding the sphere of permissibility to include the least reprehensible p-or-q worlds will lead to both p worlds and q worlds being included. Thus, (105), used performatively, leads to a context in which both eating an apple and eating a pear are permitted:

(105)   You may eat an apple or a pear.

(106)   a. You may eat an apple.
        b. You may eat a pear.

Van Rooij also implicitly addresses Ross's paradox when he cites Kamp's (1973) definition of P-ENTAILMENT.[82]

(107)   For all permission sentences p and q and for every context c,
        p **p-entails** q iff $c + p = (c + p) + q$.

Given this definition, (105) p-entails (106a), but not vice versa.

---

[82] He also notes the similarity of the definition to a more general definition of validity given by Veltman (1996).

Although Van Rooij gives insightful explanations of free choice and entailment patterns with permission sentences, he does not address the problems as they arise more generally with imperatives. It is also important to note that Van Rooij uses a classical boolean semantics for disjunction; disjunction of sentences is interpreted as a union of propositions, and free choice is derived from an additional pragmatic stipulation which requires that the disjuncts be of equal reprehensibility. In contrast to this, later work on free choice and Ross's paradox in the dynamic approach usually assumes a non-standard "choice-offering" semantics for disjunction.[83] On such approaches, disjunction of some category X yields a set of alternative meanings of the type normally assigned to X. For example, the phrase *Noah or Ben* might have the denotation $\{n, b\}$. Choice-offering theories of disjunction are often incorporated into a more general Hamblin-semantics framework on which all phrases are taken to denote sets of meanings of the type they would normally be associated with. For background on these ideas, which intersect with much broader issues in the theory of scalar implicature and free choice, see (among many other important works) Hamblin (1973), Zimmermann (2000), Kratzer and Shimoyama (2002), Aloni and van Rooij (2004), Chierchia (2004), Simons (2005), Menéndez-Benito (2005), Geurts (2005), Alonso-Ovalle (2006), Aloni (2007), Fox (2007), and Aloni and Ciardelli (2013).

Mastop (2011) is one scholar whose ideas about free choice with imperatives depend on a choice-offering analysis of disjunction. According to Mastop, a disjunctive imperative creates a commitment function with multiple sets of instructions. For example, starting with an empty commitment function s and accepting (108), we get the commitment function in (109):

(108)   Post this letter or burn it!

(109)   For every world w, $s[p \vee b](w) = \{\{\langle p, \mathrm{do} \rangle\}, \{\langle b, \mathrm{do} \rangle\}\}$

Though he does not discuss the point clearly, I believe Mastop's intention is that this commitment function represents a state in which the agent has the choice between posting the letter and burning it. More generally, in a world w, the agent has the choice to follow any of the sets of *do*'s and *don't*'s given by the commitment function in w. This framework can also avoid Ross's paradox. Mastop demonstrates this point by showing that accepting $\neg b!$ in the context of (109) yields a contradiction (since $\langle b, \mathrm{don't} \rangle$ is added to both sets in (109)).

Portner's (2011b) analysis of free choice and permission is in some ways similar to Mastop's. He suggests that contexts in which an agent is permitted but not required to do something should be represented via a to-do list which includes each option for what he may do. For example, if both *Turn left!* and *Turn right!* are incorporated into a's to-do list (and assuming that a can't both turn left and turn right), the

---

[83] I also point out Aloni and Ciardelli's (2013) work on free choice imperatives. It builds on a choice-offering semantics for disjunction, and is designed to fit into a dynamic semantics approach to imperative meaning (specifically, within inquisitive semantics); however, it does not develop a dynamic treatment or explain the properties of imperatives in terms of their sentential force.

ordering of worlds derived on Portner's analysis has two disjoint sets of "best" worlds, one in which *a* turns left and one in which *a* turns right. Since the agent's commitment principle requires that *a* take actions which tend to make the actual world one which is not worse than any other world, *a* is free to either turn left or turn right.

Portner's understanding of permission fits naturally with a choice-offering analysis of disjunctions. Assuming (108) denotes a set of exclusive properties, as in (110), and that each alternative is added to the to-do list, that to-do list will give an ordering with two maxima.

(110) $\{\{P \cap \neg B\}, \{B \cap \neg P\}\}$

Thus (108) normally leads to a context in which the addressee is permitted to post the letter, is permitted to burn it, and is required to do one or the other. Adopting a notion of consequence very similar to p-entailment (which he labels "warrant"), Portner can then solve Ross's paradox in essentially the same way as Mastop: (108) p-entails (and warrants) *Post this letter!*, but not vice versa.

Starr (2013) criticizes Portner's analysis by stating that "The fact that a reasonable speaker can place inconsistent properties on the To-Do List suggest[s] that it really isn't a To-Do List at all, that is, it is not the thing which is guiding agents' actions and practical reasoning." On the one hand, he is making the good point here that while the ordering relation is essential to the analysis as given above, the to-do list itself is not; on the other, he subsequently suggests that the possibility of having an inconsistent to-do list makes Portner's whole construct of to-do list incoherent, and I do not see why that should be. Whether empirically correct or not, the definitions of ordering and agent's commitment determine exactly what an inconsistent to-do list represents. (Note that as this book was going into production, Starr released a revised version of his paper.)

Starr has a more significant objection based on the observation that, on Portner's analysis, a disjunction warrants each of its disjuncts. This might be problematical, because it suggests that (111) should be equivalent to (108). Yet one can read the sequence of imperatives (111) as in the end requiring that the addressee burn the letter.

(111)   Post the letter or burn it! Burn it!

The fact that the final sentence of (111) has a discourse effect shows that *Burn it!* cannot be interpreted in Portner's theory by the ordinary update operation. Portner (like Mastop) would assume that the final sentence causes a retraction of *Post the letter!* $(=\{P \cap \neg B\})$ from the to-do list, not an addition of *Burn it!* (An addressee would infer that *Burn it!* must be interpreted as proposing a retraction, since it would have no effect on the context otherwise.) In contrast, Starr proposes a system in which the sequence can be interpreted by the normal update function and still lead to a context different from that derived from (108) alone. The details of his derivation are complex, however, so I will not attempt to present them here. For our purposes, the key point is that disjunction is not interpreted as a union of propositions, but rather as the union of the dynamic updates performed by the disjuncts individually. That is, (108) says to accumulate all of the effects we would get by updating the state by *Post this letter!* and by *Burn it!*[84] This move has a clear similarity to the way in which the choice-offering analysis of disjunction is used in the other dynamic theories of imperatives.

3.3.4 Minor types: optatives and exclamatives

There has been a limited amount of research on minor clause types within the dynamic approach. In this section we will look briefly at some proposals about optatives and exclamatives.[85]

Optatives.   Several scholars have studied optatives from the perspective of the dynamic approach (Biezma 2011; Grosz 2011, 2014). Even though they do not identify optatives as a distinct sentence mood, both Biezma and Grosz have interesting ideas concerning the derivation of optative meaning. Biezma builds on Roberts' version of the structured discourse context, proposing that *if* optatives like (112) receive an optative reading because they answer a certain kind of question under discussion.

(112)   If only John had driven more carefully!

Biezma argues that the compositional semantics of (112), specifically the contributions of *if* and *only*, give it a meaning which is appropriate to answering the question under discussion "How could John have gotten to the meeting on time?" (or, more precisely, "What X is such that, if X, John got to the meeting on time?"). Given that it answers this question, the implication that it is desirable that John drive more carefully follows from the desirability of the consequence for which it is a sufficient condition (that John got to the meeting on time). On Biezma's view, optatives do not constitute a true clause type, but it is an interesting question whether her approach implies that they are a sentence mood. If the job of answering a question of the kind which leads to the optative meaning is a fundamental type of update within semantic/pragmatic theory, we could see the *if (only)* pattern as a grammatically complex sentence mood.

Grosz (2014) analyzes a broader range of optative patterns and presents an intriguing game-theoretic model of how the optative meaning is marked. Unlike Biezma, who explains the presence of *if* and *only* in the optative (112) on the basis of their semantic contributions, Grosz thinks they are examples of truth-conditionally vacuous optative particles. Other such particles include *just* and *but* in English and *nur*, *bloß*, and *doch* in German. He proposes that their presence is explained not by a standard semantics, but rather by the role they play in context to

---

[84] As this manuscript was being finalized, a new article on permission by Starr (2016) appeared.

[85] As mentioned above, there is also relevant research on promissives and exhortatives; see Section 3.1.1 and Portner (2004), Mastop (2005), and Zanuttini et al. (2012). Within the dynamic approach, these minor types are treated as closely related to imperatives (or they are joined with imperatives into a broader jussive clause type), and so I will not review analyses of them here.

signal the speaker's intention that his or her utterance receive an optative meaning, as opposed to other meanings it might receive in context. In other words, the particles serve as "cues" for the optative reading. Grosz argues in favor of this perspective by showing that optative particles can only be left out in contexts in which an optative meaning is highly expected. Grosz formalizes his analysis as a signaling game using the techniques explored by Franke (2009).

Grosz's theory relies on language users being aware that the optative meaning is one alternative interpretation available to sentences like (112), and in order to assess the significance of Grosz's approach to our understanding of sentence mood generally, we would need to know exactly how the optative meaning fits into a broader paradigm of possible conversational functions. One possibility is to take as a fundamental fact about language that there is a specific inventory of such meanings, for each of which there are cues which language users may employ to signal their communicative intentions. Such a perspective can be seen as a game-theoretic analogue of the traditional view of sentence types (see Section 3.1.1), and would fit well with the construction-based approach to the marking of sentential force. Alternatively, it could be that optative meanings are cued in this way exactly because of their peripheral status within clause type systems. On this view, the basic clause types would be associated with their sentential forces in a principled way (for example, with an operator or through a pragmatic principle based on their compositional meaning), while minor types would be learned in a language-specific way on the basis of probabilistic associations. We are clearly in no position to decide if either of these possibilities is correct, but it does seem likely that game-theoretic ideas will be explored more extensively in future work on sentence mood.

Exclamatives.   A number of works have analyzed exclamatives using ideas drawn from dynamic semantics and pragmatics. In this section, we will look at the proposals of Castroviejo (2006a,b) and Zanuttini and Portner (Zanuttini and Portner 2000, 2003; Portner and Zanuttini 2000, 2006).[86]

Both Castroviejo and Zanuttini and Portner follow the compositional approach to sentence mood. Focusing on wh-exclamatives in Catalan like (113a), Castroviejo proposes that exclamatives are degree constructions containing a special high-degree morpheme TAN. Example (113a) has the truth conditions (113b) (Castroviejo 2006a, p. 141):

(113)   a. *Quina pel·lícula tan entretinguda que vaig   veure!*
           which movie   so entertaining that go.1SG see
           'What an entertaining movie I saw!'

       b. $\exists x[\text{movie}(x) \land \text{TAN}(\text{entertaining}(x))(d_i) \land \text{see}(s)(x)]$

Castroviejo cites the ontology of Ginzburg and Sag (2001), taking up their proposal that exclamatives denote facts (see Section 3.1.3). However, unlike Ginzburg and

---

[86] Readers interested in exclamatives will want to connect this section to the discussion of Rett's theory of exclamatives in Section 3.2.2.

Sag, she does not adopt a performative analysis. Instead, she derives the discourse function of the exclamative from its semantic type. On the assumption that facts cannot be asserted, asked, or ordered, it is not possible to assign exclamatives to any of the functions of the basic sentence moods. Instead, the assigned meaning is an attitude expressed by the speaker. Castroviejo (2006a, p. 142) describes this attitude as follows:

(114)   Contribution: the speaker experiences an attitude towards
$^\wedge$TAN(entretinguda$(x))(d_i)$

Castroviejo does not explain exactly how this particular contribution is derived from the factive semantics, but she does say that it is "not verbally encoded, but implicated" (Castroviejo 2006a, p. 144). This perspective identifies Castroviejo's analysis as an example of the compositional approach to sentence mood.

Zanuttini and Portner (2003) also give an analysis of exclamatives on which their discourse function is derived from their ordinary semantic meaning, and they are more explicit than Castroviejo in the consequences of their analysis for the general theory of sentence mood. Through a detailed discussion of wh-exclamatives in Italian, Paduan, and English, they argue that all such clauses contain a factive operator in CP. Their proposal is that the combination of factivity, encoded by this operator, and the standard semantics of wh-clauses is sufficient to identify the sentential force of exclamatives. I will sketch how their system works below.

The force of exclamatives, labeled WIDENING, can be given informally as follows (see Zanuttini and Portner 2003, (32) for their official definition):

(115)   **Widening:** Widen the initial domain of quantification, D_1, of the exclamative wh-operator to a new domain, D_2, in such a way that $D_2 - D_1$ only contains objects higher on the salient scale than the members of D_1.

Applied to Castroviejo's example (113a), widening affects the set of movies over which *Quina pellícula* ranges: initially, it contains some set of movies which the speaker is presupposed to have seen; after widening, it contains some more movies, which the speaker is also presupposed to have seen, and which exceed the initial set of movies in terms of how entertaining they are. This shift is meant to capture the idea that the most entertaining movies which the speaker saw were in fact so entertaining that they were not even under consideration in the initial, pre-widening context. From widening, Zanuttini and Portner derive more specific exclamative meanings like "surprise" as pragmatic inferences.

Several authors have criticized Zanuttini and Portner's theory because it does not give a central role to degrees in the semantics of wh-exclamatives (e.g. Castroviejo 2006a,b; Rett 2008a,b), and in fact the discussion of (113) above does make an unwarranted leap from the idea that certain movies were not initially in the domain of quantification to the statement that they were not because they were so highly entertaining. The adjective 'entertaining' does not make any explicit contribution to the direction of widening in Zanuttini and Portner's analysis. Assuming the criticism is valid, they might want to reformulate their theory in such a way that widening can take account of an adjective or other scalar term within the wh-phrase whose domain is being widened.[87]

Setting aside these concerns about the definition of widening, we can see how Zanuttini and Portner's analysis exemplifies the compositional approach to sentence mood. The sentential force of exclamatives, namely widening, is not syntactically encoded in all exclamatives. (They leave open the possibility that some exclamatives represent widening—for example, the *very* of English examples like *How very cute she is!*—but are clear that not all do.) Rather, they think that factivity rules out the use of the exclamative with the force of a declarative or interrogative clause, and assume that, as a result, widening is assigned as the force. Therefore, they clearly adhere to a compositional derivation of sentential force within a broadly dynamic pragmatics approach.

3.4 Theories of clause type systems and sentence mood

Having seen how scholars have sought to explain the nature of sentence mood and analyze the form and function of the most well-known clause types, we are now in a position to step back and ask a broader question: Why do languages have the sentence moods they do? Speech act theory and the dynamic approach both offer interesting perspectives on this question, and our main goal in this section will be to understand and evaluate those perspectives. Before we can do this, however, we must determine what facts a theory of clause type systems should explain. Here is a list drawn partially from the discussion throughout the chapter:

1. There are powerful crosslinguistic generalizations, including universals, concerning what clause types and sentence moods exist in natural languages.
2. There are three basic clause types, declaratives, interrogatives, and imperatives, and each of them is associated with a sentence mood.
3. The basic types may not all be equally basic. Some evidence suggests that declaratives are functionally the most basic, while imperatives are syntactically the simplest.
   (a) Declaratives are often assumed to show the most basic syntactic pattern of a given language.
   (b) Declaratives have the widest range of functions. They can easily be used to ask questions and issue directives.
   (c) On the one hand, morphologically distinct imperatives often have the least marking of verbal inflection, and this may mean that they have the simplest syntactic structure. On the other, it is very common for imperatives to share features of the morphology and syntax of some subclass of declaratives (e.g. future tense) or of non-indicative clauses (e.g. infinitives and subjunctives).

---

[87] They might retain the idea that the domain is a set of entities, but explicitly widen it according to the scale of degrees given by the adjectives. Or they might say that the domain being widened is itself a set of degrees, expanded to include higher degrees.

    (d) Imperatives have the narrowest range of functions. They can barely be used to assert information or ask questions.

4. The relations among the three basic types are controversial.

    (a) Declaratives and interrogatives are alike in many languages in the morphosyntax of their (finite, indicative, tensed) verbs. This may show that these types are more closely related to one another than either are to imperatives.

    (b) According to many syntactic theories, declaratives in a given language show its default sentential syntax, and interrogatives and imperatives are marked as distinct from declaratives by morphosyntactic means. This may show that interrogatives and imperatives are alike, and different from declaratives, in having an explicit marking of force.

5. Members of each clause type can be used in diverse ways, and though much of this diversity is certainly the result of implicature and other forms of inference, for some uses it is plausible that the type's normal sentential force is absent. Some examples:

    (a) Rising declaratives might be better classified as having the force of asking (like canonical interrogatives).

    (b) Rhetorical interrogatives might be better classified as having the force of assertion (like canonical declaratives).

    (c) Imperatives used to give instructions or express idle wishes might be thought to lack directive force.

6. There are minor clause types as well, and each of them has special properties which should also be explained:

    (a) Exhortatives are related to imperatives, and are fairly common.

    (b) Promissives may be related to imperatives or declaratives, and are quite rare.

    (c) Optatives are relatively rare as a distinct clause type, and there is debate about whether they are closely related to any basic type; constructions with optative meaning are less rare.

    (d) Exclamatives often have much in common with interrogatives, though types which are more similar to declaratives are also found. Exclamatives are not especially uncommon.

7. Certain forms of the clause types, such as morphologically distinct imperatives and verb-second declaratives and interrogatives, are the standard root clause forms of their sentence moods, but show restrictions in their ability to be embedded.

Most work on sentence types and clause type systems has assumed that a sentence can only be of one basic type; that is, they assume that the types are exclusive. However, it has been observed that it may be possible for clauses to be simultaneously of the imperative and interrogative clause types (Platzack and Rosengren 1994; Reis 1999; Kaufmann and Poschmann 2013). An example is the echo question imperative (116b), from Kaufmann and Poschmann (2013, (8)):

(116)   a. Maria to Peter:

>   *Gib   dem Lehrer   mein Buch!*
>   give.IMP the   teacher   my   book
>   'Give my book to the teacher!'

   b. Hans to Peter:

>   *WEM   gib   ihr Buch?*
>   who.DAT give.IMP her book
>   'WHO should you give her book to?'

As Kaufmann and Poschmann note, the existence of mixed types like this seems to offer support to the compositional view of clause typing. From the perspective of this section, we would wish to determine which combinations of types are possible, and then ask why just those cases allow for exceptions to exclusivity.

   When considering clause type systems, our overall goal is to understand what various ideas about the sentence mood can contribute to explaining properties of clause type systems like these. We will begin with the two major frameworks we have considered all along, speech act theory and the dynamic approach, in Sections 3.4.1–3.4.2. Each of these has some interesting consequences for understanding the most obvious properties, Points 1, 2, 5, and 6 above. The other properties require some basic linguistic analysis to become apparent; we will discuss them, Points 3, 4, and 7, in Section 3.4.3.

3.4.1 Clause type systems in speech act theory

We have already seen in Section 3.2.2 that numerous linguists argue that classical speech act theory does not provide a strong foundation for explaining the properties of clause type systems or developing a theory of sentence mood. This point is based on the assumption that sentential forces are to be identified with illocutionary forces, and follows from three basic features of the theory: First, explicit performatives can be associated with a wide variety of—possibly any— illocutionary force, even though they are grammatically of the declarative clause type. Second, even if we set aside uses which are plausibly "indirect" or the result of non-literal language use, every clause type can be used with a very large number of distinct forces. This fact implies that clause types are not closely associated with illocutionary forces, and in fact makes it difficult to maintain that there are such things as sentence moods at all. And third, the taxonomy of illocutionary forces does not align well with what we know about clause type systems. Notably, the traditional taxonomy includes a separate class for the very rare promissives (commissive acts) but groups interrogatives with imperatives (as directive acts), even though they are not a natural class in structural terms.

   In response to these points, followers of speech act theory have pursued a number of different strategies:

1. They identify sentential force with a set of illocutionary forces, an illocutionary force potential (e.g. Bach and Harnish 1979; Harnish 1994).
2. They decompose the concept of force into more primitive properties, and identify one of them with sentential force (Searle and Vanderveken 1985; Vanderveken 1990).
3. They reduce the number of fundamental forces within the theory, as is done with the dynamic force hypothesis (e.g. Kaufmann 2012; Charlow 2013).

The first strategy above addresses the problem raised by the diversity of illocutionary forces with which each clause type may be associated, but by itself does nothing to help with the other two problems. Concerning explicit performatives, it can be combined with the idea that explicit performatives have the same literal force as other declaratives (assertion or declaration), and their apparent force is derived pragmatically. It does nothing at all to deal with the overall mismatch between the speech act typology and structure of clause type systems.

The second strategy, decomposing illocutionary force, addresses the first two problems in useful ways. Concerning explicit performatives, it identifies an illocutionary point of declarations which is inferentially related to assertion; it might make sense, then, that the declarative clause type is associated with both the declarative and the assertive illocutionary points. However, it does not answer the problem posed by the mismatch between the typologies of forces and clause type systems. The theory still postulates a basic sentential force for promissives while interrogatives are still grouped with imperatives. Searle and Vanderveken nevertheless maintain their typology, holding that it is sufficiently well-motivated by fundamental philosophical considerations that these discrepancies should be explained away on functional grounds. (Recall from Section 3.2.2 that speech act theorists have argued without empirical evidence that promises are too rare or too unimportant to be associated with a grammatically distinct clause type.)

The final strategy for adjusting classical speech act theory is represented by the dynamic force hypothesis. The idea here is that there are only a few basic forces because there are just a few simple, natural ways for a speech act to affect the discourse. The sentential forces of declaratives, interrogatives, and imperatives are drawn from these simple, natural updates.

Although the strategy based on the dynamic approach (including the dynamic force hypothesis) appears to provide the best basis for explaining why we have the basic clause types we do, it is not clear which approach has the advantage when it comes to minor types. The traditional classification of speech act theory makes room for all sorts of speech acts, including lamentation, promising, expressing of wishes, and exclamation; as a result, the meanings of all of the minor types can be precisely described. The main problem which this approach faces with regard to the minor types is explaining why certain illocutionary forces such as threats and lamentations are never (as far as we know) associated with a clause type. This situation contrasts with the one we find with the dynamic force hypothesis and dynamic approach. There it is easy to explain why certain forces are not associated with minor types. The problem is to incorporate into the theory each minor type that does occur into a framework which is designed to severely restrict the range of sentential forces. In the long run, traditional speech act theory will have the advantage if the minor types are very diverse across languages, so that we conclude that any illocutionary force can in principle be associated with a syntactic structure, even if some do so only very rarely. The dynamic approaches will have an advantage if the set of possible minor types is severely constrained, so that we can extend the approach which aims to explain the typological properties of the basic types to the minor ones.

3.4.2 Clause type systems in the dynamic approach

Within the dynamic approach, it is quite common to present an explanation for the existence of three basic clause types. The core idea is that there is a notion of context relevant to semantic and pragmatic theory which encompasses less than the full richness of the situations in which communication happens. Instead, we have a structured discourse context representing the most fundamental aspects of those situations. The structured discourse context always contains some component used to represent conversational commitments concerning the way the world is (e.g. commitment slates or common ground). As the approach has developed, it is now assumed to contain a component or structural features which allow it to encode both the questions under discussion in discourse (e.g. the question under discussion set) and priorities for action to which the participants in the discourse are committed (e.g. to-do lists). A simple form of this idea takes the context to be a triple ⟨common ground, question set, to-do list function⟩, and its structure is the basis for explaining why there are three basic clause types. In this framework, the sentential forces of the basic clause types are understood to be the most natural update functions which can be defined for each of the three components. For example, if the context is such a triple, as on Portner's (2004) view, each component has one clause type specialized for updating it. Murray and Starr (2016) develop a similar idea in a system which extends Starr's (2013) theory of imperatives.

Although theories within the dynamic approach virtually all offer (or implicitly assume) this same explanation of the fundamental role played by the basic types in communication, there is much less consensus about how to deal with non-canonical functions of the basic types and the meanings of minor types. Concerning the non-canonical functions, the natural impulse within the dynamic approach is to see diversity in function as arising from implicature and inference. In other words, the literal force hypothesis remains a powerful draw within the dynamic approach—as it would have to, given that the sentential forces are so few and so simple. An example of this tendency is Portner's (2004) proposal that the various functions of imperatives differ not in force, but in the social basis which justifies their being issued; on this view, for example, orders and requests have the same force (update the to-do list), but orders are justified by authority while requests are justified by the fact that they would help the speaker achieve a goal. However, there are cases in which literal force combined with implicature and inferences does not seem sufficient to explain a sentence's discourse effects. Two clear examples here are rising declaratives and rhetorical questions, cases where linguistic features play an important role in the association of a basic type with a non-standard function.

Scholars within the dynamic approach have not reached a consensus on the analysis of rising declaratives and rhetorical questions, but it appears to me that the trend at present is to follow Gunlogson's tactic of reanalyzing the basic sentential forces in ways which allow these peripheral functions to be modeled as natural updates, even if they are rarer than the canonical functions of asserting, asking, and directing.

When it comes to the minor types, the dynamic approach has not settled on a standard treatment. In Section 3.3.4, we saw various interesting ideas for the analysis of specific minor types, but many problems remain. In the cases of exhortatives and promissives, we have a reasonable explanation within the model of the structured discourse context for why they are expressed as clause types, but not for why they are rarer than imperatives. In the cases of exclamatives and optatives, we do not have any analysis which relates the way they update the context to models of the structured discourse context used to explain the basic types. The dynamic approach should seek a theory of exclamative and optative updates which can be expressed in a natural way within the framework used to analyze the basic types, yet which makes their updates less essential in a way that explains their non-basic status.

In sum, then, dynamic theories present a promising route towards explaining those properties of clause type systems which have to do with the canonical functions of the basic types. But while there is much interesting work on the non-canonical functions and minor types, no generally accepted theory of those functions and types has yet emerged. As mentioned above, the issues facing the dynamic approach are in many ways the converse of those facing the speech act theory approach: while speech act theory leads us to expect that very many minor functions of language are equally natural, dynamic theories lead us to see only a very few functions as maximally natural. It seems to me that, overall, the dynamic approach is in a much better position to explain the full range of properties of clause type systems than speech act theory is, since I think it will prove easier for the dynamic approach to elaborate upon its simple model of the discourse context so as to allow natural updates to be associated with the minor types, without every sort of conceivable update being treated as equally natural.[88] In contrast, apart from the versions of speech act theory which follow the dynamic force hypothesis (and which follow a strategy similar to that of the dynamic approach), speech act theory has few resources internal to the theory for explaining why any particular force is not associated with a characteristic grammatical form. In the end, an extremely important difference between the dynamic approach and versions of speech act theory which accept the dynamic force hypothesis, on the one hand, and other more standard versions of speech act theory, on the other, is that the latter see many properties of clause type systems as beyond the explanatory purview of semantic/pragmatic theory, while the former continue to seek a theory of those properties.

---

[88] Of course, this evaluation accords with my own previous work, but still I think my reasons for this evaluation are sound.

3.4.3 Other properties of clause type systems

Several questions about the nature of clause type systems have not received the attention within semantic/pragmatic theory that they deserve, and before concluding this chapter I would like to call attention to them. These questions have to do with the status of clause types at the syntax/semantics interface, and for this reason fall outside of the traditional ways of thinking about sentence moods originating in philosophy. Nevertheless, they are likely quite important for understanding how clause types and sentence moods really work, and we find intriguing ideas relevant to them scattered throughout the linguistics literature.

We can begin with the issue of whether any of the three basic types is more "basic" at the grammatical level. As we have observed, declaratives are often assumed to have the most unmarked syntactic structure within a given language; for example, when we say that English is an SVO language, we say this because declaratives often have this word order. Syntactic theories will then often derive interrogatives and imperatives by adding something to declarative syntax; for example, in certain contemporary theories, a syntactic feature in C triggers the distinct word order of interrogatives and imperatives.

If interrogatives and imperatives have something extra which differentiates them from the unmarked declarative, we may ask what consequences this has for clause typing and sentence mood. It might, for example, have consequences at the level of force assignment. We see this type of approach in the analysis of Bierwisch (1980); he proposes that declaratives lack a force marker, in contrast to interrogatives (with marker *Qu*) and imperatives (*Imp*). Moreover, he allows declaratives greater latitude in force assignment; declaratives, lacking a force marker, are associated loosely with the force (or "pre-reflexive attitude") *D*, while *Qu* and *Imp* are more strictly associated with forces *Q* and *I*. Bierwisch's ideas offer hope for explaining why declaratives are more flexible in discourse function than interrogatives and, especially, imperatives.

Although declaratives are assumed to be the simplest basic type in syntactic terms, imperatives are often simpler in their morphology. In many languages, the imperative verb is very simple, as simple as or even simpler than the infinitive. For example, in Italian the canonical second person singular imperative consists in the verb stem plus the vowel indicating its conjugation class (*parl-a* 'speak'). The fact that imperatives so commonly lack tense, mood, and agreement morphology suggests that the internal structure of imperative clauses is (at least in some languages) simpler than that of declaratives. Few theories of sentence mood make anything of this relative simplicity, however.[89]

This discussion of the respects in which both declaratives and imperatives might be thought of as the "simplest" basic clause type raises the connected issue of whether there are subgroups among the three basic types which are important

---

[89] Kaufmann's (2012) theory treats imperatives as containing an unexpressed modal akin to *should*, and so the form of the verb could be explained as the result of its being selected by the modal. The property analysis of Hausser (1980, 1983) and Portner (2004) might explain it by building on the observation that subsentential constituents like VP can denote properties.

for us to recognize as we seek to understand clause type systems. There is good reason to assume that declaratives and interrogatives, with their full tense-mood-agreement paradigms, form an important subgroup apart from imperatives. We find in the literature many ideas which might connect this way of grouping clause types to the broader theory of sentence mood. For example, building on the important German tradition, scholars like Truckenbrodt (2006a) and Lohnstein (2007) aim to give theories of clause typing which assign an important role to indicative mood. From a quite different angle, we see the distinction between declaratives and interrogatives being broken down by the likes of Gunlogson (2001), Aloni and van Rooy (2002), and Ciardelli et al. (2013) (see Section 3.3.2). It seems likely that interesting results would follow from trying to link these two lines of thinking into a deeper view of the relation between declaratives and interrogatives.

A final feature of clause type systems which is not yet well understood has to do with the restrictions on embedding we find for certain clause-typing structures. In particular, researchers have long been interested in the properties of imperatives and verb-second clauses in Germanic languages:

(117) a. *Mary ordered John [leave].
       b. *Maria will,   [sie ist in diesem Fall in
          Maria wants she is in that   case in
          Berlin]. (German, Truckenbrodt 2006a)
          Berlin.

(118) a. Mary said [leave].
       b. Maria sagt [Peter geht nach Hause].
          Maria says Peter goes to   home.

Although in the past it was sometimes stated that imperatives cannot be embedded, we know now this is not the case.[90] Similarly, linguists have long known that it is simplistic to describe German as verb-second in root clauses but verb-final in embedded clauses. Nevertheless, although imperatives and V2 clauses can be embedded, the examples in (117) show that they do not do so freely.

One possible view of the data above is that imperatives and verb-second clauses contain a force-indicating operator, and that this can only be embedded when the higher predicate is able to combine with such a clause. How this plays out depends on whether one thinks that the force-indicator actually encodes force (as on Krifka's view) or some other meaning associated with force (as on Truckenbrodt's). It is also possible that the embedding restrictions are due to semantic or pragmatic properties not directly tied to force; for example, Pak et al. (2015) argue that

---

[90] For the idea that imperatives cannot be embedded, relevant references include Katz and Postal (1964), Sadock and Zwicky (1985), Palmer (1986), Rivero and Terzi (1995), Han (1998), Platzack and Rosengren (1998), Aikhenvald (2010), and Alcázar and Saltarelli (2012). For the contrary evidence, we have Rögnvaldsson (1998), Sheppard and Golden (2002), Chen-Main (2005), Rus (2005), Platzack (2007), Pak (2008), Crnič and Trinh (2011), Kaufmann and Poschmann (2013), Thomas (2014), and Medeiros (2015).

the restrictions on embedded imperatives are due to the unique properties of the imperative subject and restrictions on the marking of pragmatic features like speech style and politeness, and not directly to imperatives' sentential force.

3.5 Looking ahead

In this chapter, we have explored a variety of approaches to the analysis of sentence moods and related concepts like sentential force and clause types. We have sought to understand the major approaches to these topics and have looked in some detail at specific analyses of individual sentence moods. Though I have not touched upon a great deal of research on these topics, I hope that the presentation will provide some helpful context as readers look deeper into the literature. Here in conclusion, I would like to highlight a couple of points about the nature of this particular subfield of semantics and pragmatics.

First, since clause types and sentence mood have been studied in a serious way for such a long time and within so many different traditions, it is not an easy field to get to know. We find research whose primary orientation is syntactic, semantic, pragmatic, and philosophical. I have found it useful to organize the discussion around two approaches to discourse meaning, speech act theory and the dynamic approach, because they each offer a perspective on the nature of sentential force, and I believe that understanding sentential force is at the heart of the task. This leads to the second point: there are converging insights within proposals with very different orientations. For example, in the previous subsection we identified several analyses which suggest a close relation between declaratives and interrogatives, but which do so from very different angles. Linguists should seek to build more upon this type of convergence.

One area in which our knowledge has not developed as far as it should concerns the crosslinguistic variation of sentence moods and clause type systems. While we have good work on the typology of clause types, it does not fully incorporate the vast amount of information about sentence moods embedded in descriptions of particular languages. Descriptive and typological work often makes use of concepts of discourse modality broader than sentence mood, such as reality status and evidentiality. This separation between typological research and the formal semantics/pragmatics tradition may have begun to narrow due to more accessible presentations from the typological perspective (e.g. Aikhenvald 2010; Nuyts and van der Auwera 2016) and analyses within semantic and pragmatic theory well-informed by that perspective (e.g. Bittner 2011; Krawczyk 2012; Rett and Murray 2013; Murray 2016). Given the current trend in formal semantics towards greater crosslinguistic research, it is likely that this trend will accelerate.

4

Core mood, reality status, and evidentiality

In Chapters 2 and 3, I have reviewed and sought to clarify and sometimes to extend a range of semantic and pragmatic theories of verbal mood and sentence mood, and it has emerged that within each of those two major topics there exists a small number of cutting-edge approaches. I consider the following to be the most important of them:

1. The theory of verbal mood is dominated by a general perspective which treats the indicative/subjunctive contrast as marking features of the modal parameters of interpretation for a clause. These modal parameters can be modeled using either the method of shifting parameters or the method of derived contexts, and they track a distinction between subjunctive contexts with a comparative meaning and indicative contexts which imply truth in a designated set of worlds (or a related concept like decidedness or contextual commitment).

2. There are currently two main theoretical approaches to sentence mood. One of them is the form of the dynamic approach which aims to explain both the meanings of individual sentence moods and properties of clause type systems in terms of a structured discourse context. According to this view, we explain the function and range of the sentential forces because they are the natural ways of updating the discourse context. The other main approach is the dynamic force hypothesis, that modern branch of speech act theory which incorporates ideas from the dynamic approach to represent illocutionary force.

Verbal mood and sentence mood are by far the most well-studied categories of mood, and for the most part, they are investigated by linguists as independent, major subfields in semantics and pragmatics. In this chapter, I aim to offer some perspective on these two subfields by doing two things: In Section 4.1, I will investigate whether it is possible to synthesize theories of verbal mood and sentence mood to produce a unified theory of core mood. Then, in Section 4.2, I will attempt to situate verbal mood and sentence mood within the broader range of mood phenomena, in particular looking at the concepts of reality status and evidentiality. All of the material in this chapter will of necessity be preliminary and even rudimentary, because there has been little discussion of these issues in

Mood. First edition. Paul Portner.
© Paul Portner 2018. First published 2018 by Oxford University Press.

semantics and pragmatics, but I hope this effort helps to lay the foundations for future research on them.

4.1 Prospects for a unified theory of core mood

In this section I will show how it is possible to synthesize some of the most important theories of verbal mood and sentence mood into a unified framework. In particular, I am going to combine simplified versions of the comparison-based theory of verbal mood and the dynamic approach to sentence mood based on the structured discourse context. Roughly speaking, the goal is to produce a single framework in which both the ideas of Section 2.2.2.5 and those of Section 3.4.2 can be expressed. Doing this will show that there is some prospect for a unified theory of core mood.

Before going on, I want to emphasize that the exercise undertaken in this section is not intended to dismiss either past or future research on other approaches to verbal mood and sentence mood. As has been noted, I am not convinced that the comparison-based theory will be able to explain all of the relevant patterns (see the discussion of Portner and Rubinstein's arguments in Section 2.2.2.5). And there is most definitely exciting work being done on sentence mood which does not fit into the unified framework (for example, research on speech acts like Krifka 2014 and the dynamic force hypothesis like Kaufmann 2012). Readers should understand that my goal is to show what a unified theory would look like, and not to present a final theory. Nevertheless, I also want to be clear that I believe that the proposed synthesis explicates some deep connections between verbal mood and sentence mood, and that it therefore points in the approximate direction of a correct theory of how the two types of core mood are related.[1]

The POSW framework.   Important theories of both verbal mood and sentence mood are built on theoretical constructs which can be represented as a partially ordered set of worlds. Within the theory of verbal mood, the idea that the subjunctive marks comparison relies on an ordering relation, either a preference relation $<$ or an ordering source. Within the theory of sentence mood, imperatives are either treated as deontic modals which make use of a prioritizing ordering source or analyzed as updating a component of the structured discourse context which represents an ordering of worlds or propositions. We can abstract away from some of these differences and produce a single simplified system in which the essential ideas of various theories can be stated. We begin by defining the POSW:

(1)   A **partially ordered set of worlds** POSW is a pair $c = \langle cs_c, <_c \rangle$, where:
a. cs_c is a set of worlds, and
b. $<_c$ is a pre-order over cs_c.

---

[1] I argue in favor of a more fully developed theory in Portner (2017).

Now we define the operations and operators for the POSW. In doing so, we build on the techniques of update logic developed by Veltman (1996) and Van der Torre and Tan (1998).[2] First, the update operations:

(2) Two linguistically natural updates of a POSW c are:[3]
   a. For any POSW c and atomic sentence ϕ,
$$c + \phi = \langle cs_c \cap [\![\, \phi \,]\!]^c, <_c \rangle$$
   b. For any POSW c and atomic sentence ϕ,
$$c \star \phi = \langle cs_c, <_c \circ [\![\, \phi \,]\!]^c \rangle$$

We also have two modals:

(3) The basic necessity modals for a POSW c are:
   a. The informational modal: $[\![\, \Box_{cs}\phi \,]\!]^c = 1$ iff $cs_c \subseteq [\![\, \phi \,]\!]^c$
   b. The preference modal: $[\![\, \Box_{<}\phi \,]\!]^c = 1$ iff $m_c \subseteq [\![\, \phi \,]\!]^c$

In words: $+$ updates the set of worlds in c, $\star$ updates the ordering in c, $\Box_{cs}\phi$ says that cs entails ϕ, and $\Box_{<}\phi$ says that the best subset of cs entails ϕ. If we think of $\langle cs_c, <_c \rangle$ as a modal base and ordering source, $\Box_{cs}\phi$ expresses simple necessity and $\Box_{<}\phi$ expresses human necessity (Kratzer 1981; see Portner 2009, sect. 3.1 for background on Kratzer's theory).

The POSW framework applied to verbal mood.   The POSW framework allows us to capture important ideas in the theory of verbal mood in complement clauses. We will focus here on the role of comparativity in verbal mood selection. We begin with a definition of an AGENT'S COGNITIVE MODEL which can serve to help us express the meanings of two representative verbs, 'believe' and 'want':

(4) An agent a's **cognitive model** in situation s is a POSW $m(a, s)$ where:
   a. $cs_{m(a,s)}$ = the set of worlds compatible with a's beliefs in s; and
   b. $<_{m(a,s)}$ = the ordering of worlds which represents a's desires in s.

Now we can give meanings for the representative non-comparative predicate 'believe' and the representative comparative predicate 'want':

(5) a. $[\![\, A \text{ believes that } \phi \,]\!]^c = \{w : \exists s[s < w \text{ and } [\![\, \Box_{cs}\phi \,]\!]^{m(a,s)} = 1]\}$
   b. $[\![\, A \text{ wants } \phi \,]\!]^c = \{w : \exists s[s < w \text{ and } [\![\, \Box_{<}\phi \,]\!]^{m(a,s)} = 1]\}$

The meaning for 'believe' uses the informational modal $\Box_{cs}$, while the meaning for 'want' uses the preference modal $\Box_{<}$. Both of these entries treat the attitude predicate as a strong modal, but the one for 'want' uses the ordering component of the cognitive model in a manner similar to an ordering source.

---

[2] Compare with the 'preference structures' of Condoravdi and Lauer (2012). Recall that $\circ$ refines the ordering $<_c$ and m_c identifies the best worlds in cs_c according to $<_c$ (Section 3.3.3).

[3] To maintain $c + \phi$ as a POSW, $<_{c+\phi}$ should be restricted to $cs_{c+\phi}$. This issue will be discussed later in the section.

The central idea of the comparison-based approach to verbal mood can now be stated as follows:

1. **Indicative principle:** If a clause ϕ is operated on by the informational modal, its form is indicative.
2. **Subjunctive principle:** If a clause ϕ is operated on by the preference modal, its form is subjunctive.

An explicit theory would endorse one or both of these principles. If only one principle is active, the other mood would be selected by default. Of course, these principles can only be applied to 'believe' and 'want' so far. In order to apply them to the full lexicon, we will need a much richer structure for the cognitive model. See Sections 2.2.2.3 and 2.2.2.5 for discussion of the comparison-based approach.

This POSW framework could be combined with many different ideas about the syntax and semantics of sentence-embedding constructions. For example, we could incorporate ideas from the approach to verbal mood which states that indicative is selected by predicates which entail the truth of their argument in a designated set of worlds. To do this, we have to give the mood morpheme in ϕ access to the POSW used to interpret it. This might be done by the method of shifting contexts or by using one of the other techniques discussed in Section 2.2.

The framework is also compatible with more radical ideas about the logical forms of sentence-embedding constructions. Using techniques from Portner (1997) or Kratzer (2006, 2013), we might propose that the operators $\Box_{cs}$ and $\Box_<$ are not introduced by the matrix predicate, but rather by a morpheme in the embedded clause (the complementizer or mood morpheme itself). According to this idea, the role of the verb is to specify the precise POSW used by the modal operators. For example, we might propose that the indicative introduces the modal operator $\Box_{cs}$, and when embedded under the matrix verb 'believe', this verb assigns it the POSW $m(a, s)$. The verb 'want' would assign the same POSW, but the operator introduced by the subjunctive would be $\Box_<$.

The POSW framework applied to sentence mood.   Turning now to sentence mood, it is not difficult to give an analysis of declaratives and imperatives in the POSW framework. Building on the ideas discussed in Section 3.3, we begin with definitions of DISCOURSE COMMITMENTS, COMMITMENT SLATE, and PRIORITY SLATE:

(6)   The **discourse commitments** of an individual a are a POSW s where:
   a. $cs_s = a$'s **commitment slate**, a set of worlds compatible with all of a's factual commitments; and
   b. $<_s = a$'s **priority slate**, an ordering of worlds which represents a's to-do list.

It would also be possible to pursue this project in terms of a single common ground, rather than individual commitment slates, but in order to do so we would need to incorporate multiple priority slates (one for each participant) into the POSW framework.

A DISCOURSE CONTEXT associates each participant with discourse commitments:

(7)   The **discourse context** is a function d from a set of individuals (the participants) to discourse commitments.

This conceptualization of the discourse context allows definitions of two basic sentential forces, ASSERTION and DIRECTING:

(8)   a. Assertion of a sentence S in discourse context d: apply the update $d(speaker) + S$.

     b. Directing a sentence S in discourse context d: apply the update $d(addressee) \star S$.

We might also treat assertion as updating the commitment slate of every participant, not just the speaker's. (The way we have used the commitment slate in (8) is more in line with Gunlogson's theory than Hamblin's.)

Now we can identify the contributions of two of the basic sentence moods:

1. **Declaratives**: The sentential force of a declarative sentence is assertion.
2. **Imperatives**: The sentential force of an imperative sentence is directing.

Declaratives update the speaker's commitment slate, while imperatives update the addressee's priority slate.

This sketch of the POSW framework leaves open many basic issues in the theory of sentence mood. Most fundamentally, it does not take a stand on what grammatical properties constitute the declarative and imperative sentence moods. It does not say precisely which sentences have a sentence mood—only root clauses, root clauses and embedded clauses with root-like syntax, or all clauses? It also does not establish how sentential force is assigned to sentence moods, and it is compatible with any of the three approaches identified in Section 3.1.3 (the operator-based, construction-based, and compositional theories). All of these important issues must be settled in order to give a theory of sentence mood. What should be focused on is that this sketch gives precise form to the intuition that there are important connections between declarative sentence mood and indicative verbal mood, on the one hand, and between imperative sentence mood and subjunctive verbal mood, on the other. The connection is that declaratives/ indicatives have to do with the first component of a POSW, the set of worlds cs_c, and that imperatives/subjunctives have to do with the second component, the ordering $<_c$.

There is an obvious gap in this discussion of sentence mood—we have not said anything about interrogatives. The reason for this gap is that theories of verbal mood rarely touch on how embedded interrogatives fit into their proposals, and so a system designed to capture what is common to theories of verbal mood and theories of sentence mood naturally cannot handle them. I do not know of a single formal theory of mood selection in complement clauses which puts forth a specific proposal about the meaning of the basic question-embedding verb 'ask.'[4] Let me give a taste of what is at issue: In Italian, the verb *chiedere* takes the indicative when it means 'ask,' but the subjunctive when it means 'wonder' (example based on a sentence in Eco, *La bustina di Minerva*):

(9) a. *Gli   avevo   chiesto se ci   sono   corsi   d'inglese.*
         him have-1SG asked   if there be.3PL.INDIC course of English
         'I asked him whether there are English courses.'

     b. *Mi chiedo   se ci   siano   corsi   d'inglese.*
         me wonder-1SG if there be.3PL.SUBJ courses of English
         'I wonder whether there are English courses.'

It will be impossible to fully understand the relation between verbal mood and sentence mood until we have theories of verbal mood that can explain this difference.

We observed in Section 3.3 that certain dynamic theories of questions minimize or even eliminate the difference in sentential force between declaratives and interrogatives. For example, on the dynamic semantics theory of questions which treats the discourse context as a relation over possible worlds, assertion and asking both involve intersection; specifically, asking a question involves the update $C \cap q$ and asserting a proposition involves the update $C \cap (p \times p)$. We could integrate this view into the POSW framework by replacing the first component of the POSW with a partition or other relation appropriate to the analysis of questions. We would then have:[5]

(10) A **partitioned partially ordered set of worlds** PPOSW is a pair $c = \langle p_c, <_c \rangle$, where:
      a. p_c is a partition of some set of worlds cs_c, and
      b. $<_c$ is a pre-order over cs_c.

Then both root declaratives and root interrogatives would target the first component p_c. This might provide the basis for explaining why they both have indicative verbal mood (see Portner 2017 for an analysis along these lines). Alternatively, we could add a third component, a question set, to the basic definition of a POSW, resulting in a theory similar to Roberts' or Portner's (Roberts 1996, 2012; Portner 2004). But it would not be wise for us to spend too much time considering these options now. As observed above, if we wish to develop a unified framework for analyzing verbal mood and sentence mood, what is most needed is a theory of mood selection by interrogative-embedding predicates.

---

[4] Of course there are important theories of embedded interrogatives, some of which are mentioned in Chapter 3, but they do not try to explain verbal mood selection.
[5] This model of context is similar to Starr's (2013) preference states, but he treats the force of imperatives and interrogatives somewhat differently.

Embedded updates and embedded speech acts.   This sketch of analyses of verbal mood and sentence mood treats the two as similar only in two very abstract respects: Both types of mood are analyzed in terms of the POSW or PPOSW and make a distinction between the mood which relates to cs_c (indicative and declarative) and the mood which relates to $<_c$ (subjunctive and imperative). But the system makes room for various hypotheses which imply a tighter relation between verbal mood and sentence mood. Speaking very roughly, these hypotheses incorporate sentential force into the semantics of embedding constructions and therefore, to some extent, aim to derive the contrast between verbal moods from the distinct forces of declaratives and imperatives.

We can envision analyses which incorporate either sentential force, in the form of dynamic update potential, or full speech acts into the lexical semantics of attitude verbs. We see the first of these options, incorporating sentential force, in the analysis of verbal mood presented by Farkas (2003), as discussed in Section 2.2.2.5. In the POSW framework, we reformulate the meanings of 'believe' and 'want' as follows:

(11)   a. $[\![\ A\ believes\ that\ \phi\ ]\!]^c = \{w : \exists s[s < w\ \text{and}\ m(a,s) + \phi = m(a,s)]\}$
       b. $[\![\ A\ wants\ \phi\ ]\!]^c = \{w : \exists s[s < w\ \text{and}\ m(a,s) \star \phi = m(a,s)]\}$

These entries use the technique introduced by Heim (1992) for using an update potential to reproduce the standard semantics for attitude verbs as strong modals. (11a) is true if $cs_{m(a,s)}$ includes the content of ϕ, because it says that performing a $+$-update has no effect on $m(a,s)$, and (11b) is true if $<_{m(a,s)}$ includes the preference for ϕ. Assuming that all sentence-embedding constructions can be analyzed in a similar way, we can consider alternative mood-selection principles:

1.   **Indicative principle:** If a clause ϕ is the object of a $+$-update, its form is indicative.
2.   **Subjunctive principle:** If a clause ϕ is the object of a $\star$-update, its form is subjunctive.

An analysis based on these principles has the advantage of applying to both root and embedded clauses, and so can hope to explain the presence of indicative in declaratives and the occasional use of subjunctive form for the imperative sentence mood.[6] These principles also imply that we should develop a theory of interrogative sentence mood which treats it as using the $+$-update.

The ideas just outlined can be described as proposing that sentential force occurs in embedded contexts. The POSW framework also allows for the more radical option of incorporating full speech acts into the semantics of embedded clauses. Suppose that we think 'say' has a use which involves embedding a clause with the

---

[6] For the reasons discussed in Section 2.3.1.1, we also know that infinitives are closely related to subjunctives, and so the correct generalization is probably that subjunctives, infinitives, and imperatives fall under the same principle or closely related principles.

illocutionary force of assertion. The POSW introduced by 'say' is a reported discourse context $r(s)$, and the embedded assertion meaning can be (12):

(12) ⟦ *A says that* ϕ ⟧ $= \{w : \exists s[s < w$ and s is a saying situation and the application to $r(s)$ of the sentential force appropriate to the sentence mood of ϕ yields a transition between contexts which accurately represents A's communicative intention in $s]\}$

According to (12), the sentence *John said that Napoleon was insane* is true in a world w iff there was a situation s of John saying something in that world, and his intention in s was to add the proposition that Napoleon is insane to his commitment slate in the conversation of which s was a part. This type of meaning might be appropriate to express in the POSW framework the intuitions of authors like Wechsler (1991), Meinunger (2004), and Krifka (2014) concerning the illocutionary force of embedded verb-second declaratives.

The concept of embedded speech acts might or might not be an attractive addition to the POSW framework. But either way, the issue of embedded speech acts should be clearly distinguished from the two less radical options discussed here. Embedded indicatives could be similar to root declaratives for any of the following reasons (and similarly for subjunctives' relation to imperatives):

1. Like root declaratives, embedded indicatives are interpreted relative to the domain of a POSW, not the ordering.
2. Like root declaratives, embedded indicatives involve assertive sentential force, modeled as the $+$-update.
3. Like root declaratives, embedded indicatives involve a speech act of assertion relative to a reported context.

More than one of these possibilities could be involved in the overall explanation of the relation between verbal mood and sentence mood. For example, it's possible that a normal indicative under 'believe' should be explained in terms of 1 or 2, while an embedded clause with main-clause syntax, such as an embedded V2 declarative, might be explained in terms of 3.

Elaborations and alternatives.   The POSW framework has been developed with the goal of capturing in a single formal system the ideas of existing theories of verbal mood and sentence mood, and it is easy to think of many different formal systems in which we could express the same basic ideas. The reason I set forth the POSW is that it is just about the simplest in which the relevant ideas about verbal mood and sentence mood can be expressed. Before we close this subsection, I would like to mention several ways in which the framework could be elaborated.

1. **Mutual commitments.** The model defines a discourse context as an assignment of discourse commitments to each individual, but the analysis of sentence mood could also be based on the goal of modeling mutual commitments. The mutual commitments of a discourse would be a POSW

or PPOSW in which the first component represents the mutual assumptions about the facts and issues to be answered (the common ground and question under discussion set) and the second represents shared plans. This system would be quite similar to that of Murray and Starr (2016). Alternatively, it might be important to represent separately both mutual commitments and individual commitments, as suggested by Portner (to appear, 2017). It seems to me that, while basic declaratives and interrogatives can be analyzed using mutual commitments, imperatives are more naturally understood as relating to individual commitments (as encoded in a priority slate, to-do list, or similar).

2. **Multiple orderings.** An obvious and probably necessary elaboration of this framework would be to make room for multiple orderings of cs_c. We might think of a "multiply ordered set of worlds," a MOSW $= \langle cs_c, <^1_c, \ldots, <^n_c \rangle$. Clearly it is a dramatic oversimplification to propose that an individual's cognitive model or individual commitments can be represented using a single ordering. But beyond the issue of oversimplification, there are other reasons to adopt multiple orderings. Doing so would allow us to incorporate the proposal that modals can be sensitive to multiple ordering sources (von Fintel and Iatridou 2008), and the idea that, in some cases, ordering sources are "promoted" to modal base status (Rubinstein 2012). It would also allow us to adopt the idea that the many discourse functions of imperatives differ in that they affect distinct "sub-lists" of the to-do list (Portner 2007). We might well also want to represent expectation in discourse with an ordering relation, following Veltman (1986).

3. **Commitment sets and premise sets.** In place of the set of worlds cs_c and the ordering over worlds $<_c$, the system might utilize sets of propositions for these functions. In applying the framework to verbal mood, the set of propositions which does the job of cs_c would be a modal base; the set of propositions which does the job of $<_c$ would be the ordering source. In applying the framework to sentence mood, the former would be an individual's commitment set, and the latter would be her to-do list.[7] There are likely to be advantages in using sets of propositions for these two functions when it comes to modeling speech acts of retraction and offering permission (see, for example, Gazdar 1981 and Kamp 1973) and inconsistent priorities.

4. **The context of justification.** In Section 3.3.3, we saw that Van der Torre and Tan (1998) make an interesting distinction between the context of deliberation and the context of justification in the dynamic logic of deontic statements. The context of deliberation considers the deontic ordering of the worlds in cs_c (the worlds compatible with current information), while the context of justification considers a deontic ordering over a wider set of worlds W. In our application of the POSW framework to sentence mood, we were not explicit about whether $<_c$ represents the ordering of the context of deliberation or the ordering of the context of justification. In our definition of the assertive update in (2a), no change is made to the ordering $<_c$, and this

---

[7] In the simplest version, the to-do list would be treated as a set of propositions, rather than as a set of properties as in Portner's (2004) proposal.

means that it can order worlds not in $c + \phi$. Specifically, if we had $w <_c v$, and then an assertive update with ϕ removes w from $cs_{c+\phi}$, we still have $w <_{c+\phi} v$. At this point, $c + \phi$ will no longer technically be a POSW.

There are two ways we might adjust the definitions to bring them into alignment. Either we could revise the definition of $c+\phi$ so that $<_c$ is restricted to worlds in $[\![\phi]\!]^c$ ($<_{c+\phi} \subseteq ([\![\phi]\!]^c \times [\![\phi]\!]^c)$). Or we could maintain in our system both a context of deliberation and a context of justification. Such a move might have benefits both in the analysis of sentence mood (of optatives and counterfactual imperatives, for example) and in the analysis of verbal mood (of the complements of counterfactual attitudes like 'wish'), since we sometimes do need to pay attention to what rules, desires, and preferences have to say about worlds which are ruled out by our information.

5. **Ordering and *de se*.** The POSW framework is designed to exemplify how we might capture certain commonalities between theories of verbal mood and theories of sentence mood. These commonalities are based on the use of modal parameters to represent both cognitive states (as cognitive models) and discourse information (as individual commitment slates) in terms of orderings over possible worlds. There is another, seemingly unrelated, point of commonality between some of the theories of verbal mood and some of the theories of sentence mood which we discussed in Chapters 2–3. In both areas, we from time to time encounter the idea that one subtype of mood implies special interpretation of its subject, time, or world argument: either a *de se* reading or an "unanchored" interpretation which might be understood as a variety of *de se*. (At least, *de se* was my best attempt to understand in precise terms what the absence of anchoring amounts to.) We specifically saw ideas of these kinds applied to subjunctives, infinitives, and imperatives. We should seek ways to develop the idea that this group of clauses has something of this kind in common. A simple way of thinking about this similarity could be turned into the hypothesis that subjunctives, infinitives, and imperatives have a structure which implies that one or more of these arguments is *de se*.

If it turns out that subjunctives, infinitives, and imperatives all have in common that one or more of their clausal arguments are obligatorily interpreted as *de se*, we will be left with an important but previously-unrecognized puzzle:

- **The comparison-*de se* puzzle:** Why do those moods which are associated with a comparison-based semantics also have arguments which obligatorily receive a *de se* interpretation?

We do not yet have a very good grasp of what this link between comparison and *de se* amounts to. Consider the case of the *de se* interpretation of a complement clause's subject. A verb like 'want' can take either an infinitive or subjunctive complement, but if the embedded subject is bound by the matrix subject and *de se*, only the infinitive is possible. Matters are different with an indicative-selecting verb like 'believe'. Both the bound/*de se* and non-*de se* interpretations are available with the same mood form and pronominal subject. When it comes to tense, we find that the temporal arguments of both infinitive and subjunctive complements normally must be *de se*, while an indicative complement's temporal argument is optionally *de se* when it agrees with the matrix tense (i.e. when it is a sequence-of-tense form). Given this complexity, the way I have stated the comparison-*de se* puzzle may be incomplete, yet there is clearly something to the point that verbs like 'want', which have a modal semantics of comparison, also select *de se*-triggering infinitival and subjunctive complements, while verbs like 'know', which do not make a modal comparison, select the indicative.

6. **Probabilities and utilities.** As we have discussed in Sections 2.1 and 3.3.1, the framework of modal semantics based on premise sets (Kratzer) and the model of discourse meaning based on the common ground (Stalnaker) have been challenged recently by systems which use mathematical probabilities and utilities. We should investigate whether such systems can incorporate and improve upon the most promising hypotheses about the relationship between verbal mood and sentence mood. Within the POSW framework, there is a single major parameter which distinguishes subjunctives/imperatives from indicatives/declaratives: the presence or relevance of an ordering relation. Within the probability-based framework, we have two parameters which seem equally important: the contrast between contexts which involve probabilities alone (the complements of 'probable' and 'believe') versus those which involve both probabilities and utilities ('good'), and the contrast between contexts which involve a comparison between probabilities or utilities ('probable' and 'good') versus those which do not ('believe'). The success of the comparison-based approach to verbal mood suggests that a probability-based theory of verbal mood would see comparison of probabilities and utilities as a crucial factor. When it comes to sentence mood, however, we could entertain the idea that what sets imperatives apart from declaratives and interrogatives is that they relate to utilities. This point of view would be in contrast to the POSW framework, according to which the crucial feature of imperatives is that they affect a preference or other ordering relation.

It seems likely that one could develop a probability-based theory which incorporates the ideas of the POSW framework. A probability space is simply a pair $\langle c, P \rangle$ consisting of a set of worlds and a probability measure. Since P gives an ordering on worlds (and on propositions), this already has the power of a POSW. If we add a utility function U, we have a system which functions very similarly to a multiply ordered set of worlds. The real issue will be whether this probability-based theory can explain the properties of verbal mood and sentence mood better than those existing analyses which provide the motivation for the POSW framework. In order to make progress on this issue, a great deal of work would have to be done, since, as far as I know, the literature has not yet produced any probability-based analyses of non-indicative verbal moods or non-declarative sentence moods.

4.2 Reality status and evidentiality

We have seen that verbal mood and sentence mood, the two obvious subcategories of mood, might be properly seen as subtypes of the same linguistic category. In the terminology of this book, both are systems of mood, because they both indicate the role a clause plays in the computation of modal meaning. It even seems likely that they mark similar semantic features of the modal meanings they relate to. Verbal mood and sentence mood each can be seen as marking the presence or absence of comparison in that modal meaning, and possibly also some semantic component related to *de se* interpretation. If these formal similarities are indeed present, the reason that they exist is presumably rooted in the fact that both subsentential and discourse modality build on the same basic architecture of modal semantics. Because of the fact that they can be understood (in at least their most central features) using the fundamental concepts of modal semantics, we can describe verbal mood and sentence mood as "core mood."

In Chapter 1, we noted that a number of other grammatical categories might plausibly be recognized either as core mood or as more peripheral types of mood. Two such categories have been the subjects of important research which would allow one to consider their relation to the category of mood more generally: reality status and evidentiality. In this section, we will discuss whether reality status and evidentiality fall under the definition of mood, and whether they are similar enough to verbal mood and sentence mood to be considered examples of core mood. In neither instance will we reach a firm conclusion, but I think that the issues which get raised in the course of thinking about this topic will prove important in future research on mood and modality.

4.2.1 Reality status

Within the descriptive/typological tradition, it is common to see the terms "realis" and "irrealis" used as the labels of morphological forms or paradigms, or in the explication of forms with more specific meanings. The prevalence of this terminology, and the ways of thinking about the relation between grammatical forms and the conceptual domain of modality which go along with it, have led to an important debate concerning whether such terms should really form part of our theory of natural language meaning. If one believes that realis and irrealis are important concepts for linguistics, it will be useful to have a term which labels the conceptual domain within which they make a distinction. Elliott (2000), a supporter of the value of these concepts to linguistics, has coined the term REALITY STATUS for this category. In this section, we will examine the debate about whether reality status should be seen as a valid category for semantic/pragmatic analysis, on a par with such well-motivated categories as tense and aspect, and will consider the relation between some of the grammatical forms which have been described in terms of the opposition realis/irrealis and the category of mood as it is understood in this book.

In order to give the discussion an explicit empirical grounding, I will begin by giving an outline of some important facts from the Papuan language Amele, as presented by Roberts (1991). Amele has been brought up repeatedly in the recent literature on reality status, both by scholars who believe in the value of the realis/irrealis distinction (such as Elliott 2000) and by those who argue against it (e.g. de Haan 2012). Other work which can serve as pointers into the literature on this topic includes Givón (1994), Chafe (1995), Mithun (1995), Van Valin and

LaPolla (1997), Kinkade (1998), McGregor and Wagner (2006), the papers collected in Mauri and Sansò (2012), and Matić and Nikolaeva (2014).

In order to understand the marking of reality status in Amele, we must consider three grammatical patterns: the clause chaining construction, subordinate adverbial clauses, and sentence-level particles. We begin with the clause chaining construction, a type of sentence appearing as a series of clauses strung together with only the final one fully marked for tense and mood. Preceding clauses are dependent on the final one, and have subject agreement marking which indicates whether they have the same or a different subject from the final clause (conjunct-disjunct or switch reference marking) and whether their temporal reference is simultaneous or sequenced with that of the final clause. For example, in example (13), the initial clause 'the pig ran out' is dependent on the verb which follows, 'hit' (Roberts 1991, p. 371, (2a)):

(13) *Ho bu-busal-en   age qo-in.*
       pig SIM-run.out-3SG.DS.R 3PL hit-3PL.REM.P
       'They killed the pig as it ran out.'

The agreement marker glossed as DS.R in (13) is a different subject, simultaneous agreement form, indicating that the pig is distinct from the ones who killed the pig and that the pig's running out was simultaneous with their killing it.

There are two sub-paradigms of different subject, simultaneous agreement forms, with the choice between them determined by the tense, mood, and modal meaning marked on the final clause. Roberts associates this distinction with reality status, and so labels them the "realis" and "irrealis" forms. In (13), the realis version of third singular different subject agreement (-*en*, 'DS.R') is determined by the fact that the final clause is marked for remote past tense. Other forms of the final verb which trigger realis agreement are the present and the various other past tenses. Irrealis agreement is chosen when the final clause is marked as future tense, imperative, prohibitive, counterfactual, and others (Roberts 1991, pp. 371–2). Example (14) shows an irrealis form (Roberts 1991, (3a)):

(14) *Ho bu-busal-eb   age qo-qag-an.*
       pig SIM-run.out-3SG.DS.IR 3PL hit-3PL-FUT
       'They will kill the pig as it runs out.'

Turning now to adverbial clauses, Roberts shows that only irrealis agreement forms appear in adverbial subordinate clauses which convey such meanings as intention, desire, and purpose; realis agreement never occurs in clauses of this type. An example is (15) (his (6a)):

(15) *Ho bu-busal-eb   age qo-qag-a   bili tawe-ig-a.*
       pig SIM-run.out-3SG.DS.IR 3PL hit-3PL-REL.FUT be stand-3PL-TOD.P
       'They stood about to kill the pig as it runs out.'

The initial clause here shows irrealis marking, dependent on the overall relative future tense of the adverbial clause. In the same position as relative future tense in this construction, Roberts shows examples with imperative and infinitival marking as well. It appears that reality status marking in adverbial clauses functions in very much the same way as in clause chaining, but there is no possibility of a tense/mood form which would trigger realis agreement.

Finally, Roberts shows that sentence-level particles which can be described as indicating illocutionary force or sentence mood do not affect the marking of realis or irrealis in chained and adverbial clauses. For example, the polar question marker *fo*, the dubitative question marker *fa*, and negation might be expected to create an irrealis context, but only the realis form is possible with a realis-triggering tense, as in (16) (from Roberts 1991, (18)):

(16)   *Ho   bu-busal-en/*eb   age   qo-gi-na   fo.*
       pig   SIM-run.out-3SG.DS.R/IR 3PL   hit-3PL-PRES   DUB
       'Maybe they are killing the pig as it runs out?'

Roberts goes on to describe a number of other Papuan languages in similar terms. For example, in Anjam reality status is marked (though in different ways) in both different subject and same subject forms, and in both simultaneous and sequential temporal meaning. In Menya, according to Roberts (1991) and Whitehead (1986), reality status is marked on final verbs; for example, an imperative final verb uses the irrealis subject agreement form.

The range of clauses in Amele which employ the realis and irrealis agreement forms match up to an impressive extent with the intuitive concepts of realis and irrealis. Should the pattern found in Amele therefore be taken as evidence in favor of a linguistically important category of reality status? Elliott (2000) believes that it should. She accepts Roberts' description of the meaning of the two sets of agreement forms, and then points out the important point that, from this perspective, the marking of reality status is restricted to a specific set of morphosyntactic environments, namely in combination with the marking of different subjects and simultaneous temporal reference. De Haan (2012), in contrast, argues that the failure to mark irrealis in dubitative questions and other sentences marked as non-assertive by sentence-level particles undermines the description in terms of reality status. Moreover, Elliott's description of Amele as a language in which reality status is marked in a particular set of morphosyntactic environments does not seem quite right; the "context" can be a clause which marks switch reference and simultaneity, but if the final verb has present tense, irrealis due to a final particle will not be marked. Rather, the correct description of the facts seems to be that the morphemes DS.R and DS.IR are dependent on the tense/mood form of the final verb. They are dependent on a feature of meaning of that form which is naturally described in terms of reality status, but this does not mean that the dependent agreement forms mark the reality status of the clause they are in *per se*, since if they did, we would also expect DS.IR in (16).

Following Bybee (1998), de Haan develops a broader argument against the value of the reality status categories realis/irrealis. Perhaps most importantly, he argues that the range of contexts which are argued to trigger realis or irrealis forms is too diverse across languages to treat any one opposition as the "true" realis/irrealis opposition. This situation lends support to the idea that realis and irrealis are prototype categories, as argued by Givón (1994), if they are useful categories at all. However, as pointed out by de Haan, even such prototypically irrealis constructions as counterfactuals and imperatives are classified as realis in some languages. It is difficult to see how to understand the idea that irrealis is a prototype category if some languages mark less prototypical constructions with the irrealis form but not more prototypical ones. We might, rather, need to understand the meta-concept of irrealis as having a prototype structure, with languages representing in their grammars more or less prototypical versions of the irrealis concept (itself, a prototype concept).

There is an important issue which has not been raised adequately within this literature on reality status, namely why the category is marked in the specific range of contexts that it is. Concerning Amele, why is realis/irrealis marking limited to different subject, simultaneous clauses? Here it is worthwhile to draw a link to some of the observations about infinitives and subjunctives discussed in Chapter 2. First, recall that subjunctives often show an obviation effect, meaning that a subjunctive complement cannot be used if its subject has the same reference as that of the superordinate clause; this fact is probably best analyzed in terms of a preference for subject *de se* interpretation, realized as a control infinitive, when it is compatible with the intended meaning (see Section 2.2.2.4). And second, as pointed out in Section 2.3.1.1, the tense of a complement subjunctive is temporally dependent on that of the matrix clause, and this temporal dependence might also be analyzed as a form of temporal *de se*. Thus, it seems that Amele irrealis agreement is associated with some of the same semantic properties as the control infinitive and subjunctive.[8] This point suggests that reality status in Amele might be analyzed using some of the same ideas as have been used in semantic theories of verbal mood. A successful analysis along these lines would be quite exciting, since it is without a doubt important that reality status in Amele is realized in connection with simultaneity and different-subject marking. Stepping back, work on different languages has proposed that a wide variety of morphosyntactic categories can realize reality status, including voice and nominal morphology, in addition to verbal morphology and agreement (see de Haan 2012, sect. 3). Assuming that all of these forms really involve the semantics of mood, in the broad sense, the theory of mood must seek to explain why it is realized in all of these different ways.

This discussion of reality status has of necessity been incomplete and sketchy, but some important conclusions suggest themselves. It seems likely that the perspective of Bybee and de Haan is correct: languages do not directly mark clauses for their reality status. That is, realis marking does not literally mean "this clause is true in reality," and nor does irrealis marking mean "this clause is not (known to be) true in reality." Instead, reality status should be understood, in some cases at least, as

---

[8] Zu's (2016) work on conjunct marking in Newari and its relation to the subjunctive is relevant here. Though it does not concern a realis/irrealis system, it highlights the important relations among person marking, *de se* meaning, and obviation.

marking a clause as dependent on another element or construction which itself might imply something about the truth or falsity of the clause in reality. In such cases, reality status should be seen as related to verbal mood, and might even be correctly described as a type of verbal mood, in the general sense in which we have defined it. Given the wide variety of ways in which the terms 'realis' and 'irrealis' have been used, it is difficult to predict whether the bulk of phenomena which have been described in terms of reality status should be treated as core mood—that is, as examples of mood which can be analyzed using the basic conceptual framework used to analyze verbal mood and sentence mood.

4.2.2 Evidentiality

Evidentiality is the grammatical encoding of information source. For example, the Cuzco Quechua example (17) may be used to assert that the speaker's brother is working in Italy, and in addition, as a result of the reportative evidential *-si*, it conveys that the speaker was told this (from Faller 2002, p. 139):

(17)   *Tura-y-qa   Italia-pi-s   llank'a-sha-n kay semana-pi.*
brother-1-TOP Italy-LOC-REP work-PROG-3 this week-LOC
p= 'My brother is working in Italy this week.'
ev: speaker was told that p.

Although linguists sometimes use the term "evidentiality" to describe any expression of evidence source, semanticists typically restrict it to closed-class morphosyntactic categories. Cuzco Quechua has a typical evidential system, with three main forms referred to by Faller as the 'best possible grounds' (or 'direct'), 'conjectural,' and 'reportative' evidentials. There is significant diversity in evidential systems across languages, both with respect to their morphosyntactic realization and the meanings they express; see Aikhenvald (2006) and de Haan (2012) for recent descriptive overviews and Krawczyk (2012) for a review of the main semantic properties of evidentials and an interesting discussion of some problems with describing evidential meaning solely in terms of the source of evidence a speaker has for what she says.

As discussed by Portner (2009, sect. 5.3.2), evidentiality has been analyzed as being closely related to several other linguistic categories, in particular epistemic modality (for example, McCready and Ogata 2007 and Matthewson et al. 2007), tense/aspect (Chung 2007), and sentence mood. What is relevant to us here is the question of whether evidentiality represents a variety of mood, and so we should look at theories which treat it as related to sentence mood. We find such theories based on each of the two main theoretical frameworks for analyzing sentence mood discussed in Chapter 3, namely speech act theory and the dynamic approach. In this section, we will briefly discuss Faller's (2002, 2011) theory of evidentiality, which treats members of this category as affecting the direct, literal illocutionary force associated with a sentence, as well as Murray's (2011, 2014, 2016) theory, which treats them as affecting the update potential of a sentence within a dynamic semantics framework.

Faller's speech act theory.   In her dissertation, Faller (2002) developed an influential theory of evidentials based on speech act theory. Focusing on Cuzco Quechua, she proposes that evidentials modify various features of the illocutionary force associated with a sentence. She uses a system similar to that of Vanderveken (1990) (see Sections 1.4.2 and 3.2.2), so that a basic illocutionary act of assertion with propositional content p can be described in terms of three components: its illocutionary force, sincerity conditions, and strength (Faller 2002, p.25):[9]

(18)   *Para-sha-n*
       rain-PROG-3
       $p=$ 'It is raining.'
       ILL $=$ ASSERT$_s(p)$
       SINC $= \{Bel(s, p)\}$
       STRENGTH $= 0$

Faller proposes that evidentials modify such aspects of the speech act as its sincerity conditions and strength. The direct (best possible grounds) evidential *-mi*, for example, adjusts the speech act as follows:

(19)   *Para-sha-n-mi*
       rain-PROG-3-BPG
       $p=$ 'It is raining.'
       ILL $=$ASSERT$_s(p)$
       SINC $= \{Bel(s, p), Bpg(s, p)\}$
       STRENGTH $= +1$

While the direct evidential can be neatly analyzed as an illocutionary modifier, Faller finds that the two other main evidentials in Cuzco Quechua raise problems. According to her analysis, the conjectural *-chá* affects both the propositional content and the illocutionary act:

(20)   *Para-sha-n-chá*
       rain-PROG-3-CONJ
       $p=$ '$\Diamond$It is raining.'
       ILL $=$ ASSERT$_s(p)$
       SINC $= \{Bel(s, p), Rea(s, Bel(s, p))\}$
       STRENGTH $= -1$

Faller sees *-chá* as a combination of an epistemic modal, accounting for the '$\Diamond$' in (20), and an evidential.

    The reportative evidential proves the most difficult for Faller. The problem is that a reportative sentence like (17) is compatible with the speaker being completely non-committal as to the truth of its propositional content. For this reason, it does

---

[9] The data and descriptions of speech acts in (18)–(21) are modified from Faller (2002, pp. 25–7).

not fall under any of the types of illocutionary point described by Searle (1975b) and Vanderveken (1990), and Faller proposes a new type of illocutionary point, PRESENTATION.

(21)   *Para-sha-n-si*
       rain-PROG-3-REP
       p= 'It is raining.'
       ILL = PRESENT$_s$(p)
       SINC = {∃s_2[$Assert(s_2, p) \wedge s_2 \notin \{speaker, addressee\}$]}

In later work, Faller continues to revise her analysis of the reportative (Faller 2006a,c) and she gives more precise analyses of the sincerity conditions of all three evidentials within a possible worlds semantics for modality (Faller 2007).

Faller's theory very clearly places the evidentials of Cuzco Quechua within the semantic domain of mood as we have defined it here. Each evidential morpheme indicates how a proposition is used in the expression of modal meaning at the discourse level. Her theory presupposes that speech act theory is the correct framework for analyzing sentence mood, and if we grant this presupposition, it would be accurate to say that evidentiality of the kind exemplified by Cuzco Quechua forms part of the sentence mood system. This approach to evidentiality probably implies that evidentiality and sentence mood are not as closely related to verbal mood as suggested in Section 4.1, since there are no productive theories of verbal mood based on classical speech act theory.

Murray's dynamic theory.   Murray (2014, 2016) argues that evidentials should be analyzed as closely related to markers of sentence mood within a dynamic model of discourse meaning. She focuses on Cheyenne, a language in which both sentence mood markers and evidentials fall into a morphological paradigm known as MODE,[10] arguing that they are not merely related in their morphosyntax, but also in their interpretation. Next we will briefly examine how she proposes to give them a unified semantic analysis.

Murray's central ideal about evidentiality is that evidentials update the discourse context in a way similar to, but more "direct" than, the updates associated with sentence mood. In the case of a direct evidential declarative like the Cheyenne (22), the declarative mood leads to an update which restricts the context set to worlds in which Sandy won, while the direct evidential restricts the context set to worlds in which the speaker has direct evidence for this proposition (Murray 2014, (1a)).

(22)   *É-hó'tahéva-Ø Sandy.*
       3-win-DIR   Sandy
       'Sandy won (I witnessed).'

---

[10] To understand the range of forms covered by the category of mode in American linguistics, readers may review the way it is used by such authors as Boas (1911), Newman (1944), Bloomfield (1956), Parks (1976), Axelrod (1993), and Mithun (1999).

The analysis builds on an update semantics closely related to the dynamic semantics for questions and inquisitive semantics theories outlined in Section 3.3.2, in that the ultimate function of a declarative is to reduce the context set and that of an interrogative is to partition it. But, in comparison to other dynamic semantics models, the update proceeds in several stages, allowing her to differentiate the kind of update produced by an evidential from the kind produced by a sentence mood.

The key way in which the illocutionary update of sentence mood differs from the evidential update is that the latter but not the former is "not-at-issue," and is introduced into the discourse representation without opening up the issue of whether it should be accepted. For example, the assertive update associated with the declarative (22) initially introduces a discourse referent for the proposition that Sandy won; this step can be thought of as analogous to placing the proposition on the table and projecting it as a future commitment within the model of Farkas and Bruce (2010). Only at a later step in the process of updating the discourse context is the context set restricted to worlds in which Sandy won. In contrast, because it is not at-issue, the proposition associated with the direct evidential (that the speaker has direct evidence for the proposition that Sandy won) does not introduce a discourse referent; instead, the evidential updates the common ground directly, with no stage at which it is on the table.[11]

Murray's theory differentiates the illocutionary update from the evidential update in two ways: in the presence or absence of a discourse referent, and in whether the update proceeds in stages or is direct and immediate. It seems to me that the former difference is closer to the heart of the matter. As she remarks, the presence of the discourse referent in the illocutionary update (in the example, representing the proposition that Sandy won) makes this proposition available for "denials, objections, and challenges," while the evidential update does not produce a discourse referent to be denied or challenged (Murray 2014, p. 230). The difference between direct and staged update, on the other hand, is less clear to me. Given our understanding of the context set as representing the mutual presuppositions within a conversation, one participant can hardly impose an update without his interlocutor having any say in the matter. The evidential update is certainly somehow special; it is backgrounded in a way we would like to understand, and it concerns facts over which the speaker has more epistemic authority (i.e. the speaker usually knows what he has seen better than the addressee), but these differences do not seem to me fully captured by the notion of a direct update.

Murray's theory implies that evidentiality is a variety of mood as we have defined it in this book, and moreover that evidentials are correctly classified as sentence moods. Because she employs a dynamic semantics model closely related to the POSW framework, it is possible that her ideas could be incorporated into a theory of core mood encompassing verbal mood, sentence mood, and evidentiality.

---

[11] Other scholars have recently developed similar systems in which update proceeds in stages which vary in "directness," for example AnderBois et al. (2013). We might also draw a connection between Murray's direct update and the update of individual commitments which Coppock and Wechsler (to appear) consider for ego-marked clauses in Newari.

4.2.3 Final remarks

The literature on mood, in all of its senses, and the literature on the related concepts of reality status, evidentiality, mode, and modality, are rich and diverse. Because an analysis of some particular data concerning a language's mood system (be it a verbal mood, sentence mood, or other mood-like system) allows a researcher to express his or her more fundamental commitments about the nature of language, these analyses are often very difficult to compare, and so to some extent the literature on these topics has been fragmented into sub-literatures written by individuals with similar fundamental commitments. In this book, my primary goal has been to step back and identify many of the important ideas which underlie theories of verbal mood, sentence mood, and other phenomena which may represent types of mood, seeking to clarify them, identify their strengths and weaknesses, find common themes, and ultimately point the way towards new work which builds on the best ideas of all.

Work on mood can play an important role in helping us gain a better understanding of broader issues in linguistics. There appear to be commonalities within the analyses of verbal mood and sentence mood (and perhaps evidentiality and reality status as well), and these may point to deep facts about discourse meaning, grammar, and the relation between them. Because of the close relationship between mood and modality, a theory of modal semantics cannot be correct unless it is compatible with reasonable analyses of mood phenomena, and vice versa. Researchers should make the most of these connections as well.

References

Abusch, D. (1997). Sequence of tense and temporal de re. *Linguistics and Philosophy*, 20:1–50.

Abusch, D. (2004). On the temporal composition of infinitives. In Gueron, J. and Lecarme, J., eds, *The Syntax of Time*, pages 29–53. MIT Press, Cambridge, MA.

Aelbrecht, L., Haegeman, L., and Nye, R., eds (2012). *Main Clause Phenomena: New Horizons*. John Benjamins, Amsterdam.

Aikhenvald, A. (2006). Evidentiality in grammar. In Brown, K., ed., *Encyclopedia of Language and Linguistics*, volume 4, pages 320–5. Elsevier, Oxford.

Aikhenvald, A. (2010). *Imperatives and Commands*. Oxford University Press, Oxford and New York.

Alcázar, A. and Saltarelli, M. (2012). Why imperative sentences cannot be embedded. *Cahiers Chronos*, 25:1–23.

Allan, K. (2006). Clause-type, primary illocution, and mood-like operators in English. *Language Sciences*, 28:1–50.

Aloni, M. (2007). Free choice, modals, and imperatives. *Natural Language Semantics*, 15(1):65–94.

Aloni, M. and Ciardelli, I. (2013). A logical account of free choice imperatives. In Aloni, M., Franke, M., and Roelofsen, F., eds, *The Dynamic, Inquisitive, and Visionary Life of ϕ, ?ϕ, and ◇ϕ: A Festschrift for Jeroen Groenendijk, Martin Stokhof, and Frank Veltman*, pages 1–17. University of Amsterdam.

Aloni, M. and van Rooij, R. (2004). Free choice items and alternatives. In Bouma, G., Krämer, I., and Zwarts, J., eds, *Proceedings of KNAW Academy Colloquium: Cognitive Foundations of Interpretation*, pages 5–25. Edita KNAW, Amsterdam.

Aloni, M. and van Rooy, R. (2002). The dynamics of questions and focus. In Jackson, B., ed., *Proceedings of Semantics and Linguistic Theory 12*, pages 20–39. CLC Publications, Ithaca, NY.

Aloni, M., Butler, A., and Dekker, P., eds (2007). *Questions in Dynamic Semantics*. Elsevier, Oxford.

Alonso-Ovalle, L. (2006). Disjunction in Alternative Semantics. PhD thesis, University of Massachusetts, Amherst.

Altmann, H. (1987). Zur Problematik der Konstitution von Satzmodi als Formtypen. In Meibauer, J., ed., *Satzmodus zwischen Grammatik und Pragmatik*, pages 22–58. Niemeyer, Tübingen.

Ambar, M. (2016). On finiteness and the left periphery: Focusing on subjunctive. In Błaszczak, J., Giannakidou, A., Klimek-Jankowska, D., and Migdalski, K., eds, *Mood, Aspect, Modality Revisited: New Answers to Old Questions*, pages 125–76. University of Chicago Press, Chicago, IL.

Anand, P. and Brasoveanu, A. (2010). Modal concord as modal modification. In Prinzhorn, M., Schmitt, V., and Zobel, S., eds, *Proceedings of Sinn und Bedeutung 14*, pages 19–36. Vienna.

Anand, P. and Hacquard, V. (2013). Epistemics and attitudes. *Semantics and Pragmatics*, 6(8):1–59.

Anand, P. and Nevins, A. (2004). Shifty operators in changing contexts. In Watanabe, K. and Young, R. B., eds, *Proceedings of Semantics and Linguistic Theory 14*, pages 20–37. CLC Publications, Ithaca, NY.

AnderBois, S., Brasoveanu, A., and Henderson, R. (2013). At-issue proposals and appositive impositions in discourse. *Journal of Semantics*, 32(1):93–138.

Anderson, A. R. (1951). A note on subjunctive and counterfactual conditionals. *Analysis*, 11:35–8.

Åqvist, L. (1967). Good Samaritans, contrary-to-duty imperatives, and epistemic obligations. *Noûs*, 1(4):361–79.

Asher, N. (1987). A typology for attitude verbs and their anaphoric properties. *Linguistics and Philosophy*, 10(2):125–98.

Asher, N. and Bonevac, D. (2005). Free choice permission is strong permission. *Synthese*, 145(3):303–23.

Asher, N. and Lascarides, A. (1998). Questions in dialogue. *Linguistics and Philosophy*, 23(3):237–309.

Asher, N. and Lascarides, A. (2001). Indirect speech acts. *Synthese*, 128(1–2): 183–228.

Austin, J. (1962). *How to do Things with Words*. Oxford University Press, New York.

Avrutin, S. and Babyonyshev, M. (1997). Obviation in subjunctive clauses and agr: Evidence from Russian. *Natural Language and Linguistic Theory*, 15:229–62.

Axelrod, M. (1993). *The Semantics of Time: Aspectual Categorization in Koyukon Athabaskan*. University of Nebraska Press, Lincoln, NE.

Bach, K. (1975). Performatives are statements too. *Philosophical Studies*, 28:229–36.

Bach, K. and Harnish, R. M. (1979). *Linguistic Communication and Speech Acts*. MIT Press, Cambridge, MA.

Baker, M. and Travis, L. (1997). Mood as verbal definiteness in a tenseless language. *Natural Language Semantics*, 5:213–69.

Ballmer, T. (1978). *Logical Grammar*. North Holland, Amsterdam.

Barker, C. (2010). Free choice permission as resource-sensitive reasoning. *Semantics and Pragmatics*, 3(10):1–38.

Barker, C. (2012). Imperatives denote actions. In Guevara, A. A., Chernilovskaya, A., and Nouwen, R., eds, *The Proceedings of Sinn und Bedeutung 16*, pages 57–70. MITWPL, Cambridge, MA.

Barwise, J. (1981). Scenes and other situations. *Journal of Philosophy*, 78:369–97.

Beaver, D. and Clark, B. (2008). *Sense and Sensitivity: How Focus Determines Meaning*. Wiley-Blackwell, Oxford.

Bell, A. (1984). Language style as audience design. *Language in Society*, 13(2): 145–204.

Beyssade, C. and Marandin, J.-M. (2006). The speech act assignment problem revisited: Disentangling speaker's commitment from speaker's call on addressee. In Bonami, O. and Hofherr, P. C., eds, *Empirical Issues in Syntax and Semantics 6*, pages 37–68. http://www.cssp.cnrs.fr/eiss6/.

Bhat, D. (1999). *The Prominence of Tense, Aspect, and Mood*. John Benjamins, Amsterdam.

Bierwisch, M. (1980). Semantic structure and illocutionary force. In Searle, J. R., Kiefer, F., and Bierwisch, M., eds, *Speech Act Theory and Pragmatics*, pages 1–35. Reidel, Dordrecht.

Biezma, M. (2011). Optatives: Deriving desirability from scalar alternatives. In Reich, I., ed., *Proceedings of Sinn und Bedeutung 15*. Universaar–Saarland University Press, Saarbrücken.

Biezma, M. and Rawlins, K. (2012). Responding to alternative and polar questions. *Linguistics and Philosophy*, 35(5):361–406.

Bittner, M. (2011). Time and modality without tenses or moods. In Musan, R. and Rathert, M., eds, *Tense across Languages*. Niemeyer, Tübingen.

Blanco, M. T. (2011). *Causatives in Minimalism*. John Benjamins, Amsterdam.

Bloomfield, L. (1956). *Eastern Ojibwa: Grammatical Sketch, Texts and Word List*. The University of Michigan Press, Ann Arbor.

Boas, F. (1911). *Handbook of American Indian Languages, Part 1*. Smithsonian Institution, Bureau of American Ethnology, Washington; Reprint: Thoemmes Press, 2002. Bristol, England.

Boër, S. E. and Lycan, W. G. (1980). A performadox in truth-conditional semantics. *Linguistics and Philosophy*, 4(1):1–46.

Bolinger, D. (1967). The imperative in English. In Halle, M., Lunt, H., and MacLean, H., eds, *To Honor Roman Jakobson: Essays on the Occasion of his Seventieth Birthday*, volume 1 of *Janua Linguarum*, pages 335–62. Mouton, The Hague and Paris.

Bolinger, D. (1976). Again—one or two subjunctives? *Hispania*, 59(1):41–9.

Bolinger, D. L. (1968). Post-posed main phrases: An English rule for the Romance subjunctive. *Canadian Journal of Linguistics*, 14:3–30.

Bolinger, D. L. (1974). One subjunctive or two? *Hispania*, 57(3):462–71.

Brandner, E. (2004). Head-movement in minimalism and V2 as force-marking. In Lohnstein, H. and Trissler, S., eds, *The Syntax and Semantics of the Left Periphery*, pages 97–138. Mouton de Gruyter, Berlin.

Brandt, M., Reis, M., Rosengren, I., and Zimmermann, I. (1992). Satztyp, Satzmodus, und Illokution. In Rosengren, I., ed., *Satz und Illokution*, volume 1, pages 1–90. Niemeyer, Tübingen.

Brasoveanu, A. (2006). Temporal and propositional de se: Evidence from Romanian subjunctive mood. In Ebert, C. and Endriss, C., eds, *The Proceedings of Sinn und Bedeutung 10*, pages 55–70. ZASPIL.

Bresnan, J. (1972). Theory of Complementation in English Syntax. PhD thesis, MIT.

Brown, C. (2011). Narrow mental content. In Zalta, E. N., ed., *The Stanford Encyclopedia of Philosophy*. Fall 2011 edition. http://plato.stanford.edu/archives/fall2011/entries/content-narrow/.

Brown, M. (1988). On the logic of ability. *Journal of Philosophical Logic*, 17(1): 1–26.

Büring, D. (2003). On D-trees, beans, and B-accents. *Linguistics and Philosophy*, 26:511–45.

Bybee, J. L. (1998). "Irrealis" as a grammatical category. *Anthropological Linguistics*, 40(2):257–71.

Castroviejo, E. (2006a). A degree-based account of wh-exclamatives. In Puig-Waldmüller, E., ed., *Proceedings of Sinn und Bedeutung 11*. Universitat Pompeu Fabra.

Castroviejo, E. (2006b). Wh-exclamatives in Catalan. PhD thesis, University of Barcelona.

Chafe, W. (1995). The realis–irrealis distinction in Caddo, the northern Iroquoian languages, and English. In Bybee, J. L. and Fleischman, S., eds, *Modality in Grammar and Discourse*. John Benjamins, Amsterdam.

Charlow, N. (2011). Practical Language: Its Meaning and Use. PhD thesis, University of Michigan.

Charlow, N. (2013). What we know and what to do. *Synthese*, 190:2291–323.

Charlow, S. and Sharvit, Y. (2014). Bound "de re" pronouns and the LFs of attitude reports. *Semantics and Pragmatics*, 7(3):1–43.

Chellas, B. (1969). *The Logical Form of Imperatives*. Perry Lane Press, Stanford, CA.

Chellas, B. (1971). Imperatives. *Theoria*, 37:114–29.

Chen-Main, J. (2005). Characteristics of Mandarin imperatives. In Brandstetter, C. and Rus, D., eds, *Georgetown University Working Papers in Theoretical Linguistics*, volume IV, pages 1–51. Georgetown University Department of Linguistics, Washington, DC.

Cheng, L. L.-S. (1991). On the typology of WH-questions. PhD thesis, MIT, Cambridge.

Chierchia, G. (1989). Anaphora and attitudes "de se". In Bartsch, R., van Benthem, J., and van Emde Boas, P., eds, *Semantics and Contextual Expressions*, pages 1–31. Foris, Dordrecht.

Chierchia, G. (2004). Scalar implicatures, polarity phenomena, and the syntax/pragmatics interface. In Belletti, A., ed., *Structures and Beyond*. Oxford University Press, Oxford.

Christidis, A. (1981). Oti/pos–pu: complementizer choice in Modern Greek. *Studies in Greek Linguistics*, 2:113–77.

Chung, K.-S. (2007). Spatial deictic tense and evidentials in Korean. *Natural Language Semantics*, 15:187–219.

Ciardelli, I., Groenendijk, J., and Roelofsen, F. (2013). Inquisitive semantics: a new notion of meaning. *Language and Linguistics Compass*, 7(9).

Clark, B. (1993). Relevance and "pseudo-imperatives". *Linguistics and Philosophy*, 16(1):79–121.

Condoravdi, C. and Lauer, S. (2011). Performative verbs and performative acts. In Reich, I., Horch, E., and Pauly, D., eds, *Proceedings of Sinn und Bedeutung 15*, pages 149–64. Universaar–Saarland University Press, Saarbrücken.

Condoravdi, C. and Lauer, S. (2012). Imperatives: Meaning and illocutionary force. In Piñón, C., ed., *Empirical Issues in Syntax and Semantics 9*. Colloque de Syntaxe et Sémantique à Paris, Paris.

Coppock, E. and Wechsler, S. (to appear). The proper treatment of egophoricity in Kathmandu Newari. In Jaszczolt, K. M. and Huang, M., eds, *Expressing the Self: Cultural Diversity and Cognitive Universals*. Oxford University Press, Oxford.

Costantini, F. (2006). Obviation in subjunctive argument clauses and the first-personal interpretation. In Frascarelli, M., ed., *Phases of Interpretation*, pages 295–319. Mouton de Gruyter, Berlin.

Cresswell, M. J. and von Stechow, A. (1982). De re belief generalized. *Linguistics and Philosophy*, 5(6):503–35.

Crnič, L. and Trinh, T. (2009). Embedded imperatives in English. In Riester, A. and Solstad, T., eds, *Proceedings of Sinn und Bedeutung 13*, pages 113–27. University of Stuttgart.

Crnič, L. and Trinh, T. (2011). Embedding imperatives. In Lima, S., Mullin, K., and Smith, B., eds, *Proceedings of NELS 39*, volume 1. GLSA, University of Massachusetts, Amherst.

Cross, C. and Roelofsen, F. (2014). Questions. In Zalta, E. N., ed., *The Stanford Encyclopedia of Philosophy*. Fall 2014 edition. http://plato.stanford.edu/archives/fall2014/entries/questions/.

Cui, Y. (2015). Modals in the Scope of Attitudes: A Corpus Study of Attitude–Modal Combinations in Mandarin. PhD thesis, Georgetown University.

Davidson, D. (1979). Moods and performances. In Margalit, A., ed., *Meaning and Use*, pages 9–20. Reidel, Dordrecht.

Davies, E. (1986). *The English Imperative*. Croom Helm, London.

Dayal, V. (2016). *Questions*. Oxford University Press, Oxford and New York.

Deal, A. R. (2011). Modals without scales. *Language*, 87(3):559–85.

de Haan, F. (2012). Irrealis: fact or fiction? *Language Sciences*, 34(2): 107–30.

Dench, A. (1991). Panyjima. In Dixon, R. and Blake, B. J., eds, *The Handbook of Australian Languages*, volume 4, pages 125–244. Oxford University Press, Melbourne.

Dixon, R. M. W. (1982). *Where Have All the Adjectives Gone? And Other Essays in Semantics and Syntax*. Mouton, Berlin.

Dobrovie-Sorin, C. (2001). Head-to-head merge in Balkan subjunctives and locality. In Rivero, M.-L. and Ralli, A., eds, *Comparative Syntax of Balkan Languages*, pages 44–73. Oxford University Press, New York.

Donnellan, K. (1966). Reference and definite descriptions. *Philosophical Review*, 75:281–304.

Downing, B. T. (1969). Vocatives and third-person imperatives in English. *Papers in Linguistics*, 1:570–92.

Dudman, V. H. (1970). Frege's judgment-stroke. *The Philosophical Quarterly*, 20(79): 150–61.

Dudman, V. H. (1972). Frege on assertion. *The Philosophical Quarterly*, 22(86): 61–4.

Elliott, J. (2000). Realis and irrealis: forms and concepts of the grammaticalisation of reality. *Linguistic Typology*, 4:55–90.

Emonds, J. E. (1969). Root and Structure-preserving Transformations. PhD thesis, MIT.

Fabricius-Hansen, C. and Saebø, K. J. (2004). In a mediative mood: The semantics of the German reportative subjunctive. *Natural Language Semantics*, 12(3): 213–57.

Faller, M. (2002). Semantics and Pragmatics of Evidentials in Cuzco Quechua. PhD thesis, Stanford University.

Faller, M. (2006a). The Cusco Quechua reportative evidential and rhetorical relations. Ms., University of Manchester.

Faller, M. (2006b). Evidentiality and epistemic modality at the semantics/pragmatics interface. Paper presented at the 2006 Workshop on Philosophy and Linguistics, University of Michigan.

Faller, M. (2006c). Evidentiality below and above speech acts. Ms., University of Manchester.

Faller, M. (2007). The Cuzco Quechua conjectural, epistemic modal or evidential? or both? Talk given at SULA 4, Universidade de São Paulo.

Faller, M. (2011). A possible worlds semantics for Cuzco Quechua evidentials. In Li, N. and Lutz, D., eds, *The Proceedings of SALT 20*, pages 660–83. Linguistic Society of America.

Farkas, D. (1985). *Intensional Descriptions and the Romance Subjunctive Mood.* Garland, New York.

Farkas, D. (1992a). On obviation. In Sag, I. and Szabolsci, A., eds, *Lexical Matters*, pages 85–109. CSLI Publications, Stanford, CA.

Farkas, D. (1992b). On the semantics of subjunctive complements. In Hirschbueler, P. and Koerner, K., eds, *Romance Languages and Modern Linguistic Theory*, pages 69–104. Benjamins, Amsterdam and Philadephia.

Farkas, D. (2003). Assertion, belief, and mood choice. Paper presented at the workshop on conditional and unconditional modality, Vienna.

Farkas, D. and Bruce, K. B. (2010). On reacting to assertions and polar questions. *Journal of Semantics*, 27(1):81–118.

Farkas, D. and Roelofsen, F. (2017). Division of labor in the interpretation of declaratives and interrogatives. *Journal of Semantics*, 34(2): 237–89.

Fine, K. (2016). Survey of truthmaker semantics. Ms., New York University.

Finlay, S. (2010). What *ought* probably means, and why you can't detach it. *Synthese*, 177:67–89.

von Fintel, K. and Gillies, A. S. (2010). *Must . . . stay . . . strong. Natural Language Semantics*, 18:351–83.

von Fintel, K. and Iatridou, S. (2008). How to say *ought* in foreign: The composition of weak necessity modals. In Guéron, J. and Lecarme, J., eds, *Time and Modality*, pages 115–41. Springer, Berlin.

von Fintel, K. and Iatridou, S. (2015). A modest proposal for the meaning of imperatives. Ms., MIT.

Fox, D. (2007). Free choice disjunction and the theory of scalar implicatures. In Sauerland, U. and Stateva, P., eds, *Presupposition and Implicature in Compositional Semantics*, pages 71–120. Palgrave-Macmillan, Basingstoke.

Franke, M. (2005). Pseudo-imperatives. Ms., University of Amsterdam.

Franke, M. (2009). Signal to Act: Game Theory in Pragmatics. PhD thesis, University of Amsterdam.

Gärtner, H.-M. (2002). On the force of V2 declaratives. *Theoretical Linguistics*, 28:33–42.

Gazdar, G. (1979). *Pragmatics: Implicature, Presupposition, and Logical Form.* Academic Press, London.

Gazdar, G. (1981). Speech act assignment. In Joshi, A., Weber, B. H., and Sag, I. A., eds, *Elements of Discourse Understanding*, pages 64–83. Cambridge University Press, Cambridge.

Geach, P. T. (1958). Imperative and deontic logic. *Analysis*, 18:49–56.

Geurts, B. (2005). Entertaining alternatives: Disjunctions as modals. *Natural Language Semantics*, 13(4):383–410.

Geurts, B. and Huitink, J. (2006). Modal concord. In Dekker, P. and Zeijlstra, H., eds, *Proceedings of the ESSLLI Workshop Concord Phenomena at the Syntax–Semantics Interface, Malaga*, pages 15–20. Available at www.ru.nl/ncs/janneke/modalconcord-essllio6.pdf.

Giannakidou, A. (1994). The semantic licensing of NPIs and the modern Greek subjunctive. In *Language and Cognition 4: Yearbook of the Research Group for Theoretical and Experimental Linguistics*, pages 55–68. University of Groningen, Groningen.

Giannakidou, A. (1995). Subjunctive, habituality, and negative polarity items. In Simons, M. and Galloway, T., eds, *The Proceedings of SALT 5*, pages 94–111. CLC Publications, Cornell University Linguistics Department.

Giannakidou, A. (1997). The Landscape of Polarity Items. PhD thesis, Groningen.

Giannakidou, A. (1998). *Polarity Sensitivity as (Non)veridical Dependency*. John Benjamins, Amsterdam.

Giannakidou, A. (1999). Affective dependencies. *Linguistics and Philosophy*, 22(3):367–421.

Giannakidou, A. (2009). The dependency of the subjunctive revisited: Temporal semantics and polarity. *Lingua*, 119(12):1883–908.

Giannakidou, A. (2011). Nonveridicality and mood choice: subjunctive, polarity, and time. In Musan, R. and Rathert, M., eds, *Tense across Languages*. Niemeyer, Tübingen.

Giannakidou, A. (2014). (Non)veridicality, Evaluation, and event actualization: Evidence from the subjunctive in relative clauses. In Taboada, M. and Trnavac, R., eds, *Nonveridicality and Evaluation: Theoretical, Computational, and Corpus Approaches*, Studies in Pragmatics. Brill, Leiden.

Giannakidou, A. (2016). Evaluative subjunctive and nonveridicality. In Błaszczak, J., Giannakidou, A., Klimek-Jankowska, D., and Migdalski, K., eds, *Mood, Aspect, Modality Revisited: New Answers to Old Questions*, pages 177–217. University of Chicago Press, Chicago, IL.

Giannakidou, A. and Mari, A. (2015). Mixed veridicality and mood choice in complement clauses. Ms, University of Chicago. Available at home.uchicago.edu/giannaki/pubs/GM.subjunctive.typology.pdf.

Ginet, C. (1979). Performativity. *Linguistics and Philosophy*, 3(2):245–65.

Ginzburg, J. (1995a). Resolving questions, part I. *Linguistics and Philosophy*, 18(5):459–527.

Ginzburg, J. (1995b). Resolving questions, part II. *Linguistics and Philosophy*, 18(6):567–609.

Ginzburg, J. (1996). Dynamics and the semantics of dialogue. In Seligman, J., ed., *Language, Logic and Computation, Volume 1*, CSLI Lecture Notes. CSLI, Stanford, CA.

Ginzburg, J. and Sag, I. A. (2001). *Interrogative Investigations: The Form, Meaning, and Use of English Interrogatives*. The University of Chicago Press, Chicago, IL.

Giorgi, A. and Pianesi, F. (1997). *Tense and Aspect: From Semantics to Morphosyntax*. Oxford University Press, Oxford.

Givón, T. (1994). Irrealis and the subjunctive. *Studies in Language*, 18:265–337.

Gordon, D. and Lakoff, G. (1971). Conversational postulates. In *Papers from the Seventh Regional Meeting of the Chicago Linguistic Society*, pages 63–84. University of Chicago Press, Chicago, IL.

Gordon, D. and Lakoff, G. (1975). Conversational postulates. In Cole, P. and Morgan, J. L., eds, *Syntax and Semantics, Volume 3: Speech Acts*, pages 83–106. Academic Press, New York.

Gregory, A. E. and Lunn, P. (2012). A concept-based approach to the subjunctive. *Hispania*, 95(2):333–43.

Groenendijk, J. (2009). Inquisitive semantics: Two possibilities for disjunction. In Bosch, P., Gabelaia, D., and Lang, J., eds, *Seventh International Tbilisi Symposium on Language, Logic, and Computation*. Springer.

Groenendijk, J. and Roelofsen, F. (2009). Inquisitive semantics and pragmatics. Presented at the Stanford workshop on Language, Communication and Rational Agency.

Groenendijk, J. and Stokhof, M. (1982). Semantic analysis of wh-complements. *Linguistics and Philosophy*, 5:175–233.

Groenendijk, J. and Stokhof, M. (1984). Studies on the Semantics of Questions and the Pragmatics of Answers. PhD thesis, University of Amsterdam.

Groenendijk, J. and Stokhof, M. (1990). Dynamic Montague grammar. In Kálman, L. and Pólos, L., eds, *Papers from the Symposium on Logic and Language*, pages 3–48. Adakémiai Kiadó, Budapest.

Groenendijk, J. and Stokhof, M. (1991). Dynamic predicate logic. *Linguistics and Philosophy*, 14:39–100.

Groenendijk, J. and Stokhof, M. (1997). Questions. In van Benthem, J. and ter Meulen, A., eds, *Handbook of Logic and Language*, pages 1055–124. Elsevier/MIT Press, Amsterdam and Cambridge, MA.

Groenendijk, J., Stokhof, M., and Veltman, F. (1996). Coreference and modality. In Lappin, S., ed., *The Handbook of Contemporary Semantic Theory*, pages 179–213. Blackwell Publishers, Oxford.

Groenendijk, J., Stokhof, M., and Veltman, F. (1997). Coreference and modality in multi-speaker discourse. In Kamp, H. and Partee, B., eds, *Context Dependence in the Analysis of Linguistic Meaning*, pages 195–216. I.M.S., Stuttgart.

Grosz, P. (2010). Grading modality: A new approach to modal concord and its relatives. In Prinzhorn, M., Schmitt, V., and Zobel, S., eds, *Proceedings of Sinn und Bedeutung 14*, pages 185–201. Vienna.

Grosz, P. (2011). On the Grammar of Optative Constructions. PhD thesis, Massachusetts Institute of Technology.

Grosz, P. (2014). Optative markers as communicative cues. *Natural Language Semantics*, 22(1):89–115.

Gunlogson, C. (2001). *True to Form: Rising and Falling Declaratives as Questions in English*. Routledge, Abingdon.

Gutiérrez-Rexach, J. (1996). The semantics of exclamatives. In Garret, E. and Lee, F., eds, *Syntax at Sunset*, UCLA Working Papers in Linguistics. Department of Linguistics, UCLA, Los Angeles, CA.

Hacquard, V. (2010). On the event-relativity of modal auxiliaries. *Natural Language Semantics*, 18(1):79–114.

Haegeman, L. (2006). Conditionals, factives and the left periphery. *Lingua*, 116(10):1651–69. (Special issue: Language in Mind: A Tribute to Neil Smith on the Occasion of his Retirement.)

Halpern, J. (2003). *Reasoning about Uncertainty*. MIT Press, Cambridge, MA.

Hamblin, C. L. (1958). Questions. *Australasian Journal of Philosophy*, 36: 159–68.

Hamblin, C. L. (1971). Mathematical models of dialogue. *Theoria*, 37(2): 130–55.

Hamblin, C. L. (1973). Questions in Montague English. *Foundations of Language*, 10:41–53.

Han, C.-H. (1998). The Structure and Interpretation of Imperatives: Mood and Force in Universal Grammar. PhD thesis, University of Pennsylvania.

Han, C.-H. (2011). Imperatives. In von Heusinger, K., Maienborn, C., and Portner, P., eds, *Semantics: An International Handbook of Natural Language Meaning*. Mouton de Gruyter, Berlin.

Han, C.-H. and Lee, C. (2007). On negative imperatives in Korean. *Linguistic Inquiry*, 38(2):373–95.

Hansson, S. O. (1990). Preference-based deontic logic (pdl). *Journal of Philosophical Logic*, 19(1):75–93.

Hansson, S. O. (2001). *Structures of Values and Norms*. Cambridge University Press, Cambridge.

Harner, H. (2016). The Modality of Desire Predicates and Directive Verbs. PhD thesis, Georgetown University.

Harnish, R. M. (1994). Mood, meaning, and speech acts. In Tsohatzidis, S. L., ed., *Foundations of Speech Act Theory: Philosophical and Linguistic Perspectives*, pages 407–459. Routledge, London.

Harper, W. L. (1976). Ramsey test conditionals and iterated belief change. In Harper, W. L. and Hooker, C. A., eds, *Foundations of Probability Theory, Statistical Inference, and Statistical Theories of Science*. Reidel, Dordrecht.

Hausser, R. (1980). Surface compositionality and the semantics of mood. In J. Searle, F. Kiefer, and M. Bierwisch, eds, *Speech Act Theory and Pragmatics*, pages 71–95. Reidel, Dordrecht and Boston.

Hausser, R. (1983). The syntax and semantics of English mood. In Kiefer, F., ed, *Questions and Answers*. Reidel, Dordrecht.

Haverkate, H. (2002). *The Syntax, Semantics and Pragmatics of Spanish Mood*. John Benjamins, Amsterdam.

Heim, I. (1982). The Semantics of Definite and Indefinite Noun Phrases. PhD thesis, University of Massachusetts, Amherst.

Heim, I. (1983). File Change Semantics and the familiarity theory of definiteness. In Bauerle, R., Schwarze, C., and von Stechow, A., eds, *Meaning, Use, and Interpretation of Language*, pages 164–89. Mouton de Gruyter, Berlin. Reprinted in Portner, P. and Partee, B. H., eds (2002). *Formal Semantics: The Essential Readings*. Blackwell, Oxford.

Heim, I. (1988). On the projection problem for presuppositions. In Barlow, M., Flickinger, D., and Wiegand, N., eds, *Proceedings of WCCFL 2*, pages 114–25. Stanford University. Reprinted in Portner, P. and Partee B. H., eds (2002). *Formal Semantics: The Essential Readings*. Blackwell, Oxford.

Heim, I. (1992). Presupposition projection and the semantics of attitude verbs. *Journal of Semantics*, 9:183–221.

Higginbotham, J. (2003). Remembering, imagining, and the first person. In Barber, A., ed., *Epistemology of Language*, pages 496–533. Oxford University Press, Oxford.

Hintikka, J. (1961). Modality and quantification. *Theoria*, 27:110–28.

Holliday, W. H. and Icard, T. F. (2013). Measure semantics and qualitative semantics for epistemic modals. In Snider, T., ed., *The Proceedings of SALT 23*. CLC Publications, Ithaca, NY.

Hooper, J. and Thompson, S. A. (1973). On the applicability of root transformations. *Linguistic Inquiry*, 4:465–97.

Huitink, J. (2012). Modal concord: A case study of Dutch. *Journal of Semantics*, 29(3):403–37.

Hulstijn, J. (1997). Structured information states: Raising and resolving issues. In Benz, A. and Jager, G., eds, *Proceedings of MunDial97*. University of Munich.

Huntley, M. (1980). Propositions and the imperative. *Synthese*, 45(2):281–310.

Huntley, M. (1984). The semantics of English imperatives. *Linguistics and Philosophy*, 7:103–34.

Iatridou, S. (2000). The grammatical ingredients of counterfactuality. *Linguistic Inquiry*, 31(2):231–70.

Jäger, G. (1996). Only updates: On the dynamics of the focus particle *only*. In Dekker, P. and Stokhof, M., eds, *Proceedings of the 10th Amsterdam Colloquium*. ILLC, University of Amsterdam.

Jary, M. (2011). Assertion, relevance and the declarative mood. In Escandell-Vidal, V., Leonetti, M., and Ahern, A., eds, *Procedural Meaning: Problems and Perspectives*, pages 267–89. Brill, Leiden.

Jary, M. and Kissine, M. (2014). *Imperatives*. Cambridge University Press, Cambridge.

Jary, M. and Kissine, M. (2016). Imperatives as (non-)modals. In Blaszczak, J., ed., *Cross-linguistic Approaches to Tense, Aspect and Mood*. University of Chicago Press, Chicago, IL.

Jensen, B. (2003). Syntax and semantics of imperative subjects. *Nordlyd*, 31:150–64.

Kamp, H. (1973). Free choice permission. *Proceedings of the Aristotelian Society, N.S.*, 74:57–74.

Kamp, H. (1981). A theory of truth and semantic representation. In Groenendijk, J., Janssen, T., and Stokhof, M., eds, *Formal Methods in the Study of Language*, pages 277–322. Mathematical Centre, Amsterdam.

Kamp, H. and Reyle, U. (1993). *From Discourse to Logic: Introduction to Model-theoretic Semantics of Natural Language, Formal Logic and Discourse Representation Theory*. Kluwer, Dordrecht.

Kanger, S. (1971). New foundations for ethical theory. In Hilpinen, R., ed., *Deontic Logic: Introductory and Systematic Readings*, pages 36–58. D. Reidel, Dordrecht.

Karttunen, L. (1971). Some observations on factivity. *Papers in Linguistics*, 5:55–69.

Karttunen, L. (1973). Presuppositions of compound sentences. *Linguistic Inquiry*, 4:169–93.

Karttunen, L. (1976). Discourse referents. In McCawley, J., ed., *Notes from the Linguistic Underground*, volume 7 of *Syntax and Semantics*. Academic Press, New York.

Karttunen, L. (1977). Syntax and semantics of questions. *Linguistics and Philosophy*, 1:3–44.

Karttunen, L. and Peters, S. (1975). Conventional implicature. In Oh, C.-Y. and Dinneen, D., eds, *Syntax and Semantics, vol. 11: Presupposition*, pages 1–56. Academic Press, New York.

Katz, G. (2005). Attitudes toward degrees. In Maier, E., Barry, C., and Huitink, J., eds, *Proceedings of Sinn und Bedeutung 9*. Nijmegen Centre of Semantics (NCS).

Katz, G., Portner, P., and Rubinstein, A. (2012). Ordering combination for modal semantics. In Chereches, A., ed., *The Proceedings of SALT 22*, pages 488–507. CLC Publications, Stanford, CA.

Katz, J. J. and Postal, P. M. (1964). *An Integrated Theory of Linguistic Descriptions*. MIT Press, Cambridge, MA.

Kaufmann, M. (2012). *Interpreting Imperatives*. Springer.

Kaufmann, M. (2016). Free choice as a form of dependence. *Natural Language Semantics*, 24(3):247–90.

Kaufmann, M. and Poschmann, C. (2013). Embedded imperatives: Empirical evidence from colloquial German. *Language*, 89(3):619–37.

Kempchinsky, P. (1985). The subjunctive disjoint reference effect. In Neidle, C. and Nuñez Cedeño, R., eds, *Studies in Romance Linguistics*, pages 123–40. Foris, Dordrecht.

Kempchinsky, P. (2009). What can the subjunctive disjoint reference effect tell us about the subjunctive? *Lingua*, 119(12):1788–810.

Keshet, E. (2011). Split intensionality: A new scope theory of de re and de dicto. *Linguistics and Philosophy*, 33(4):251–83.

Kinkade, M. D. (1998). Is irrealis a grammatical category in Upper Chehalis? *Anthropological Linguistics*, 40(2):234–44.

Klamer, M. (2012). Reality status in Teiwa (Papuan). *Language Sciences*, 34(2): 216–28.

Klecha, P. (2012). Positive and conditional semantics for gradable modals. In Guevara, A. A., Chernilovskaya, A., und Nouwen, R., eds, *Proceedings of Sinn und Bedeutung 16*, volume 2, pages 363–76. MITWPL.

Klecha, P. (2014). Bridging the Divide: Scalarity and Modality. PhD thesis, University of Chicago.

Kolodny, N. and MacFarlane, J. (2010). Ifs and oughts. *The Journal of Philosophy*, 108(3):115–43.

König, E. and Siemund, P. (2007). Speech act distinctions in grammar. In Shopen, T., ed., *Language Typology and Syntactic Description*, volume 1, pages 276–324. Cambridge University Press, Cambridge.

Kratzer, A. (1977). What "must" and "can" must and can mean. *Linguistics and Philosophy*, 1(1):337–55.

Kratzer, A. (1981). The notional category of modality. In Eikmeyer, H.-J. and Rieser, H., eds, *Words, Worlds, and Contexts*, pages 38–74. de Gruyter, Berlin.

Kratzer, A. (1991). Modality. In von Stechow, A. and Wunderlich, D., eds, *Semantik/Semantics: An International Handbook of Contemporary Research*, pages 639–50. de Gruyter, Berlin.

Kratzer, A. (2006). Decomposing attitude verbs. Talk at The Hebrew University of Jerusalem honoring Anita Mittwoch on her 80th birthday. Available at semanticsarchive.net/Archive/DcwY2JkM/attitude-verbs2006.pdf.

Kratzer, A. (2012). *Modal and Conditionals: New and Revised Perspectives*. Oxford University Press, Oxford.

Kratzer, A. (2013). Constructing domains for deontic (and other) modals. Slides for a talk given at the USC deontic modality workshop.

Kratzer, A. and Shimoyama, J. (2002). Indeterminate phrases: The view from Japanese. In Otsu, Y., ed., *The Proceedings of the Third Tokyo Conference on Psycholinguistics*, pages 1–25. Hituzi Syobo, Tokyo.

Krawczyk, L. (2012). Inferred Propositions and the Expression of the Evidence Relation in Natural Language: Evidentiality in Central Alaskan Yup'ik Eskimo and English. PhD thesis, Georgetown University.

Krifka, M. (2001). Quantifying into question acts. *Natural Language Semantics*, 9:1–40.

Krifka, M. (2011). Questions. In von Heusinger, K., Maienborn, C., and Portner, P., eds, *Semantics: An International Handbook of Natural Language Meaning*, volume 2, pages 1742–85. Mouton de Gruyter, Berlin.

Krifka, M. (2014). Embedding illocutionary acts. In Roeper, T. and Speas, M., eds, *Recursion: Complexity in Cognition*. Springer.

Laca, B. (2010). Mood in Spanish. In Thieroff, R. and Rothstein, B. eds, *Mood in the Languages of Europe*, pages 199–220. John Benjamins, Amsterdam and Philadelphia.

Lascarides, A. and Asher, N. (2003). Imperatives in dialogue. In Kühnlein, P., Rieser, H., and Zeevat, H., eds, *Perspectives on Dialogue in the New Millennium*, pages 1–24. Benjamins, Philadelphia.

Lasersohn, P. (2017). *Subjectivity and Perspective in Truth-Conditional Semantics*. Oxford University Press, Oxford.

Lassiter, D. (2011). Measurement and Modality: The Scalar Basis of Modal Semantics. PhD thesis, New York University.

Lassiter, D. (2016). *Graded Modality*. Oxford University Press, Oxford.

Lauer, S. (2013). Towards a Dynamic Pragmatics. PhD thesis, Stanford University.

Lemmon, E. J. (1965). Deontic logic and the logic of imperatives. *Logique et Analyse*, 8:39–71.

Levinson, S. C. (1980). Speech act theory: The state of the art. *Language Teaching and Linguistics: Abstracts*, pages 5–24.

Levinson, S. C. (1981). The essential inadequacies of speech act models of dialogue. In Parret, H., Sbisà, M., and Verschueren, J., eds, *Possibilities and Limitations of Pragmatics: Proceedings of the Conference on Pragmatics, Urbino, July 8–14, 1979*, pages 473–92. John Benjamins, Amsterdam.

Levinson, S. C. (1983). *Pragmatics*. Cambridge University Press, Cambridge.

Lewis, D. (1972). General semantics. In Davidson, D. and Harman, G., eds, *Semantics of Natural Language*. Reidel, Dordrecht.

Lewis, D. (1975). Adverbs of quantification. In Keenan, E., ed., *Formal Semantics of Natural Language*, pages 3–15. Cambridge University Press, Cambridge.

Lewis, D. K. (1979a). Attitudes de dicto and de se. *Philosophical Review*, 88:513–43.

Lewis, D. K. (1979b). A problem about permission. In Saarinen, E., Hilpinen, R., Niiniluoto, I., and Hintikka, M. P., eds, *Essays in Honour of Jaakko Hintikka*, pages 163–75. Reidel, Dordrecht.

Lewis, D. K. (1979c). Scorekeeping in a language game. *Journal of Philosophical Logic*, 8:339–59.

Lohnstein, H. (2000). *Satzmodus-kompositionell. Zur Parametrisierung der Modusphrase im Deutschen*. Akademie Verlag, Berlin.

Lohnstein, H. (2007). On clause types and sentential force. *Linguistische Berichte*, 209:63–86.

Luján, M. (1979). Clitic promotion and mood in Spanish verbal complements. IULC, Bloomington, Indiana.

Luján, M. (1980). Clitic promotion and mood in Spanish verbal complements. *Linguistics*, pages 381–484.

Lunn, P. V. (1995). The evaluative function of the Spanish subjunctive. In Bybee, J. and Fleischman, S., eds, *Modality in Grammar and Discourse*, pages 429–49. Benjamins, Amsterdam.

McCready, E. and Ogata, N. (2007). Evidentiality, modality and probability. *Linguistics and Philosophy*, 30(2):147–206.

McGregor, W. B. and Wagner, T. (2006). The semantics and pragmatics of irrealis mood in Nyulnyulan languages. *Oceanic Linguistics*, 45(2):339–79.

McKay, T. and Nelson, M. (2014). Propositional attitude reports. In Zalta, E. N., ed., *The Stanford Encyclopedia of Philosophy*. Spring 2014 edition. http://plato.stanford.edu/archives/spr2014/entries/prop-attitude-reports/.

Maier, E. (2010). Presupposing acquaintance: a unified theory of *de dicto*, *de re* and *de se* belief reports. *Linguistics and Philosophy*, 32:429–74.

Malamud, S. and Stephenson, T. (2015). Three ways to avoid commitments: Declarative force modifiers in the conversational scoreboard. *Journal of Semantics*, 32:275–311.

Mascarenhas, S. (2009). Inquisitive Semantics and Logic. Master's thesis, University of Amsterdam.

Mastop, R. (2005). What Can You Do: Imperative Mood in Semantic Theory. PhD thesis, University of Amsterdam.

Mastop, R. (2011). Imperatives as semantic primitives. *Linguistics and Philosophy*, 34(4):305–40.

Matić, D. and Nikolaeva, I. (2014). Realis mood, focus, and existential closure in Tundra Yukaghir. *Lingua*, 150:202–31.

Matthewson, L., Rullmann, H., and Davis, H. (2007). Evidentials as epistemic modals: Evidence from St'át'imcets. In Craenebroeck, J. V. and Rooryck, J., eds, *The Linguistic Variation Yearbook 7*, pages 201–54. John Benjamins, Amsterdam.

Mauri, C. and Sansò, A., eds (2012). *Language Sciences*, 34.2, Special issue, Papers selected from the workshop "What do languages encode when they encode reality status?" at the 41st Annual Meeting of the Societas Linguistica Europaea, Forlì, Italy, 17–20 September 2008.

Medeiros, D. J. (2015). Embedded Ancient Greek imperatives: A feature transfer analysis. *Syntax*, 18(2):124–56.

Meibauer, J. (1989). Ob sie wohl kommt? Zum Satzmodus von selbständigen Sätzen mit Endstellung des finiten Verbs. In Katny, A., ed., *Studien zur kontrastiven Linguistik und literarischen Übersetzung*, pages 11–33. Lang, Frankfurt am Main.

Meinunger, A. (2004). Verb position, verbal mood and the anchoring (potential) of sentences. In Lohnstein, H. and Trissler, S., eds, *The Syntax and Semantics of the Left Periphery*, pages 313–41. Mouton de Gruyter, Berlin.

Menéndez-Benito, P. (2005). *The Grammar of Choice*. PhD thesis, University of Massachusetts, Amherst.

Merin, A. (1991). Imperatives: linguistics vs. philosophy. *Linguistics*, 29(4): 669–702.

Merin, A. (1994). Algebra of elementary social acts. In Tsohatzidis, S. L., ed., *Foundations of Speech Act Theory: Philosophical and Linguistic Perspectives*, pages 234–66. Routledge, London.

Michaelis, L. A. and Lambrecht, K. (1996). Toward a construction-based theory of language function: The case of nominal extraposition. *Language*, 72(2):215–47.

Mithun, M. (1995). The relativity of irreality. In Bybee, J. L. and Fleischmann, S., eds, *Modality in Grammar and Discourse*, pages 367–88. John Benjamins, Amsterdam and Philadelphia.

Mithun, M. (1999). *The Languages of Native North America*. Cambridge University Press, Cambridge.

Moretti, G. and Orvieto, G. (1981). *Grammatica Italiana*. Benucci, Perugia.

Morgan, J. L. (1970). On the criterion of identity for noun phrase deletion. In *Papers from the Sixth Regional Meeting, Chicago Linguistic Society*, pages 380–9. Chicago Linguistic Society.

Morgan, J. L. (1977). Two types of convention in indirect speech acts. Technical Report 52, University of Illinois at Urbana-Champagne.

Morzycki, M. (2012). Adjectival extremeness: Degree modification and contextually restricted scales. *Natural Language and Linguistic Theory*, 30(2):567–609.

Moss, S. (2015). On the semantics and pragmatics of epistemic vocabulary. *Semantics and Pragmatics*, 8(5):1–81.

Mulder, W. D. (2010). Mood in French. In Thieroff, R. and Rothstein, B. eds, *Mood in the Languages of Europe*, pages 157–78. John Benjamins, Amsterdam and Philadelphia.

Murray, S. (2011). A Hamblin semantics for evidentials. In Ito, S. and Cormany, E., eds, *Proceedings from Semantics and Linguistic Theory XIX*. CLC Publications, Ithaca, NY.

Murray, S. and Starr, W. B. (2016). The structure of communicative acts. Manuscript, Cornell University.

Murray, S. E. (2014). Varieties of update. *Semantics and Pragmatics*, 7(2):1–53.

Murray, S. E. (2016). Evidentials and illocutionary mood in Cheyenne. *International Journal of American Linguistics*, 82(4):487–517.

Newman, S. (1944). *Yokuts Language of California*. Viking Fund Publications in Anthropology, Number 2. Johnson Reprint Corporation, New York.

Nuyts, J. and van der Auwera, J., eds (2016). *The Oxford Handbook of Modality and Mood*. Oxford University Press, Oxford.

Obenauer, H.-G. (2004). Nonstandard wh-questions and alternative checkers in Pagotto. In Lohnstein, H. and Trissler, S., eds, *Syntax and Semantics of the Left Periphery*, Interface Explorations 9, pages 343–83. Mouton de Gruyter, Berlin.

Ogihara, T. (1996). *Tense, Attitudes, and Scope*. Reidel, Dordrecht and Boston.

Ogihara, T. (2007). Attitudes without monsters: A Japanese perspective. In Tancredi, C., Kanazawa, M., Imani, I., and Kusumoto, K., eds, *Proceedings of SALT 16*. CLC Publications, Cornell University Linguistics Department.

Pagin, P. (2014). Assertion. In Zalta, E. N., ed., *The Stanford Encyclopedia of Philosophy*. Spring 2014 edition. http://plato.stanford.edu/archives/spr2014/entries/assertion/.

Pak, M. (2008). Types of clauses and sentence end particles in Korean. *Korean Linguistics*, 14:113–55.

Pak, M., Portner, P., and Zanuttini, R. (2008a). Agreement and the subjects of jussive clauses in Korean. In Elfner, E. and Walkow, M., eds, *Proceedings of NELS 37*, volume 2, pages 127–38. GLSA, Amherst.

Pak, M., Portner, P., and Zanuttini, R. (2008b). Agreement in promissive, imperative, and exhortative clauses. *Korean Linguistics*, 14:157–75.

Pak, M., Portner, P., and Zanuttini, R. (2015). Course notes for "The syntax and semantics of discourse oriented features". LSA Summer Institute, University of Chicago.

Palmer, F. (1986). *Mood and Modality*. Cambridge University Press, Cambridge.

Palmer, F. (1990). *Modality and the English Modals*. Longman, New York.

Palmer, F. (2001). *Mood and Modality*, second edition. Cambridge University Press, Cambridge.

Parks, D. R. (1976). *A Grammar of Pawnee*. Garland Publishing.

Pearson, H. (2013). *The Sense of Self: Topics in the Semantics of De Se Expressions*. PhD thesis, Harvard University.

Pendlebury, M. (1986). Against the power of force: Reflections on the meaning of mood. *Mind*, 95(379):361–72.

Percus, O. and Sauerland, U. (2003). On the LFs of attitude reports. In *Sinn und Bedeutung 7*, pages 228–42.

Perry, J. (1977). Frege on demonstratives. *Philosophical Review*, LXXXVI: 474–97.

Pesetsky, D. (1992). *Zero Syntax*. MIT Press, Cambridge, MA.

Pica, P. (1984). On the distinction between argumental and non-argumental anaphors. In de Geest, W. and Putseus, Y., eds, *Sentential Complementation*, pages 185–93. Foris, Dordrecht.

Picallo, C. (1984). The infl node and the null subject parameter. *Linguistic Inquiry*, 15:75–101.

Picallo, C. (1985). Opaque Domains. PhD thesis, CUNY.

Pierrehumbert, J. B. and Hirschberg, J. (1990). The meaning of intonational contours in the interpretation of discourse. In Cohen, P., Morgan, J., and Pollack, M., eds, *Intentions in Communication*, pages 271–311. Bradford Books, MIT Press, Cambridge, MA.

Platzack, C. (2007). Embedded imperatives. In van der Wurff, W., ed., *Imperative Clauses in Generative Grammar: Studies Offered to Frits Beukema*, volume 103 of *Linguistik Aktuell/Linguistics Today*, pages 181–203. John Benjamins, Amsterdam and Philadelphia.

Platzack, C. and Rosengren, I. (1994). On the subject of imperatives: A minimalist account of the imperative pronoun and negated imperatives. *Sprache und Pragmatik*, 34:26–67.

Platzack, C. and Rosengren, I. (1998). On the subject of imperatives: A minimalist account of the imperative clause. *The Journal of Comparative Germanic Linguistics*, 1(3):177–224.

Portner, P. (1992). Situation Theory and the Semantics of Propositional Expressions. PhD thesis, University of Massachusetts, Amherst.

Portner, P. (1997). The semantics of mood, complementation, and conversational force. *Natural Language Semantics*, 5:167–212.

Portner, P. (2004). The semantics of imperatives within a theory of clause types. In Watanabe, K. and Young, R. B., eds, *Proceedings of Semantics and Linguistic Theory 14*, pages 235–52. CLC Publications, Cornell University Linguistics Department.

Portner, P. (2007). Imperatives and modals. *Natural Language Semantics*, 15(4): 351–83.

Portner, P. (2008). Beyond the common ground: The semantics and pragmatics of epistemic modals. In Yoon, J.-Y. and Kim, K.-A., eds, *The Perspectives of Linguistics in the 21st Century*. Hankook Publishing Company, Seoul.

Portner, P. (2009). *Modality*. Oxford University Press, Oxford.

Portner, P. (2011a). Perfect and progressive. In von Heusinger, K., Maienborn, C., and Portner, P., eds, *Semantics: An International Handbook of Natural Language Meaning*, volume 1. Mouton de Gruyter, Berlin.

Portner, P. (2011b). Permission and choice. In Grewendorf, G. and Zimmermann, T. E., eds, *Discourse and Grammar: From Sentence Types to Lexical Categories*, Studies in Generative Grammar. Mouton de Gruyter, Berlin.

Portner, P. (2011c). Verbal mood. In von Heusinger, K., Maienborn, C., and Portner, P., eds, *Semantics: An International Handbook of Natural Language Meaning*, volume 2, pages 1262–91. Mouton de Gruyter, Berlin.

Portner, P. (2016). Imperatives. In Aloni, M. and van Rooij, R., eds, *Cambridge Handbook of Semantics*. Cambridge University Press, Cambridge.

Portner, P. (2017). On the relation between verbal mood and sentence mood. Ms., Georgetown University. http://semanticsarchive.net/Archive/GFiYjAwZ/.

Portner, P. (to appear). Commitment to priorities. In Fogel, D., Harris, D., and Moss, M., eds, *New Work on Speech Acts*. Oxford University Press, Oxford.

Portner, P. and Partee, B. H., eds (2002). *Formal Semantics: The Essential Readings*. Blackwell Publishers, Oxford.

Portner, P. and Rubinstein, A. (2013). Mood and contextual commitment. In Chereches, A., ed., *The Proceedings of SALT 22*, pages 461–87. CLC Publications, Cornell, NY.

Portner, P. and Rubinstein, A. (2016). Extreme and non-extreme deontic modals. In Charlow, N. and Chrisman, M., eds, *Deontic Modals*. Oxford University Press, Oxford.

Portner, P. and Zanuttini, R. (2000). The force of negation in Wh exclamatives and interrogatives. In Horn, L. and Kato, Y., eds, *Studies in Negation and Polarity: Syntactic and Semantic Perspectives*, pages 201–39. Oxford University Press, New York and Oxford.

Portner, P. and Zanuttini, R. (2006). The semantics of nominal exclamatives. In Elugardo, R. and Stainton, R., eds, *Ellipsis and Non-sentential Speech*. Kluwer Academic Publishers, Dordrecht and Boston.

Potsdam, E. (1996). Syntactic Issues in English Imperatives. PhD thesis, University of California at Santa Cruz.

Progovac, L. (1993). The (mis)behavior of anaphora and negative polarity. *The Linguistic Review*, 10:37–59.

Quer, J. (1998). *Mood at the Interface*. Holland Academic Graphics, The Hague.

Quer, J. (2001). Interpreting mood. *Probus*, 13:81–111.

Quer, J. (2009). Twists of mood: The distribution and interpretation of indicative and subjunctive. *Lingua*, 119:1779–87.

Quer, J. (2010). Mood in Catalan. In Thieroff, R. and Rothstein, B. eds, *Mood in the Languages of Europe*, pages 221–36. John Benjamins, Amsterdam and Philadelphia.

Quine, W. V. O. (1956). Quantifiers and propositional attitudes. *Journal of Philosophical Logic*, 53(5):177–87.

Raposo, E. (1986a). On the null object in European Portuguese. In Jaeggli, O. and Silva-Corvalan, C., eds, *Studies in Romance Linguistics*, pages 373–90. Foris, Dordrecht.

Raposo, E. (1986b). Some asymmetries in the binding theory in Romance. *The Linguistic Review*, 5:75–110.

Rawlins, K. (2013). (Un)conditionals. *Natural Language Semantics*, 21:111–78.

Reis, M. (1999). On sentence types in German: An enquiry into the relationship between grammar and pragmatics. *IJGLSA*, 4(2):195–236.

Reis, M. (2003). On the form and interpretation of German wh-infinitives. *Journal of Germanic Linguistics*, 15(2):155–201.

Rett, J. (2008a). A degree account of exclamatives. In Rett, J., Friedman, T., and Ito, S., eds, *The Proceedings of SALT 18*, pages 601–18.

Rett, J. (2008b). Degree Modification in Natural Language. PhD thesis, Rutgers University.

Rett, J. (2011). Exclamatives, degrees and speech acts. *Linguistics and Philosophy*, 34(5):411–42.

Rett, J. (2014). Attitude markers and sincerity conditions in an update semantics. Ms., UCLA.

Rett, J. and Murray, S. (2013). A semantic account of mirative evidentials. In Snider, T., ed., *The Proceedings of SALT 23*, pages 453–72. CLC Publications, Cornell University Linguistics Department.

Rivero, M. L. (1994). Clause structure and V-movement in the languages of the Balkans. *Natural Language and Linguistic Theory*, 12(1):63–120.

Rivero, M. L. and Terzi, A. (1995). Imperatives, V-movement and logical mood. *Journal of Linguistics*, 31:301–32.

Rizzi, L. (1997). The fine structure of the left periphery. In Haegeman, L., ed., *Elements of Grammar: Handbook of Generative Syntax*. Kluwer Academic Publishers, Dordrecht.

Roberts, C. (1996). Information structure in discourse: Towards an integrated formal theory of pragmatics. In Toon, J.-H. and Kathol, A., eds, *Papers in Semantics*, OSU Working Papers in Linguistics, Vol. 49, pages 91–136. Department of Linguistics, the Ohio State University, Columbus.

Roberts, C. (2004). Context in dynamic interpretation. In Horn, L. and Ward, G., eds, *The Handbook of Pragmatics*, pages 197–220. Blackwell, Oxford and Malden, MA.

Roberts, C. (2012). Information structure in discourse: Towards an integrated formal theory of pragmatics. *Semantics and Pragmatics*, 5(6):1–69.

Roberts, C. (to appear). Speech acts in discourse context. In Fogal, D., Harris, D., and Moss, M., eds, *New Work on Speech Acts*. Oxford University Press, Oxford.

Roberts, J. R. (1991). Modality in Amele and other Papuan languages. *Journal of Linguistics*, 26(2):363–401.

Roelofsen, F. and Farkas, D. (2015). Polarity particle responses as a window onto the interpretation of questions and assertions. *Language*, 91(2):359–414.

Rögnvaldsson, E. (1998). The syntax of the imperative in Old Scandinavian. www.academia.edu/2861283/The_syntax_of_the_imperative_in_Old_Scandinavian.

Rooth, M. (1992). A theory of focus interpretation. *Natural Language Semantics*, 1(1):75–116.

Rosengren, I., ed. (1992a). *Satztyp, Satzmodus, und Illokution*, volume 1. Niemeyer, Tübingen.

Rosengren, I., ed. (1992b). *Satztyp, Satzmodus, und Illokution*, volume 2. Niemeyer, Tübingen.

Ross, A. (1944). Imperatives and logic. *Philosophy of Science*, 11(1):30–46.

Rothschild, D. (2012). Expressing credences. *Proceedings of the Aristotelian Society*, 112(1):99–114.

Rubinstein, A. (2012). Roots of Modality. PhD thesis, University of Massachusetts, Amherst.

Rubinstein, A., Harner, H., Krawczyk, E., Simonson, D., Katz, G., and Portner, P. (2013). Toward fine-grained annotation of modality in text. In *Proceedings of IWCS 2013 Workshop on Annotation of Modal Meanings in Natural Language (WAMM)*, pages 38–46, Potsdam, Germany. Association for Computational Linguistics.

Rupp, L. (2003). *The Syntax of Imperatives in English and Germanic: Word Order Variation in the Minimalist Framework*. Palgrave Macmillan, Basingstoke.

Rus, D. (2005). Embedded imperatives in Slovenian. In Brandstetter, C. and Rus, D., eds, *Georgetown University Working Papers in Theoretical Linguistics*, volume IV, pages 153–83. Georgetown University Department of Linguistics, Washington, DC.

Russell, B. (2007). Imperatives in conditional conjunction. *Natural Language Semantics*, 15(2):131–66.

Ruwet, N. (1984). Je veux partir / *je veux que je parte: On the distribution of finite complements and infinitival complements in French. *Cahiers de Grammaire*, 7:75–138.

Sadock, J. M. (1974). *Toward a Linguistic Theory of Speech Acts*. Academic Press, New York.

Sadock, J. M. (1985). On the performadox, or a semantic defense of the performative hypothesis. In *University of Chicago Working Papers in Linguistics*, volume 1, pages 160–9. Department of Linguistics, University of Chicago.

Sadock, J. M. (2004). Speech acts. In Horn, L. and Ward, G., eds, *The Handbook of Pragmatics*, pages 53–73. Blackwell, Oxford.

Sadock, J. M. and Zwicky, A. (1985). Speech act distinctions in syntax. In Shopen, T., ed., *Language Typology and Syntactic Description*, pages 155–96. Cambridge University Press, Cambridge.

Šafářová, M. (2005). The semantics of rising intonation in interrogatives and declaratives. In Maier, E., Bary, C., and Huitink, J., eds, *Proceedings of Sinn und Bedeutung 9*, pages 355–69.

Šafářová, M. (2007). Nuclear rises in update semantics. In Aloni, M., Butler, A., and Dekker, P., eds, *Questions in Dynamic Semantics*, pages 355–69. Elsevier, Oxford.

Šafářová, M. and Swerts, M. (2004). On the recognition of declarative questions in English. In *Speech Prosody 2004*, pages 313–16.

Schlenker, P. (2003). A plea for monsters. *Linguistics and Philosophy*, 26:29–120.

Schlenker, P. (2005). The lazy Frenchman's approach to the subjunctive (speculations on reference to worlds and semantic defaults in the analysis of mood). In Geerts, T., van Ginneken, I., and Jacobs, H., eds, *Romance Languages and Linguistic Theory 2003: Selected Papers from "Going Romance"*, pages 269–310. John Benjamins, Amsterdam.

Schlenker, P. (2010). Presuppositions and local contexts. *Mind*, 119(474):377–91.

Schlenker, P. (2011). Indexicality and de se reports. In von Heusinger, K., Maienborn, C., and Portner, P., eds, *Semantics: An International Handbook of Natural Language Meaning*, volume 2. de Gruyter, Berlin.

Schmerling, S. (1982). How imperatives are special, and how they aren't. In Schneider, R., Tuite, K., and Chameltzy, R., eds, *Papers from the Parasession on Nondeclaratives*. Chicago Linguistics Society, The University of Chicago.

Searle, J. R. (1965). What is a speech act? In Black, M., ed., *Philosophy in America*, pages 221–239. Unwin Hyman, London.

Searle, J. R. (1969). *Speech Acts*. Cambridge University Press, Cambridge.

Searle, J. R. (1975a). Indirect speech acts. In Cole, P. and Morgan, J. L., eds, *Syntax and Semantics, volume 3: Speech Acts*, pages 59–82. Academic Press, New York.

Searle, J. R. (1975b). A taxonomy of illocutionary acts. In Gunderson, K., ed., *Language, Mind and Knowledge*, Minnesota Studies in the Philosophy of Science, Vol. VII, pages 344–69. University of Minnesota Press, Minneapolis.

Searle, J. R. (1989). How performatives work. *Linguistics and Philosophy*, 12(5): 535–58.

Searle, J. R. (2001). Réponses de Searle. *Revue internationale de philosophie*, 2(216):277–97.

Searle, J. R. (2010). http://youtu.be/-9bxhqiosni.

Searle, J. R. and Vanderveken, D. (1985). *Foundations of Illocutionary Logic*. Cambridge University Press, Cambridge.

Segerberg, K. (1990). Validity and satisfaction in imperative logic. *Notre Dame Journal of Formal Logic*, 31(2):203–21.

Sheppard, M. M. and Golden, M. (2002). (Negative) imperatives in Slovene. In Barbiers, S., Beukema, F., and van der Wurff, W., eds, *Modality and its Interaction with the Verbal System*, volume 47 of *Linguistik Aktuell/Linguistics Today*, pages 245–59. John Benjamins Publishing Company, Amsterdam and Philadelphia.

Siegel, L. (2009). Mood selection in Romance and Balkan. *Lingua*, 119(12):1859–82.

Simons, M. (2005). Dividing things up: The semantics of *or* and the modal/*Or* interaction. *Natural Language Semantics*, 13(3):271–316.

Smirnova, A. (2011). Evidentiality and Mood: Grammatical Expressions of Epistemic Modality in Bulgarian. PhD thesis, The Ohio State University.

Smirnova, A. (2012). The semantics of mood in Bulgarian. In *Proceedings of the Chicago Linguistics Society 48*. Chicago Linguistics Society.

Soames, S. (1982). How presuppositions are inherited: A solution to the projection problem. *Linguistic Inquiry*, 13:483–545.

Sperber, D. and Wilson, D. (1986). *Relevance: Communication and Cognition*. Blackwell, Oxford.

Squartini, M. (2004). Disentangling evidentiality and epistemic modality in Romance. *Lingua*, 114(7):873–95.

Stalnaker, R. (1970). Pragmatics. *Synthese*, 22:272–89.

Stalnaker, R. (1974). Pragmatic presuppositions. In Munitz, M. and Unger, P., eds, *Semantics and Philosophy*, pages 197–213. New York University Press, New York.

Stalnaker, R. (1975). Indicative conditionals. *Philosophia*, 5:269–86.

Stalnaker, R. (1978). Assertion. In Cole, P., ed., *Syntax and Semantics 9: Pragmatics*, pages 315–32. Academic Press, New York.

Stalnaker, R. (1984). *Inquiry*. MIT Press, Cambridge, MA.

Stalnaker, R. (1988). Belief attribution and context. In Grimm, R. H. and Merrill, D. D., eds, *Contents of Thought*, pages 140–56. University of Arizona Press, Tucson. Reprinted in: R. C. Stalnaker. *Context and Content*. Oxford: Oxford University Press, 1999, 150–66.

Stalnaker, R. (2014). *Context*. Oxford University Press, Oxford and New York.

Stalnaker, R. (to appear). Dynamic pragmatics, static semantics. In Fogel, D., Harris, D., and Moss, M., editors, *New Work on Speech Acts*. Oxford University Press, Oxford.

Starr, W. B. (2010). Conditionals, Meaning, and Mood. PhD thesis, Rutgers University.

Starr, W. B. (2013). A preference semantics for imperatives. Ms., Cornell University.

Starr, W. (2016). Expressing permission. *Semantics and Linguistic Theory*, 26: 325–49.

Steele, S. (1975). Past and irrealis: Just what does it all mean. *International Journal of American Linguistics*, 41:200–17.

Stenius, E. (1967). Mood and language game. *Synthese*, 17:254–74.

Stowell, T. (1982). The tense of infinitives. *Linguistic Inquiry*, 13(3):561–70.

Suñer, M. (1986). On the referential properties of embedded finite clause subjects. In Bordelois, I., Conteres, H., and Zagona, K., eds, *Generative Studies in Spanish Syntax*, pages 183–203. Foris, Dordrecht.

Suñer, M. and Padilla-Rivera, J. (1987). Sequence of tenses and the subjunctive, again. *Hispania*, 70(3):634–42.

Swanson, E. (2007). The language of subjective uncertainty. Ms., University of Michigan. Revised version of Ch. 2 of his 2006 MIT dissertation.

Swanson, E. (2011a). How not to theorize about the language of subjective uncertainty. In Egan, A. and Weatherson, B., eds, *Epistemic Modality*, pages 249–69. Oxford University Press, Oxford.

Swanson, E. (2011b). Propositional atitudes. In von Heusinger, K., Maienborn, C., and Portner, P., eds, *Semantics: An International Handbook of Natural Language Meaning*, volume 2. Mouton de Gruyter, Berlin.

Swanson, E. (2015). The application of constraint semantics to the language of subjective uncertainty. *Journal of Philosophical Logic*, pages 1–26.

Terrell, T. and Hooper, J. (1974). A semantically based analysis of mood in Spanish. *Hispania*, 57(3):486–94.

Thieroff, R. (2010). *Moods, Moods, Moods: Mood in the Languages of Europe*, pages 1–29. In Thieroff, R. and Rothstein, B., eds, John Benjamins, Amsterdam and Philadelphia.

Thieroff, R. and Rothstein, B., eds (2010). *Mood in the Languages of Europe*. John Benjamins, Amsterdam and Philadelphia.

Thomas, G. (2014). Embedded imperatives in Mbyà. In Huang, H.-L., Poole, E., and Rysling, A., eds, *Proceedings of NELS 43*, Amherst. GLSA, University of Massachusetts.

Thomason, R. H. (1981a). Deontic logic and the role of freedom in moral deliberation. In Hilpinen, R., ed., *New Studies in Deontic Logic*, pages 177–86. D. Reidel Publishing Co., Dordrecht.

Thomason, R. H. (1981b). Deontic logic as founded on tense logic. In Hilpinen, R., ed., *New Studies in Deontic Logic*, pages 165–76. D. Reidel Publishing Co., Dordrecht.

Trinh, T. and Crnič, L. (2011). The rise and fall of declaratives. In Reich, I., ed., *Proceedings of Sinn und Bedeutung 15*, pages 645–60. Saarland University Press, Saarbrücken.

Truckenbrodt, H. (2006a). On the semantic motivation of syntactic verb movement to C in German. *Theoretical Linguistics*, 32(3):257–306.

Truckenbrodt, H. (2006b). Replies to the comments by Gärtner, Plunze and Zimmermann, Portner, Potts, Reis, and Zaefferer. *Theoretical Linguistics*, 32(3): 257–306.

Tsoulas, G. (1996). The nature of the subjunctive and the formal grammar of obviation. In Zagona, K., ed., *Linguistic Theory and Romance Languages*, pages 295–306. John Benjamins, Amsterdam/Philadelphia.

van Benthem, J. and Liu, F. (2004). Dynamic logic of preference upgrade. *Journal of Applied Non-Classical Logics*, 14(2):1–26.

van der Auwera, J. and Devos, M. (2012). Irrealis in positive imperatives and in prohibitives. *Language Sciences*, 34(2):171–83.

van der Torre, L. W. N. and Tan, Y.-H. (1998). An update semantics for deontic reasoning. In *Proceedings of DEON'98*, pages 409–26.

van Fraassen, B. C. (1973). Values and the heart's command. *Journal of Philosophy*, 70(1):5–19.

van Rooij, R. (2000). Permission to change. *Journal of Semantics*, 17:119–45.

Van Valin, R. D. and LaPolla, R. J. (1997). *Syntax: Structure, Meaning and Function*. Cambridge University Press, Cambridge.

Vanderveken, D. (1990). *Meaning and Speech Acts, Volume 1: Principles of Language Use*. Cambridge University Press, Cambridge.

Vanderveken, D. (1991). *Meaning and Speech Acts, Volume 2: Formal Semantics of Success and Satisfaction*. Cambridge University Press, Cambridge.

Vanderveken, D. (2002). Universal grammar and speech act theory. In Vanderveken, D. and Kuno, S., eds, *Essays in Speech Act Theory*, pages 25–62. John Benjamins, Amsterdam.

Veltman, F. (1986). Data semantics and the pragmatics of indicative conditionals. In Traugott, E., ter Meulen, A., and Snitzer, A., eds, *On Conditionals*, pages 147–68. Cambridge University Press, Cambridge.

Veltman, F. (1996). Defaults in update semantics. *Journal of Philosophical Logic*, 25:221–61.

Villalta, E. (2000). Spanish subjunctive clauses require ordered alternatives. In Jackson, B. and Matthews, T., eds, *The Proceedings of SALT 10*, pages 239–56. CLC Publications, Ithaca, NY.

Villalta, E. (2006). *Context Dependence in the Interpretation of Questions and Subjunctives*. PhD thesis, Tübingen.

Villalta, E. (2008). Mood and gradability: An investigation of the subjunctive mood in Spanish. *Linguistics and Philosophy*, 31(4):467–522.

von Stechow, A. (1995). On the proper treatment of tense. In Simons, M. and Galloway, T., eds, *The Proceedings of SALT 5*, pages 362–86. Cornell University, Ithaca, NY.

von Stechow, A. (2003). Deletion under semantic binding. Ms., University of Tübingen; text of NELS 33 talk.

von Stechow, A. (2004). Binding by verbs: Tense, person and mood under attitudes. In Lohnstein, H. and Trissler, S., eds, *The Syntax and Semantics of the Left Periphery*, pages 431–88. Mouton de Gruyter, Berlin and New York.

Vranas, P. (2008). New foundations for imperative logic i: Logical connectives, consistency, and quantifiers. *Noûs*, 42:529–72.

Vranas, P. (2011). New foundations for imperative logic: Pure imperative inference. *Mind*, 120:369–446.

Wechsler, S. (1991). Verb second and illocutionary force. In Leffel, K. and Bouchard, D., eds, *Views on Phrase Structure*, pages 177–91. Kluwer, Dordrecht.

Whitehead, C. R. (1986). Tense, Aspect, Mood and Modality: Verbal Morphology in Menya. Master's thesis, University of Manitoba.

Wiklund, A.-L., Bentzen, K., Hrafnbjargarson, G. H., and Hróarsdóttir, T. (2009). On the distribution and illocution of v2 in Scandinavian that-clauses. *Lingua*, 119(12):1914–38.

Willer, M. (2014). Dynamic thoughts on ifs and oughts. *Philosophers' Imprint*, 14(28):1–30.

Wilson, D. and Sperber, D. (1988). Mood and the analysis of non-declarative sentences. In Dancy, J., Moravcsik, J. and Taylor, C., eds, *Human Agency: Language, Duty and Value*, pages 77–101. Stanford University Press, Stanford, CA.

Wiltschko, M. (2016). The essence of a category: Lessons from the subjunctive. In Błaszczak, J., Giannakidou, A., Klimek-Jankowska, D., and Migdalski, K., eds, *Mood, Aspect, Modality Revisited: New Answers to Old Questions*, pages 218–54. University of Chicago Press, Chicago, IL.

Wittgenstein, L. (1953). *Philosophical Investigations*. G. E. M. Anscombe and R. Rhees (eds) and translated by G. E. M. Anscombe. Blackwell, Oxford.

Yalcin, S. (2007). Epistemic modals. *Mind*, 116(464):983–1026.

Yalcin, S. (2010). Probability operators. *Philosophy Compass*, 5(11):916–37.

Yalcin, S. (2011). Nonfactualism about epistemic modality. In Egan, A. and Weatherson, B., eds, *Epistemic Modality*. Oxford University Press, Oxford.

Yalcin, S. (2012). Context probabilism. In Aloni, M., Kimmelman, V., Roelofsen, F., Sassoon, G., Schulz, K., and Westera, M., eds, *Proceedings of the 18th Amsterdam Colloquium*, pages 12–21.

Yamada, T. (2007a). Acts of commanding and changing obligations. In Inoue, K., Satoh, K., and Toni, F., eds, *Computational Logic in Multi-Agent Systems, 7th International Workshop, CLIMA VII, Hakodate, Japan*, volume 4371 of *Lecture Notes in Artificial Intelligence*, pages 1–19. Springer, Berlin.

Yamada, T. (2007b). Logical dynamics of commands and obligations. In Takashi-Washio, Sato, K., Takeda, H., and Inokuchi, A., eds, *New Frontiers in Artificial Intelligence, JSAI 2006 Conference and Workshops, Tokyo, Japan, June 2006*, volume 4384 of *Lecture Notes in Artificial Intelligence*, pages 133–46. Springer, Berlin.

Yamada, T. (2007c). Logical dynamics of some speech acts that affect obligations and preferences. In van Benthem, J., Ju, S., and Veltman, F., eds, *A Meeting of Minds: Proceedings of the Workshop on Logic, Rationality and Interaction, Beijing, 2007*, volume 8 of *Texts in Computer Science*, pages 275–89. King's College Publications, London.

Zaefferer, D. (1981). On a formal treatment of illocutionary force indicators. In Parret, H., Sbisà, M., and Verschueren, J., eds, *Possibilities and Limitations of Pragmatics: Proceedings of the Conference on Pragmatics, Urbino, July 8–14, 1979*, pages 779–98. John Benjamins, Amsterdam.

Zaefferer, D. (1983). The semantics of sentence mood in typologically differing languages. In Hattori, S. and Inoue, K., eds, *Proceedings of the XIIIth International Congress of Linguists*, pages 553–7. CIPL, Tokyo.

Zaefferer, D. (1986). The grammar of clause type and the pragmatics of illocution type. In *Proceedings of the Twenty-Second Regional Meeting of the Chicago Linguistic Society*, volume 2, pages 29–39. University of Chicago, Chicago, IL.

Zaefferer, D. (1998). On a formal treatment of illocutionary force indicators. In Kasher, A., ed., *Pragmatics: Critical Concepts, Volume II: Speech Act Theory and Particular Speech Acts*, pages 250–67. Routledge, London.

Zaefferer, D. (2001). Deconstructing a classical classification: A typological look at Searle's concept of illocution type. *Revue internationale de philosophie*, 2(216):209–25.

Zaefferer, D. (2006a). Conceptualizing sentence mood—two decades later. In Brandt, P. and Fuß, E., eds, *Form, Structure, and Grammar: A Festschrift Presented to Günther Grewendorf on Occasion of his 60th Birthday*, Studia Grammatica 67, pages 367–82. Akademie, Berlin.

Zaefferer, D. (2006b). Types, moods, and force potentials: Towards a comprehensive account of German sentence mood meanings. *Theoretical Linguistics*, 32(3): 335–52.

Zaefferer, D. (2007). Deskewing the Searlean picture: A new speech act ontology for linguistics. In *The Proceedings of BLS 32*. Berkeley Linguistics Society.

Zanuttini, R. (1997). *Negation and Clausal Structure: A Comparative Study of Romance Languages*. Oxford University Press, New York and Oxford.

Zanuttini, R. (2008). Encoding the addressee in the syntax: Evidence from English imperative subjects. *Natural Language and Linguistic Theory*, 26(1):185–218.

Zanuttini, R. and Portner, P. (2000). The characterization of exclamative clauses in Paduan. *Language*, 76(1):123–32.

Zanuttini, R. and Portner, P. (2003). Exclamative clauses: At the syntax–semantics interface. *Language*, 79(1):39–81.

Zanuttini, R., Pak, M., and Portner, P. (2012). A syntactic analysis of interpretive restrictions on imperative, promissive, and exhortative subjects. *Natural Language and Linguistic Theory*, 30(4):1231–74.

Žarnić, B. (2003a). Imperative change and obligation to do. In Segerberg, K. and Sliwinski, R., eds, *Logic, Law, Morality: Thirteen Essays in Practical Philosophy in Honour of Lennart Åqvist*, volume 51 of *Uppsala Philosophical Studies*, pages 79–95. Department of Philosophy, Uppsala University.

Žarnić, B. (2003b). Imperative logic, moods and sentence radicals. In Dekker, P. and van Rooij, R., eds, *Proceedings of the Fourteenth Amsterdam Colloquium*, pages 223–8. ILLC, Amsterdam.

Zeijlstra, H. (2008). Modal concord is syntactic agreement. In Gibson, M. and Friedman, T., eds, *The Proceedings of SALT XVII*. CLC Publications, Cornell University Linguistics Department.

Zimmermann, T. E. (2000). Free choice disjunction and epistemic possibility. *Natural Language Semantics*, 8:255–90.

Zu, V. (2016). Competition and obviation from French to Newari. In *Proceedings of NELS 46*. GLSA, University of Massachusetts.

Index

Note: The most important page references are indicated in bold type.